THE INTERNATIONAL MONETARY SYSTEM AND ITS REFORM

Part IV

CONTRIBUTIONS
TO
ECONOMIC ANALYSIS

197

Honorary Editor:
J. TINBERGEN

Editors:
D. W. JORGENSON
J. WAELBROECK

NORTH-HOLLAND
AMSTERDAM · NEW YORK · OXFORD · TOKYO

THE INTERNATIONAL MONETARY SYSTEM AND ITS REFORM

Papers prepared for the Group of Twenty-Four by a
United Nations project directed by Sidney Dell
1979-1986

Published in cooperation with the United Nations

PART IV

1990

NORTH-HOLLAND
AMSTERDAM · NEW YORK · OXFORD · TOKYO

ELSEVIER SCIENCE PUBLISHERS B.V.
P.O. Box 211, Sara Burgerhartstraat 25,
1000 AE Amsterdam, The Netherlands

Distributors for the United States and Canada:

ELSEVIER SCIENCE PUBLISHING COMPANY INC.
655 Avenue of the Americas
New York, N.Y. 10010, U.S.A.

ISBN: 0 444 88847 0

Library of Congress Cataloging-in-Publication Data

(Revised for vol. 4 & 5)
The International monetary system and its reform.

  (Contributions to economic analysis ; 162,
  "Published in cooperation with the United Nations."
  Includes bibliographies.
    1. International finance. 2. Debts, External.
3. International Monetary Fund. 4. Economic stabilization – Developing
countries. 5. Balance of payments – Developing countries. I. Dell, Sidney
Samuel. II. Group of Twenty-four.   III. United Nations. IV. Series:
Contributions to economic analysis ; 162, etc.
HG3881.I57672   1987   332.4'5   87-6737
ISBN 0-444-70227-X (Vols. 1, 2 & 3)
ISBN 0-444-88847-O (Vols. 4 & 5)

PRINTED IN THE NETHERLANDS

Introduction to the series

This series consists of a number of hitherto unpublished studies, which are introduced by the editors in the belief that they represent fresh contributions to economic science.

The term 'economic analysis' as used in the title of the series has been adopted because it covers both the activities of the theoretical economist and the research worker.

Although the analytical methods used by the various contributors are not the same, they are nevertheless conditioned by the common origin of their studies, namely theoretical problems encountered in practical research. Since for this reason, business cycle research and national accounting, research work on behalf of economic policy, and problems of planning are the main sources of the subjects dealt with, they necessarily determine the manner of approach adopted by the authors. Their methods tend to be 'practical' in the sense of not being too far remote from application to actual economic conditions. In addition they are quantitative.

It is the hope of the editors that the publication of these studies will help to stimulate the exchange of scientific information and to reinforce international cooperation in the field of economics.

The Editors

PREFACE

In 1987 North-Holland published three volumes containing studies of international monetary problems originally prepared for submission to the Group of Twenty-four (G-24) over the period from 1979 to 1986. As noted in the Preface to these volumes, the Group had been established in November 1971 to increase the negotiating strength of developing countries in discussions taking place from time to time among IMF members on the future of the international monetary system. Parts IV and V are now being published to continue the series up to the end of 1987.

The first four papers in Part IV were prepared for a special session of the Group of Twenty-four convened in Buenos Aires in March 1986 in order to address the world debt problem. A second group of papers in Parts IV and V was prepared to assist a Working Group which was established by the Group of Twenty-four in August 1986 in order to examine and report on the role of the International Monetary Fund in adjustment with growth. These papers provide a comprehensive review of all major aspects of the Fund's activities, with particular emphasis on the concerns of developing countries. The report of the Working Group based on these papers was adopted by the Group of Twenty-four itself at ministerial level and was published in the IMF Survey, Supplement on the Group of 24 Deputies' Report (10 August, 1987.)

A third group of papers consists of studies of the experience of selected developing countries in adjusting to external shocks during the ten-year period ending in 1984. These papers were used as a basis for the general study of balance of payments experience and growth prospects prepared by Professor G.K. Helleiner and included in Part III of the present series, at pp. 961-1011. The terms of reference for these country studies were set out in a paper by Professor E.L. Bacha which can also be found in Part III at pp. 1012-1030.

Since considerable interest has been expressed in having the entire series of studies accessible in the public domain, Parts IV and V are now being made available to the public at large in the present form.

Acknowledgements are due to Maureen Henderson who was responsible for the onerous task of preparing for publication the contents of Parts IV and V, as well as of the earlier Parts I-III.

TABLE OF CONTENTS

Page

PART IV

Preface   vii

EXTERNAL SHOCKS AND GROWTH PROSPECTS:
THE CASE OF BRAZIL: 1973-1989   1
   by E. Bacha

1.   Introduction   1
2.   External shocks and domestic policies, 1973-1983   2
     (a) The 1973-1978 experience   3
     (b) The 1978-1983 experience   7
     (c) Adjustment Brazilian style: an interpretation   8
3.   Economic prospects through 1989   10
     (a) Income multipliers in the simulation model   11
     (b) Simulations for 1984-1989   15
4.   Conclusions   23

BALANCE OF PAYMENTS ADJUSTMENT IN INDIA:
1970-71 TO 1983-84   35
   by M. Ahluwalia

1.   Introduction   35
2.   The balance-of-payments from 1970-71 to 1983-84   36
     (a) The first oil shock   36
     (b) The second oil shock   43
3.   Decomposition of current-account changes   48
     (a) The first oil shock   49
     (b) The second oil shock   52
4.   Prospects and constraints up to 1990-91   54
     (a) The structure of the model   54
     (b) Model simulations up to 1990-91   55

THE BALANCE OF PAYMENTS ADJUSTMENT PROCESS IN DEVELOPING
COUNTRIES: THE EXPERIENCE OF THE IVORY COAST   83
   by A. Ouattara

1.   Introduction   83
2.   Evolution of the economic and social situation from
     1974 to 1981   83
3.   Evolution of the balance of payments   85
     (a) Review of the general trend   85
     (b) Trade balance   86
     (c) Current account: 1975-1983   94
     (d) Financing of the deficit   96
4.   Macroeconomic policies from 1974 to 1976   99
     (a) Policies with regard to the external sector   101

(b) The impact of the current account deficit
    on the internal situation   102
(c) Adjustment policies   103
(d) Factors hampering the adjustment   104
(e) Results of the adjustment policy   104
5. The outlook for the Ivory Coast's external debt,
    balance of payments and economic situation in
    the years 1983 to 1990   105
(a) The simulation model   106
(b) Main assumptions used in the simulation   108
(c) Results of the simulations   110

FOREIGN DEBT, BALANCE OF PAYMENTS, AND GROWTH
PROSPECTS: THE CASE OF THE REPUBLIC OF KOREA,
1965-1988   139
  by Yungchul Park

1. Introduction   139
2. Evolution of the Republic of Korea's external
    indebtedness, 1960-1983: an overview   140
3. Evolution and causes of the Republic of Korea's foreign
    debt accumulation   144
(a) Debt-financed development strategy   144
(b) High import intensity of exports   146
(c) Preference of debt financing over foreign direct
    investment   148
(d) Interest rate differential between home and
    international financial markets   149
4. Adjustment to internal shocks and debt accumulation 151
(a) Interest rate reform and foreign loan guarantees,
    1965-1970   151
(b) Promotion of capital-intensive industries, and
    debt accumulation, 1975-1979   156
5. Policy response and adjustment to external shocks   158
(a) Policy response and adjustment to the first oil
    crisis, 1973-1977   158
(b) Policy response and adjustment to the second oil
    crisis and high interest rates, 1979-1983   162
6. Efficiency and optimality of foreign borrowing in the
    Republic of Korea   169
(a) Growth and foreign borrowing   169
(b) Efficiency of foreign loan allocation in the 1960s 170
(c) Efficiency of foreign loan allocation in the 1970s 171
7. Economic prospects and macro-simulations for 1984-1988 173
(a) Revision of the Fifth Five-Year Development Plan,
    1982-1986, and macro-projections through 1988   173
(b) A simulation model for Korea   174
(c) Simulation scenarios and exercises   181
8. Summary and concluding remarks   184

Page

MEXICO'S RECENT BALANCE-OF-PAYMENTS EXPERIENCE
AND PROSPECTS FOR GROWTH   207
   by E.Z. Ponce de Leon

1.   Introduction   207
2.   The period 1973-1977   208
     (a) The current account   208
         (i) The foreign debt   210
         (ii) Domestic economic policy   211
3.   The period 1978-1981   214
     (a) The current account during the boom years   214
     (b) The foreign debt, 1978-1981   215
     (c) The domestic environment   216
4.   The events since 1982   221
     (a) The disorderly and involuntary adjustment of 1982   221
     (b) The economic adjustment programme of 1983   223
     (c) Foreign debt management   224
     (d) The performance in 1983 and 1984   226
     (e) More recent developments on the debt front   227
5.   Prospects   229

FOREIGN DEBT, BALANCE OF PAYMENTS AND THE ECONOMIC
CRISIS OF THE PHILIPPINES IN 1983-84   261
   by E. Remolona, M. Mangahas and F. Pante, Jr.

1.   Introduction   261
2.   An overview of the balance of payments   262
     2.1 Balance-of-payments experience, 1971-83   262
     2.2 The role of external shocks   264
     2.3 The role of domestic policies   266
         2.3.1 The growth strategy   266
         2.3.2 Management of the external debt   268
         2.3.3 Foreign exchange rate policy   270
         2.3.4 Trade and industrial policies   271
3.   Analysis of the current account, 1971-1982   272
     3.1 The 1971-73 episode   272
     3.2 The 1974-76 episode   273
     3.3 The 1977-82 episode   273
4.   Counterfactual scenarios, 1979-83   274
     4.1 External shocks   274
     4.2 Policy responses   275
5.   Simulations with a forecasting model   276
     5.1 The model   276
     5.2 Predetermined variables   279
     5.3 Simulation results   281
6.   Concluding remarks   283

ZIMBABWE: TRANSITION TO ECONOMIC CRISES 1981-1983
RETROSPECT AND PROSPECT   315
  by R.H. Green and X. Kadhani

1.   Growth, recession, recovery and imbalance: an
        introduction   315
2.   Zimbabwe: some aspects of the pre-1980 experience   318
3.   The structural heritage: Rhodesia to Zimbabwe   319
4.   Independence, transition and boom 1980-1982   323
5.   1982-1984: the macroeconomics of crisis management   329
6.   Current account deficit 1978/80 - 1981/83: a causal
        decomposition   332
7.   Political and economic policy: prospects and parameters   337
8.   Zimbabwe 1984: macro policy issues   340
9.   Policy issues and perspectives: sectoral   346
10.   Prospects 1985-1990   351
11.   Conclusion   355

THE WORLD DEBT PROBLEM: A DIAGNOSIS
  by Sidney Dell   359

      Introduction and summary   359
      The situation at the end of 1985   362
      Historical parallels   364
      The origins of the debt crisis   366
      Factors in the debt crisis   370
      The response to the crisis   374
      The external environment for adjustment   378
      The nature of the adjustment process   381
      Problems of the official borrowers   386
      Prospects for the debt problem   388
      The common interest in co-operative solutions   395
      Conditions for solving the debt problem   396
      The case for an intergovernmental dialogue   399

PROSPECTS FOR INTERNATIONAL DEBT REFORM   411
  by P. Krugman

I.   Background to the problem   411
        The two debt crises   411
        The Latin American debt crisis   412
        The African debt crisis   412
        Coping with the debt problem   413
          The Latin American strategy   413
          The African strategy   413
          The results of ad hoc strategies   414
        Prospects for the ad hoc strategy   415
          The financial outlook for market borrowers   415
          1986 vs. 1983   415
          Africa's prospects   417

Page

II.   A conceptual framework for debt reform   417
      The narrow financial argument for an official role   418
        The case for defensive lending   419
        The free rider problem   421
        Bargaining and mediation   422
        The case for official lending   423
      Broader arguments for intervention   424
        Safeguarding the financial system   424
        Trade-finance linkages   425
        Political and security consequences   426
        Social and humanitarian concerns   426
      The interests of the debtor countries   427
      Possible dimensions of debt reform   428
        Procedural reform vs. reduced adjustment burden   429
        Stretch-out vs. write-down   429
        Reforming conditionality   430
        Who pays for reform?   431
      A preliminary view of reform options   431
        Changing the nature of the claims   432
        Changing the ownership of claims   432
        Changing the value of claims   433
III. A survey of major reform proposals   433
      Procedural reforms   434
        Multi-year rescheduling   434
        Longer maturities   434
        Insurance and secondary markets   435
      Changing the nature of claims   436
        Interest capitalization   436
        Indexed loans   437
        Exchange participation notes   437
      Changing the ownership of claims   438
        Official incremental lending   438
        Official takeover of debt   438
      Changing the value of claims   439
IV.   Evaluating reform proposals   440
      Procedural reforms   440
        Multi-year rescheduling and extension of maturities   440
        Secondary markets and insurance   441
      Changing the nature of claims   442
        Interest capitalization   442
        Exchange participation   443
      New institutions   445
        Advantages of a new intermediary   445
        Disadvantages of an intermediary   446
      Debt relief   447
        Quantitative tradeoffs   448
        Critique of debt relief plans   449
        Combining debt relief with new money   450
V.   Conclusions   451
      The current state of international debt   451
      Procedural reform   452

              Changing the nature of claims   452
              A new intermediary   453
              Debt relief   453
              Prospects for debt reform   454

                              PART V

EXTERNAL DEBT AND THE REFORM OF THE
INTERNATIONAL MONETARY SYSTEM   459
   by Arturo O'Connell

              Introduction   459
I.   Commercial banking vis-à-vis public institutions
         in the provision of finance to the developing
         countries   460
II.   Economic policy co-ordination among countries, the
         reform of the international monetary system and
         the fundamental solution to the external debt problem 469
III. The adjustment process in highly indebted countries,
         conditionality and the debt problem in the
         transition to a growing world economy   474
IV.   Concluding comments   476

TRANSFER OF RESOURCES TO DEVELOPING COUNTRIES   483
   by D. Avramovic

              Summary   483
I.   Resource flows: recent experience   484
         World aggregates: DAC resource flow measurements   484
         World aggregates: World Bank net transfer estimates 485
         Latin America: reverse transfers   485
         Sub-Saharan Africa: declining positive transfers   486
         Resource transfer effects of falling commodity prices 488
II.   Current initiatives for resource mobilization   489
         Baker Plan   489
         Africa   492
III. Need for Special Drawing Rights (SDRs)   494

TARGET ZONES AND INDICATORS AS INSTRUMENTS FOR
INTERNATIONAL ECONOMIC POLICY CO-ORDINATION   501
   by J. Williamson

1.   Introduction   501
2.   The position to date   501
3.   Target zones   507
4.   Possible roles of indicators   509
5.   The selection and structuring of indicators   512

   Page

6.   Comparison and implementation   520
7.   The interests of the developing countries   523
8.   Concluding remarks   524

THE TERMS OF TRADE AND THE EXTERNAL FINANCING
PROBLEMS OF COMMODITY-EXPORTING DEVELOPING
COUNTRIES   529
   by Alfred Maizels

I.   Introduction   530
II.   Factors influencing commodity prices   531
          Structural changes   531
          Prices and the commodity terms of trade   532
III.   Prospects for foreign exchange earnings   539
          Demand   539
          Supply   540
          Dollar depreciation   541
          Import requirements and the terms of trade   542
IV.   International policy   547

UNSETTLED QUESTIONS ABOUT ADJUSTMENT WITH GROWTH   551
   by Tony Killick

       Summary   551
I.   Background   555
II.   The international environment   559
III.   The design of adjustment with growth   562
          The new orthodoxy   562
          Conceptualising the strategy   565
          Consistency with long-run development   571
          Other issues of design   576
IV.   Questions of finance   580
          The adequacy of financial flows   580
          The sequencing of financial flows   583
V.   Institutional issues   584
          Debt management   585
          Role and resources of IMF and the World Bank   586
          Co-ordination of creditor country responses   589
VI.   Questions of consistency   589

THE DESIGN AND IMPLEMENTATION OF IMF CONDITIONALITY   601
   by J. Williamson

1.   Introduction   601
2.   Is conditionality necessary?   601

  Page

3.   Programme design   606
     (a) Improved terms of trade   607
     (b) Output   608
     (c) Reduced absorption with constant output   608
     (d) Reduced absorption with lower output   608
          (i)   Overkill   609
          (ii)   Import liberalization   611
          (iii) Income distribution   612
          (iv)   Inflation   613
4.   Performance criteria and preconditions   614
     (a) External balance alone   615
     (b) External balance plus   616
     (c) Supply-side variables   617
     (d) Real variables   617
     (e) Growth   618
     (f) Real exchange rate   618
5.   Preconditions   619
6.   Repayment provisions   622
7.   Policy initiatives   623

THE CHANGING RELATIONSHIP BETWEEN THE WORLD BANK
AND THE INTERNATIONAL MONETARY FUND   631
   by R. Feinberg

1.   Introduction   631
2.   Origins of the Bretton Woods institutions   632
3.   A division of labour: the "Primary responsibilities"
     rule of the 1960s   633
4.   The drift toward ambiguity   634
5.   Cross-conditionality   639
6.   The Structural Adjustment Facility   643
7.   Future directions for Bank-Fund relations   645
     (a) Merger   645
     (b) The status quo ante   646
     (c) Redefining responsibilities   646
8.   A new division of labour   646
     (a) Staff collaboration   647
     (b) Issue demarcation   647
     (c) Target selectivity   648
     (d) Country or regional specialization   648
     (e) Separate ineligibility decisions   648
     (f) Fund stand-by arrangements and Bank
          project loans   651
9.   Generating additional resources   651
10. Summary of main conclusions and recommendations   653

DEBT, GROWTH AND STRUCTURAL ADJUSTMENT IN LATIN
AMERICA: AN APPRAISAL OF THE BAKER INITIATIVE   657
  by M. Abreu, W. Fritsch and E. Modiano

    Introduction   657
I.   Economic fluctuations in the OECD countries
    and their impact on Latin American debtor
    countries   659
   A. Demand fluctuations   660
      1. Export volumes   660
      2. Export prices   663
   B. Interest rate fluctuations   664
II. Structural adjustment policies: rationale
    and facts   668
   A. Policies aimed at increasing domestic savings,
      capital productivity and growth of capacity
      output   668
      1. Interest rate policy and savings performance   669
      2. Fiscal policy and domestic savings   670
      3. Public investment and the role of public
        enterprises   672
      4. Capital-output ratios   675
   B. Policies aimed at increasing allocative efficiency 677
      1. Exchange-rate policies   678
      2. Pricing policies   682
III. The Baker Plan: a quantitative assessment   684
   A. The model   686
   B. Scenarios   688
   C. Simulation results   691
IV. Conclusions   697

THE ROLE OF THE SPECIAL DRAWING RIGHT IN THE
INTERNATIONAL MONETARY SYSTEM   703
  by Alec Chrystal

A.   The SDR as an idea   704
B.   International reserves post-floating   707
      1. The floating option   707
      2. Borrowed reserves   709
      3. Currency status   710
C.   The SDR as a reserve asset   711
      1. The drawing right   712
      2. Valuation   714
      3. The interest rate   716
      4. Liquidity   717
D.   Ways forward   718
      1. Steps possible within the existing structure   719
      2. A new structure for the SDR facility   719
      3. Allocation method   721
E.   Conclusions   722

  Page

ADJUSTMENT WITH GROWTH AND THE ROLE OF
THE INTERNATIONAL MONETARY FUND   729
    by A. Buira

        Introduction   729
I.   Adjustment with growth   730
        1. Initial approach to the international
                debt crisis   730
        2. Towards a strategy of adjustment with growth   732
            (a) The international environment   732
            (b) Domestic adjustment requirements of
                    developing countries   733
            (c) Financial flows to developing countries   735
II.   The role of the IMF   737
        1. Fund surveillance   737
        2. Integration of the growth objective in IMF
                programmes   738
III.   The financing role of the Fund   739
        1. The size of Fund quotas   739
        2. Allocation of SDRs   740
        3. Access policy   741
        4. The catalytic role of the Fund   742
        Conclusion   746

IMF CONDITIONALITY: CONCEPTUAL PROBLEMS AND
POLICY ALTERNATIVES   751
    by E. Bacha

1.   Conceptual problems   751
2.   A proposal for a hands-off approach   754
            The proposal in detail   758
3.   Preconditions for a hands-on approach   760
4.   Summary   761

THE FINANCIAL ROLE OF THE INTERNATIONAL MONETARY
FUND IN PROMOTING ADJUSTMENT WITH GROWTH   769
    by C. Gwin and D. Sobol

        Introduction   769
I.   Quotas   771
II.   Access   781
III.   Compensatory Financing Facility   790
IV.   Structural Adjustment Facility   796
V.   Rate of charge   802
VI.   Repayment obligations   808
VII.   Borrowing   811
VIII.   Conclusions   815

  Page

ADJUSTMENT WITH GROWTH IN AFRICA: UNSETTLED QUESTIONS
OF DESIGN AND FINANCE   827
  by Tony Killick

       Summary   827
       Introduction   831
I.   Symptoms   832
           The dangers of over-generalization   832
           Trade and the balance of payments   832
           The debt overhang   836
           Domestic economic performance   840
II.   Diagnoses   843
III.   Prescriptions: the design of adjustment   847
           The spread of adjustment-related lending   847
           Programme content   848
           Programme effectiveness   848
           Outstanding issues in the design of adjustment   851
       Questions relating to conditionality   851
       (a) The conditionality explosion   851
       (b) The modalities of conditionality and uniformity
           of treatment   855
       (c) The IMF's limited capacity to adjust   857
       Questions relating to the new orthodoxy   858
       (a) Getting prices right: the example of the
           exchange rate   858
       (b) Roles of the public and private sectors: para-
           statal performance and privatization   863
       (c) The role of exports in African adjustment   866
       (d) Industrialization, adjustment and development   868
       (e) Poverty, income distribution and political
           sustainability   871
IV.   The role of external finance   875
           The case for external support   875
           Estimates of need   878
           Prospects for capital inflows   880
           Prospects for debt relief   882
V.   Concluding observations   884

EXTERNAL SHOCKS AND GROWTH PROSPECTS:
THE CASE OF BRAZIL, 1973-1989

Edmar L. Bacha*

1. INTRODUCTION

This is a study of the factors underlying the current-account deficits experienced by Brazil since the mid-1970s. It also explores the country's economic prospects through 1989, with the help of a simple macro-simulations model.

The current-account deficit is identically equal to the excess of domestic spending over national income. Provided that net external financing is available, this excess may increase for a number of reasons. Prominent among them is an expansion of real domestic spending, associated with increases either of real consumption expenditures or of real domestic capital formation. Even if domestic absorption is invariant, the external deficit may worsen because of inadequate domestic pricing policies. These may make it impossible for local firms to compete with cheaper foreign products, thus forcing a contraction of national income and employment. A temporary reduction of GNP below its potential value may also be caused by domestic supply shocks of a climatic or other nature. However, other factors can also cause a deterioration of the current account.

First, worsening terms of trade cause an increase in the nominal value of domestic spending (which includes imports), relative to the nominal value of national output (which includes exports), even as the relevant real magnitudes remain constant. Second, if the country is a net debtor, increased real international interest rates reduce the value of national income for a given domestic income. And thirdly, for a given domestic spending level, national income is reduced as real exports fall in consequence of a world recession or of external protectionism.

For example, the current account may be in deficit even when domestic prices are "right" and a country's real expenditure is the limits of its GNP (after discounting external shocks). Under these circumstances, external debt may accumulate because of suddenly deteriorating terms of trade, interest rate shocks, and world recession.

*The author is Professor of Economics, Pontifícia Universidade Católica, Rio de Janeiro. June 1985.

In this context, this study investigates the factors underlying the evolution of the external accounts of Brazil since the mid-1970s, following an approach suggested in the Dell Report and elaborated by Balassa. 1/ The reasons for a deterioration of the current account are divided into three groups: external shocks, burden of accumulated debt, and domestic policy actions. The first group comprises terms of trade, international interest rates, and world recession. The second includes the accumulated effect of past shocks and domestic policy actions. Finally, the third group encompasses the variables supposedly under the control of local policy makers: domestic absorption and the economy's tradeability.

This frame of reference is developed in the next section and is applied to the balance-of-payments experience of Brazil from 1973 to 1983. Two periods are considered, 1973-1978 and 1978-1983, the first corresponding to the first oil-shock and subsequent adjustments, and the second, to the shock wave of the late 1970s and early 1980s, leading to the debt crisis of 1982-1983. A tentative evaluation of adjustment Brazilian-style is attempted at the end of the section.

The third section considers the economic prospects for the country through 1989, with the help of a simple macro-simulation model. The discussion starts with the income multipliers revealed by the model, as the magnitudes of these are essential for an appropriate understanding of the factors affecting the growth prospects of the country in the next few years. A summary of the results of the simulations follows for the 1984-1989 period, under three alternative scenarios. Conclusions are summarized in the fourth section. The algebra of the current-account decomposition exercises and the structure of the model used in the simulations are presented in appendices.

2. EXTERNAL SHOCKS AND DOMESTIC POLICIES, 1973-1983

Brazil's balance-of-payments and growth experience since the late 1960s can be summarized as follows 2/:

1968-1970:   Strong economic recovery, following the 1963-1967 stabilization period, when economic activity slowed down. Serious export promotion activities begin with the institution of mini-devaluations. New mechanisms are introduced to facilitate the access of domestic residents to the Eurodollar market.

1971-1973:   "Brazilian economic miracle" period, during which growth rates attain previously unrecorded magnitudes. Primary exports boom and heavy borrowing abroad starts. Inflation stabilizes at under 20 per cent per year.

1974-1975:   First oil-shock and its immediate aftermath. Recrudescence of inflation. There is turmoil and indecision in Brazilian policy-making.

1976-1978:   Adjustment Brazilian-style is put into practice. Imports are restricted and relatively high GDP growth rates are maintained. Inflation rates reach a new level of 40 per cent per year.

1979-1980:   Second oil-shock and the October 1979 "Monetarist Revolution" in United States monetary policy. Brazil considers slowing down under Simonsen, but an expansionist policy course is favoured under Delfim Netto. Inflation skyrockets to 100 per cent per year.

1981-   :   Drastic adjustment to rapidly deteriorating external circumstances and galloping domestic inflation. An "Extended Arrangement" is signed with the IMF in January 1983.

This section skips the 1968-1973 experience to deal initially with the first oil-shock period, from 1974 to 1978. The second part discusses the shock wave and domestic adjustments of the late 1970s and early 1980s. A tentative evaluation of the failures and accomplishments of the adjustment policies followed by Brazil closes the section.

(a) The 1973-1978 experience

The first oil shock hit the Brazilian economy at the height of a formidable economic expansion, stretching from 1968 to 1973. Worsening terms of trade were, however, by no means alone in accounting for the massive deterioration of Brazil's external accounts after 1973. A rise in import volume in 1974 and a decline of world trade in 1975 largely explain why Brazil's current-account deficit more than tripled from 2.0 per cent of potential GDP in 1973 to 6.3 per cent in 1974, while declining only to 5.1 per cent in the following year. 3/

More precise estimates are displayed in table 1. A breakdown has been made of the factors underlying the worsened external accounts of the country after 1973. The variations in the ratio of the current-account deficit to potential GDP between each year in the 1974-1978 period and the 1973 base-year are analyzed in the light of the behaviour of three groups of explanatory factors: external shocks, burden of accumulated debt, and domestic policy actions.

The first group - external shocks - is subdivided into terms-of-trade deterioration, interest rate shocks, and retardation of world trade growth. The measurement of the first two effects is quite standard, but an explanation is needed for the computation of the effect of the deceleration of world trade growth, which may be controversial.4/ First the ratio of Brazil's exports to potential GDP is expressed as a product of the ratio of Brazil's export to world

Table 1

BRAZIL: Decomposition of the current-account deficit increases between each year in the 1974-1978 period and the 1973 base-year* (All variables are ratios to potential GDP)

Explanatory Factors	1974	1975	1976	1977	1978
1. External shocks	2.46	3.90	1.43	.46	2.00
1.1 Terms-of-trade deterioration a/	2.01	2.45	.60	-.70	.75
1.2 Interest rate shocks b/	.03	.18	-.06	-.04	-.03
1.3 Retardation of world trade growth	.42	1.27	.89	1.20	1.28
2. Burden of accumulated debt c/	-.07	.33	.59	.57	.67
3. Domestic policy actions d/	2.18	-1.09	-.19	-.85	-2.06
3.1 Domestic recession e/	.46	.23	.37	.02	-.14
3.1.1. Fixed investment cuts f/	(.16)	(.31)	(.30)	(.09)	(-.06)
3.1.2. Domestic output contraction g/	(.00)	(-.08)	(-.07)	(-.07)	(-.20)
3.2 Increased tradeability h/	2.00	-1.30	-.60	-.92	-1.95
3.2.1. Export deepening i/	(.11)	(-1.06)	(-.01)	(-.05)	(-.41)
3.2.2. Import replacement j/	(1.89)	(-.24)	(-.61)	(-1.42)	(-1.54)
3.3 Profit remittances compression k/	.02	-.02	.04	.05	.03
4. Calculated deficit increase [(1) + (2) + (3)]	4.57	3.14	1.83	.18	.61
5. Interaction effects and adding-up errors	-.28	-.11	-.06	.02	.17
6. Observed deficit increase [(4) + (5)]	4.29	3.03	1.77	.20	.78

Note: *The decomposition factors were calculated using an average of current-year and 1973 weights.

a/ Negative value means terms-of-trade improvement.
b/ Negative value means interest rate reduction.
c/ Negative value means reduced foreign liabilities ratio to potential GDP.
d/ Positive value means deficit increasing policy.
e/ Positive value means domestic expansion.
f/ Positive value means investment increases.
g/ Positive value means output expansion.
h/ Positive value means reduced tradeability.
i/ Positive value means export contraction.
j/ Positive value means import additions.
k/ Positive value means profit remittances decompression.

exports, multiplied by the ratio of world exports to potential GDP (all variables in constant dollar terms). Thus, the variations in the ratio of Brazilian exports to potential GDP can be (approximately) written as the sum of two components, one related to changes in the ratio of Brazil's exports to world exports, the other to changes in the ratio of world exports to Brazil's potential GDP. It is the latter which is designated as the <u>retardation of world trade growth</u> effect in table 1. The former appears as <u>export deepening</u>, among the domestic policy actions in the table. The appearance of the world trade growth effect as an external shock in table 1 presumes that the growth rate of Brazil's potential GDP in the period (of about 7.6 per cent per year) was in line with the normal behaviour of world trade growth. Hence, if the ratio between the two fell, the explanation lies in an insufficient growth of world trade after the first oil shock, rather than in any excessive expansion of Brazil's potential GDP in the period.

The second group of factors consists of only one component - <u>the burden of accumulated debt</u> - which measures the deterioration in the service accounts explained by an increase in the (end-of-past-year) debt to potential GDP. This effect is calculated on the assumption of unchanged interest rates, as the effects of the latter are captured by the <u>interest rate shocks</u>, in the first group of factors

<u>Domestic policy actions</u> designate the third and last group of explanatory factors. The <u>domestic recession</u> component accounts for a shrinkage of imports, explained either by a lowering of the fixed investment ratio, or by a reduction of the overall capacity utilization rate. Fixed investment is given privileged attention because its materialization is assumed to require complementary capital goods imports, in addition to the imports of other goods and services which are associated with the generation of aggregate domestic output. <u>Increased tradeability</u> measures the effects of both an expansion of Brazil's market share in world exports, and a replacement of imports by domestic substitutes. <u>Import replacement</u> is measured by a reduction of the import coefficients in the production of domestic output and in the composition of fixed investment. Underlying the classification of import replacement as an increased tradeability phenomenon is the assumption that the resources for the production of the domestic substitutes were drawn either out of idleness or the home goods sector, not of potential export activities. The final domestic policy component relates to changes in the ratio of profit remittances to potential GDP. Such changes may be due to factors only remotely associated with domestic policy actions, but their relatively small magnitude in the period seemed to make unnecessary a more precise classification procedure.

The sum of the effects of external shocks, accumulated debt burden, and domestic policy actions is equal to the observed variations in the ratio of the current-account deficit to potential GDP, after allowance for interaction effects and adding-up errors, as in table 1.

After the sharp rise in the current-account deficit ratio in 1974-1975, a significant improvement occurred in the 1976-1977 period, by and large explained by a temporary recovery of the terms of trade, in the wake of the mini-commodity boom and the coffee frosts of the period. In spite of a considerably improved domestic policy performance, the deficit situation worsened again in 1978, as these temporary factors faded away, and the growth of world trade continued to lag behind the expansion of Brazil's productive capacity.

The economy was kept in high gear during the period, as is witnessed by the positive signs and values in the "domestic recession" line except for 1978. Also, the negative impacts of external shocks and increased debt were not at all compensated by a deeper penetration of Brazil's exports in foreign markets. Hence, the bulk of the adjustment was effected through import replacement, which proceeded at an expanding rate after 1975. The following two comments should, however, be made. First, the dismal performance of Brazilian exports in the period is entirely explained by the very poor quantitative behaviour of coffee exports. Indeed, the following picture is obtained, if we break down the figures for export deepening in table 1 into coffee and non-coffee exports:

	1974	1975	1976	1977	1978
Export deepening	.11	-1.06	.01	.50	-.41
Coffee exports	.64	.36	.65	1.51	1.01
Non-coffee exports	-.53	-1.42	-.64	-1.01	-1.42

Hence, non-coffee exports were indeed promoted but not on a sufficient scale to compensate for the coffee market losses in the period.

Second, the decomposition below of the import replacement effect clearly indicates that practically nothing was done to substitute domestic products for oil imports in the short run, hence, the emphasis of import substitution fell on items the relative prices of which did not in fact increase over the period under consideration.

	1974	1975	1976	1977	1978
Import replacement	1.89	-.24	-.61	-1.42	-1.54
Capital goods	.43	.64	-.33	-.87	-.95
Other imports	1.59	-.76	-.27	-.52	-.57
Oil	-.13	-.12	-.01	-.03	-.02

The final picture is of a developing economy that decided not to ride a recession as a means of coping with an adverse external environment. Having made that decision, it proceeded to adjust its balance of payments through a significant replacement of capital goods and other non-oil imports after 1975. Its efforts to substitute domestic for foreign energy sources and to penetrate foreign markets were, however, much less than required under the circumstances. Hence, foreign debt piled up, and the problem was essentially postponed for the future.

(b) The 1978-1983 experience

The future did not prove to be particularly accommodating. Much to the contrary, after 1978 Brazil was hit by a renewed series of external shocks of increasing strength, which finally forced its Government to apply for help to the International Monetary Fund.

The relevant facts are synthesized in table 2. As in the previous exercise, this table decomposes the variations in the current-account deficit in each year of the 1979-1983 period, taking 1978 as the base-year from which changes are measured.

The increasing strength of the external shocks is clearly revealed in this table. Everything else remaining constant, these shocks would have produced a deterioration of the ratio of the current-account deficit to potential GDP of no less than 5.6 percentage points, when 1978 is compared either with 1982 or 1983. Terms-of-trade deterioration accounts for the bulk of the total shock, while interest rate increases and retardation of world trade growth share responsibility for the remaining losses.

As in the early 1970s, domestic policy-making was slow to react to these shocks, and in 1979 actually managed to magnify their effect on the current account. However, once forced into action by a deteriorating international reserves position, Brazil's policy-makers displayed a considerable capacity both to slow down the economy and to expand its tradeability. The extent of both export deepening and import replacement in the 1981-1983 period is impressive indeed.

Domestic reaction was eventually very forceful, but unfortunately it came too late. In view of the extent of the damage done by the external shocks, it certainly was not enough to maintain the country's creditworthiness in international credit markets, after the Malvinas (Falklands) War and the Moratorium on the Mexican debt. Owing to the disruption of the international private financial market precipitated by these events, Brazil suddenly became unable not only to finance its current-account deficits but also to roll-over its previously accumulated debts. In a short space of time after "Black September" 1982, the country had to be rescued by a hastily composed package of short-term official credits, while negotiations took place for a restructuring of its previously accumulated private and public debt. Fresh money was also required, given the permanence of the current-account deficit and the exhaustion of Brazil's international reserves. Unable to honour its debt-service commitments, the country was thus forced to submit an adjustment programme to the International Monetary Fund. 5/

(c) Adjustment Brazilian style: an interpretation

There is no denying the tardiness in Brazil's adjustment efforts. But the reluctance to adjust should be viewed in the light of the severity of the external shocks suffered by the country in the mid-1970s and early 1980s. A less exuberant response would certainly have been welcome both in 1974-1976 and 1979/80. Even in those years, the negative effect of domestic growthmanship on the current account was relatively minor when compared with the impact of external shocks. (See the values in lines 1.1 and 3.1, in tables 1 and 2). The Brazilian Government is certainly guilty of excessive optimism, perhaps also of complacency in the matter of exchange rate policy, but much less guilty of excessive spending

There is, however, one sense in which this is perhaps too lenient an evaluation of Brazil's pattern of adjustment to external shocks. In hindsight, a more export-oriented strategy would have paid handsome dividends indeed. To illustrate this with a somewhat extreme example, let us assume that, after 1975, Brazil's non-coffee exports would have managed to maintain their share in world exports growing at the same rate as in 1973-75, that is, at 11.4 per cent per year. Not much would be involved in terms of external market penetration: in 1978, the share of Brazil's non-coffee exports in total world exports would have been 1.6 per cent, rather than the observed 1.2 per cent. Relative magnitudes would also have been small, in comparison to Brazil's productive potential: the ratio of non-coffee exports to potential GDP in 1978 would have climbed to 9.0 per cent from the observed 6.7 per cent. In 1978, the Brazilian economy was operating at 96 per cent of its capacity, hence there was some room for expansion, but not much. This means that if exports were higher, domestic absorption needed to be somewhat lower, but then (ignoring differences in product composition between exports and domestic absorption) the maximum contraction required would have been 2.7 percentage points, distributed over a period of three years. This would hardly seem to imply an austerity programme of major dimensions. 6/ While austerity and external market penetration would have been minor, the results in terms of reduced current-account deficits would have been extraordinary. Even without taking into account the lesser debt burden, the current-account deficits would have been cut in half in 1976, disappeared in 1977, and turned into a surplus in 1978.

Similarly, the deterioration in the external accounts of the country after 1978 could have been lessened substantially, if a prompter response to the external shocks had taken place already in 1979, as was indeed the plan of the ousted Planning Minister, Mario Simonsen. 7/

There are, of course, good economic reasons explaining why the Brazilian Government chose not to push exports more aggressively. On the one hand, in the mid-1970s there was no reason to foresee the complete reversal (which eventually occurred in 1979) of the cheap money policy traditionally followed by the industrial countries since

Table 2

BRAZIL: Decomposition of the variations in the current-account
deficit between each year in the 1979-1983 period and the 1978
base-year[a]
(percentage points)

Explanatory Factors	1979	1980	1981	1982	1983
1. External shocks	1.08	3.42	5.00	5.64	5.31
1.1 Terms-of-trade deterioration	.85	2.35	2.87	2.98	3.19
1.2 Interest rate shocks	.30	.80	1.23	1.47	.60
1.3 Retardation of world trade growth[b]	-.07	.27	.90	1.19	1.52
2. Burden of accumulated debt	.21	.62	.65	.90	.83
3. Domestic policy actions[c]	.12	-2.06	5.00	4.53	-6.35
3.1 Domestic recession[d]	-.04	.13	-.86	-1.13	-1.39
3.1.1 Fixed investment cuts	(-.04)	(-.06)	(-.28)	(-.34)	(-.40)
3.1.2 Domestic output contraction[e]	(0.00)	(.19)	(-.58)	(-.79)	(-.99)
3.2 Increased tradeability[f]	.13	-2.02	-3.96	-3.34	-4.90
3.2.1 Export deepening	(.00)	(-1.40)	(-2.35)	(-1.65)	(-2.25)
3.2.2 Import replacement	(.13)	(-.62)	(-1.61)	(-1.69)	(-2.65)
3.3 Profit remittances compression[h]	.03	-.17	-.18	-.06	.06
4. Calculated deficit increase[i]	1.41	1.98	.65	2.01	-.21
5. Interaction effects and adding-up errors	-.07	.09	-.02	-.64	-.99
6. Observed deficit increase[i]	1.34	2.07	.63	1.37	-1.20

a/ The decomposition factors were calculated using current weights.
b/ Negative value means acceleration of world trade growth.
c/ Positive value means deficit increasing policies.
d/ Positive value means domestic expansion.
e/ Positive value means output expansion.
f/ Positive value means reduced tradeability.
g/ Positive value means import additions.
h/ Positive value means profit remittances decompression.
i/ Negative value means deficit decrease.

the Second World War. Hence, if the international banks made credit
available, it seemed to pay to get into debt,even at floating rates of
interest. On the other hand, boosting non-traditional exports would
require either more subsidies or exchange rate devaluation. Costs
would be measured in terms of larger budget deficits and increased
inflationary pressures, at a time when both were already getting out of
hand.

These economic calculations are real enough, but in the end a
broader political economy question seems to be at stake. The
alternative programme of export expansion which was previously outlined
seems reasonable when measured against Brazil's tiny share in world
markets or the country's potential GDP. But it implies that non-coffee
exports would have had to grow at an average real rate of 20 per cent
per year, sustained over the entire period from 1973 to 1978. It might
have been realizable, but it would have required a fundamental
commitment of the Government, both in political and organizational
terms. However, before the current crisis, a strong political movement
has never developed in Brazil that would defend at the same time a
vigorous policy of both import substitution and export promotion, as
the 1970s required. Historically, it has always been one or the
other. Import substitution comes together with export discrimination,
as exemplified by the traditional Latin American rule of privileged
access of residents to national products. In inward-oriented growth
strategies, non-traditional exports typically are only the residual
which is left over from domestic production after local demand has been
satisfied. By contrast, export orientation tends to be associated with
import liberalization. In the late 1970s in Latin America, this
association was carried to its extremes by the Southern Cone
monetarists' misuse of traditional comparative advantage theory, as a
justification for their naive attempt to promote exports by opening up
domestic markets to competitive imports. At a more mundane level,
Northern neo-protectionism increasingly seems to require North-South
trade in manufactures to be based on "reciprocity" of trade
regulations, except when, as in the case of East Asian newly
industrializing countries, the geopolitics of the East-West conflict
determine otherwise. These considerations help to explain why in
Brazil it has always been so difficult to work out a compromise between
a "nationalist" (i.e., pro-import substitution) and an
"internationalist" (i.e., pro-export promotion) growth strategy. They
also help to explain why Brazil, when deciding to promote manufactured
exports in the 1970s, also chose to diversify its customers, giving
less prominence to OECD and more to developing and socialist countries.

3.   ECONOMIC PROSPECTS THROUGH 1989

This section investigates the aftermath of the debt crisis. The
first part initially establishes the fact that, as a consequence of
this crisis, Brazil has become an economy subject to foreign exchange
constraints. The income multipliers extracted from the simulation
model are then used to investigate the sensitivity of Brazil's actual
and potential GDP to variations in relevant exogenous variables. The
second part presents a summary of medium-term GDP growth simulations

under three alternative scenarios. The first represents a continuation of current trends in the world economy and in the debt renegotiation process, assuming a passive stance of domestic policy-making vis-à-vis the tradeability of the Brazilian economy. The second scenario illustrates the effects of additional export promotion efforts, and the third contemplates the consequences of an enhanced access of Brazil to external sources of finance.

(a) Income multipliers in the simulation model

Brazil's industrial economy has been in deep recession since the last quarter of 1980. In November 1983, industrial production was 11 per cent lower than its average value in 1980. Most severely hit was the capital goods sector, the production index of which stood in November 1983 at 55 per cent of its average value in 1980 The Vargas Foundation's quarterly industrial survey estimates that only 72 per cent of Brazil's manufacturing capacity was in operation in January 1984. 8/ For the economy as a whole, Bonelli and Malan (1984) estimate an overall output gap of 22 per cent in 1983.

These figures indicate that there is considerable slack capacity in the Brazilian economy in early 1984. Hence, up to a point, in the near future output growth can indeed be demand-driven, provided that sufficient foreign exchange is made available to balance the external accounts. 9/

The dynamics of a large economy constrained by the availability of foreign exchange, like Brazil in the mid-1980s, are peculiar indeed. For the relevant marginal import coefficients are unlikely to exceed 10 per cent of Brazil's GDP in the near future. The implication is that each additional dollar of imports (apart from inventory replenishment) will tend to be associated with about 10 additional dollars of GDP. This example helps to explain why the income multipliers for foreign exchange related variables are as large as shown in the first line of table 3. (All figures in this table are derived from the simulation model for the Brazilian economy presented in appendix 2.) For example, each additional 1 per cent increase in world interest rates leads to a decline of $11.4 billion in Brazil's GDP (or 3.8 per cent of its estimated dollar value in 1983).

Table 3 displays the income multipliers of export demand, foreign savings (i.e., current-account deficit financing), foreign capital income (i.e., interest on foreign debt and profit remittances), domestic savings, and import substitution (i.e., reductions of the import coefficients both in the production of domestic output and in the composition of fixed investment). A distinction is made between the values of the multipliers when the economy is constrained by foreign exchange (implying that actual GDP is less than potential GDP) and when it is contrained by domestic capacity (which implies that actual GDP is equal to potential GDP). In the first case, separate multipliers are shown for (current-year) actual GDP and (next-year)

External Shocks and Growth Prospects: Brazil Case

Table 3

BRAZIL: Income multipliers in the simulation model,
with and without a foreign exchange constraint

	Exogenous changes at time t						
	$ billion increase in real export demand	$ billion increase in current-account deficit financing	$ billion increase in factor-service payments	1 percentage point increase in dollar interest rates a/	1 percentage point increase in domestic savings rate	1 percentage point reduction in capital goods import coefficient	1 percentage point reduction in current goods import coefficient
Endogenous variations							
Case A							
Foreign exchange constraint applies							
. Variation of GDP in $ billions at time t	11.2	10.2	-11.0	-11.3	-2.9	11.5	33.7
. Variation of potential GDP in $ billions at time t + 1	1.7	2.6	-1.9	-1.9	.83	.38	4.2
Case B							
Domestic capacity constraint applies							
. Variation of GDP and of potential GNP in $ billions at time t + 1	N/A b/	.41	-.06	-.06	1.5	N/A b/	N/A b/

a/ Calculated for the estimated value of net foreign liabilities in December 1982 ($ 103 billion).
b/ Not applicable because the trade balance is endogenously determined by the difference between potential output and domestic absorption. This implies, first, that actual exports do not increase when export demand goes up and, second, that actual exports decline when domestic demand shifts out of imports into domestic output.

potential GDP. In the second, the same multipliers apply to both concepts, as income-generating capacity is fixed in the short run and, in Harrod-Domar fashion, a function of fixed investment in the long run (which in our case occurs next year, because a simple one-year lag is assumed for the maturation of investment).

The values of the multipliers in the first line of table 3 were derived from a one-sector fixed-price macroeconomic model. Hence, they tend to overstate the importance of the foreign exchange constraint, as they are unable to capture the possibilities for import substitution which exist in a real-world multisectoral flexible-price economy. For example, Brazil succeeded in significantly compressing its import coefficients in the 1980-1983 period, even though the values of these coefficients were already relatively low, in comparison with the mid-1970s. Nonetheless, with the exception of the energy sector, Brazil seems now to have exhausted its limits for import substitution, within the confines of its open developing capitalist economy model. Hence the restriction on imports should indeed be a critical determinant of the growth prospects of the country in the remainder of the 1980s. The thrust of this conclusion is appropriate captured by the multipliers in table 3, even though the "real world" importance of the foreign exchange constraint probably is exaggerated by the numbers in the table.

In this context, it should also be pointed out that the multipliers in Case A assume that each and every dollar added to (or subtracted from) the Brazilian economy is used only to increase (or reduce) necessary imports. No room is allowed either for luxury imports (defined negatively as those not required to increase domestic production or to complement domestic investment) or for induced variations in net international assets. Thus, for example, if part of an additional $1 billion of export earnings is used to allow some luxury imports, or to replenish international reserves, or to anticipate foreign debt repayments, the relevant income multipliers should be reduced accordingly, i.e. they should be multiplied by the share of the additional $1 billion which is actually used to increase necessary imports.

If the provision of foreign exchange is critical, the impact of domestic savings on growth is more intricate. An increase in domestic savings releases both domestic and imported resources from the consumption goods sector. The foreign exchange thus saved can be used to expand domestic investment. But the capital goods sector is much more import-intensive than the consumption goods sector. Hence, not all domestic resources released from consumption can be redeployed to expand investment. The result is that national income falls as domestic savings expand, when the economy is subject to foreign exchange constraints. Notice that the underlying mechanism is rather distinct from the "paradox of parsimony" in simple macro-Keynesian models. For investment does respond to an increase in savings, as indicated by the positive multiplier of domestic savings on (next year's) potential output in table 3. The problem here has to do not with a postulated insensitivity of investment to domestic savings, but with distinct sectoral import intensities in a foreign exchange constrained context. The underlying assumption is that the government has full control over the investment activities in the economy; hence, that it can connect or disconnect them at will, according to the availability of foreign exchange. However, in a mixed developing economy, like Brazil, a government-sponsored credit expansion may fail to bring forth private investment, if the situation is one of generalized unused capacity in the industrial sector. In this "Keynesian" context, more than the mere provision of foreign exchange would be required to reignite the private economy, after a prolonged recession.

The magnitudes of the income multipliers vary greatly, depending on whether the economy is constrained by foreign exchange or by domestic capacity. Multipliers are generally much lower in the latter case, with the notorious exception of the situation where the domestic savings rate increases, which has its strongest impact on income when the economy is constrained by available capacity. Furthermore, export demand increases and import coefficient reductions have a very strong impact on income when the economy is foreign exchange constrained, but not when the domestic capacity constraint applies. The reason is that in the latter case the trade balance is endogenously determined by the difference between potential GDP and domestic absorption. Hence, an increase in export demand cannot materialize in higher exports unless domestic absorption falls by an equal amount. Similarly, a reduction of import coefficients must be read as a switch of domestic demand from imports into domestic output. But as potential output is given, this implies a reduction of actual exports, which nullifies the effect of import replacement both on the trade balance and on income levels.

The results in table 3 help to illuminate the question of how to measure the foreign contribution to domestic growth: by foreign savings (i.e., the current-account deficit), or by net resource transfers (i.e., the trade-cum-non-factor-services deficit).

The first measurement should be favoured in Case B in table 3, when growth is constrained by domestic capacity. In this case, factor-service payments have only a very marginal impact on domestic growth, when compared to current-account deficit financing. Each additional one-billion dollars of current account deficit financing generates $451 million in potential GDP, whereas an increase of the same amount in foreign capital income reduces domestic growth by only $60 million. The reason is that a dollar of current-account deficit financing adds a full dollar to the financing of domestic investment, whereas an additional dollar of foreign capital income reduces domestic savings only in proportion to the marginal propensity to save of domestic residents, from whose income the additional dollar was subtracted.

By contrast, Case A illustrates a situation in which net resource transfers or the so-called resources gap is the relevant concept. In this case, in which both multipliers are much higher than previously, factor-service payments level off with foreign savings in its importance for domestic growth. Measured in terms of actual output, the impact of factor services is in fact marginally higher than that of foreign savings: each additional $1 billion of factor service payments reduces GDP by a full $11 billion, whereas additional deficit finance of the same amount is capable of adding $10.2 billion to domestic income. The underlying reason is that a dollar is a dollar, independently of where it comes from. The important thing is that it is used to increase imports, which are assumed to be the only factor constraining growth in Case A.

The differences in magnitude and even in signs of the relevant multipliers help to explain the fierceness of the debate in Latin America in general and in Brazil more particularly, about the nature of IMF conditionality. Specifically in the case of Brazil, the priority target of the IMF programme is a significant increase in the domestic savings rate. 10/ The justification is that this is supposed to be the only way to maintain economic growth when foreign savings dry up. The advice is unobjectionable where the economy is constrained by domestic capacity, as table 3 indicates: to each percentage point increase in the domestic savings rate, there will correspond an increase of $1.5 billion in GDP starting the following year. A different picture, however, emerges when the economy is working below capacity because it lacks foreign exchange. Sure enough, to more domestic austerity there still will correspond an increase in the capacity to produce, though more moderate than in the first case: for each percentage point increase in the domestic saving rate there is an addition of $830 million to potential output. However, in this case it is not only the sacrifice of current consumption that is at stake. For an income drop is required in order to accommodate the foreign exchange constraint, when the import-intensive investment sector partially replaces the consumption sector as a user of the available pool of foreign exchange. To each one-percentage increase in domestic savings, there corresponds a drop in actual GDP of $2.9 billion, according to the figures in table 3. More capacity to produce is forthcoming from an increase in domestic savings, but less of it is put to productive use. Under these circumstances those of us who do not expect Brazil to be soon out of its present foreign exchange bind will naturally tend to be much less sanguine about domestic austerity than the IMF is.

(b) Simulations for 1984-1989

We start from the assumptions, which are reasonably grounded in facts, first, that in early 1984 the Brazilian economy is not fully employing its available productive capacity; secondly, that the most important reason for this is the compression of domestic demand, particularly fixed investment, which results from the tight fiscal and monetary policies applied by the Government since the last quarter of 1980; and thirdly, that these policies are by and large a response to the balance-of-payments difficulties starting in 1980 and reaching a crisis situation in the last quarter of 1982. Hence, we assume that these policies will be reversed, to the extent that the foreign exchange constraint abates, as long as the Brazilian economy continues working below capacity.

Starting from the assumed economic conditions for the base-year 1983, the simulation model generates projections until 1989. Estimates of both actual and potential GDP are produced. The former is normally constrained by the availability of foreign exchange (except when it happens to hit its ceiling, i.e., the level of potential output). The latter is driven by accumulated fixed investment minus depreciation. Imports are of two types. Capital goods imports depend on the level of investment. Non-capital goods imports depend on the level of domestic output. Domestic consumption (which includes inventory changes) is a fixed fraction of national income. Fixed investment is generated jointly with GDP, as a function of domestic savings and the availability of foreign exchange. 11/

Exports are given by an exogenous foreign demand, except when the overall economy or the export sector happens to operate at capacity. In these cases, exports are respectively assumed to be equal to the residual between total supply and domestic absorption, or to the domestic exportable capacity.

Foreign capital inflows are also given exogenously, together with international reserves accumulation. This means that the current-account deficit is exogenous. Dollar interest rates are also exogenous. The year-end external liabilities are equal to those existing at the beginning of the year plus this year's current-account deficit.

In the following scenarios, terms of trade are assumed constant, and dollar inflation is put at 5 per cent per annum. The savings rate (gross of depreciation but net of inventory changes) is kept constant at 15.5 per cent of national income. The income elasticity of employment is a constant 0.4, as suggested in Bonelli and Malan (1984). In line with the results of these same authors, the degree of capacity utilization (ratio between actual and potential GDP) is set equal to 80 per cent in 1983. In view of the diversified nature of Brazilian exports, export capacity is arbitrarily set at 10 per cent of potential GDP (or 3.7 percentage points above its observed value in 1983).

The growth of real export demand initially is assumed to be related only to GDP growth in industrialized countries. This is projected at 3 per cent per annum, as in the base cases of the recent world forecasts of different international organizations. In line with the econometric results of Cline (1983), as qualified in Leven and Roberts (1983) and Fishlow (1984), an income elasticity of 1.67 is assumed for the growth of Brazilian exports vis-à-vis industrial countries' growth. There results a growth of real export demand at 5 per cent per annum. However, in view of the good export results for 1983 and the Brazilian Government's projections for 1984/85, a higher real growth rate of 7 per cent per annum is postulated for exports in both years.

The projections assume that the extremely compressed import coefficients obtaining in 1983 are unsustainable in a growing economy. At the margin, $9 of capital goods imports are assumed to be required for each $100 of fixed investment. This is a good deal higher than the $7.50-to-$100 ratio calculated for 1983, but it is comparable to the coefficients observed immediately before 1982. Also, $7.50 of non-capital goods imports are assumed to be required, at the margin, for each $100 of GDP. This contrasts with a ratio of $5.60 to $100 obtaining in 1983, and assumes that additional gains in energy substitution will be more than compensated for by an abatement of the current restriction of non-oil imports.

World interest rates are assumed to remain relatively constant at their current high levels, as no dramatic departures are expected from the neo-conservative posture of monetary policy in the main industrial countries. This means that Brazil is assumed to pay a dollar rate of return on its net foreign liabilities of 10.5 per cent per year, throughout the simulation period. This compares with an implicitly estimated 10 per cent rate of return on Brazil's net debt plus direct investment from abroad in 1983. Thus, it allows for the upward interest rate drift which has taken place since the last quarter of 1983. 12/

Except for trade financing, private international credit markets are assumed to remain closed to Brazil. This means that only "involuntary" lending will continue to take place, at a rapidly dwindling rate. Squeezed between reduced budgets, on the one hand, and increased demands from the least developed countries, on the other, multilateral credit agencies are also assumed to contribute progressively less to financing Brazil's current-account deficit. Direct investment, however, is predicted to grow continuously from its current depressed levels. Finally, a significant build-up of international reserves is predicted throughout the period, in order to compensate for the dramatic losses since the beginning of the decade. These assumptions are spelled out in numerical terms in table 4. Altogether, they imply that current-account deficit financing for Brazil declines sharply during the decade. In fact, Brazil is assumed to be in need of starting to generate current-account surpluses as early as 1987. These projections seem to be in line with the medium-term outlook of Brazil's extended arrangement with the IMF.

Under this set of external circumstances, the short and medium term prospects of Brazil are dismal indeed. As shown in table 5, it is only in 1989 that Brazil will be able to resume GDP growth rates above the rate of growth of its population. These simulations imply that in 1989 real GDP per capita will be 6 per cent lower than in 1983, and 19 per cent lower than in 1980. 13/

The simulations are based on current trends of Brazil's extended arrangement with the IMF, assuming, moreover, an essentially passive domestic policy stance vis-à-vis the tradeability of the Brazilian economy. Their purpose, thus, is not to project what is actually going to happen, but rather to dramatize the need both for a relaxation of external constraints and for an expanded tradeability of the Brazilian economy.

As the multipliers under Case A in table 3 make abundantly clear, the Brazilian economy should rebound dramatically if external circumstances are improved, and renewed efforts are devoted to increasing the country's tradeability.

Table 4

BRAZIL: Projections for current account deficit
financing, 1984-1989
(in $ billions)

Year	Gross loan Disbursements a/ (1)	Amortizations (2)	Direct Invest- ment b/ (3)	Gross foreign reserves accumula- tion c/ (4)	Current- account deficit financing d/ (5)
1984	17.2	-8.3	.7	-4.3	5.3
1985	14.9	-9.6	.7	-2.0	4.0
1986	14.1	-12.2	.8	-.9	1.8
1987	12.5	-12.5	.9	-1.0	-.1
1988	9.8	-11.9	1.0	-1.0	-2.1
1989	6.4	-9.6	1.1	-1.7	-3.8

a/ Net of errors and omissions and of Brazilian lending abroad.
b/ Excluding reinvestments.
c/ Minus sign means increase.
d/ Excluding reinvested profits.

Table 5

BRAZIL: External constraints and growth prospects, 1984-1989[a]

Year	Current-account deficit financing ($ billion)	Real growth rate of exports (%)	GDP ($ billion) (1983 prices)	GDP growth rate (%)
1983	6.3	7.1[b]	300	-3.3
1984	5.3	7.0	306	1.9
1985	4.0	7.0	311	1.7
1986	1.8	5.0	306	-1.5
1987	-.1	5.0	309	.9
1988	-2.1	5.0	315	2.0
1989	-3.8	5.0	327	3.9

[a] Dollar inflation : 5 per cent p.a. Dollar rate of return on net foreign liabilities: 10.5 per cent p.a.

[b] Growth rate of purchasing power of exports.

Memo: End of period values	1989
Employment (1983 = 100)	104
Foreign capital stock/GDP (1983 = .34)	.25
Foreign capital stock/exports (1983 = 4.4)	2.5
Factor services/exports (1983 = .44)	.27
Capacity use (1983 = .80)	.79
Imports/GDP (1983 = 0.65)	.065
Exports/potential GDP (1983 = .063)	.079

The limitations on the latter should, however, be pointed out. First, import coefficients are already rather low. Hence, with the exception of energy substitution, not much should be expected from import replacement as a means of increasing the tradeability of Brazil's economy. Export deepening is the way out. But there are two related difficulties here. There is first the generalized lack of foreign exchange in Brazil's clients in the Third World and socialist countries. Special payments arrangements and trade agreements will need to be worked out, before these markets can regain the importance which they had in the 1970s for the growth of Brazilian exports. This means that Brazil in the 1980s will depend much more than before on a successful penetration of the highly competitive markets of the First World. The problem is that, as Brazil succeeds in doing so, both its terms of trade are likely to decline, and the pressures from the North for reciprocity of trade arrangements are likely to intensify. To the extent that these imply a reduction in the purchasing power of exports and an increse in Brazil's import coefficients, a corresponding reduction will obtain in the foreign exchange constrained growth rate of GDP.

At most, Brazilian exports might be expected to expand in real terms at 7 per cent per annum after 1985, which is 1.5 times higher than the forecast growth rate of world trade in the period. As indicated in table 6, this would improve the country's medium-term prospects considerably, but would still leave Brazilians at the end of the decade with a real per capita income barely above those obtaining in 1983.

This discussion suggests that a relaxation of the external constraint needs in fact to take place, in order to ensure a better performance of the Brazilian economy in the remainder of the 1980s. One possibility is displayed in table 7, where simulations are carried out on exactly the same assumptions as in table 6, except that current-account deficit financing is assumed to remain constant in real dollar terms, at the level of $5.3 billion in 1984 prices. As indicated in the second column in the table, this essentially amounts to capitalizing half of the factor services bill in each year of the period. To put it in another way, the negative resource transfers implicit in tables 5 and 6 need to be cut in half to guarantee the GDP growth rates displayed in table 7.

These growth rates average 6.5 per cent per year after 1984. Although quite high when compared with the recent experience of the country, they would be no more than sufficient to guarantee to Brazilians, at the end of the decade, the same per capita income which they enjoyed in 1980.

These GDP growth rates are accompanied by an improvement in the relevant debt ratios. As indicated in the memoranda accompanying the table, the foreign capital stock to GDP ratio (a proxy for the debt to GDP ratio) falls from .34 to .25 between 1983 and 1988, while the factor services to export ratio (a proxy for the ratio of interest to exports) drops from .44 in 1983 to .29 in 1988.

Table 6

BRAZIL: Growth prospects with additional export
promotion, 1984-1989[a]/

Year	Current-account deficit financing ($ billion)	GDP ($ billion) (1983 prices)	GDP growth rate (%)
1983	6.3	300	-3.3
1984	5.3	306	1.9
1985	4.0	311	1.7
1986	1.8	312	.5
1987	-.1	322	3.1
1988	-2.1	336	4.2
1989	-3.8	356	6.1

a/ Real export growth rate: 7 per cent p.a. Dollar inflation: 5 per
cent p.a. Dollar rate of return on net foreign liabilities: 10.5%
p.a.

Memo: End of period values	1989
Employment (1983 = 100)	107
Foreign capital stock/GDP (1983 = .34)	.23
Foreign capital stock/exports (1983 = 4.4)	2.3
Factor services/exports (1983 = .44)	.25
Capacity use (1983 = .80)	.85
Imports/GDP (1983 = .065)	.067
Exports/potential GDP (1983 = .063)	.084

Table 7

BRAZIL: Growth prospects with export promotion and constant
real capital inflows, 1984-1989[a]

Year	Current-account deficit financing		GDP	GDP
	($ billion)	(As a ratio to factor services)	($ billion) (1983 prices)	growth rate (%)
1983	6.3	.61	300	-3.3
1984	5.3	.49	306	1.9
1985	5.6	.49	325	6.4
1986	5.8	.49	346	6.5
1987	6.1	.49	369	6.5
1988	6.4	.49	393	6.6
1989	6.8	.49	419	6.6

a/ See note a/ in table 6.

Memo: End of period values	1989
Employment (1983 = 100)	114
Foreign capital stock/GDP (1983 = .34)	.25
Foreign capital stock/exports (1983 = 4.4)	2.9
Factor services/exports (1983 = .44)	.29
Capacity use (1983 = .80)	.96
Imports/GDP (1983 = .065)	.072
Exports/potential GDP (1983 = .063)	.081

A final point needs to be stressed. Notice in table 7 that, with a 6.5 per cent growth rate after 1984, the level of capacity utilization is 96 per cent in 1989. This means that towards the end of the decade, the currently low rate of domestic savings in Brazil will start preventing the economy from sustaining such a GDP growth rate. When domestic capacity becomes fully utilized actual GDP cannot grow more than potential GDP does. And the pace of the latter is determined by the sum of domestic and foreign savings. In the simulation in table 7, potential GDP is growing at 3 per cent per year in 1989, while the ratio of foreign savings to GDP is only 1 per cent. Hence, domestic savings would need to increase significantly at that stage, to keep the economy growing at 6.5 per cent per year.

Domestic austerity will thus be eventually required, if sufficient foreign exchange is provided during the remainder of the 1980s. Currently, however, domestic austerity only ensures that the economy is kept in a recessionary state, hence, that it negatively adjusts to the external shocks of the late 1970s and early 1980s. Undoubtedly, domestic recession helps to tame inflation, but the careful econometric study of Modiano (1983) confirms that the Phillips curve pay-offs are very low indeed in the highly-indexed Brazilian economy. In fact, the main result until early 1984 of the monumental monetary squeeze implemented since 1980 has been a spectacular near doubling of the velocity of circulation of money accompanying a more than doubling of the rate of inflation. In spite of this evidence, the IMF is still insisting on lowering the target rate of money supply growth for 1984 to 50 per cent, even as it acknowledges the need to raise the expected inflation range from 75-100 to 100-130 per cent. 14/ This stance may succeed in halting even the mild recovery of the Brazilian economy in 1984/85 suggested in tables 5-7. More generally, the whole posture of the IMF programme ignores the fact that the indispensable condition for the resumption of growth is the provision not of savings but of foreign exchange. Significant increases in Brazil's savings rate will be required only if external circumstances in the mid- and late 1980s turn out to be much better than forecasters are currently daring to expect or statesmen willing to deliver.

4. CONCLUSIONS

Practical orthodoxy will often start an analysis of the external debt problem of the developing countries by inquiring whether the debt was incurred to increase consumption or to expand investment. Consumption increases are immediately castigated. Investment expansion may be condoned, provided that the rate of return on capital was expected to be higher than the interest rate.

This approach disregards the actual reasons for external debt accumulation in the 1970s and early 1980s, certainly in the case of Brazil, probably in other non-oil-producing developing countries as well. For the worsening of Brazil's external accounts was by and large unrelated to real domestic spending excesses. Foreign debt accumulated throughout the period mostly because of deteriorating terms of trade, interest rate shocks, and world recession.

It is true that, faced with adverse external circumstances, Brazil opted for external financing rather than domestic adjustment. This adventurous option was doomed by the shock wave of the late 1970s and early 1980s. But it must be evaluated in the context of the development strategy of a country whose previous successful growth experience led it to believe in the possibility of catching up with the industrial leaders of its time.

Brazil is now in the fourth consecutive year of declining GDP per capita. If the Central Bank of Brazil (1984) prediction of a flat GDP in 1984 is confirmed, the standard of living of the average Brazilian this year will be 17.4 per cent lower than in 1980. This is calculated by adding to an estimated 14.1 per cent decline in GDP per capita the additional real income losses implied by lower external terms of trade and higher factor payments to abroad.

The Brazilian population is estimated to grow at 2.5 per cent per year. Hence, total GDP would need to grow at an average rate of 6.5 per cent per year, after 1984, simply to recover by the end of the decade the average standard of living enjoyed by Brazilians in 1980. Coincidentally, as indicated in table 7, this is also the rate of demand growth which would achieve nearly full utilization of available domestic capacity by the end of the decade.

Brazil will not achieve this objective if it is compelled to start generating current-account surpluses as early as 1987. With exports growing initially at 7 per cent and, after 1985, at 5 per cent a year in real terms, the average GDP growth rate will be only 1.8 per cent per year in the 1985-1989 period. According to this scenario, in 1989 Brazilians stand to be 20 per cent poorer than they were in the beginning of the decade.

Part of the distance between this scenario and the target 6.5 per cent GDP growth rate can be covered by higher export growth rates, but not all of it. A realistic possibility is the maintenance, until 1989, of the 7 per cent real growth rate of exports which Brazil achieved in 1983, and which the Brazilian Government hopes to maintain both in 1984 and 1985. Inserting this hypothesis, we calculated an average GDP growth rate of 3.1 per cent for the remainder of the decade, assuming constant international interest rates.

Very little at an aggregate level can be expected from additional import substitution. Barring first prizes in the oil lottery, the energy substitution that Brazil is likely to achieve will only leave room for the necessary decompression of non-oil imports, which are at present at levels 50 per cent below those of 1980, in real terms.

Hence, the rest of the distance will have to be covered by additional finance. If the current-account deficit remains constant in real terms -- that is, if it grows at the rate of 5 per cent per year from its $5.3 billion base in 1984 -- then Brazil's GDP will grow at the required 6.5 per cent, if exports expand at 7 per cent in real terms, and LIBOR remains constant.

World trade may expand more vigorously than predicted, LIBOR may fall, and international banks may flow back to Latin America. However, as the multipliers in table 3 make abundantly clear, for Brazil these questions are too critical to be left floating in the air. An international understanding needs to be reached, guaranteeing Brazil the access to external markets and the additional finance which it requires for an adequate resumption of GDP growth rates.

According to our calculations, the successful implementation of the latter scenario will result not only in satisfactory GDP growth rates, but also in considerable improvement in debt ratios. The ratio of foreign liabilities to exports would fall from 4.4 in 1983 to 2.9 in 1984, whereas the ratio of factor services (mostly interest) to exports would decline from .44 in 1983 to .29 in 1989. Thus, under this programme, Brazil would start the 1990s with both a renovated economy and a good balance-of-payments situation.

APPENDIX 1

ALGEBRA OF THE CURRENT-ACCOUNT DECOMPOSITION EXERCISES

The current account deficit (excluding reinvested profits) at time t, in dollars, is initially expressed as the difference between imports of goods and non-factor services (NFS) plus net factor services, minus exports of goods and NFS, inclusive of unrequited transfers.

$$D(t) = M(t) + V(t) - E(t) \tag{1}$$

Imports are decomposed into capital goods, oil and other imports, each of them being expressed as the product of price and volume indexes (in 1975 dollars):

$$M(t) = P_k(t) \, J_k(t) + P_o(t) J_o(t) + P_j(t) J_y(t) \tag{2}$$

Import coefficients relate the capital goods import volume to fixed investment in real terms, and the volumes of oil and other imports to real GDP:

$$J(t) = j_k(t) I(t) \tag{3}$$

$$J_o(t) = j_o(t) Z(t) \tag{4}$$

$$J_y(t) = j_y(t) Z(t) \tag{5}$$

Net factor services are divided into net interest and other investment income (excluding reinvested profits), with the former expressed as the product of an implicit dollar interest rate and the net stock of foreign debt at the end of the previous year:

$$V(t) = V_i(t) + V_d(t) \tag{6}$$

$$V_i(t) = r_i(t) F_1(t-1) \tag{7}$$

Exports are decomposed into coffee and non-coffee exports, each of them being expressed as the product of price and volume indexes (in 1975 dollars):

$$E(t) = P_c(t) \, X_c(t) + P_n(t) X_n(t) \tag{8}$$

Export coefficients relate the volume of both coffee and non-coffee exports to the real value of world trade (as measured by the United Nations volume index of world exports of developed market economies, in 1975 dollars):

$$X_c(t) = x_c(t) W(t) \tag{9}$$

$$X_n(t) = x_n(t) W(t) \tag{10}$$

Substituting (2) to (10) in (1) and dividing the result by the dollar value of potential output, there results:

$$D(t)/Y^*(t) = j_k(t)I(t)/Z^*(t) + j_y(t)p_j(t)Z(t)/Z^*(t) +$$

$$j_o(t)p_o(t)Z(t)/Z^*(t) + r_i(t)F_i(t-1)/Y^*(t) + V_d(t)/Y^*(t) -$$

$$x_c(t)p_c(t)W(t)/Z^*(t) + x_n(t)p_n(t)W(t)/Z^*(t) \qquad (11)$$

where the dollar value of potential output is related to its real value
by use of the implicit GDP price deflator, expressed in dollars:

$$Y^*(t) = P_y(t)Z^*(t) \qquad (12)$$

and where the small p's result from the division of the respective big
P's by P_y.

Except for 1983, the conversion of the cruzeiro value of potential
GDP (as calculated by Bonelli and Malan, 1984) into dollars was done by
use of the average dollar/cruzeiro exchange rate in the Boletim Mensal
of the Central Bank of Brazil. The maxi-devaluation of February 1983
significantly changed the real parity of the cruzeiro in that year.
Consequently, for 1983, the decision was taken to calculate the value
of potential GDP by adding the rise in the United States wholesale
price index to the real change of potential GDP, as estimated in
Bonelli and Malan (1984). Thus, the value of potential GDP in 1983 in
table 2 differs from that used in the simulations.

The final formula, as numerically expressed in tables 1 and 2, is
obtained by taking first differences in equation (11):

$$[d(D(t)/Y^*(t))] = [j_k(s)(I(s)/Z^*(s))dp_k(t) +$$

$$j_y(s)(Z(s)/Z^*(s))dp_j(t) + j_o(s)(Z(s)/Z^*(s))dp_o(t) -$$

$$x_c(s)(W(s)/Z^*(s))dp_c(t) - x_n(s)(W(s)/Z^*(s))dp_n(t)] +$$

$$[(F_i(s-1)/Y^*(s))dr_i(t)] - [(p_c(s)x_c(s) +$$

$$p_n(s)x_n(s))d(W(t)/Z^*(t))] +$$

$$[r_i(s)d(F_i(t-1)/Y^*(t))] + [p_k(s)j_k(s)d(I(t)/Z^*(t)) +$$

$$(p_k(s)j_y(s) + p_o(s)j_o(s))d(Z(t)/Z^*(t)) +$$

$$((p_k(s)(I(s)/Z^*(s))dj_k(t) + p_j(s)(Z(s)/Z^*(s))dj_y(t) +$$

$$p_o(s)(Z(s)/Z^*(s))dj_o(t)) - (p_c(s)(W(s)/Z^*(s))dx_c(t) +$$

$$p_n(s)(W(s)/Z^*(s))dx_n(t)) + d(V_d(t)/Y^*(t))] +$$

[interaction terms] $\qquad (13)$

where "d" stands for the difference in the value of the magnitude
following this sign between each year of the 1974-1978 period and 1973
(or between 1979-83 and 1978), and where the bracketed terms are
identified in tables 1 and 2 as follows:

[variation in the current—account deficit ratio to potential GDP between year ____ and base-year 1973 (or 1978)] = [terms-of-trade deterioration] + [interest rate shock] + [retardation of world trade growth] + [burden of accumulated debt] - [fixed investment cuts + domestic output contraction + import replacement + export deepening + profit remittances compression] + [interaction effects and adding-up errors].

Note also the symbol "s" in equation (13), which indicates the year for which the "weights" of the decomposition terms were calculated. In this research, both a "Laspeyres" procedure, or base-year weights, and a "Paasche" procedure, or current-year weights, were initially adopted. The procedure finally selected was that which minimized the value of the interaction effects in equation (13).

APPENDIX 2

SIMULATION MODEL FOR BRAZIL

(Constant terms-of-trade version)

1. IMPORT FUNCTIONS

$$M(t) = P(t)J_z(t) + P(t)J_k(t)$$

$$J_z(t) = .091(t) - 1,578 \qquad [e_z(1983) = 1.27]$$

$$J_k(t) = .75Z(t) - 4,820 \qquad [e_k(1983) = 1.50]$$

(the constant terms are in millions of 1983 dollars)

2. EXPORT FUNCTIONS

$$E(t) = P(t)X(t)$$

$$X(t) = X(t-1)(1+h(t)) < X_{max}(t)$$

3. CURRENT ACCOUNT DEFICIT

$$D(t) = M(t) + V(t) - E(t)$$

4. DOMESTIC ABSORPTION

$$P(t)A(t) = D(t) + P(t)Z(t) - V(t)$$

5. FIXED INVESTMENT

$$P(t)I(t) = P(t)A(t) - P(t)C(t)$$

6. CONSUMPTION

(domestic absorption other than fixed investment)

$$P(t)C(t) = .845 \ [P(t)Z(t) - V(t)]$$

7. FACTOR SERVICES

$$V(t) = r(t)F(t-1)$$

8. NET FOREIGN CAPITAL STOCK

$$F(t) = F(t-1) + D(t)$$

9. DOLLAR PRICE LEVEL

$$P(t) = P(0)(1.05)^t \ ; \ P(0) = 1$$

10. POTENTIAL OUTPUT

$$Z^*(t) = .967Z^*(t-1) + .413I(t-1)$$

11.   EMPLOYMENT

$$N(t) = q[Z(t)]^{.4} \quad ; \quad N(0) = 100$$

DEFINITIONS OF VARIABLES IN APPENDICES 1 AND 2

The following symbols appear in the two previous appendices:

M   = dollar value of imports of goods and non-factor services (NFS)

J_z = Non-capital goods imports in constant dollars, which subdivided into:

  J_0 = oil imports in constant dollars

  J_y = other imports in constant dollars

J_k = capital goods imports in constant dollars

I   = fixed investment in constant dollars

Z   = GDP in constant dollars

E   = dollar value of exports of goods and NFS

C   = consumption (private consumption plus government consumption plus inventory changes) in constant dollars

D   = current-account deficit in dollars, excluding reinvested profits

V   = factor services in dollars, which subdivides into:

  V_i = net interest

  V_d = other investment income (excluding reinvested profits)

r   = rate of return of foreign capital (per cent)

r_i = rate of interest on net debt (per cent)

F   = net stock of foreign liabilities (net of international reserves on the balance-of-payments concept) in dollars

F_i = net foreign debt in dollars

Y*   = potential output in dollars

Z*   = potential output in constant dollars

P   = dollar price level

P_y = implicit price deflator, in dollars

P_k = dollar price index of capital goods imports

P_j = dollar price index of other imports

P_o = dollar price of oil imports

P_c = dollar price index of coffee exports

P_n = dollar price index of non-coffee exports

X_{max} = equal to the minimum between 10 per cent of potential GDP, and the sum of potential GNP plus imports minus domestic absorption, in constant dollars

h = growth rate of real export demand

e_k = elasticity of capital goods imports with respect to fixed investment

e_z = elasticity of current goods imports with respect to GDP

N = employment index with $N(0) = 100$

q = conversion factor such that $N(0) = 100$; or $q = 100/Z(0)^{.4}$

FOOTNOTES

1/   Cf. Dell and Lawrence (1980) and Balassa (1983).

2/   For details, see Bacha (1980) and Bacha and Malan (1984).

3/   Figures for Brazil's potential GDP are taken from Bonelli and
      Malan (1984). Departing from a popular procedure in the
      literature, we replace actual GNP by potential GDP, as the
      appropriate scalar to measure the size of current-account
      deficits. This is done on the assumption that potential GDP is a
      better measure than actual GNP of the permanent income of a
      country. Potential GNP would perhaps be a better scalar than
      either of them, if measures were available of the 'permanent'
      rates of return on net foreign liabilities for each year of the
      observation period. With the exception of 1983, observed exchange
      rates are used to convert into dollars the potential GDP initially
      measured in cruzeiros. This implies the assumption that market
      exchange rates adequately reflect the external purchasing power of
      both actual and potential domestic production. A better
      alternative would have been to calculate the dollar value of
      potential GDP using "equilibrium" exchange rates, if these were
      available for the period under consideration. See appendix 1 for
      additional methodological details.

4/   A similar procedure to calculate the impact of world recession was
      used by Balassa (1983).

5/   More details are provided in Bacha (1983b).

6/   This calculation assumes that domestic absorption was equal to
      potential GDP, which was roughly the case in the late 1970s.

7/   For further evaluation of post-1979 Brazilian economic policies,
      see Bacha (1983a) and Diaz-Alejandro (1983).

8/   Interpretation of this figure should take into account that 90 per
      cent was the highest capacity utilization rate ever reported by
      Brazilian industrialists in this survey, which has been conducted
      by the Vargas Foundation since 1968.

9/   Most of the 20-odd percentage points of excess capacity in the
      Brazilian economy in 1983 consists of non-exportables. However,
      in 1983, only 6.3 per cent of available capacity was used to
      generate exports, and in none of the following simulations does
      the expansion of exports require the use of more than 8.4 per cent
      of the contemporaneously available domestic productive capacity.
      Hence, specific capacity limitations in exportable production are
      also unlikely to be a major constraint on Brazil's economic growth
      in the remainder of the decade.

10/   Cf. appendix to Galveas (1983).

11/   See appendix 2 for a specification of the model.

12/ The implicit rate of return for 1983 subdivides into an implicit interest rate on net foreign debt of 11.5 per cent, and an implicit profit remittances rate on foreign direct investment from abroad of 3.8 per cent. The latter is very low by historical standards and likely to increase in the near future, as foreign exchange controls are relaxed. Thus, the assumption of a constant rate of return presupposes that this effect will be compensated by a higher share of direct investment in foreign liabilities, and by lower international interest rates in the outer years of the projections period.

13/ These figures assume that Brazil's population grows at 2.5 per cent per annum, and that the current revision of the national accounts will confirm the Bonelli-Malan (1984) estimate of a 3.5 per cent drop in real GDP in 1981.

14/ Cf. data in Central Bank of Brazil, 1983 and 1984.

REFERENCES

Bacha, E. (1980). "Selected Issues in Post-1964 Brazilian Economic Growth." Models of Growth and Distribution for Brazil. Lance Taylor et al. (New York: Oxford University Press), pp. 17-48.

Bacha, E. (1983a). "Vicissitudes of Recent Stabilization Attempts in Brazil and the IMF Alternative." IMF Conditionality. Ed. J. Williamson (Washington, D.C.: Institute for International Economics/MIT Press).

Bacha, E. (1983b). "The IMF and the Prospects for Adjustment in Brazil." Prospects for Adjustment in Argentina, Brazil and Mexico: Responding to the Debt Crisis. Ed. J. Williamson. Washington, D.C.: Institute for International Economics/MIT Press).

Bacha, E. and P. Malan (1984). "Brazil's Debt: From the Miracle to the Fund". Unpublished manuscript, forthcoming in Democratizing Brazil?. Ed. A. Stepan. (New Haven: Yale University Press).

Balassa, B. (1983). "Policy Responses to External Shocks in Sub-Saharan African Countries". Journal of Policy Modelling, 5(1), (March), pp. 75-106.

Bonelli, R. and P. Malan (1984). "Economic Growth, Industrialization, and the Balance of Payments: Brazil in the 1970s and 1980s". Unpublished manuscript (74 pages).

Central Bank of Brazil (1983). Brazil Economic Program: Internal and External Adjustment, vol. 1, October.

Central Bank of Brazil (1984). Brazil Economic Program: Internal and External Adjustment, vol. 2, March.

Dell, S. and R. Lawrence (1980). Balance of Payments Adjustment in
    Developing Countries (Elmsford, N.Y.: Pergamon).

Cline, W. (1983). International Debt and the Stability of the World
    Economy. Institute of International Economics Policy Analyses in
    International Economics, vol. 4, September, 134 pp.

Diaz-Alejandro, Carlos F. (1983). "Some Aspects of the 1973-83
    Brazilian Payments Crisis". Brookings Papers on Economic
    Activity, 2:515-52.

Fishlow, A. (1984). "Coping with the Creeping Crisis of Debt".
    Department of Economics, Working Paper No. 181. (Berkeley:
    University of California, February, 60 pp).

Galveas, E. (1983). A Crise Mundial e a Estratégia Brasileira de
    Ajustamento do Balanco de Pagamentos (Brasília, D.F., March).

Leven, R. and D. Roberts (1983). "Latin America's Prospects for
    Recovery". Federal Reserve Bank of New York Quarterly Review,
    Autumn, 8(3):6-13.

Modiano, E. (1983). "A Dinâmica de Salários e Precos na Economia
    Brasileira, 1966-81". Pesquisa e Planejamento Economico, 13(1),
    April.

BALANCE-OF-PAYMENTS ADJUSTMENT IN INDIA
1970-71 TO 1983-84

Montek Singh Ahluwalia*

1. Introduction

In common with other oil-importing developing countries, India experienced a severe external shock in 1973 when oil prices quadrupled and again after 1979, when oil prices more than doubled. India was able to adjust to both shocks somewhat more easily than other oil-importing developing countries, but there were important differences between the adjustments in the two cases. The adjustment to the first oil shock was remarkably easy, so much so that the current deficit, which peaked in 1974-75, turned to a substantial surplus within two years. The second external shock was more severe, and although a substantial degree of adjustment has taken place since then, especially in comparison with the severe difficulties faced by many developing countries, the adjustment is not yet complete (1984). The current-account deficit has been reduced as a percentage of GDP, but with present prospects for the availability of external finance, it will be necessary to reduce the current deficit further in the rest of the decade. This will not be easy to achieve.

This paper examines India's adjustment experience after each of the two oil shocks with a view to identifying the factors at work in each case. It also examines the balance-of-payments prospects in the period up to 1989-90. Section 2 provides an overview of India's balance-of-payments experience in the context of developments in the domestic economy and the evolution of policy. Section 3 presents a quantitative analysis of the factors underlying the observed changes in the current-account deficit which followed the first shock and the second, using the decomposition technique outlined in the terms of reference appended to G. Helleiner's synthesis paper. Section 4 presents the results obtained from using the simulation model in the said "terms of reference" to explore the prospects for the Indian economy in the rest of the decade.

*The author is Economic Adviser in the Department of Economic Affairs, Ministry of Finance of the Government of India. July 1985.

2. The balance of payments from 1970-71 to 1983-84

India's balance of payments in the period 1970-71 to 1983-84 is presented in detail in table 1. A summary view is presented in table 2 which shows movements in the current-account deficit in value terms and also as a proportion of both GDP and exports of goods and services. The two phases of external imbalance are clearly identifiable in Table 2, the first beginning in 1974-75 immediately after the first oil shock, and the second in 1980-81 following the second oil shock in 1979.

(a) The first oil shock

The first oil shock hit the economy at a time when economic performance had been weak for some years. A succession of indifferent harvests, first in 1971-72 and again in 1972-73, had depressed agricultural production and GDP growth (table 3) and also generated inflationary pressure well before the rise in oil prices. The rate of inflation in wholesale prices rose to 10 per cent in 1972-73 and reached 20 per cent in 1973-74 (table 3), with much of the price rise in 1973-74 occurring before the impact of higher oil prices.

The fourfold increase in international crude oil prices between September 1973 and April 1974 raised the petroleum import bill (crude and products) from Rs.203 crores in 1972-73 to Rs.1157 crores in 1974-75, an increase of Rs.954 crores in two years. The current-account deficit deteriorated by almost the same amount in those years from a surplus of Rs.28 crores in 1972-73 to a deficit of Rs.961 crores in 1974-75. Since oil prices were not the only import prices that increased it is more appropriate to assess the effect of the higher oil prices on the current-account deficit by considering what would have happened had the unit value of oil imports increased by the same proportion as the unit value of all other imports. This calculation confirms that the oil price increase was indeed the dominant factor in the current-account deterioration. Had unit values of oil imports increased between 1972-73 and 1974-75 by the same proportion as unit values of other imports, the current deficit in 1974-75 would have been only Rs.111 crores, or less than 0.2 per cent of GDP, whereas in fact it amounted to 1.4 per cent of GDP.

The current-account deficit of 1.4 per cent of GDP in 1974-75 represented a considerable deterioration from the average level of 0.4 per cent in the preceding three years. The deficit appears small as a percentage of GDP compared with figures for other countries, but this impression is due to the fact that trade flows are small relative to GDP in India, as is the case in most other large economies. The financing problem posed by the larger deficit is better seen when expressed as a percentage of total exports of goods and services. This shows an increase from an average of 8 per cent in 1970-71 to 1972-73 to just over 25 per cent in 1974-75 (table 2).

As it happened, the economy was able to adjust to tne external shock in a remarkably short time. From the peak level of Rs.961 crores in 1974-75, the deficit declined to Rs.579 crores in 1975-76 and was converted into a surplus in 1976-77 amounting to 1.3 per cent of GDP. Thereafter, the current account remained in surplus (though declining as a percentage of GDP) until 1979-80, when the economy experienced the second oil shock. As shown in table 4, the level of foreign exchange reserves rose in 1975-76, and the pace of reserve accumulation accelerated in the next two years.

This turnaround in the external payments situation was the result of a combination of three very favourable developments which were partly a reflection of favourable external circumstances and partly a reflection of domestic policy. To begin with, there was relatively easy availability of external financing to meet the larger deficit arising from the terms-of-trade deterioration. The availability of finance would normally be expected to reduce the compulsion for adjustment, but in fact there was an impressive adjustment in the trade account resulting from a rapid expansion of exports combined with a slowing down of import growth. There was also a steady and largely unexpected increase in private transfers. Each of these factors, and its contribution to the adjustment process, is discussed below.

(i) External financing

The immediate financing problem posed by the larger current-account deficit in 1974-75 was easily met by reliance upon official financing flows, both short term and long term. India drew Rs.293 crores (SDR 311 million) from its gold tranche and first credit tranche in the IMF early in 1974-75 and subsequently drew Rs.194 crores (SDR 200 million) under the 1974 Oil Facility. Thus almost half the current deficit in 1974-75 could be financed from unconditional or low conditionality facilities from the IMF. An additional amount of Rs.207 crores (SDR 201 million) was made available in 1975-76 from the 1975 Oil Facility.

Along with short-term official financing, the flow of external assistance (including loans from multilateral institutions) increased significantly. There was a substantial increase in total aid commitments after 1973-74 (table 10), including special assistance in the form of concessional loans from some OPEC countries. There was also a shift towards quick disbursing non-project assistance, such as programme loans and debt relief, which led to a considerable acceleration in utilization of external assistance flows. As a result of these developments, gross external assistance flows from bilateral donors and multilateral institutions increased from Rs.342 crores (0.7 per cent of GDP) in 1972-73 to Rs.834 crores (1.2 per cent of GDP) in 1974-75 and further to Rs.1220 crores (1.6 per cent of GDP) in 1975-76 (table 1).

(ii)   <u>Reduction of the trade deficit</u>

In spite of the comfortable financing position, there was a truly remarkable adjustment in the trade account: the trade deficit, which had peaked in 1974-75, turned into a surplus within two years. This surprisingly quick turnaround occurred because of a combination of rapid export growth and a slowdown in imports, both of which had much to do with domestic policy.

Export growth played an extremely important role in the trade account adjustment. In fact, export performance had improved even before the oil shock from 1972-73 onwards, and this helped to cushion the impact of the oil shock. Exports had grown at an average rate of 25 per cent in 1972-73 and 1973-74 (table 5). Most of the growth in these two years was attributable to rising unit values, whereas export volumes grew by less than 7 per cent per year; part of the growth reflected aid-financed exports to Bangladesh. In 1974-75 there was an increase of 36 per cent in export values, again mainly due to rising unit values, but with slightly better volume growth of 8 per cent. The rapid growth in export earnings in this period clearly helped to moderate the impact of the oil shock when it came, for the growth acted as a form of advance adjustment. However, to the extent that the export growth was accounted for mainly by higher prices, it had less to do with conscious policy than with favourable world market conditions.[1]/

Exports continued to rise rapidly after 1974-75, and the growth in this period was much more due to rising export volumes. In 1975-76 and 1976-77 export earnings grew at an average annual rate of 26 per cent, with volume growing at about 18 per cent. There was a slight decline in volume terms in 1977-78, but exports picked up again in the next two years (table 5). Between 1973-74 and 1978-79, export growth averaged about 20 per cent per year in value terms and over 9 per cent per year in volume terms. Indian exports in this period expanded considerably faster than world trade, which grew by only a little over 4 per cent per year in volume terms.

While exports grew rapidly, imports moderated immediately after the oil shock. The import bill increased by 50 per cent in 1974 when the full impact of the oil shock was felt, but in volume terms imports actually declined in 1974-75 and remained stagnant at about the depressed level of 1974-75 for the next two years. During this period the trade deficit actually turned into a trade surplus. Imports picked up again in both volume and value terms after 1977-78, and the trade account turned into a modest deficit by 1978-79, but even so the deficit was only 0.3 per cent of GDP, a considerable reduction from the peak level of 1.3 per cent of GDP in 1974-75.

Domestic economic policy had an important role to play in the trade account adjustment, and two aspects of policy were particularly important. Macro-economic policy shifted to a restrictive stance early in 1974-75, and this affected both exports and imports. A second factor was that exchange rate movements were highly favourable to exports from 1972 onwards.

The shift to restrictive macro-economic policy occurred not because of the compulsions of external adjustment but principally because of the need to counteract domestic inflationary pressure, which had built up after 1972-73, with the rate of inflation reaching 20 per cent in 1973-74. Inflationary pressures were further intensified early in 1974-75, when the rabi (winter) crop of 1973-74, which came into the market in the first quarter of 1974-75, proved to be disappointing. The budgetary balance was also threatened because project costs were being revised upward in consequence of the inflation of the previous year, and cost-of-living adjustments of government and public sector wages were considerably higher than expected.

The government took a series of measures in the second quarter of 1974-75 to reduce private disposable income. The measures included the freezing of all wage increases and half of additional cost-of-living increases in the public sector, limitations on dividend distributions by companies, and a new scheme of compulsory (frozen) deposits on the basis of a graduated "slab" for all income tax payers. Excise duties were increased, a tax was imposed on interest income of commercial banks and was to be passed on in the form of higher lending rates, and railway freight rates were raised. These post-budget measures reduced disposable income by about 1 per cent of GDP in 1974-75. Deficit financing by the Central and State governments combined was reduced below the previous year's level, and money supply (M3), which had expanded about 18 per cent in each of the previous two years, grew by only about 11 per cent in 1974-75 (table 7).

Aggregate demand restraint combined with increased imports succeeded in dampening inflation, and prices, which had been rising steadily for over two years, fell in September and continued to decline in the rest of the year (although the average level of prices in 1974-75 was nevertheless 25 per cent above the level in 1973-74 because of rapid inflation up to September 1974). Fiscal policy remained cautious in 1975-76, and in terms of deficit financing by the Centre and States combined there was a shift from a modest deficit to a surplus in 1975-76. The growth of high-powered money was reduced to 2.7 per cent. However, overall monetary policy was not restrictive and M3 increased by 15 per cent, which was not excessive since GDP increased by 9.4 per cent in real terms (table 3). The average level of prices declined in 1975-76, reflecting the impact of cautious fiscal policy combined with continued food imports and a good harvest which promised increased supplies in the second half of the year.

The policy of demand restraint undoubtedly provided a short run stimulus to exports by reducing the pressure of demand in the domestic market and thus increasing export availability and also enhancing the relative incentive to export as domestic sales and profitability declined. A stimulus of this type, based on the short-run consideration of exporting to cover variable cost when domestic demand weakens, is not of course the same thing as longer-term dynamism in the export sector, which depends upon sustainable cost competitiveness. However, it certainly helps to reduce the balance-of-payments deficit and in the longer run it also helps to expose industry to foreign market opportunities. Both these features were evident in the export performance after 1974-75.

The restrictive stance of fiscal policy also helped to reduce imports (other than food imports) in volume terms, though import values increased sharply. Lower import volumes resulted from the depressive effect of fiscal restraint upon public investment, which has a higher import content than private investment because of its sectoral composition. 2/ Public fixed capital formation in nominal terms increased by 6.6 per cent in 1974-75 and by 31 per cent in 1975-76 (table 8). However, in real terms there was a decline of 14.5 per cent in 1974-75 followed by a recovery in 1975-76 which did no more than restore public investment to the level of 1973-74. Private investment increased in real terms in 1974-75 but it did not offset the decline in public investment, so that total fixed capital formation in the economy in 1974-75 declined by about 3 per cent. It increased by 9.6 per cent in 1975-76, but this raised it only to 6.4 per cent above the level of two years earlier, and even that rise was mainly accounted for by the private investment component. The slackening of investment, especially public investment, in these years was clearly one of the factors underlying the low level of capital goods imports after 1974-75 (table 6).

Exchange rate movements in the mid-1970s were an important factor underlying the very favourable export performance in that period. In June 1972 the rupee was delinked from the dollar and pegged to the pound sterling, which proved to be a weak currency, depreciating substantially against most currencies in the subsequent two years. As the rupee depreciated with the pound, the index of the nominal exchange rate of the rupee against the currencies of India's major trading partners depreciated by about 11 per cent from the average level in 1972 to the average in 1975 (table 7). The index of the real effective exchange rate (which corrects for relative price movements) also depreciated by 8 per cent in this period. In September 1975 the rupee was pegged to a basket of currencies of India's major trading partners. The shift to a multi-currency basket stabilized exchange rate movements to some extent, and the nominal effective exchange rate index depreciated by only 8 per cent between 1975 and 1979. However, the real effective exchange rate depreciated by 17 per cent because prices in India remained remarkably stable in this period, rising at an average rate of less than 2 per cent per year in the four years after 1974-75. This price stability was achieved initially because of the success of the anti-inflationary policy in 1974-75 and 1975-76, and was maintained subsequently even when fiscal policy became expansionary, because of relatively good agricultural production in 1977-78 and 1978-79. In any event, the combination of a mild nominal depreciation combined with remarkable price stability provided a strong stimulus for exports.

Apart from exchange rate movements, there were other policy initiatives taken in this period to give additional incentives to exporters, especially through a series of steps providing preferred access to imports for exporters to enable them to meet their import needs. These schemes were undoubtedly important, but the change in the level of these incentives was quantitatively probably much less important as a stimulus to exports than the movement in the real effective exchange rate.

In retrospect the trade account adjustment that took place after 1974-75 had many of the ingredients of a "classical" adjustment programme. Fiscal policy emphasized demand restraint at an early stage creating conditions of price stability which were broadly conducive to external adjustment. Overall incentives to exports increased substantially as reflected in movements in the real effective exchange rates. There was a depressive effect upon investment in the first two years after which investment levels began to recover.

(iii) <u>Private transfers</u>

The third major element in the current-account adjustment after 1974-75 was the growth in private transfers. These had been a modest element in the balance of payments earlier, but rose spectacularly after 1974-75 because of the foreign currency remittances from Indian workers who had gone abroad, especially to the Gulf countries in the wake of the oil boom. As shown in table 1, these transfers constituted the most dynamic item on the receipts side, growing at an average rate of over 40 per cent per year in the five years after the first oil shock. In 1978-79 private transfers were three times as large as the trade deficit, turning the modest trade deficit into a substantial current-account surplus.

The rapid growth of private transfers reinforced the trade account adjustment to make the current-account situation that much more comfortable. The current account moved from a deficit of Rs.961 crores in 1974-75 to a surplus of Rs.1031 crores a mere two years later, and continued in substantial surplus for the next two years. The result of the unexpectedly rapid turnaround combined with the expanded financial inflows was a substantial build-up of foreign reserves. Some reserve build-up was desirable because total reserves at the end of 1974-75 were equivalent to just over two months' imports of goods and services, but the build-up that actually took place was clearly excessive in that foreign reserves were equivalent to more than nine months' imports by the end of 1978-79 (table 4).

The rapid growth in private transfers was clearly unforeseen, and there was considerable uncertainty in the initial stages about the continuation of these flows. These flows really did not form part of the government's strategy for adjustment. They were simply superimposed on the strong trade account adjustment taking place and produced a build-up of excess reserves. In time, however, as these flows gained acceptance as an important element of foreign exchange receipts which was likely to continue, the question of how to utilize these flows began to be asked. The Government's Economic Survey for 1977-78, presented to Parliament in February 1978, explicitly noted "the paradoxical situation of a poor country lending abroad - which is what the growth in foreign exchange reserves really amounts to" and in this context called for "an overall strategy of growth which will utilize the increasing foreign exchange reserves".

The logical policy response to the problem of utilizing available foreign resources for development is some combination of raising investment and liberalizing access to imports. Both were tried, with different degrees of success.

A conscious effort at import liberalization was indeed made in a series of steps taken after 1976-77 but most clearly articulated in the import policy for 1978-79, which embodied many of the recommendations of the Alexander Committee. The new policy was not intended as a radical liberalization of imports in the sense of an abandonment or sharp curtailment of the system of import licensing. It was more in the nature of a major simplification of procedures and rationalization of licensing, combined with some reduction in the degree of import control, especially with respect to imported intermediate inputs into industry. A major change was the shift from a system with positive lists of permitted imports to a negative list system in which whatever is not specifically restricted or licensed is freely allowable. However, this change was accompanied by a fairly extensive list of imports subject to licence. Nevertheless the new framework of import policy was more liberal than in the past, and provided much greater flexibility to producers for obtaining access to imports.

The response in terms of accelerating the pace of investment activity fell short of what was feasible. Total fixed investment in the economy, which had increased by almost 13 per cent in real terms in 1976-77 thus recovering substantially from the restrictive phase in 1974-75 and 1975-76, slowed to 9.8 per cent growth in 1977-78 and then remained stagnant in 1978-79. The stagnation was common to both Government and private fixed investment. 3/ At a time when foreign reserves were mounting and good agricultural performance had created large stocks of foodgrains, the slow-down in investment was clearly a lost opportunity. In retrospect, it is clear that public investment activity could have been more expansionary in 1977-78 and 1978-79.

Perhaps the most remarkable feature of the adjustment after the first oil shock is that it was accomplished with an acceleration in economic growth, with GDP growth averaging about 5.1 per cent in the period 1974-75 to 1978-79 compared with the earlier trend rate of about 3.5 per cent. The main reason for this acceleration was the improvement in agricultural performance in this period, when agricultural production rose at a rate averaging 4.6 per cent per year compared with the earlier trend rate of 2.5 per cent (table 3). Improved agricultural performance reflected the success of the strategy consistently followed since the late 1960s of expanding irrigation and the supply of bio-chemical inputs, including especially high-yielding wheat and rice varieties and fertilizers. This strategy had produced an acceleration in output growth in the late 1960s, followed by an apparent setback in the early 1970s because of poor weather. There was a strong revival after the mid-1970s, when the weather was more normal and the expansion in agriculture in turn stimulated industrial production, especially as there was an element of excess capacity in industry in the mid-1970s.

To summarize, the economy adjusted to the first oil shock faster and more easily than might have been expected. This result was partly due to exogenous factors such as private transfers, but there was also a very strong trade account adjustment which was helped by the adoption of policies characteristic of traditional adjustment packages, including especially demand restraint in the early stages and improved incentives to export. This strategy was effective in achieving external adjustment with growth because supply elasticities in the economy were favourable, with a substantial growth in agricultural production, and also because external demand conditions permitted rapid growth of exports in response to improved incentives.

(b)   The second oil shock

Oil prices more than doubled in the course of 1979, raising India's oil import bill from Rs.1678 crores in 1978-79 to Rs.5264 crores in 1980-81. The current-account position in those years moved from a surplus of Rs.575 crores to a deficit of Rs.2020 crores respectively (table 1). As a percentage of GDP, the current account moved from a surplus of 0.6 per cent to a deficit of 1.6 per cent, a deterioration of 2.2 per cent compared with a deterioration of 1.4 per cent between 1972-73 and 1974-75. In this respect the magnitude of the second shock was greater than that of the first.

The adjustment to the second oil shock differed greatly from the adjustment to the first one. Whereas earlier the current-account deficit was turned into a surplus within two years, it declined only gradually on the second occasion from the peak level of 1.6 per cent of GDP in 1980-81 and 1981-82, to a little over 1 per cent in 1983-84. Impressive as it is, the adjustment will have to be carried further. The high deficits after 1980-81 had to be covered by recourse to short- to medium-term financing and this has led to a build-up of debt-service payments for the rest of the decade. Owing to severe constraints on long-term flows, the amount of net financing available from likely levels of gross borrowings in the future will be limited, and hence the current deficit will have to be reduced further in the years ahead.

(i)   External financing

The external financing environment facing India after the second oil shock has been much less supportive than it was in the mid-1970s.

The immediate financing needs of the economy were adequately met by short- and medium-term finance from the IMF, but there has been a distinct deterioration in the current and future availability of long-term concessional flows, the effects of which will be felt in the years ahead.

A large part of the current deficits in the period 1980-81 to 1983-84 was effectively covered by short- and medium-term resources from various IMF facilities. In 1980-81 India drew Rs.541 crores (SDR 530 million) from the Trust Fund and Rs.274 crores (SDR 266 million) from the Compensatory Financing Facility, both low conditionality facilities. In November 1981 India entered into an extended arrangement with the Fund in support of a medium-term adjustment programme under which India could draw up to SDR 5 billion over a three-year period. An important feature of this adjustment programme was that it was much more oriented to the requirements of structural adjustment, with particular emphasis upon achieving investment targets in critical sectors, especially energy. Actual drawings under this arrangement up to the end of 1983-84 amounted to SDR 3.7 billion. 4/ Thus in the four-year period 1980-81 to 1983-84, India obtained a total of about Rs.4700 crores from IMF sources, equivalent to about 55 per cent of the cumulative deficit in those years.

While short- to medium-term finance was adequate, long-term concessional flows, which traditionally have been India's main source of external financing, did not respond as earlier. Gross external assistance flows as recorded in the balance of payments increased by 50 per cent between 1978-79 and 1981-82 whereas they had increased by 120 per cent between 1972-73 and 1975-76 (table 1). Much of the increase after 1980-81 reflects growing disbursements in consequence of the earlier growth of assistance committed in the past. New aid commitments, which will determine disbursements in the years ahead, have been far more sluggish increasing from about Rs.2336 crores in 1978-79 to Rs.2903 crores in 1982-83, an increase of only 24 per cent in four years (table 10).

This limited increase in volume hides a considerable deterioration in average terms. The International Development Association (IDA), which was India's major source of concessional assistance has run into difficulties. The term of the sixth replenishment of IDA (IDA VI), originally envisaged as three years, had to be stretched to four years ending in 1983-84. New commitments from IDA declined after 1981-82 and though they were offset by higher IBRD funding, the compositional shift represents a major deterioration in the average terms of the financial flows from the World Bank Group to India. Nor is this only a temporary phenomenon. As the funds for IDA VII have been settled at $9 billion, and as India's share has been reduced in consequence of China's entry as an eligible borrower, the new commitments from IDA will be no more than $700 million per year up to 1986-87. Although IBRD flows are expected to expand, the total commitments of IDA and IBRD will show only a modest increase and average terms will deteriorate further as the IBRD share rises. 5/

Aid commitments from bilateral sources have been more or less stagnant in recent years and are expected to show only very modest growth in nominal terms in the years ahead.

These developments have forced India to resort to commercial borrowing, in order to supplement the finance available from traditional sources. In the past, commercial borrowing was restricted to a few special areas, such as the purchase of ships and aircraft, and amounted to only a few hundred million dollars a year. From 1981-82 onwards commercial borrowings have been used to finance selected projects in the public sector, and the volume of new commitments has increased to an average of about $1 billion a year. 6/

(ii)   Current-account adjustment

The slower current-account adjustment after 1980-81 reflects a reversal in the behaviour of the major elements in the current account compared with the experience after the first oil shock. Earlier, there was a rapid growth in export volumes and a slow-down in imports, reinforced by rapidly growing private transfers. By contrast, export growth slowed down after 1978-79 while imports accelerated and private transfers ceased to grow. Different factors were at work in each case.

Private transfers did not increase in the way they had done after 1974-75, entirely because of changed international circumstances. Unlike the first oil price rise, the second one did not generate a sustained oil boom in the Gulf, partly because the world economy slowed down considerably, and consequently the volume of oil exports declined, and partly also because of political developments in the Gulf region, especially the Iran-Iraq war. In addition, labour and employment policies in many countries of the Gulf region were changed in a manner restricting the absorption of foreign labour into the region. For all these reasons the flow of private transfers, while remaining at a fairly high level, slowed down after 1980-81 and hence an important corrective factor which had operated after the first oil shock, was inoperative after the second. There was a sharp increase in 1983-84, but this reflects a once-and-for-all increase representing capital transfers as workers returned home from the Gulf.

The growth rate of exports slowed down dramatically from 9.4 per cent in volume terms in the period 1973-74 to 1978-79 to only 3.6 per cent in the period 1978-79 to 1983-84. The available evidence suggests that the slow-down was largely due to the behaviour of world trade. In the period 1973-74 to 1978-79, when Indian exports grew by 9.4 per cent in volume terms, world exports had grown by about 4.1 per cent (table 5). In the second period, the rate of growth of India's exports slowed down to 3.6 per cent, but that of world exports had also slowed down to a rate of only 1.6 per cent in volume terms. In both periods, India's exports grew faster than world exports, and with a very respectable elasticity of 2.3 in each case, clearly suggesting that India's slower export growth in the second period was primarily due to slower growth in world markets.

Domestic policy towards exports remained broadly supportive after 1980-81, with a further strengthening of the policy of giving exporters specially favourable access to imports of raw materials, capital goods and also technology. Special schemes such as the scheme of 100 per cent Export-Oriented Units were introduced offering facilities similar to free-trade zones for bonded units located anywhere in the country, with provisions for declaring a part of an existing unit as a 100 per cent EOU provided that bonding could be ensured. The import policy for exporters was also liberalized with a view to expanding the volume, as well as the flexibility in use, of special licences (replenishment licences) issued to exporters for the import of otherwise restricted items.

Exchange rate movements after the second oil shock were not as favourable as after the first. There was a mild appreciation in the nominal exchange rate in 1980, which was reversed in 1981. However, the domestic rate of inflation in India in 1980 exceeded inflation rates in India's main trading partners, so that the real effective exchange rate index showed a significant appreciation in 1980. It stayed at that level in 1981 but there was a depreciation in 1982 followed by a slight appreciation again in 1983 (table 7). In general, the real effective exchange rate has been somewhat higher than in the years immediately preceding the second oil shock though it remains below the level of 1977. Real effective exchange rates are not, however, the only relevant index for export competitiveness. Account must also be taken of other incentives which were strengthened, especially the liberalization of import policy for exporters, and when allowance is made for this factor it is likely that the total level of incentives after the second oil shock was at about the same level as before.

The third reason for the slower current-account adjustment after 1980-81 was that imports grew much faster than after the first oil shock. The volume growth in imports in the period 1973-74 to 1978-79 had averaged only 4.5 per cent per year. It increased to 10.6 per cent in the period 1978-79 to 1983-84. This increase in total imports was composed of a decline in the volume of oil imports, a very rapid growth in capital goods imports and rapid growth in other imports.

	Annual average growth rate of import volume (percentages)	
	1973-74 to 1978-79	1978-79 to 1983-84
Oil imports (net)	1.5	-6.6
Capital goods	-0.4	19.9
Others	7.5	10.0
Total	4.5	10.6

The acceleration in import growth in volume terms in the second period reflects developments in the domestic economy and especially the strategy of external adjustment.

The reduction in oil imports reflects the success of one of the key elements in the Government's adjustment programme. The Sixth Five-Year Plan launched in 1980 emphasized the need for increased production in the energy sectors, especially petroleum. Shortly after the Plan had been approved an "accelerated programme" of petroleum production and development was adopted with increased investments for the petroleum sector and the objective of raising domestic production of petroleum even beyond the original targets of the Sixth Plan. The programme succeeded in raising crude production from 11.6 million tons in 1978-79 to over 26 million tons in 1983-84 (table 13). Domestic crude production as a proportion of domestic consumption of petroleum products (in crude equivalent) increased from 38 per cent in 1978-79 to 68 per cent in 1983-84, a major success in import substitution in a critical area.

The rapid growth of other imports, including especially capital goods, must be ascribed to two factors. One was the liberalization of import policy in the late 1970s, which provided easier access to imports needed either as inputs into production or as capital goods. These features of the import policy were strengthened in subsequent years in recognition of the need to upgrade and modernize production and technology in Indian industry. The growth of capital goods and other imports was especially rapid up to 1980-81, reflecting the once-and-for-all adjustment to a higher level of imports after which the rate of expansion slowed down in line with GDP. These developments are reflected in the behaviour of the coefficient (Jec) relating capital goods imports to investment which shows a strong increase up to 1981-82 and only a modest increase thereafter (table 11). The effect of import liberalization is also evident in the movement of the coefficient (Jyno) relating other non-oil imports to GDP which rose sharply up to 1980-81.

The second factor behind the rapid growth of imports was the growth and sectoral composition of public investment after 1980-81. Total fixed investment in the economy in constant prices did not rise faster after the second shock than after the first, but public investment rose more rapidly, and the sectors which received priority in public investment were petroleum, coal, power and fertilizers. These were seen as critical sectors in which capacity and production had to be increased in order to remove key supply bottlenecks in the economy. They also happened to be sectors which were relatively import-intensive in terms of their capital goods requirements.

The behaviour of public investment after the second oil shock was in marked contrast to the experience after the first oil shock and reflects a basic difference in the stance of macro-economic policy. On the earlier occasion there had been a shift to a restrictive macro-economic policy principally because of the perceived dangers of inflation, and this policy had depressed public investment in real terms. By contrast, macro-economic policy in 1980-81 was not restrictive, and public investment in 1981-82 was 13.5 per cent higher than in 1979-80. There were superficial similarities in the economic situation, which might have argued for a restrictive response as on the earlier occasion. There was an upsurge of inflation in 1979-80 caused by the severe drought in 1979, and control of inflation received high priority attention. However, the approach to controlling inflation on this occasion placed much more emphasis on removing short-term and medium-term supply bottlenecks. One reason for this change of emphasis is that the balance of macro-economic policy was set in the light of priorities outlined in the Sixth Five-Year Plan which covered the period 1980-81 to 1984-85. The Plan emphasized the importance of investment in several critical areas, especially in the energy transport infrastructure. These areas had suffered from a measure of underinvestment in earlier years which needed to be corrected, and in any case, the second oil price increase made these investments even more urgent so as to reduce dependence on imported energy as a means of external adjustment.

On the whole, economic policy after the second oil shock was consciously designed to achieve the objective of medium-term structural adjustment. This meant a continuation of the relatively liberalized import regime of 1978-79 in the interest of industrial productivity and ambitious targets for public investment aimed at expanding capacity in critical areas. It was recognized that this strategy implied a high requirement for imports of capital goods as well as intermediate inputs, and even after allowing for import savings from higher oil production, it would imply a current-account deficit of substantial size for some years. It was to finance this deficit that India negotiated the extended arrangement with the IMF as a source of temporary financing.

The adjustment strategy also envisaged an acceleration in export growth which is necessary to finance higher levels of imports directly, and also indirectly by permitting higher levels of borrowing consistent with debt-service norms. The Sixth Five-Year Plan had set a target of 9 per cent volume growth of exports, but actual performance was much lower because of the sharp deceleration in world trade. Continued slow growth of world trade combined with the present prospects for long-term concessional flows will put severe constraints on the economy in the rest of this decade. The nature of these constraints is examined in detail in Section 4 on the basis of a simple projection model.

3.   Decomposition of current-account changes

In this section we present a quantitative analysis of the relative importance of different elements which affected the current account during each of the two oil shocks. The technique used is a modification of the decomposition scheme outlined in the terms of reference appended to G. Helleiner's synthesis paper.

A detailed statement of the decomposition scheme is given in Appendix I. In essence the change in the deficit expressed as a per cent of GDP, over any given period, is decomposed into the following components plus second order terms, which constitute an unexplained residual. (i) A set of terms-of-trade effects which measure the impact of changes in the price indices of exports and various categories of imports, relative to the index of the GDP deflator. 7/ (ii) The contribution of export volume growth to the change in deficit as a percent of GDP. This consists of two terms, one reflecting the domestic export effort, which raises export share in world trade, and another reflecting the growth of world demand relative to the growth of real GDP. (iii) Import saving which measures the effect of changes in the propensity to import as measured by changes in various import coefficients relating the volume of imports to various real variables in the economy. (iv) The effect of remittances which have been an extremely important source of foreign exchange over this period. (v) The impact of interest payments which consists of the effect of changes in the average interest rate, and the effect of the accumulation of debt on which interest payments have to be made. (vi) The effect of domestic demand policies which is measured essentially by the ratio of investment to GDP. 8/ Needless to say, the decomposition scheme is essentially an accounting framework based upon identities rather than causal relationships, and interpretation in terms of causal relationships has to be attempted with caution. The results presented in this section must be viewed primarily as illustrating the qualitative account of developments in Section 2.

(a)   The first oil shock

The experience of the first oil shock may be analyzed in terms of three sub-periods: 1972-73 to 1974-75 when the current account deteriorated sharply, 1974-75 to 1976-77 when there was a rapid turnaround bringing the current account as a percentage of GDP to a peak surplus position of 1.3 per cent, and 1976-77 to 1978-79 when the current account adjusted towards a more normal level, with the surplus declining as a percentage of GDP. Table 14 shows the change in the current account in each period decomposed into the contribution of individual elements.

(i)   1972-73 to 1974-75

The deterioration of 1.4 percentage points in the current deficit in this period was the result of a number of factors, some of which moved in an offsetting manner. The items identified in the decomposition in table 14 account for 140 per cent of the actual change. 9/

The largest single element contributing to the deterioration was clearly the rise in oil prices which had an adverse impact of 1.9 percentage points. Oil prices were not, however, the only import prices which increased. Prices of non-oil imports, especially in the non-capital goods category, also rose sharply and although the extent of this increase was much less than for oil imports (table 12), it had a relatively large adverse impact of about 1.6 percentage points of GDP because the price increase affected a larger volume. The rise in non-oil import prices was itself a reflection of boom conditions in the international economy which had offsetting advantages in terms of higher export prices and expanding export volumes. These factors offset the adverse effect of higher import prices to some extent. The net effect of the changes in non-oil import prices, export prices and export volumes was an adverse impact of about 0.8 percentage points. This was much less than the adverse impact of the oil price increase.

Parallel with these developments there were other important factors operating to improve the current deficit. There were import savings resulting from a reduction in import propensities which had a combined favourable impact of 0.3 percentage points. There was also a reduction in the relative burden of interest payments which grew much less than GDP.

(ii)   1974-75 to 1976-78

In this two-year period the current account moved from a deficit of 1.4 per cent of GDP to a surplus of 1.3 per cent - a massive improvement of 2.7 percentage points. The decomposition accounts for 95 per cent of the actual change.

Terms-of-trade effects were more or less neutral in this period as improvements in export prices were largely offset by increases in non-oil import prices with a marginal net favourable impact. However, there were other significant favourable developments. The most important single factor was the dynamic export performance which contributed an improvement of about 1.5 percentage points. This was the result of a very strong export effort, contributing an improvement of 1.8 percentage points, which was partially offset by a deterioration of 0.3 percentage points because world trade slowed down. Apart from export expansion, the trade account also benefited from a slow-down in import volumes arising from reductions in the import propensities for capital goods and other non-oil imports. As pointed out in Section 2, the reduced propensity to import capital goods probably reflected the reduction in public investment as a proportion of total investment. Total investment as a percentage of GDP actually increased in these years. The reduced propensity to import other goods reflects import savings in the case of fertilizers and iron and steel, where there were large increases in domestic production.

The combined effect of terms-of-trade changes, export volume changes and import propensity changes was a favourable impact of 2 percentage points. To this was added an improvement of 0.5 percentage points from the growth of private transfers.

(iii) 1976-77 to 1978-79

The current account in this period deteriorated by 0.7 percentage points, a move in the right direction from the excessively large surplus of 1.3 per cent of GDP in 1976-77, though it left the current account still in a surplus of 0.6 per cent in 1978-79. The decomposition explains 119 per cent of the observed change.

The major factors underlying the deterioration were a slow-down in export performance relative of GDP growth and, even more important, higher import propensities. The slow-down in exports was the result of a weakening in the export effort and a slowing down of world trade, which together had an adverse impact of 0.8 percentage points. Even more important was the large increase in the propensity to import non-oil non-capital goods after 1976-77, reflecting the import liberalization measures introduced in this period. This contributed an adverse impact on the current account of about 1.2 percentage points. There was some increase in the propensity to import oil, whereas the propensity to import capital goods declined slightly. Taken together, these changes in import propensities contributed a deterioration of about 1.4 percentage points. Thus the slow-down in export volumes relative to GDP growth and the greater propensity to import jointly contributed to a deterioration of almost 2.2 percentage points.

There was an offsetting improvement of about 1 percentage point arising from favourable terms-of-trade effects as export prices rose faster than the GDP deflator while prices of oil and other non-oil imports rose more slowly. Other favourable developments were a continuing growth of remittances, some improvement in debt servicing, and a reduction in the investment ratio.

(iv)   1974-75 to 1978-79

Taking the adjustment phase after 1974-75 as a single four-year period, we find that the current account improved by about 2 percentage points, moving from a deficit of 1.4 per cent in 1974-75 to a surplus of 0.6 per cent in 1978-79. The decomposition in col. 4 of table 14 explains about 93 per cent of this improvement. The following elements are important: (i) Improvements in export performance, arising mainly from an improved export effort, contributed 0.9 percentage points. Export prices contributed a further improvement of 0.9 percentage points while import price movements largely offset each other. Thus export volumes and prices together contributed an improvement of 1.8 percentage points; (ii) This was offset to the extent of almost 1 percentage point by an increase in overall import propensity reflecting a higher import propensity for "other imports" and also for oil. Thus the developments related to the trade account contributed to a net improvement in the current deficit of 0.8 percentage points; (iii) Rapid growth in remittances reinforced the trade account improvement and contributed a further improvement of 0.6 percentage points. The sense in which the growth of remittances was not essential to the adjustment in this period is evident from the fact that had remittances grown at only the same rate as GDP in nominal terms, the contribution of this item would have been zero, and the current account, instead of being in surplus, would have been exactly balanced in 1978-79.

(b) The second oil shock

     The experience of the second oil shock can be analyzed in terms of
the deterioration phase from 1978-79 to 1980-81 and the subsequent
adjustment phase 1980-81 to 1983-84. The decomposition of the change
in the current account in each of these periods is shown in table 15.

     (i) 1978-79 to 1980-81

     The current account in this period deteriorated by 2.2 percentage
points compared with only 1.4 percentage points between 1972-73 and
1974-75. The decomposition explains 100 per cent of the actual change.

     The direct impact of the oil price increase is a deterioration of
1.5 percentage points, which is somewhat less than the size of the
impact of the first oil shock. Nevertheless, it accounts for about 70
per cent of the observed deterioration in the current account.
However, there were other changes taking place in various elements
affecting the current account, some of which were offsetting.

     As far as price movements are concerned, non-oil import prices
grew much more slowly than the GDP deflator, with a favourable impact
on the current deficit as a percentage of GDP. However, this was
almost entirely offset by the fact that export prices also grew more
slowly. The net terms-of-trade effects were, therefore, dominated by
the adverse impact of the oil price increase.

     There was a substantial favourable impact on the current deficit
from three factors: rapid export growth, rising remittances and a
turnaround in net factor payments from an outflow to a net inflow
because of earnings from rising foreign reserves. These had a combined
favourable impact of about 2.5 percentage points. However, this was
more than offset by an adverse impact of 3.1 percentage points arising
from larger import volumes reflecting the effect of import
liberalization. The net effect of all these developments was an
adverse movement of 0.6 percentage points.

     This suggests that there would have been a deterioration in the
current deficit even if oil prices had not increased in 1979. However,
as there was considerable cushion in the current-account position in
1978-79, this deterioration would not have presented a problem. For
example, taking the deterioration in the current account because of the
oil price increase at 1.5 percentage points, it could be argued that if
oil prices had increased only at the same rate as the GDP deflator,
then other things being the same the current account would have
deteriorated from a surplus of 0.6 per cent to a deficit of only about
0.1 per cent in 1980-81. This would still have been comfortable and
would have left room for further expansionary policies given the
availability of long-term flows.

This illustration is undoubtedly simplistic since it implies that individual items in the decomposition can be treated as separable elements. In fact, the oil price increase had other effects on the world economy, which are reflected in the observed movements in export volumes, export prices, remittances, etc., and the counterfactual situation without an oil price rise can be properly quantified only when all these effects are taken into account. Such an analysis is beyond the scope of the paper, but the decomposition certainly suggests that while the net effect of other factors affecting the current account would have led to a deterioration in the current deficit, this could have been accommodated since the current account was in surplus in 1978-79. It is the oil price increase which pushed the current deficit beyond the level consistent with availability of long-term flows, which would have been around 0.5 per cent of GDP.

(ii)   1980-81 to 1983-84

There was a modest improvement in the current-account deficit amounting to about 0.54 percentage points over this period. The decomposition explains 131 per cent of the actual change and there are striking differences in the individual components accounting for the improvement compared with those that operated after the first oil shock.

Two factors which had operated strongly in support of adjustment after the first oil shock operated in reverse in this period. Export performance, which was highly favourable in 1974-75 to 1976-77, was much poorer on the second occasion, mainly because of the very considerable slow-down in world trade after 1981-82. The export effort succeeded in increasing India's share in world trade in this period, but world demand actually declined, which contributed an adverse impact of 1.1 percentage points on the current deficit. Remittances, which had grown rapidly earlier, grew more slowly after the second oil shock; this deceleration contributed to a widening of the current deficit. In addition, factor income payments (mainly interest payments on foreign debt), which had declined even in absolute terms through the 1970s when reserves were building up, and net foreign debt was therefore declining, began to increase after 1980-81 as interest payments on IMF borrowing built up.

The most important favourable influence on the current account after 1980-81 was the massive saving on petroleum imports resulting from the large increase in domestic crude production (table 13), an increase which contributed a favourable impact of as much as 2.2 percentage points of GDP. This was partially offset by rising import intensity of investment, reflecting the shift in composition of investment towards public investment, which in turn was concentrated in sectors such as energy, petroleum exploration and development and fertilizers, all of which are heavily import-intensive. However, even after allowing for the rising import intensity of investment there was a net favourable impact of about 1.8 percentage points.

Terms-of-trade changes were also marginally favourable in this period. Prices for imports of petroleum and capital goods rose less rapidly than the GDP deflator and this had a favourable impact. Most of this was offset by the fact that export prices also grew more slowly, but the net effect was a favourable impact of about 0.3 percentage points.

4.   Prospects and constraints up to 1990-91

In this section we examine the nature of the external constraints affecting India's performance in the rest of the decade. As shown in Section 2, although India was able to adjust to the second oil shock somewhat more easily than most other countries, this adjustment is not yet complete and India is likely to face a difficult situation in the rest of the decade. Export prospects are to some extent limited by the expected slow growth of world trade and, at the same time, the amount of external finance on concessional terms is unlikely to increase rapidly in future. India can resort to commercial borrowings to finance the current-account deficit, but the extent of such recourse must be kept within limits imposed by prudent debt management.

Thus the total amount of foreign exchange available to the economy in the years ahead will be limited. Yet the overall import propensity of the economy has been increasing under the influence of import liberalization. Inadequate access to external financing in the years ahead could impose severe constraints either on the utilization of existing production capacity by denial of maintenance inputs, or on the levels of investment because of the inability to import capital goods. These constraints are explored through a simple projection model of the type outlined in the terms of reference appended to the synthesis paper.

(a)   The structure of the model

The model is designed primarily to quantify the reaction of the economy to scarcity of foreign exchange. Its basic features may be summarized as follows. 10/ The level of export demand and the size of the current deficit are specified exogenously, reflecting the nature of the external environment facing the economy. This determines the level of foreign exchange available to the economy. The model then chooses an allocation of this foreign exchange between "maintenance imports", which are needed to produce GDP, and capital goods imports needed for investment. The allocation ensures that the level of GDP is consistent with the level of investment in terms of the requirement that savings plus the current deficit must equal investment. In effect, this means that the level of GDP is determined by the level of demand (i.e. the multiplier relationship) allowing for import leakages and exports. This demand-determined income level is subject to capacity constraints determined by the level of past investment. If in any year the level of demand is such that demand-determined GDP hits the "full capacity" constraint, then the excess demand "spills over" into a reduction in exports which reduces foreign exchange availability and forces a contraction. If the level of GDP is significantly below full capacity, this implies a foreign exchange constraint, since higher levels of GDP could be produced by raising the level of demand through higher investment levels but for the inability to finance imports.

The model quantifies some of the choices involved in the face of a foreign exchange constraint. Starting from an equilibrium position, a reduction in foreign exchange availability reduces import capacity and forces the following changes. There will be a reduction in the level of investment which will directly reduce the requirement of capital goods. It will also reduce GDP via the multiplier, thus indirectly reducing maintenance imports. A reduction in foreign exchange availability therefore reduces investment and lowers utilization of productive capacity. The reduction in GDP via the multiplier can be avoided by measures to reduce the rate of saving (stimulate domestic consumption), but this will only force the burden of reducing imports on reduction in investment levels, which will be larger than otherwise. There is therefore a trade-off between maintaining the level of investment in the interest of future growth on the one hand, and maintaining current GDP levels on the other.

With the size of the current-account deficit specified exogenously, the model also generates a financing pattern on the capital account, with a build-up of external debt and a debt-service profile. The availability of concessional flows is exogenously specified in terms of (i) disbursements from past commitments and (ii) disbursements from new commitments. Amortization due on these flows is computed year by year. This determines the net availability of concessional assistance. The difference between net concessional flows and the exogenously specified current deficit has to be filled by net commercial borrowing. Amortization on past commercial borrowing being known, gross commercial borrowing is determined year by year to ensure financing of the exogenously specified current deficit. Thus the stock of concessional and non-concessional debt in the simulation period is built up separately, and interest payments on these debts are determined on the basis of average interest rates. These interest payments figure in the current account and affect the import capacity of the economy given the exogenously specified level of exports and remittances. The interest and amortization streams together determine the debt-service profile.

(b) Model simulations up to 1990-91

The nature of the external constraints upon India's performance can be explored in terms of a base solution of the Model and some alternative simulations making different assumptions about the availability of external financing and also the growth of exports. The base solution as defined here is purely a reference solution and not a normative projection in any sense.

(1) The base solution

The base solution makes the following critical assumptions about the external environment: (i) demand for India's exports is projected to grow at about 5 per cent per year in real terms, which is broadly consistent with relatively optimistic scenarios of world trade expansion over the period, given the prospects of a trend growth in the OECD countries of only about 3.5 per cent per year; (ii) the current deficit is allowed to expand at about 10 per cent per year in nominal terms over the rest of the decade; (iii) new commitments of concessional assistance and long-term multilateral flows have been projected as follows: IDA commitments are assumed to stabilize at about $700 million per year, IBRD commitments are projected to rise at about 8 per cent per year in nominal terms from a level of $1100 million in 1983-84 and bilateral assistance is assumed to rise at 5 per cent per year in nominal terms.

The main results of the base solution in terms of rates of growth of GDP, the degree of capacity utilization and movements in the debt-service ratio are summarized in table 16. The following features are worth noting.

(1) It is clear that with exports constrained to 5 per cent real growth and the current deficit expanding by 10 per cent in nominal terms, the economy will experience a severe foreign exchange constraint. This is reflected in the fact that the degree of capacity utilization, which is the ratio of GDP to potential GDP as determined by the capacity created by past investments, declines from almost 100 per cent in the base year to about 92 per cent by 1990-91. A larger availability of foreign exchange would have permitted higher levels of output and also higher volumes of investment. Thus while the level of investment in the base solution generates a growth of 4.4 per cent in potential output (i.e. full capacity GDP) over the period 1983-84 to 1990-91, actual GDP growth over this period is only 3.2 per cent per year reflecting the effect of the foreign exchange constraint. This is considerably lower than the average growth rate of 4.3 per cent achieved over the ten-year period 1973-74 to 1983-84.

(2) There is a marked deterioration in the debt-service ratio from 13 per cent of exports in 1983-84 to 30 per cent in 1990-91. This reflects the fact that with repayments falling due on the medium-term financing undertaken after 1980-81, and the continuing unfavourable prospects for concessional flows, the projected current-account deficit can only be financed through increasing resort to commercial borrowing. This produces a major change in the structure of debt over the period. The outstanding debt in the Base Solution rises only modestly from Rs.20,000 crores in 1983-84 or 10.6 per cent of GDP to Rs.43,149 crores in 1990-91 or 13.1 per cent of GDP, but the proportion of commercial debt in the total increases dramatically from less than 10 per cent in 1983-84 to over 30 per cent by 1990-91. This is in addition to the considerable hardening of average terms on long-term multilateral flows resulting from the expected switch from borrowings from IDA to borrowings from IBRD.

In short, the base solution implies a deceleration in GDP growth and a steady worsening in the debt-service ratio if exports grow no faster than world trade and external financing remains constrained.

(ii)   Enlarged financing

Although the economy suffers from a foreign exchange constraint it is not possible to finance larger imports by running larger deficits because any increase in the size of the current deficit would have highly adverse consequences for the debt-service ratio. The simulation in table 17 shows the implications of allowing the current deficit to expand by 15 per cent in nominal terms. This increases the import capacity of the economy which allows further utilization of capacity by expanding investment and raising GDP. The average growth rate over the period 1983-84 to 1990-91 rises from 3.2 per cent in the Base Solution to 3.7 per cent and the growth of potential output also increases from 4.4 per cent to 4.6 per cent. However, the debt-service ratio reaches 36 per cent in 1990-91 compared with 30 per cent in the base solution. Since even 30 per cent is excessive, it is clear that enlarged financing through additional commercial borrowing is not a sound proposition.

(iii) Forced contraction

The implications of living within a reasonable level of the debt-service ratio are explored in the simulation reported in table 18 in which the current-account deficit is allowed to expand by only 5 per cent per year in nominal terms. Since the rate of export growth remains at 5 per cent in real terms, the enforced reduction in the current deficit reduces the foreign exchange available to the economy during the simulation period. Investment levels are reduced and the degree of underutilization of capacity also increases. GDP growth in this simulation is reduced to 2.9 per cent per year compared with 3.2 per cent in the base solution. The debt-service ratio in the terminal year declined to 26 per cent compared with 30 per cent in the Base Solution but the improvement is achieved at the expense of a considerable reduction in the rate of growth.

(iv)   Faster export growth

More rapid export growth has a highly beneficial effect upon the economy as is shown by the simulation in table 19, in which the demand for India's exports is projected to grow by 7 per cent per year in real terms instead of 5 per cent in the base solution. This leads to a substantial increase in import capacity which allows higher levels of investment and GDP, with near 100 per cent utilization of capacity. The growth of GDP over the period 1983-84 to 1990-91 increases from 3.2 per cent in the base solution to 4.8 per cent. It is important to emphasize that this acceleration is not due to the direct stimulus of exports to production, but to the fact that the additional foreign exchange earnings permit greater access to imports, which in turn permits higher levels of investment and GDP. In this simulation the level of capacity utilization is near 100 per cent over the whole period.

Faster export growth also helps to improve the debt-service profile consistent with the exogenously specified levels of the current-account deficit. The debt-service ratio in this simulation reaches a maximum of 27 per cent in 1990-91 compared with 30 per cent in the base solution. However, even at this level, the debt-service ratio is far too high.

The debt-service profile can be improved by restraining the growth in the current deficit. In table 18, reducing the growth in the current deficit to 5 per cent per year in nominal terms compared with 10 per cent in the base solution lowers the debt-service ratio in the terminal year by about 4 percentage points and lowers the growth rate by about 0.3 percentage points. This suggests that with 7 per cent export growth, it would be necessary to keep the current deficit more or less constant in nominal terms (instead of growing at 10 per cent as in table 19), to lower the debt service ratio by 8 percentage points so as to bring it within the 20 per cent limit. This contractionary adjustment would also involve a reduction in GDP growth by about 0.6 percentage points per year.

Thus even with 7 per cent real growth in exports, which is considerably faster than the likely growth in world trade, India is likely to experience a foreign exchange constraint in the rest of the decade because it will have to keep the current deficit more or less constant in nominal terms if the debt service ratio is to be kept within the limit of 20 per cent of exports of goods and services. The overall rate of growth of the economy in these circumstances is unlikely to exceed 4.2 per cent per year which is lower than the growth rate achieved in recent years and is also below the economy's potential.

The broad conclusions to be drawn from the simulations discussed above are that India's growth performance is likely to be severely constrained by the external environment. Improved export performance should be a major objective of policy but it will be difficult to achieve sufficiently high rates of export growth in an environment of relatively slow growth in world trade and rising protectionism in the developed countries. India will also suffer from the effects of the deterioration in the terms of external financing that began after 1980-81, and is likely to continue, which will make it difficult for India to finance a large enough current deficit. India is not at present burdened with excessive debt-service obligations, but as repayments of recent medium-term borrowings fall due in the rest of the decade, there is only limited room for undertaking additional commercial borrowings within the usual constraints regarding debt-service ratios.

Precise numerical results are naturally sensitive to the particular structure and calibration of the model from which they are generated and the model used in this paper is not rich enough to explore a wide range of policy alternatives which need to be examined in practice. Subject to this qualification, however, it appears that even if India is able to expand exports at a rate of about 7 per cent in volume terms (and what is more, to do so without any deterioration in the terms of trade), GDP growth may still be constrained to a little over 4 per cent, if the debt-service ratio is not to exceed 20 per cent. India would have to finance an expansion in the current deficit of about 10 per cent per year in nominal terms to provide the degree of access to imports needed to achieve about 5 per cent GDP growth. However, with the existing limitations on concessional flows, and the hardening of terms on multilateral flows, this would require an excessive amount of commercial borrowing, which raises the debt-service ratio beyond permissible limits. This would not have been the case had there been an adequate expansion of long-term concessional flows.

The potential undoubtedly exists for GDP growth of around 5 per cent. The actual growth rate achieved in the Fifth Plan period 1974-75 to 1978-79 was around 5.1 per cent. The growth rate in the Sixth Plan period 1980-81 to 1984-85 is expected to be around 5 per cent. These two Plan periods exclude 1979-80 which was an exceptionally bad year, but even so the average growth rate over the period 1974-75 to 1984-85 is likely to be around 4.5 per cent. This represents an acceleration over the earlier trend rate of about 3.5 per cent and further acceleration to 5 per cent can surely be achieved if the external environment does not force a contraction.

Appendix I

Decomposition of Current Deficit

The decomposition of the current-account deficit used in this paper differs slightly from the version presented in Bacha (1983). The deficit D may be written as follows: where the successive terms in square brackets are obviously equal to the value of imports, exports, net factor payments and remittances respectively.

$$D = [M_o^* P_{jo} + M_k^* \cdot P_k + M_{jno}^* \cdot P_{jno}] - [X^* \cdot P_x] + [r \cdot NF] - [R]$$

where M_o^* = oil imports in constant prices, M_k^* = capital goods imports in constant prices, M_{jno}^* = all other imports in constant prices.

P_{jo}, P_k, P_{jno} are the corresponding prices, X^* = exports in constant prices, P_x = export prices, r = the rate of return on net foreign debt, NF is the stock of foreign assets, R is the value of remittance inflows.

The above equation can be further expanded as follows:

$$D = [J_{yo} \cdot z^* \cdot P_{jo} + J_{yk} \cdot I^* \cdot P_k + J_{yno} \cdot z^* \cdot P_{jno}] -$$

$$[X^*/W^*) \cdot P_x \cdot W^*] - [R] + [r \cdot NF]$$

where $J_{yo} = M_o^*/z^*$, $J_{yk} = M_k^*/I^*$, $J_{yno} = M_{jno}^*/z^*$, z^* is GDP at constant prices.

Dividing both sides by $Z = z^* P_y$, where Z is GDP in current prices and P_y is the GDP deflator, and then differentiating, the change in the current deficit can be written as the sum of the following terms:

$$\Delta D = [J_{yk} \cdot \frac{I^*}{z^*}] \cdot \Delta [\frac{P_k}{P_y}]$$

$$+ J_{yo} \Delta [\frac{P_{jo}}{P_y}]$$

$$+ J_{yno} \Delta [\frac{P_{jno}}{P_y}]$$

$$- \frac{X^*}{z^*} \Delta [\frac{P_x}{P_y}]$$

$$- [\frac{P_x W^*}{P_y z^*}] \Delta [\frac{X^*}{W^*}] \qquad \text{Export effort}$$

$$- \left[\frac{P_x}{P_y} \frac{X^*}{W^*} \right] \Delta \left[\frac{W^*}{Z^*} \right]$$ World demand

$$+ \left[\frac{P_{jo}}{P_y} \right] \cdot \Delta J_{yo}$$ Import propensity (oil)

$$+ \left[\frac{I^*}{Z} \cdot \frac{P_{jk}}{P_y} \right] \Delta J_{yk}$$ Import propensity (capital goods)

$$+ \left[\frac{P_{jno}}{P_y} \right] \Delta J_{yno}$$ Import propensity (other imports)

$$- \Delta \left[\frac{R}{Z^* \cdot P_y} \right]$$ Remittance effect

$$+ \left[\frac{NF}{Z^* P_y} \right] \Delta r$$ Interest rate effect

$$+ r \Delta \left[\frac{NF}{Z^* P_y} \right]$$ Debt accumulation effect

$$+ \left[\frac{J_{yk} \cdot P_{jk}}{P_y} \right] \Delta \left[\frac{I^*}{Z^*} \right]$$ Domestic demand effect

An important difference between this decomposition and that used by Bacha is that no distinction is made between actual domestic GDP and potential domestic GDP. It is extremely difficult to measure potential domestic GDP especially in a situation where losses of GDP due to adverse weather conditions or supply bottlenecks in critical infrastructure sectors such as power have to be distinguished from losses of GDP due to the effect of the foreign exchange constraint. Bacha's distinction between actual and potential GDP relates entirely to the underutilization of potential due to the foreign exchange constraint and it is not easy to isolate this element.

FOOTNOTES

1/   This is not strictly correct as unit value increases are not the same as price increases. Unit values may increase because of quality upgrading which is a reflection of export effort.

2/   Private investment in the national accounts includes investment in housing, the unorganized sector and all farm investment, all of which have a very small direct import content.

3/   The change in Government in 1977 after the general election in
      that year probably had some effect on the pace of investment
      activity in the public sector. The Fifth Five-Year Plan, which
      was scheduled to end in 1978-79, was terminated prematurely and
      work began on a new Five-Year Plan reflecting the new Government's
      priorities. However, the plan was never formally adopted.

4/   A further drawing of SDR 200 million was made under this
      arrangement in May 1984, taking the total amount drawn to SDR 3.9
      billion before India terminated the arrangement.

5/   The comparative terms of IDA and IBRD flows are as follows: IDA
      loans are for 50 years with a 10-year grace period with an
      interest charge of 1/4 per cent. IBRD flows for India are for 25
      years' maturity, with a five-year grace period and a
      market-related interest rate.

6/   Disbursements from these borrowings are not separately reported in
      table 1 as they were quite modest up to 1982-83.

7/   The use of the GDP deflator as a reference price follows from the
      fact that the decomposition relates to the change in the current
      deficit as a percentage of GDP.

8/   The decomposition in the "terms of reference" was "potential GDP"
      rather than actual GDP where "potential GDP" is defined as that
      level of GDP which could have been sustained had the economy not
      been "foreign exchange constrained". As pointed out in Appendix
      I, it is difficult to measure this concept and in any case, as
      mentioned in Section 2 of this paper, the Indian economy was
      probably not constrained by foreign exchange availability in the
      1970s in the sense of the terms of reference.

9/   The sum of the individual items can be greater than or less than
      100 per cent of the actual change in the deficit because the
      decomposition is based on the difference equation obtained from an
      expanded equation for the current deficit which ignores second and
      third order terms.

10/   The equations of the model are not reported here as they are
      common to the other countries studies and are set out in the terms
      of reference. The equations have not been estimated formally
      through econometric techniques. Instead we have calibrated the
      model by choosing key parameters which appear consistent with
      recent observed behaviour and which, together with the constant
      terms chosen, replicate the base year 1983-84 when the model is
      solved for exogenous variables corresponding to the base year.
      The incremental output capital ratio (taking incremental capital
      stock after allowing for depreciation at 3.33 per cent per year)
      is 0.38. The marginal rate of savings out of disposable income
      (GDP minus factor payments plus remittances) is 22 per cent.

Tables

1. Balance of payments

2. Movements in the current account deficit

3. Selected indicators of economic performance

4. India's foreign exchange reserves

5. Export performance

6. Imports at current prices

7. Nominal and real effective exchange rate index

8. Rate of growth of money supply

9. Gross domestic fixed capital formation

10. Aid commitments

11. Import coefficients

12. Movements in import and export prices

13. Petroleum production and demand balances

14. Decomposition of current account changes: the first shock

15. Decomposition of current account changes: the second shock

16. The base solution

17. Enlarged financing

18. Forced adjustment of current deficit

19. Faster export growth

Table 1   BALANCE OF PAYMENTS a/   (Rs. crores)

	1970-71	1971-72	1972-73	1973-74	1974-75	1975-76	1976-77	1977-78	1978-79	1979-80	1980-81	1981-82	1982-83	1983-84
I. CURRENT ACCOUNT														
Exports of goods and n.f.s.	1771	1838	2225	2829	3834	4813	6140	6635	7118	8381	9029	10003	10450	11200
Imports of goods and n.f.s.	1816	2006	2049	3175	4778	5665	5615	6521	7429	10094	13604	14566	14817	15900
Resource Balance	-45	-168	176	-346	-944	-852	525	114	-311	-1713	-4575	-4563	-4367	-4700
Factor Income (net)	-284	-291	-302	-325	-291	-255	-233	-233	-156	153	298	-7	-140	-300
Private Transfers (net)	123	163	154	192	274	528	739	1022	1042	1624	2257	2221	2375	3000
Current Balance	-206	-296	28	-479	-961	-579	1031	903	575	64	-2020	-2349	-2132	-2000
II. CAPITAL ACCOUNT														
External Assistance (net)	492	461	342	572	834	1220	1090	761	631	799	870	1004	1405	1620
(Gross)	(723)	(711)	(629)	(869)	(1104)	(1540)	(1452)	(1243)	(1115)	(1334)	(1556)	(1658)	(2067)	
(Repayments)	(231)	(250)	(287)	(298)	(270)	(320)	(362)	(481)	(464)	(535)	(686)	(654)	(662)	
IMF (net)	-154	-	-	62	485	207	-303	-289	-207	-84	808	602	1893	1330
Allocation of SDRs	75	75	-	-	-	-	-	-	126	126	121	-	-	-
Other Capital (net)	-39	104	-48	48	-364	-473	-371	-362	-8	96	-62	-227	-304	250
Errors and Omissions	-257	-245	-355	-119	13	455	-51	542	-137	-632	-233	-648	-237	
Change in Reserves (- increase)	89	-99	33	-84	-7	-810	-1396	-1555	-1000	-369	516	1618	-625	-1200

a/ The balance-of-payments data presented in the table differ from the data as presented by the Reserve Bank of India because the latter are based on payments data whereas for our exercise we need data corresponding to trade flows. Trade data are obviously more appropriate for integration in the expenditure flows of the national accounts and in any case import breakdowns are only available from trade data. Accordingly, we have used trade data for merchandise exports and imports and combined them with payments data on service payments and remittances. The current-account deficit in the table is therefore not the same as in the published data of the Reserve Bank of India. The difference shows up as part of the errors and omissions. Data for 1982-83 and 1983-84 were not fully available at the time of completing this study in July 1984 and they are essentially author's estimates based on preliminary information.

Table 2

MOVEMENTS IN THE CURRENT ACCOUNT DEFICIT
(- indicates a surplus)

Year	Rs. Crores	As % GDP	As % Exports of goods and non-factor services
1970-71	206	0.51	11.63
1971-72	296	0.68	16.50
1972-73	-28	-0.06	-1.26
1973-74	479	0.81	16.93
1974-75	961	1.38	25.07
1975-76	579	0.78	12.03
1976-77	-1031	-1.29	-16.79
1977-78	-903	-1.01	-13.61
1978-79	-575	-0.59	-8.08
1979-80	-64	-0.06	-0.76
1980-81	2020	1.58	22.37
1981-82	2349	1.58	23.48
1982-83	2132	1.30	20.40
1983-84	2000	1.04	17.86

Balance-of-Payments Adjustment in India

Table 3

SELECTED INDICATORS OF ECONOMIC PERFORMANCE
(Annual growth rates)

Year	GDP in constant prices	Index of agricultural production	Index of industrial production	Wholesale price index	Consumer price index	GDP deflator
1970-71	5.6	7.4	n.a.	5.5	5.1	3.2
1971-72	1.6	-0.3	5.7	5.6	3.2	5.2
1972-73	-1.1	-8.1	4.0	10.0	7.8	11.2
1973-74	4.7	10.0	0.8	20.2	20.8	18.9
1974-75	0.9	-3.2	3.2	25.2	26.8	17.9
1975-76	9.4	14.9	7.2	-1.1	-1.3	-3.0
1976-77	0.8	-7.0	9.6	2.1	-3.8	6.7
1977-78	8.8	14.3	3.3	5.2	7.6	3.4
1978-79	5.8	3.8	7.6	No ch.	2.2	2.2
1979-80	-5.3	-15.2	-1.4	17.1	8.8	15.8
1980-81	7.8	15.7	4.0	18.2	11.4	11.4
1981-82	5.3	5.6	8.6	9.3	12.5	10.2
1982-83	1.8	-4.0	3.9	2.6	7.8	7.8
1983-84	7.5	13.0	5.5	9.3	12.6	n.a.

Table 4

INDIA'S FOREIGN EXCHANGE RESERVES
(Rs. crores)

End of period	Foreign Currency Assets 1	Gold 2	SDRs 3	Total a/ Reserves (1+2+3)	Reserves in terms of months of imports of goods and n.f.s.
1970-71	438	183	112	733	4.8
1971-72	480	183	186	849	5.1
1972-73	479	183	185	847	5.0
1973-74	581	183	184	948	3.6
1974-75	611	183	176	970	2.4
1975-76	1492	183	211	1886	4.0
1976-77	2863	188	191	3242	6.9
1977-78	4500	193	169	4862	9.0
1978-79	5220	220	383	5823	9.4
1979-80	5164	225	542	5931	7.1
1980-81	4822	226	494	5542	4.9
1981-82	3355	226	442	4023	3.3
1982-83	4265	226	290	4781	3.9
1983-84	5498	226	247	5971	4.5

a/ Changes in reserves based on these figures differ from reserve changes shown in Table 1 since the latter include reserve valuation changes.

Table 5

EXPORT PERFORMANCE
(Rs. crores)

Year	Indian Exports of Goods and Services		World Exports a/		India's share in World Exports (%)	
	Current Prices	Constant Prices	Current Prices (x10³)	Constant Prices (x10³)	Current Prices	Constant Prices
1970-71	1771	1771	215.1	215.1	0.82	0.82
1971-72	1794	1805	239.4	223.0	0.75	0.79
1972-73	2225	1966	287.6	249.1	0.78	0.79
1973-74	2829	2055	417.7	282.5	0.68	0.73
1974-75	3834	2222	628.3	301.2	0.61	0.74
1975-76	4813	2590	705.9	284.3	0.68	0.91
1976-77	6140	3099	828.3	316.5	0.74	0.98
1977-78	6635	2981	899.9	332.2	0.74	0.90
1978-79	7118	3224	992.8	346.1	0.72	0.93
1979-80	8381	3765	1,240.5	372.8	0.74	1.01
1980-81	9029	3753	1,483.8	382.8	0.61	0.98
1981-82	10,003	3816	1,654.4	379.8	0.60	1.00
1982-83	10,450	4115	1,646.2	364.4	0.63	1.13
1983-84	11,200	3853	1,716.4	375.4	0.65	1.03

a/ Source: International Financial Statistics published by the IMF. The constant price series in rupees has been calculated by converting the current price series into rupees and deflating by a unit value index in rupees obtained from the dollar unit value index by adjusting for changes in the rupee/dollar rate.

Table 6

IMPORTS AT CURRENT PRICES[a]/
(Rs. crores)

	1970-71	1971-72	1972-73	1973-74	1974-75	1975-76	1976-77	1977-78	1978-79	1979-80	1980-81	1981-82	1982-83	1983-84
1. Petroleum	136.0	194.1	204.0-	560.3	1156.9	1226.1	1413.4	1551.8	1686.9	3332.9	5263.5	4939.5	4440.7	3285
2. Capital Goods	404.0	482.7	550.8	673.5	723.3	967.7	1079.4	1148.8	1306.1	1458.5	1910.3	2096.2	2368.3	2804
3. Others	1276.0	1328.9	1294.2	1941.6	2898.2	3471.4	3122.4	3820.8	4436.0	5302.8	6430.2	7530.3	8008	9811
4. Total	1816.0	2005.7	2049.0	3175.4	4778.4	5665.2	5615.2	6521.4	7429.0	10094.2	13604.0	14566.0	14817.0	15900
IMPORTS AT CONSTANT PRICES														
1. Petroleum	136.0	204.3	261.5	287.3	196.1	200.7	237.6	250.3	309.5	366.2	402.4	311.2	268.2	220.5
2. Capital Goods	404.0	502.8	487.4	552.1	428.0	434.0	437.0	524.6	464.8	429.0	819.9	957.2	1025.0	1154.0
3. Others	1276.0	1451.7	1374.5	1454.7	1366.9	1380.3	1384.4	1837.7	2086.5	2005.8	2877.1	2817.9	2883.6	3364.5
4. Total	1816.0	2158.8	2123.4	2294.1	1991.0	2015.0	2059.0	2612.6	2860.8	2801.0	4099.4	4086.3	4176.8	4739.0

a/ Comprises imports of goods and services. Service imports are included in other imports. For computing imports at constant prices, unit values for this category have been assumed to be the same as the unit values for other imports of goods only.

Table 7

NOMINAL AND REAL EFFECTIVE EXCHANGE RATE INDEX

Year	Nominal	Real
1970	120.5	108.9
1971	199.0	109.2
1972	112.3	108.5
1973	104.7	105.4
1974	102.4	107.9
1975	100.0	100.0
1976	97.3	89.4
1977	96.8	89.6
1978	93.3	82.5
1979	92.2	82.7
1980	94.3	89.2
1981	90.2	89.5
1982	88.3	86.6
1983	84.6	88.3

Note: The indices are based on exchange rate movements vis-à-vis the US dollar, the pound Sterling, Deutsche Mark and Yen using export weights. The exchange rate is defined as foreign currencies per rupee, hence a downward movement in the index implies a depreciation.

Table 8

RATE OF GROWTH OF MONEY SUPPLY
(Per cent)

Year	Narrow Money M1	Broad Money M3	High Money
1970-71	11.2	13.2	8.5
1971-72	12.9	15.2	11.6
1972-73	16.6	18.3	12.1
1973-74	15.5	17.4	20.6
1974-75	6.9	10.9	4.6
1975-76	11.3	15.0	2.7
1976-77	20.3	23.6	25.5
1977-78	a/	18.4	11.7
1978-79	20.2	21.9	28.7
1979-80	15.7	17.7	17.7
1980-81	17.1	18.1	17.4
1981-82	6.5	12.5	7.9
1982-83	14.4	16.1	10.1
1983-84 b/	14.7	17.0	24.8

Note: Reserve Bank of India data are on the basis of closure of Government accounts from 31 March 1971 onwards. Therefore, the growth rates given for 1970-71 have been worked out from the earlier series which was not adjusted for the closure of Government accounts.

a/   It is not possible to compare the growth rate of M1 in 1977-78 because of a change in definition which affects the distribution of savings deposit into demand and time components. The series incorporating the new definition is available from 1977-78 onwards and the old series up to 1976-77.

b/   Refers to growth rates computed from 31 March 1983 up to the last Friday of 1984.

Table 9

GROSS DOMESTIC FIXED CAPITAL FORMATION
(Rs. crores)

Year	At Current Prices			At 1970-71 Prices		
	Public	Private	Total	Public	Private	Total
1970-71	2394	3911	6305	2394	3911	6305
1971-72	2802	4272	7074	2648	4038	6686
1972-73	3619	4447	8066	3166	3893	7059
1973-74	4009	5020	9029	3134	3926	7060
1974-75	4272	6658	10930	2680	4176	6856
1975-76	5600	7648	13248	3176	4338	7514
1976-77	7048	8219	15267	3918	4567	8485
1977-78	7697	9449	17146	4181	5134	9315
1978-79	8376	10449	18825	4186	5223	9409
1979-80	9974	10928	20902	4312	4726	9038
1980-81	11629	13588	25217	4486	5242	9728
1981-82	14489	15227	29716	4895	5145	10040
1982-83	17787	16162	33949	5419	4924	10343
1983-84	-	-	-	5961*	5416*	11377*

* Author's estimate.

Table 10

AID COMMITMENTS
(In terms of Agreements signed)
(Rs. crores)

| Fiscal Year | World Bank Group | | Other Consortium Countries | Others | Total |
	IDA	IBRD			
1970-71	126	41	592	3	762
1971-72	335	45	547	2	929
1972-73	200	–	476	–	676
1973-74	437	55	577	102	1171
1974-75	582	129	707	253	1671
1975-76	714	84	764	1092	2654
1976-77	–	285	815	186	1286
1977-78	712	163	693	329	1897
1978-79	1287	228	757	64	2336
1979-80	421	204	989	246	1860
1980-81	1539	362	783	622	3306
1981-82	1307	533	862	141	2843
1982-83	758	1081	951	113	2903

Note: Commitments are recorded according to the date of signature of aid agreements; this method of recording frequently causes spillovers across fiscal years especially since the fiscal years of many important donors (including the multilateral institutions) run from July to June.

Table 11

IMPORT COEFFICIENTS

Year	Capital Goods Jyk	Oil Imports Jyo	Non-Oil Imports Jyno
1970-71	.064	.003	.032
1971-72	.075	.005	.035
1972-73	.069	.006	.034
1973-74	.078	.007	.034
1974-75	.062	.005	.032
1975-76	.058	.004	.030
1976-77	.052	.005	.029
1977-78	.056	.005	.036
1978-79	.049	.006	.038
1979-80	.048	.007	.039
1980-81	.084	.007	.052
1981-82	.095	.005	.048
1982-83	.099	.004	.048
1983-84	.101	.003	.053

Note: Jyk is the coefficient relating the capital goods imports to fixed investment in 1970-71 prices. Jyo and Jyno are coefficients relating oil imports and other imports, respectively, to GDP in constant 1970-71 prices.

Table 12

MOVEMENTS IN IMPORT AND EXPORT PRICES
As ratios of the GDP deflator Pyt

Year	Price of Capital Goods Imports (Pkt/Pyt)	Price of Oil Imports (Pjot/Pyt)	Price of Other Imports (Pjnot/Pyt)	Export Prices (Pxt/Pyt)	Terms of Trade (Pxt/Pmt)
1970-71	1.0	1.0	1.0	1.0	1.0
1971-72	.912	.903	.870	.968	1.10
1972-73	.966	.667	.805	.968	1.17
1973-74	.877	1.402	.959	.990	0.99
1974-75	1.031	3.597	1.293	1.052	0.72
1975-76	1.402	3.841	1.581	1.168	0.66
1976-77	1.455	3.504	1.329	1.167	0.73
1977-78	1.247	3.531	1.184	1.268	0.89
1978-79	1.567	3.039	1.185	1.231	0.85
1979-80	1.637	4.382	1.273	1.072	0.62
1980-81	1.007	5.653	0.966	1.040	0.72
1981-82	.859	6.222	1.048	1.054	0.75
1982-83	.841	6.024	1.011	1.026	0.79
1983-84	.808	4.952	.969	0.966	0.87

Note: For definitions of the symbols used in the ratios in this table
see the "Terms of reference" for the country studies appended to
the synthesis paper by G. Helleiner.

Table 13   PETROLEUM PRODUCTION AND DEMAND BALANCES (Million Tons)

	1970-71	1971-72	1972-73	1973-74	1974-75	1975-76	1976-77	1977-78	1978-79	1979-80	1980-81	1981-82	1982-83	1983-84
I. CRUDE														
1. Domestic Production	6.82	7.30	7.32	7.19	7.68	8.45	8.90	10.76	11.63	11.77	10.51	16.19	21.06	26.02
2. Exports	-	-	-	-	-	-	-	-	-	-	-	0.84	4.35	4.99
3. Net Imports	11.68	12.95	12.08	13.87	14.02	13.62	14.05	14.51	14.66	16.12	16.25	14.46	12.60	10.98
4. Refinery Throughput a/	18.38	20.04	19.33	20.96	21.09	22.28	23.00	24.90	25.97	27.47	25.84	30.15	33.16	35.26
II. PRODUCTS														
5. Domestic Production (from refining of 4 above)	17.11	18.64	17.83	19.50	19.60	20.83	21.43	23.22	24.19	25.79	24.12	28.18	31.07	32.89
6. Imports	1.08	2.15	3.53	3.55	2.65	2.22	2.62	2.88	3.88	4.72	7.29	4.88	5.03	4.05
7. Exports	0.32	0.14	0.13	0.16	0.18	0.17	0.07	0.05	0.04	0.09	0.04	0.06	0.80	1.33
8. Net Imports	0.76	2.01	3.40	3.39	2.47	2.05	2.55	2.83	3.84	4.63	7.25	4.82	4.22	2.72
9. Total availability	17.87	20.65	21.23	22.89	22.07	22.88	23.98	26.05	28.03	30.42	31.37	32.94	35.29	35.52
III.														
10. Total Consumption a/ b/	17.91	20.07	21.72	22.35	22.11	22.45	24.10	25.54	28.24	29.88	30.90	32.52	34.66	35.60
11. Domestic crude petroleum production as % of domestic consumption in crude equivalent.	35.45	33.83	31.09	29.93	32.28	35.19	34.41	39.29	38.36	36.98	31.75	46.53	56.93	68.18

a/ Adjusted for inventory and loss.

b/ Exclude consumption of refinery fuel.

Table 14

DECOMPOSITION OF CURRENT ACCOUNT CHANGES: THE FIRST SHOCK
(Percentages of GDP)

	1972-73 to 1974-75	1974-75 to 1976-77	1976-77 to 1978-79	1974-75 to 1978-79
1. Total Terms of Trade Effect	3.20	-0.10	-0.97	-1.00
1.1 Oil Price Change	1.88	-0.04	-0.23	-0.26
1.2 Price of capital goods imports	0.08	0.42	0.10	0.54
1.3 Price of other imports	1.64	0.12	-0.42	-0.35
1.4 Export price effect	-0.40	-0.60	-0.42	-0.93
2. Export Volume	-0.48	-1.49	0.79	-0.88
2.1 Export effort	0.29	-1.79	0.38	-1.45
2.2 World demand	-0.77	0.30	0.41	0.57
3. Import Intensity	-0.34	-0.40	1.37	0.95
3.1 Import propensity (oil)	-0.12	0.14	0.25	0.38
3.2 Import propensity (capital goods)	-0.11	-0.18	-0.06	-0.22
3.3 Import propensity (other imports)	-0.11	-0.36	1.18	0.79
4. Remittance Effect	-0.07	-0.53	-0.14	-0.67
5. Interest Payments on Debt	-0.22	-0.14	-0.15	-0.31
5.1 Interest rate effect	-0.04	-0.12	-0.07	-0.18
5.2 Acc. debt effect	-0.18	-0.02	-0.08	-0.13
6. Domestic Demand	-0.07	0.13	-0.07	0.07
A. TOTAL EXPLAINED CHANGE (1+2+3+4+5+6)	2.02	-2.53	0.83	-1.84
B. ACTUAL CHANGE (Percentage explained)	1.44 (140)	-2.67 (95)	0.70 (119)	-1.97 (93)

Table 15

DECOMPOSITION OF CURRENT ACCOUNT CHANGES: THE SECOND SHOCK
(Percentages of GDP)

	1978-79 to 1980-81	1980-81 to 1983-84
1. Total Terms of Trade Effect	1.31	-0.28
1.1 Oil Price Change	1.49	-0.51
1.2 Price of Capital Goods Imports	-0.47	-0.29
1.3 Price of Other Imports	-0.84	0.02
1.4 Export Price Effect	1.13	0.50
2. Export Volume	-1.05	0.77
2.1 Export Effort	-0.38	-0.34
2.2 World Demand	-0.67	1.11
3. Import Intensity	3.07	-1.84
3.1 Import Propensity (Oil)	0.49	-2.18
3.2 Import Propensity (capital goods)	0.93	0.31
3.3 Import Propensity (Other imports)	1.65	0.03
4. Remittance Effect	0.70	0.22
5. Interest Payments on Debt	-0.52	0.39
5.1 Interest Rate Effect	-0.48	0.39
5.2 Acc. Debt Effect	-0.04	-
6. Domestic Demand	0.05	0.03
A. TOTAL EXPLAINED CHANGE (1+2+3+4+5+6)	2.16	-0.71
B. ACTUAL CHANGE	2.17	-0.54
Percentage explained (A as % of B)	(100)	(131)

Table 16

THE BASE SOLUTION

Export demand growing at 5 per cent in real terms
Current deficit growing at 10 per cent in nominal terms

Year	GDP		Capacity Utilisation (%)	Current Deficit as % of GDP	Debt Service as % of Exports of goods and services
	Rs. crores in 1983-84 prices	Growth rate (%)			
1983-84	187646	-	99.6	1.2	13
1984-85	191887	2.3	97.3	1.2	16
1985-86	197837	3.1	95.9	1.2	19
1986-87	204601	3.4	95.0	1.2	24
1987-88	211572	3.4	94.1	1.3	27
1988-89	218868	3.4	93.3	1.3	29
1989-90	226661	3.6	92.7	1.3	29
1990-91	234445	3.4	91.9	1.3	30

Average Annual Growth: 1983-84 to 1990-91

Actual GDP   3.2%

Potential GDP   4.4%

Imports   5.0%

Table 17

ENLARGED FINANCING

Export demand growing at 5 per cent in real terms
Current deficit growing at 15 per cent in nominal terms

Year	GDP		Capacity Utilisation (%)	Current Deficit as % of GDP	Debt Service as % of Exports of goods and services
	Rs. crores in 1983-84 prices	Growth rate (%)			
1983-84	187646	–	99.6	1.2	13
1984-85	192868	2.8	97.8	1.3	16
1985-86	199813	3.6	96.8	1.3	20
1986-87	207588	3.9	96.2	1.4	25
1987-88	215592	3.9	95.6	1.5	29
1988-89	223946	3.9	95.0	1.6	31
1989-90	232826	4.0	94.5	1.6	33
1990-91	241731	3.8	93.8	1.7	36

Average Annual Growth: 1983-84 to 1990-91

Actual GDP   3.7%

Potential GDP   4.6%

Imports   5.0%

Table 18

FORCED ADJUSTMENT OF CURRENT DEFICIT

Export demand growing at 5 per cent in real terms
Current deficit growing at 5 per cent in nominal terms

Year	GDP		Capacity Utilisation (%)	Current Deficit as % of GDP	Debt Service as % of Exports of goods and services
	Rs. crores in 1983-84 prices	Growth rate (%)			
1983-84	187646	-	99.6	1.2	13
1984-85	190906	1.7	96.8	1.2	16
1985-86	195955	2.6	95.1	1.1	19
1986-87	201895	3.0	93.9	1.1	23
1987-88	208118	3.1	92.9	1.1	26
1988-89	214738	3.2	92.0	1.0	26
1989-90	221928	3.3	91.3	1.0	26
1990-91	229178	3.3	90.7	1.0	26

Average Annual Growth: 1983-84 to 1990-91

Actual GDP   2.9%

Potential GDP   4.3%

Imports   4.9%

Table 19

FASTER EXPORT GROWTH

Export demand growing at 7 per cent in real terms
Current deficit growing at 10 per cent in nominal terms

Year	GDP		Capacity Utilisation (%)	Current Deficit as % of GDP	Debt Service as % of Exports of goods and services
	Rs. crores in 1983-84 prices	Growth rate (%)			
1983-84	187646	–	99.6	1.2	13
1984-85	194483	3.6	98.6	1.2	16
1985-86	203341	4.6	98.5	1.2	19
1986-87	213352	4.9	98.8	1.2	23
1987-88	223941	5.0	99.0	1.2	25
1988-89	235258	5.1	99.3	1.2	26
1989-90	247511	5.2	99.7	1.2	26
1990-91	260234	5.1	100.0	1.2	27

Average Annual Growth: 1983-84 to 1990-91

Actual GDP   4.8%

Potential GDP   4.8%

Imports   7.0%

THE BALANCE OF PAYMENTS ADJUSTMENT PROCESS IN DEVELOPING
COUNTRIES: THE EXPERIENCE OF THE IVORY COAST

Alassane D. Ouattara*

1. INTRODUCTION

From 1960 to 1975, the Ivory Coast, a medium size country in West
Africa, applied a dynamic economic development policy that resulted in
an annual average growth rate of its GDP of 7 per cent. This dynamic
policy was continued and reinforced as from 1976, thanks to a
considerable increase in the price of cocoa and coffee. Several
projects were undertaken in the agricultural and industrial sectors,
and investment grew at an average annual rate of 19 per cent during the
period under study.

However, owing to the difficult international environment
prevailing since 1978 economic growth has considerably slowed down and
the country's financial situation has worsened seriously.

As a result, the Authorities adopted in 1981, in consultation with
the International Monetary Fund, a number of adjustment measures
intended to restore the equilibrium of the economic and financial
situation and to create the required conditions for a smooth growth of
the economy of the Ivory Coast.

2. EVOLUTION OF THE ECONOMIC AND FINANCIAL SITUATION FROM 1974 TO 1981

After the 1960s, when the economy experienced an exceptionally
strong growth as reflected in an annual real growth rate of GDP of 7.7
per cent, the pace of the economic growth slowed down during the period
1970-1974. Thus GDP in constant prices grew at 2.8 per cent (annual
rate) increasing from $758 million in 1970 to $780 million in 1974.

The weak performance in 1974 is attributable to the adverse
weather conditions which affected the agricultural sector and brought
about stagnation and even a decrease in the production of food and cash
crops. Coffee production decreased from 301,800 tons in 1973 to
195,200 tons. Timber production declined from 5,169 m^3 to 4,629 m^3
on a year to year basis.

*The author is Vice Governor, Central Bank of the West African
States. July 1985.

From 1975, the upward trend of the annual growth of GDP in constant prices resumed and rose to 7.6 per cent during the period 1975-1980. The agricultural sector, the industrial sector as well as commerce were the main factors contributing to this growth. The output of the principal productive activities recovered to levels well above those recorded during the 1974 decline. Timber production increased and stood at satisfactory levels in 1978 and 1979. Similarly, coffee production rose steadily between 1975 and 1977.

Despite the relative decrease of its share in GDP, agriculture remains the dominant sector of the economy. The main cash crops are: coffee, cocoa, cotton, pineapple, bananas, palm-products and sugar, while food products grown locally comprise rice, corn, yams, banana plantain and cassava.

Gross capital formation in constant prices experienced two stages. Up to 1974, its growth was relatively slow, at an average year-to-year rate of 5.7 per cent, because of the considerable slowdown of economic growth.

As from 1975, the trend of capital formation, which in that year stood at $858 million, was characterised by high growth rates: 15 per cent in 1975, 22.4 per cent in 1974 and 42.7 per cent in 1977 and 22.3 per cent in 1978, or an annual average rate of 23.7 per cent (cf. table XV). This trend reflected the desire of the national authorities to maintain a constant pace of investment growth.

These investments, essentially aimed at creating industrial production units, developing the industrial and transportation sectors and setting up of an important infrastructure programme, were financed up to 1977 from the substantial resources of the Ivory Coast's Caisse de Stabilisation et de Soutien des Prix des Produits Agricoles (Stabilization Fund) which benefited during that period from the high level of prices of the main agricultural products, notably coffee and cocoa.

Since 1977, the Stabilization Fund has played a marginal part in the financing of the capital budget because its resources have diminished as a consequence of the deterioration of the terms of trade due to the steady decline of the prices of export products. As a result, for the purpose of financing its investment programme the Ivory Coast resorted to massive external borrowing.

From $778.2 million in 1974, the Ivory Coast's outstanding debt rose to $926 million in 1975, an increase of 19 per cent. The debt increased at even steeper rates as high as 79.5 per cent and 56.67 per cent by year end in 1978 and 1979, respectively (cf. table XII).

This state of affairs inevitably had a negative impact on the situation of the Ivory Coast. The ample liquidities generated by massive borrowing led to an increase of public and semi-public expenditures, while at the same time, the burden of debt service, comprising interest and repayment of principal, became more onerous. In these circumstances, the authorities decided in 1980 to reduce the public investment programme and to restructure the state corporations.

Consequently, in 1980 the growth rate of outstanding debt declined to 31 per cent, compared to 56.6 per cent a year before. In the following years, the pace slowed down further by 9 per cent in 1981 and 15 per cent in 1982.

On the monetary side, credit expansion was particularly rapid during 1975-1980, when domestic credit (granted by the banking system to both the State and to the private sector) expanded at an annual average rate of 60 per cent. The Government's net credit balance shrank from $535.4 million in 1979 to $263.9 million in 1980 before turning into a deficit of $225.9 million in 1981 and $561.1 million in 1983.

The rapid credit expansion recorded from 1975, far from being the result of an excess of liquidity, actually reflected the deliberate intention of the monetary authorities to promote economic development and integration through a more active monetary policy more in keeping with the needs of the member countries of the West African Monetary Union.

The slackening of the growth of credit expansion since 1980 is attributable to a restrictive monetary and credit policy dictated by the difficult international economic environment.

Net foreign assets of the banking system have declined steadily from a positive figure of $75.8 million in 1974 to a negative figure of $1.6645 million in 1983.

The analysis of the economic situation of the Ivory Coast during the period 1975-1983 shows that an expansionary policy continued to be applied despite the decrease in both agricultural production and international commodity prices; actually, producer prices were raised slightly and the level of investment rose steadily, thanks at first to substantial export earnings, and later to external borrowing. All these factors contributed to the increase of total demand which led to a weakening of the balance of payments, as reflected in the shrinking of the external reserves of the banking system.

3.   EVOLUTION OF THE BALANCE OF PAYMENTS

(a) Review of the general trend

The balance of payments of the Ivory Coast showed large deficits in the period between 1974 and 1983. Surpluses were recorded only in

1976 and 1978 of respectively $32.6 and 88.6 million, in current prices, due essentially to an improvement of the trade balance and to higher net capital inflows.

Unlike that of most of the developing countries, the trade balance of Ivory Coast has always been in surplus, exports rising generally at a faster rate than imports. The substantial increase in the trade surplus recorded in 1977 (+ 42 per cent) explains the low current account deficit despite the surge in imports during the same year attributable to the oil crisis and to inflation in the industrialized countries. The deficit habitually recorded by the balance of payments of the Ivory Coast is accounted for essentially by the large net outflow in respect of services, which increased considerably during the period from $33.6 million in 1974 to $116 million in 1983.

Unrequited transfers are also characterized by net outflows in consequence of large transfers of private capital, estimated at $70.6 million for the year 1980 alone.

The inflow of capital, consisting largely of long-term private and public borrowings as well as direct investments contributed to the financing of the current payments deficit and, in some years, made it possible to achieve a surplus both in the basic balance and in the total balance of payments (cf. table I).

(b) Trade balance

(i) Trend of imports

Capital goods, textiles, foodstuffs, chemicals and energy-related products are the main components of the Ivory Coast's imports.

The imports structure during the period 1975-1983 is set out in table III (imports are calculated on a c.i.f. basis, whereas in the balance of payments they are valued on an f.o.b. basis). The table shows that the total value of imports almost doubled between 1975 and 1982.

In current prices, the value (f.o.b.) of imports rose steadily at an average rate of 9.7 per cent from $ 1,011.6 million in 1975 to $ 2,613.5 million in 1980.

Imports of petroleum products in current prices increased from $157 million in 1975 to $495.3 million in 1982.

From 1975 to 1978, imports of petroleum products in constant prices grew at an average rate of 12 per cent, which is a reasonable pace.

IVORY COAST: IMPORTS BY PRODUCTS (in constant 1975 prices)

	1975	1976	1977	1978	1979	1980	1981	1982
			(in millions of dollars)					
Capital goods	343	390	566	625	493	546	331	292
Consumer goods	1,257	1,527	1,825	2,175	2,210	1,426	2,407	1,165
of which energy- related products	157	168	196	195	260	241	207	203
Total imports	1,600	1,917	2,391	2,800	2,703	2,972	2,738	2,477

The value of all the other import items (chemicals, textiles, steel products, machinery and appliances etc.) increased steadily during the period under review.

For the purpose of estimating the impact of the rise in import prices the following method was used: the value of imports in current prices was compared with the value of imports expressed in constant 1975 prices.

This method is based on the assumption that price increases that have occurred since 1975 were due to external shocks, mainly the consequences of the fourfold increase in oil price and exchange rate fluctuations.

Thus, it appears that the import price effects may be said, in the aggregate, to account for more than one-third of the total 1983 imports in constant terms.   In 1982, imports in current prices amounted to $3,378 million, while in constant terms they amounted to $2,247 million, i.e. a difference of $901.8 million; this illustrates the magnitude of the external shock effects.

It is clear from table XI that the price increases were mainly attributable to imports of oil and capital goods; in their case the impact of the price effect accounts for more than 50 per cent of imports in constant terms.

The phenomenon was not invariable during the period 1975-1983. From 1975 to 1977, the impact was very weak: 2.7 per cent in 1976, 6.5 per cent in 1977.

As from 1978, the trend was reversed and the price effect exerted a considerable impact, as is shown by the following figures: 22 per cent in 1978, 27 per cent in 1979, 52 per cent in 1980, 36 per cent in 1981 and 1982, which reflect clearly the incidence of runaway inflation and of the instability of foreign exchange rates on the country's economy.

Furthermore, the analysis of imports of goods in constant prices indicates an upward trend of imports in quantitative terms.   The rates at which the volume of imports increased advanced to 19 per cent in 1976, 24 per cent in 1978 and 17 per cent in 1979.

Despite the direct and indirect effects of oil price increases and of the fluctuations of exchange rates the Ivory Coast did not reduce its imports between 1975 and 1978.

This state of affairs can be explained by the abundance of the country's financial resources that were obtained thanks to the outstanding performance of exports and to the high level of drawings on external credit which made it possible to finance the Government's huge investment programme referred to above.

A comparative analysis of the evolution of imports, particularly those of capital goods, and the evolution of investments and gross domestic production, yields conclusive evidence in support of this statement.

The analysis of the following table shows a correlation between the trend of imports of capital goods and that of the level of investments.

In 1976, imports of capital goods by the Ivory Coast in constant terms grew by 13.7 per cent, while the level of investments rose by 22.5 per cent.   The phenomenon is more perceptible in 1977, when imports in constant terms grew by 45 per cent and the volume of investments by 42 per cent.   The correlation held true in 1981 and 1982, when both aggregates declined.

This reflects the determination of the authorities of the Ivory Coast to carry on the ambitious development programme, as shown by the dominant share of capital goods in total imports (19 per cent in 1976; 14 per cent in 1977 and 17 per cent in 1978).

Starting from 1978, a reversal of the trend took place: the share of capital goods in total imports declined gradually, as did the value in constant prices, the rate of decline being 9.5 per cent in 1982.   In effect, the impact of external shocks has seriously affected the financial situation of the Ivory Coast and greatly contributed to jeopardizing the country's ambitious investment programme.

IVORY COAST'S IMPORTS
(in millions of current dollars)

	1975	1976	1977	1978	1979	1980	1981	1982	1983
Imports	1,600	1,917	2,391	2,800	2,703	2,973	2,738	2,477	...
Variation in %		+ 19	+ 24	+ 17	+ 9	+ 10	- 7.9	- 9.5	...
Imports of capital goods	343	390	566	625	493	546	331	292	...
Variation in %	- 3.7	+13.7	+ 45	+10.4	- 21	+10.7	- 30	-11.8	...
Investment	858	1,051	1,499	1,833	1,657	1,525	1,351	1,771	935
Variation in %	+15.4	+22.5	+42.6	+22.2	- 9.6	- 8	-11.4	- 31	-47.2
GDP	3,894	4,361	5,566	5,018	5,113	5,508	5,519	5,298	5,064
Variation in %	+9.05	+ 12	+ 4.7	+ 9.9	+ 1.9	+ 7.7	+ 0.1	- 41	-4.4

(ii) Trend of exports

Unlike most developing countries, the Ivory Coast has always recorded a surplus in its balance of trade because exports have grown faster than imports.

The current value of exports, according to the official trade statistics, doubled between 1975 and 1982, rising from $1,238 million to $2,419 million, reaching a peak of $3,012 million in 1980 (see table IV).

Tables V and VII relating to the export structure during the period 1975 to 1983 show that the Ivory Coast's main export products were coffee, cocoa, timber, which together represented between 60 per cent and 79 per cent of total exports during these years. Their share tended to decline towards the end of the period, particularly in 1982, when they accounted for only 55 per cent of total exports.

This can be easily explained by analysing the trend of the country's exports in constant terms based on 1975 prices. Exports expressed in constant dollars, which make it possible to assess the trend in quantitative terms, rose slightly in 1975-1982, from $1,239 million in 1975 to $1,791 million in 1982, that is, at an average growth rate of 6.3 per cent, by contrast with a rate of 13.6 per cent if the calculation is made on a current dollar basis (tables III and IV).

This slow growth of exports in volume terms was the result of the combination of adverse climatic conditions, the fall in international commodity prices, the poor demand in the international market and some specific policies adopted by the authorities of the Ivory Coast.

Since most of the Ivory Coast's exports consist of agricultural products, local weather conditions play an important role in export performance. Because of severe droughts, coffee and cocoa production dropped sharply in 1977, 1982 and 1983; coffee production totalled only 264,500 tons in 1982, compared to 353,000 tons in 1981, and the output of cocoa amounted to 471,000 tons in 1982, compared to 486,200 tons in 1981. Timber production increased substantially in 1976 (38 per cent), but at a slower rate in 1977 (2.5 per cent) and then gradually declined in consequence of the Government's decision to protect certain species and of the unfavourable trend of world markets affected by the recession in the industrial countries.

Exceptional price developments also affected the country's exports during the period under review. In 1976, exports in volume terms, particularly of coffee, cocoa and lumber, were following a distinctly upward trend, increasing at rates of 26.6 per cent, 11.8 per cent and 34 per cent, respectively. The notable improvement in world prices in 1976 contributed to the increase in export earnings to $1,735 million from $1,238 million in current dollars, an improvement of 40 per cent. This situation continued to prevail in 1977 when, despite the slight decrease in the volume of exports, the firm prices of the main export products were responsible for a rise in export receipts (cf. Table IV).

As from 1978, exceptional factors began to influence prices: the trend was reversed, the level of prices of the main export products (coffee, cocoa and lumber) deteriorated gradually, leading to a strong reaction on the part of the authorities.

The comparative method of analysing the trend of exports in constant and current dollars makes it possible to assess the impact of external shocks, notably the price effects, on the volume of exports and total export receipts.

In 1978, total exports in constant value terms, which reflect the trend in volume terms, grew by 1.5 per cent; when expressed in current value terms, the growth rate is only 8.5 per cent because of the price fall. This phenomenon was aggravated in 1980 when, in spite of the larger volume actually exported, current export receipts fell.

A product-by-product analysis shows even more clearly the impact of the fall of commodity prices on the volume of exports and on export earnings.

The volume of coffee exported by the Ivory Coast increased substantially, as reflected in the trend of exports expressed in constant terms. From 1979 to 1982, these exports went up from $222 million to $427 million.

As regards cocoa, after the fall in production recorded in 1979, from 341,900 tons in 1978 to 298,800 tons in 1979, and the consequential decline of exports, cocoa output increased gradually to 420,900 tons in 1980, 486,200 in 1981 and 471,000 tons in 1982; the output then decreased again to 355,000 tons in 1983, resulting in an average growth rate of 7.2 per cent between 1979 and 1983.

Despite the steady expansion of the volume of exports of cocoa, made possible by a favourable production environment, export receipts in current dollars dropped gradually from $713 million and $793 million in 1970 and 1980 to $497 million in 1983, or a fall of 46 per cent in current dollars (cf. table IV).

This substantial fall of receipts from cocoa exports was essentially due to the continuous fall of prices on the international markets (see table IV). Accordingly, in late 1979, the authorities of the Ivory Coast instituted a policy of retaining stocks of cocoa beans, as shown in the following table.

Ivory Coast: Production and exports of cocoa
(in thousands of tons)

	1975	1976	1977	1978	1979	1980	1981	1982	1983
Production (calendar year)	239.4	257.4	243.1	341.9	298.8	420.9	486.2	471.0	355
Export (calendar year)	169.7	194.9	158.5	244.0	170.8	283.7	438.4	326.4	170.4

Source:　　Official statistics: Caisse de Stabilisation et de Soutien des Prix des Produits Agricoles; European Community; Ministère des Eaux et Forêts.

It is worth mentioning that whereas it is possible to store coffee for the purpose of ensuring uniform and regular exports, such storage is not practicable in the case of cocoa beans. The only alternative to the immediate export of cocoa beans is to convert them into cocoa butter.

It follows that the policy of retaining stocks of cocoa beans has had a net positive effect on the raw material processing industry in the Ivory Coast.

As a result of the adverse movement of the prices of the main traditional export products and its impact on the volume of exports the relative share of exports of coffee, cocoa and lumber in total exports has declined substantially; on the other hand, however, exports of petroleum products to neighbouring countries have risen.

The share of exports of petroleum products in total exports, which stood at 3.8 per cent in 1978, increased to 13 per cent in 1983. Expressed in terms of current dollars, exports of petroleum products grew substantially, rising from $67 million in 1975 to $296 million in 1982.

Changes in import controls or other protectionist measures in importing countries have not, however, affected the export performance of the Ivory Coast in the period studied. Almost 70 per cent of its exports were shipped to countries members of the European Economic Community and the United States of America, where the Ivory Coast's exports are not subject to any restriction. In fact, most of the goods exported by the Ivory Coast enjoy preferential treatment in the Common Market. 1/

In the light of the review of the trend of Ivory Coast's imports and exports during the period 1975-1983 it may be said that despite the steady decline in the prices of the main export commodities and despite the rise of the prices of import goods, which have greatly added to the cost of imports and materially affected the level of export earnings, the country's trade balance remains structurally in surplus.

A strong growth of the trade balance was recorded in 1976 (53 per cent) and even in 1977 (41 per cent), when it attained a record surplus of $815 million compared to $227 million in 1975.

1/ Cf. A.D. Ouattara, "Trade effects of the association of African countries with the European Economic Community", International Monetary Fund, Staff Papers, July 1973.

This substantial expansion of the country's external trade is attributable to a rapid growth of both the volume and the value of exports after the rise of commodity prices which occurred during that period. Between 1978 and 1981, the trade balance, while still in surplus, declined slightly because of adverse climatic conditions and the fall in prices.

(iii) Services

The trend of the invisibles balance was influenced largely by the movement of payments for freight and insurance and, since 1978, by the considerable rise of net outflows in respect of payments of interest on the foreign debt.

More specifically, the deficit of the services balance deteriorated rapidly, almost doubling from 1975 to 1978, when it reached $994.1 million. From 1978 to 1980, the deficit continued to rise at a fast rate, and payments for services totalled $1,518.3 million in 1980. After a period of relative stability in 1981 and 1982, the deficit in dollar terms was greatly reduced.

(iv) Unrequited transfers

The analysis of the trend of unrequited transfers yields evidence of the same general aggravation of the chronically adverse balance. Unrequited transfers almost tripled between 1975 and 1979, the increase being due mainly to the net outflows of savings out of the earnings of foreign residents. Rising continually, they totalled $ 705.7 million in 1980. In 1981, the net transfers began to decline appreciably, and in consequence of the strong appreciation of the dollar the downward trend was particularly pronounced in 1982. It should be noted that during the entire period under review, unrequited transfers (in dollar terms) increased at an annual average rate of 12.7 per cent and workers' remittances increased by 16.2 per cent.

(v)   Capital account

Net capital inflows into the Ivory Coast increased slowly between 1975 and 1977, when the country held large resources generated by export receipts.

In 1978, the balance-of-payments deficit increased from $341 million to $921 million, a 241 per cent deterioration, attributable mainly to the public sector and parastatals, which borrowed massively from the international financial markets in order to finance the country's ambitious investment programmes.

This trend continued until 1982, when the current account deficit reached a record $1,092 million. The substantial decline which occurred in 1983 is the result of the determination of the authorities of the Ivory Coast to curb the country's external indebtedness.

(c) Current account: 1975-1983

The current account deficit has greatly deteriorated during recent years, increasing from $175.8 million in 1977 to $840.7 million in 1978 and $1,378 million in 1979. The deterioration of the current account was more pronounced in 1980, when the deficit reached $1,824.9 million. For the past three years, the deficit has been decreasing. It stood at $1,181 million in 1981, $1,087 million in 1982 and $738.5 million in 1983.

The gradual deterioration of the current account during the period 1977-1981 is attributable to several factors. The deficit being essentially dependent upon the country's imports and exports, payments in respect of services and unrequited transfers, we shall consider below the main factors that have affected the current account.

The trend of the Ivory Coast's current account deficit can be divided into three time periods:

from 1975 to 1977:   characterized by a fall of the current account deficit;

from 1978 to 1980:   characterized by a strong growth of the deficit;

from 1981 to 1983:   characterized by a gradual decrease of the deficit.

(i) - From 1975 to 1977

In 1975, the current account deficit shrank by 35 per cent, from $384 million to $249 million. This fall, however, reflected a growth of both investments and GDP in constant dollars, which grew by 15.5 per cent and 9.5 per cent respectively.

The explanation for this trend might well be found in the behaviour of imports and exports as well as in the conditions of investment financing and the external borrowing policy.

- Imports

The assumptions used in this study led us to integrate non-service factors and unrequited transfers into total imports, in order to isolate payments in respect of service factors.

In 1975 and 1979, the trend of imports affected substantially the level of the current account deficit. Imports in constant terms increased in 1975 and 1976 by 19.7 per cent and 24 per cent. This increase was mainly due to capital goods imports whose growth rate during the period under review reached 14 per cent and 45 per cent respectively. However, it can be noted that the import ratio increased slightly between 1975 and 1976 from 0.3 per cent to 0.4 per cent.

- Exports

Exports in constant terms likewise increased in 1976 by 15 per cent. When expressed in current terms, the year-to-year growth rate reached 35 per cent. This favourable trend can be explained by the good agricultural harvests in 1975 and 1976 as well as by the sustained international demand for Ivory Coast's export commodities. This sharp rise in export receipts provided the Stabilization Fund with large resources.

- External debt

Outstanding debt during this period was characterized by steady growth rates: 19 per cent in 1975, 20 per cent and 21 per cent in 1976 and 1977.

In the final analysis, it can be said that the deterioration of the current account between 1976 and 1977 was mainly due to the imports, particularly capital goods imports, which were increased to meet the needs of the country's huge investment programme, despite the slight decrease of import ratios.

These massive imports by the Ivory Coast raised the level of its external debt and stimulated economic growth, as is indicated by the growth of GDP in real terms by 9 per cent and 12 per cent in 1975 and 1977, respectively.

(ii) - From 1978 to 1980

The current account deterioration recorded during the preceding period went on at a faster speed. The deficit grew by 478 per cent in 1978, or more than fourfold, by 167 per cent in 1979 and 132 per cent in 1980.

- Imports

Imports in constant terms increased appreciably at an annual average rate of 22 per cent. The breakdown of imports reveals that this progression was mainly due, in 1978, to imports of current consumer goods, which grew at a rate of 38 per cent, as well as to capital goods imports the growth rate of which was also on the rise.

Capital goods being dependent on the level of investments and import prices, the figures reflecting higher imports of these goods are easily explained by the continuation of the investment programme and the increase in import prices.

Moreover, since imports of current consumer goods are regarded as being dependent on GDP and import prices, the high level of GDP rose further in response to higher investments, which are themselves due to the rising trend of imports.

On the other hand, exports in real terms suffered a marked decline because of adverse climatic conditions and the fall in prices.

- External debt

The period 1978-1980 being characterized by a slowdown in exports, the continuation of investment necessitated massive external borrowing, resulting in the sharp rise of the outstanding debt from $1,350 million in 1978 to $2,423 million in 1980, an increase of more than 79 per cent.

All these factors, therefore, contributed directly to the worsening of the deficit, which reached its highest level in 1980 ($1,825 million).

(iii) - From 1981 to 1983

This period, characterized by the economic slowdown due to the country's financial difficulties and the international environment, recorded a general decrease of all the aggregates: imports, exports, investments and GDP.

All these factors explain the gradual decline of the current deficit, which reached $758.5 million in 1983 compared to $1087.0 million the year before.

(d)   Financing of the deficit

The current account deficit was financed mainly by non-monetary assets which reached record levels in 1980, 1981 and 1982 of $1,063.9 million, $636.5 million and $932.1 million, respectively.   Moreover, in order to finance the deficit, the country resorted to loans from commercial banks 2/ which had been able to accumulate reserves during 1975-1977.

What happened was that in the 1970s the Ivory Coast began to follow a policy of borrowing heavily abroad in order to ensure the development of the country's agricultural sector and infrastructure. Its outstanding debt (public and private debt) increased from $926 million in 1974 to $4,986 million in 1980, before dropping slightly from 1981 to 1983. The outstanding debt, which had represented only 23 per cent of GDP at current prices in 1974, reached 30 per cent and 49 per cent in 1978 and 1980, respectively.

However, the capital inflow from external borrowing (drawings less amortization), which had been trending strongly upwards until 1980, slowed down gradually in 1980-1983 in which period it ranged from $1,420 million to $780 million. The changes in the borrowing conditions, notably the high interest rates on the international markets, were largely responsible for the downturn.

Moreover, thanks to its membership to the West African Monetary Union and the Franc Zone, the Ivory Coast has become less dependent on foreign lenders. The reason is that the six member countries of the West African Monetary Union (Benin, Burkina Faso, Ivory Coast, Niger, Senegal and Togo) have pooled their foreign exchange reserves, thus giving to each of these countries the possibility to use the resources of the pool when it experiences balance-of-payments difficulties. Furthermore, under the Convention on the Operations Account between B.C.E.A.O. (the Central Bank of the West African States, which is the Ivory Coast's issuing institution) and the French Treasury, member States of the West African Monetary Union are eligible for advances from the French Treasury on concessional terms to meet their balance of payments needs. In this way, the Ivory Coast has been able to benefit from advances from the French Treasury for balance-of-payments purposes. In consequence of the persisting external payments difficulties, these advances rose rapidly and reached $632 million in December 1983.

As regards the use of the resources of the IMF, these played a marginal role up to 1979 in the financing of the current account deficit.

2/ In general, commercial banks in the Ivory Coast are subsidiaries or branches of foreign commercial banks, mainly French banks. When the Central Bank adopts restrictive monetary policies, the banks use their lines of credits abroad and borrow on special terms in order to maintain the level of credit granted to the private sector.

Financing of current account deficit
1975-1983

	1975	1976	1977	1978	1979
Current account deficit	-384.0	-249.0	-175.8	-840.7	-1378.8
Financing	384.0	249.0	175.8	840.7	1378.8
Non-monetary assets	205.8	272.4	382.2	921.0	762.0
Monetary assets	165.2	-47.7	-172.2	-71.4	645.0
Central Bank	-30.8	9.6	-92.4	-179.1	299.0
C.A.A.	134.6	-56.1	-16.3	62.5	20.2
Commercial banks	71.4	-1.2	-63.5	45.2	325.8
Use of IMF resources	-	14.2	-9.8	-17.3	-
SDR allocations	-1.4	-	-	-	-9.9
Errors and omissions	14.4	9.7	-24.4	8.4	38.1
	1980	1981	1982	1983	
Current account deficit	-1825.0	-1181.0	-1087.0	-758.5	
Financing	1825.0	1181.0	1087.0	758.5	
Non-monetary assets	1047.4	636.5	931.2	417.3	
Monetary assets	801.5	544.6	155.8	341.2	
Central Bank	603.6	-	-	-	
C.A.A.	3.8	-	-		
Commercial banks	194.1	-	-		
Use of IMF resources	-	-	-	-	
SDR allocations	9.4	14.7	39.6	36.9	
Errors and omissions	45.1	16.2	-	-	

Source: B.C.E.A.O.

In September 1974, the Ivory Coast borrowed the equivalent of $26 million in foreign exchange from the Fund through the first oil facility and its gold tranche. Up to 1979, the member States of the West African Monetary Union were always reluctant to resort to the Fund's facilities because the commitments stipulated in the programmes, though applied flexibly and often liberally, imply political decisions in certain specific areas and such decisions may not be compatible with the general political and social objectives of the Government.

Then, the new facilities created by the Fund (e.g. the extended facility, the supplementary facility and the Trust Fund), which meet better the needs of developing countries wishing to use the resources of the IMF, encouraged Ivory Coast to apply to the Fund for assistance in financing its balance-of-payments deficits. By 1981, the Fund's loans to the Ivory Coast stood at $348 million and in 1982 they rose to $454 million.

4. MACROECONOMIC POLICIES FROM 1974 TO 1976 3/

Although worldwide economic conditions were unfavourable, an expansionary policy was adopted during the period 1974-1976. By increasing its investment programme especially in the export sector, the Government succeeded in sustaining economic growth, albeit at a slow rate. Measures were taken to expand the home production of traditionally imported foodstuffs (e.g. sugar and rice). The Government was therefore in a favourable position to take advantage of the recovery in the demand for the Ivory Coast's exports and to reduce the country's dependence on imported foodstuffs, immediately after the petroleum crisis thus avoiding a compression of the volume of the country's imports.

Furthermore, because of the small size of the country's manufacturing sector, the impact of the oil price increase was bound to be limited. The Ivory Coast, which does not produce petroleum in its territory, relies heavily on petroleum imports to cover its energy needs. At present, the petroleum refinery has a capacity of about 2 million tons and part of its production is exported to Mali and Burkina Faso. As a result, net imports of petroleum and petroleum products amounted to less than 10 per cent of total imports in 1974.

These factors enabled the Government to weather the crisis without having to resort to a general austerity programme. The use of the IMF resources made available through the oil facility in 1974/75, led to

---

3/ See Dr. A.D. Ouattara: "The Balance-of-Payments Adjustment Process in Developing Countries: the Case of Ivory Coast", in UNCTAD/MFD/TA/5, March 1978.

the adoption of a financial programme designed to narrow the balance-of-payments deficit in 1976. As previously mentioned, the undertakings required by the financial programme were rather limited and concerned essentially policies in the energy and monetary sectors, which for the most part had been implemented before the negotiations with the IMF.

In the energy sector, the Government authorized oil price increases at the consumer level in order to reflect the whole of the increase in costs and the higher ad valorem duties and taxes in the turnover. The retail price of premium gasoline is used as the retail price index for oil products, which are numerous (for example, regular gasoline, kerosene, diesel fuel etc.). Since oil prices increased fourfold, the index related to refining costs and taxes (which generally account for 80 per cent of the retail price) closely followed the movements in the "African" consumer price index for that period. Consequently, Government policy in this area was neutral as it did not try to reduce consumption by increasing taxes, or to counter the rise in the retail price by lowering import duties. At the same time, the authorities tried to reduce oil import dependency by developing off-shore prospecting and building a hydroelectric complex at Taabo (on the Bandama river, downstream from Kossou).

In the monetary sector steps were taken to reduce the balance-of-payments deficit. The State's financial transactions reflected the impact of the measures pertaining to wage increases granted to civil servants and the expansion of the investment budget from 1974 to 1976. The financial programme limited the opportunities for the Government to tap the banking system in order to finance its deficit and reduced the growth rate of domestic credit. However, sufficient credit was provided to finance the increased agricultural output, while oil corporations were urged to finance their additional needs by using suppliers' credit and digging into their reserves before applying to local banks for credit.

The new instruments of monetary and credit policy adopted by the Central Bank in July 1975 had a major impact on the course of the policy in that period. The Central Bank's rediscount rate was raised from 8.5 per cent to 10 per cent and interest paid on deposits of the private sector with banks were also raised to take into account the movement of foreign interest rates. Banks were no longer authorized to hold foreign exchange reserves outside the countries of the West African Monetary Union and the rediscount policy became restrictive enough to induce them to borrow more on a short-term basis from parent banks or from their correspondents. In addition, contrary to past practices, the Central Bank stopped notifying the banks of the amount of resources it was willing to inject and advised them to reduce substantially their lending to large clients, whose requests for loans were subject to prior approval by the Central Bank.

Between 1974 and 1977, the monetary and credit policy yielded mixed results as far as the liquidity objective and the reduction in the balance-of-payments deficit were concerned. Except in 1975, money growth was much more rapid than the rise of GDP in current prices. The export surplus deposited with banks by the Caisse de Stabilisation et de Soutien des Prix des Produits Agricoles and the increased monetization of the country's economy were largely responsible for these differences. The rates of growth of credit to the private sector and domestic credit are more closely related to the increase in GDP, but the ability of banks to borrow abroad when credit policies tightened influenced these developments significantly. The Central Bank's refinancing of banks did not increase in 1975, and while there was only a moderate 17.1 per cent growth in 1976, there was, in contrast, an almost twofold increase of GDP and private sector credit. Thus during this period, credit policy was generally motivated by considerations that were not solely concerned with the reduction of the balance-of-payments deficit. The Ivory Coast's membership of the West African Monetary Union and of the Franc Zone no doubt facilitated a smooth adjustment of the country's balance of payments, and there was no need to take drastic measures in these circumstances.

(a) <u>Policies with regard to the external sector</u>

As a member of the Franc Zone, the Ivory Coast does not have an exchange rate policy of its own. Its currency, the CFA franc, is pegged to the French franc by a fixed rate: 1 CFA franc = 0.02 French franc or 1 French franc = 50 CFA francs. The French franc is the only intervention currency and transactions in other currencies are carried out at the rates ruling on the Paris market between the French franc and these currencies.

Movements in the exchange rate of the CFA franc during this period reflect those recorded for the French franc.

Table XVII shows the U.S. dollar rates against the CFA franc from 1975 to 1983, on the basis of the yearly average. The figures indicate that between 1975 and 1980, the CFA franc appreciated against the dollar at an average rate of 2.9 per cent a year. Thereafter, yearly fluctuations, wider than previously, brought about a very pronounced depreciation averaging 26.7 per cent yearly between 1981 and 1983.

On this basis, the CFA franc fluctuations during the period under review tended to increase the cost of imports denominated in foreign currencies, especially after 1980 when the CFA franc depreciation against the dollar exceeded 26 per cent.

The depreciation of the exchange rate had apparently little or no impact on the level of imports. As mentioned earlier, the volume of imports was not affected by the oil crisis and growth was consistent with the "normal" development of the economy. Besides, a large part of imports is not affected by short-term exchange rate fluctuations, as France is the first supplier of the Ivory Coast.

The Ivory Coast has a very liberal payments system. With the exception of a few local products (e.g. coffee, rice, etc.) and the ban on imports from South Africa, goods may be imported freely from any country, subject only to the filing of a declaration of intention to import. Despite the rapid growth of imports, no controls or restrictions were introduced during the period under review. However, the spectacular rise in the prices of a few foodstuffs forced the Government, in 1975, to employ the services of the Swiss Société Générale de Surveillance to check prices of imports before they entered the Ivory Coast. It seems that the unit values of imports were affected by this measure, especially in 1976, but their origin and composition were not.

When exports are analysed, the impact of the exchange rate depreciation is even less significant, since three products (cocoa, coffee and timber) account for 70 per cent to 75 per cent of total export receipts. The prices of these commodities are determined by the conditions prevailing in world markets, and crop production is more dependent on climatic conditions than on price fluctuations. Exports of finished goods, which might be sensitive to exchange rate fluctuations, account for a marginal share of the Ivory Coast's total exports.

Export promotion is still the main objective of the Government's policy. The authorities have persistently tried over the past decade to diversify the country's export products and markets. The Ivory Coast is the third coffee producer in the world (after Brazil and Colombia), the leading cocoa exporter and a major exporter of high-grade timber; other export products include cotton, pineapple, bananas, palm oil, etc. The large-scale production of these commodities began only in the 1960s, after independence. The search for new markets in the United States has led to a decrease in the volume of total exports to the EEC countries (particularly France). Neighbouring African States are also beginning to become important customers of the Ivory Coast. It is difficult to estimate the quantitative effect of these various measures, but the sustained growth of exports recorded earlier corroborates their positive influence.

(b) The impact of the current account deficit on the internal situation

The financing of the Ivory Coast's current account deficit by massive recourse to external resources inevitably had negative repercussions on the country's financial situation. Between 1977 and 1980, the global financial situation of the public sector, which had previously been in slight surplus, began to show a deficit, which rose to a record high equivalent to 15.2 per cent of GDP.

Moreover, the debt structure also changed during the period under study, in that the Ivory Coast resorted increasingly to private financial institutions and to suppliers' credits, at the expense of public institutions. Loans with very high interest rates and shorter terms and grace periods greatly aggravated the debt service burden.

This aggravation of the debt service burden is attributable not only to the high level of international interest rates but also to the depreciation of the CFA franc vis-à-vis the dollar.

As regards foreign trade, the cumulative deficit of the balance of payments since 1979 depleted the Ivory Coast's foreign exchange reserves. The country's net foreign assets dropped heavily, with a negative foreign position amounting to $1,655 million being recorded at the end of December 1983.

(c) Adjustment policies

As early as 1980, the national authorities grasped the seriousness of this financial situation. They decided to undertake thorough structural changes, within the framework of a strict economic and financial recovery programme, backed by an extended facility of the IMF. The programme had three objectives:

- the gradual reduction of the deficit of the public finances;

- the restoration of the balance-of-payments equilibrium;

- the control of domestic liquidity.

It is evident, however, that to achieve such goals more than political will would be required. The adjustment process is bound to be affected by external factors, beyond the control of the local authorities. For example, the evolution of the terms of trade, climatic conditions and the situation on foreign exchange and capital markets - all these are factors which may further or impede the national recovery effort.

With regard to public finance, the adjustment programme adopted by the Government required a reinforcement of budgetary discipline, a revision of the investment programme and a reorganization of the employment system. The overall financial deficit was to be progressively reduced from 15.2 per cent of GDP in 1980, to 6.3 per cent, while arrears and net borrowing from the banking system were to decrease.

As far as the balance of payments is concerned, the scaling down of the investment programme should result in an appreciable drop in imports.

As regards monetary policy, even though net credit rose again sharply in 1981, credit extended to the private sector increased only slightly and the rate of growth of the banking system's net domestic assets declined in 1981. The Ivory Coast has respected all the credit ceilings set as performance criteria within the framework of the 1981 financial programme.

However, the growth of monetary demand diminished more significantly than credit, in consequence of the recession, and the Central Bank's net foreign liabilities went up sharply. Although the Central Bank raised the money market rates by 4 points in 1981, to almost 15 per cent, the global structure of interest rates remained linked to the normal discount rate, fixed at 10.5 per cent. Because of the negative differential between interest rates charged on domestic credit and the rates on foreign markets, the banks in the Ivory Coast, by suddenly reversing the trend of capital flow in 1982, limited the net inflow of capital.

(d) Factors hampering the adjustment

The implementation of the Ivory Coast's adjustment programme was hampered by a number of factors beyond the Government's control.

First of all, the country's terms of trade worsened by 12 per cent in 1981, not by the 9 per cent initially expected. In the light of recent forecasts of the trend of prices of the major export commodities, an improvement in the terms of trade is not foreseen.

Secondly, the interest paid on the external public debt was higher in 1982 and 1983 than had been forecast in the initial programme, mainly because of the high level of international interest rates and the depreciation of the CFA franc with regard to the dollar.

Finally, the coffee export quotas imposed by the International Coffee Agreement led to a contraction of coffee exports and to stockpiling in Ivory Coast.

In order to offset the adverse effects of these various factors, the authorities have adopted additional budgetary measures and set limits on investment expenditures by cutting out or postponing projects with low rates of return.

(e) Results of the adjustment policy

Despite the unfavourable trend of external factors (deterioration of the terms of trade, poor climatic conditions), the Ivory Coast's recovery efforts have yielded some positive results.

In 1981 and 1982, economic activity slackened. In real terms GDP increased by 0.2 per cent in 1981 and decreased by 4 per cent in 1982. However, wide variations were recorded from one sector to another. Excellent coffee and cocoa harvests boosted agricultural incomes. In contrast, the abrupt reduction of investments, due to the tighter budgetary discipline, upset the building industry and public works, which had both been over-expanding in earlier years.

In the field of public finance, the control of public expenditure, despite the stagnation of receipts, was reflected in a slight shrinkage of the deficit; similarly, arrears of payments decreased markedly and investments in constant terms declined significantly.

The results achieved, which are attributable primarily to the tightening of budgetary discipline and to the application of a vigorous policy of better budget management and control, may contribute in the medium term to the successful realization of the plan for repairing the country's finances.

In contrast, the external trade situation turned out to be less satisfactory in 1981 and 1982 than had been forecast when the initial targets of the adjustment programme were established. In 1981, the country's balance of payments improved, thanks to the recovery of the current balance, the deficit of which decreased from $1,825 million in 1980 to $1,181 million in 1981.

The improvement of the current balance can be explained by the fact that imports dropped faster than exports, because of weak economic growth and the restrictive credit policy.

In 1982 and 1983, the level of net capital inflows determined the size of the balance-of-payments deficit. The deficit went down to $228 million in 1982, but in 1983 rose again to $402 million.

It is possible that the balance-of-payments difficulties were aggravated by the appreciation of the real exchange rate, which was mainly attributable to the expansionary policies adopted by Ivory Coast in previous years.

5. THE OUTLOOK FOR THE IVORY COAST'S EXTERNAL DEBT, BALANCE OF PAYMENTS AND ECONOMIC SITUATION IN THE YEARS 1983 TO 1990

The global economic outlook of the Ivory Coast for the remainder of this decade has been assessed by means of various simulation exercises. These exercises, based on various assumptions regarding the trend of the various elements of the international environment, made it possible to visualize to some extent the effects of improved or deteriorating world economic conditions on the Ivory Coast's economy which, until recently, had performed well.

After a brief review of the simulation model and the assumptions underlying the forecast, this last part of the study will discuss the main results of the different simulations appearing in the Appendix.

(a) The simulation model

In the simulation model, the country's economy is assumed to be heavily dependent on the conditions of trade with foreign countries, at least during the years covered by the forecast. This implies that the levels of exports and of the current deficit are given as exogenous variables. The model then generates forecasts for the trend of imports, GDP, investment, domestic demand and domestic consumption, which result from the assumptions concerning economic behaviour adopted as regards exports, terms of trade, remuneration of foreign capital (factor services), the level of the current deficit and the savings rate. The main definitions used in the model are:

- The value of imports (M) equals the sum of the values of imports of consumer goods and capital equipment, which are respectively a function of real GDP levels (Z) and investment (I);

- The current deficit is defined as the sum of imports, net outflows in respect of factor services (V) and of migrant workers' remittances (R) minus the value of exports (X);

- The current deficit is further defined as the difference between domestic absorption (A) and the dollar value of the national income. This last term is equal to GDP minus payments due to foreign production factors, i.e. capital and labour;

- Domestic absorption equals the sum of gross fixed investment and other components of domestic absorption (C): private and government consumption and variation of stocks;

- Total consumption is linked to national income by the marginal propensity to consume (1 - s);

- Payments in respect of income on foreign capital are calculated by applying to the debt (NF) outstanding at the end of the year preceding the estimates, the coefficient r, which stands for the current rate of return on capital;

- Besides the level of the current account deficit, three constraints have been imposed:

- the investment level cannot be negative; if it should happen to be negative, it is assumed to be zero;

- GDP may not exceed the potential GDP (Z^*), for that would imply the full utilization of the country's available capacity;

- the real level of exports may not exceed the country's potential exports (X^*), which are a function of potential GDP.

- Lastly, the estimated employment level (N) was based on an output elasticity of employment (h).

On this basis, the main equations of the model are as follows:

The basic equations of the model[a/]

$$M_t = P_{jt}.j_y.Z + J_o + P_{kt}.J_k.I_t + K_o$$

$$D_t = M_y + V_t - P_x X_t + R_t$$

$$D_t = P_{at}. A_t - (P_{yt} + Z_t - V_t - R_t)$$

$$P_{at}A = P_{it}.I_t + P_{ct}.C_t$$

$$C_t = (1 - s) (P_{yt}Z_t - V_t - R_t) / P_{ct} + C_o$$

$$V_t = r_t. NF_{t-1}$$

$$NF_{t-1} = NF_{t-2} + D_{t-1}$$

$$I_t \geq 0$$

$$Z_t \leq Z_t^* \text{ with } Z_t^* = (1-d) + al_{t-1}$$

$$X_t \leq X_t^* \text{ with } X^* = eZ_t^*$$

$$N_t = Z_t^h$$

The following assumptions were made with regard to the calculations of the real value of GDP, consumption and investment (see footnote to the preceding equations):

$$P_{yt} = P_{xt}$$

$$Pct = P_{jt}^b . P_{yt}^{1-b} \text{ with } b = P_{jo} J_{yo} / (P_{jo}J_{yo} + P_{yo}.Z_o)$$

$$Pit = P_{kt}^g . P_{yt}^{1-g} \text{ with } g = P_{ko} . J_{ko} / P_{io}I_o$$

a/ For the definitions of the variables and values of the parameters see tables XX and XVIII in the appendix.

(b) <u>Main assumptions used in the simulation</u>

For the purpose of the simulation, available data concerning the future course of the Ivory Coast's economic and monetary policy, as well as various assumptions regarding the future trend of the main parameters of the international economic environment, have been used in this study.

(1)   <u>Implementation of the Ivory Coast's economic and monetary policy from 1983 to 1990</u>

It has been decided that from 1983 to 1990, which is the period covered by the simulations, the national authorities should continue and strengthen the economic recovery measures already introduced.

This policy is consistent with the targets fixed by the governing body of the West African Monetary Union, the purpose of which is to achieve a global balance-of-payments equilibrium in each member State by 1984. The policy should make it possible to avoid any increase in the present level of the current account deficit, which should actually decline gradually as from 1984. It is envisaged that the deficit should decrease:

- by 5 per cent per annum under the conditions assumed in scenarios 1 and 2, so as to bring the current deficit down to $530 million in 1990 as compared to $753 million in 1983;

- by 10 per cent per annum under the conditions assumed in scenarios 3 and 4, in order to bring down the level of the current deficit to $383 million by 1990, as compared to $753 million in 1983.

This change in the current account deficit should be the outcome of measures applied at national levels. The measures in question should ensure greater selectivity in imports, control domestic demand and channel it towards local goods and products, particularly consumer goods.

In view of the country's level of industrialization, no significant evolution of the share of imported capital goods in global investment is envisaged for the forthcoming years. Thus, the value of the marginal import ratio for capital goods was maintained at 0.252 during the period for which the projections are made.

Lastly, the high level of the net outflow of savings of foreign residents in recent years has materially affected the evolution of the Ivory Coast's current payments.

In view of the measures taken by the Government, no increase in the level of transfers is expected; their decline should contribute to the achievement of the common monetary policy in the coming years. The following assumptions were made:

- a decrease of 5 per cent per annum under scenarios 1 and 2, in order to bring this outflow to $427 million in 1990 from $611 million in 1983;

- a decrease of 10 per cent per annum under scenarios 3 and 4, in order to reduce their level to $292 million in 1990.

(ii) <u>Assumptions made with regard to the international environment</u>

The following main factors related to the international economic environment were taken into account:

- international demand for the primary commodities exported by the Ivory Coast;

- the level of interest rates on international capital markets;

- the level of the prices of the primary commodities exported by the Ivory Coast (coffee, cocoa, timber);

- the level of import prices.

With regard to the various scenarios, the assumptions used are based on the following:

<u>With regard to scenarios 1 and 3</u>

- an increase in real terms of 5 per cent per annum in Ivory Coast's exports during the entire period;

- and a stabilization of the terms of trade from 1983 to 1990, including an increase of 5 per cent in the prices of both exports and imports.

<u>With regard to scenarios 2 and 4</u>

- an increase of 5 per cent in the volume of the country's exports during 1983-1990;

- and an improvement of Ivory Coast's terms of trade with a rise of export and import prices of 7 per cent and 5 per cent, respectively.

During the entire period of the projections, the level of interest rates was kept unchanged at 17.6 per cent per annum.

(c) Results of the simulations

It appears from the results obtained that the economy of the Ivory Coast should, over the next few years, significantly reflect various developments in international economic conditions. The impact of external shocks on the country's economy may be assessed through developments in:

- economic growth,

- employment level,

- external debt level.

(i)   Economic growth of the Ivory Coast from 1983 to 1990

Simulations based on the four scenarios focussed on the weight of internal factors but also of the international environment on the country's economic growth. For notwithstanding the evolution of internal factors, the level of economic activity will be perceptibly affected by the behaviour of demand and by the movement of the prices of the primary commodities exported by the Ivory Coast.

Thus, from a comparison of the results of scenarios 1 and 2, which both suppose that action taken at the internal level should bring about a reduction of the current deficit level and a 5 per cent drop in the outflow of workers' remittances, the following inferences may be drawn:

- GDP is likely to increase only very slightly after a sharp decline in 1983 if the international environment does not contribute to a betterment of the terms of trade (scenario 1). The real growth rate should be at 3.8 per cent per annum from 1984 to 1990. The 1983 GDP level - $6.95 billion - will not be reached again before 1990. Because of the relatively high rate of population growth, per capita income is likely to be seriously eroded;

- If, however, the international economic environment was to improve, then (see scenario 2) the yearly average growth rate should reach 9.7 per cent from 1984 to 1990. The capacity utilization ratio should benefit from the recovery and reach 98 per cent as opposed to 71.8 per cent in scenario 1;

- The relatively higher investment level (scenario 2) would make it possible to raise the country's potential GDP appreciably.

Moreover, an analysis of the results of scenarios 3 and 4 (both based on the assumption of a 10 per cent yearly decrease in the current deficit and in the outflow of workers' remittances), leads to the same conclusions:

- The yearly growth rate of GDP is higher in scenario 4 (10 per cent), which assumes a more favourable international environment than does scenarios 3 (4.5 per cent);

- Similarly, productive capacity increases more rapidly in scenario 4, in response to the high level of investment and would be fully utilized by the end of the decade; in scenario 3, productive capacity would only be used at 75.2 per cent in 1990.

(ii) Employment in the Ivory Coast from 1983 to 1990

With regard to employment, results from the various scenarios remain identical to those obtained with respect to economic activity, since employment is assumed to be related to the level of real GDP.

Hence, if 1983 = 100, the 1990 employment level will, according to the different scenarios, be equal to:

Scenarios	1990 employment level (1983 = 100)
1	116 (+ 2.1 per cent yearly average)
2	145 (+ 5.4 per cent yearly average)
3	119 (+ 2.5 per cent yearly average)
4	147 (+ 5.6 per cent yearly average)

Only a substantial recovery in the international economic environment (see scenarios 2 and 4) will make it possible to achieve a higher level of employment in the years to come.

If, on the contrary, the yearly growth rates of employment are 2.1 per cent and 2.5 per cent as obtained in scenarios 1 and 3, then the Ivory Coast will not be able to satisfy the increased demand for employment.

(iii) External debt situation of the Ivory Coast from 1983 to 1990

On the basis of the different scenarios, the percentage ratio of payments on the external debt to exports, which reached 14.8 per cent in 1980, should by 1990 reach the following figures:

Scenarios

1	:	32 per cent
2	:	26 per cent
3	:	30 per cent
4	:	25 per cent.

These data show that for the Ivory Coast's economy, the most disturbing consequences of the lack of a substantial improvement in external factors are those concerning the country's external indebtedness.

The implication is that by the end of the present decade, interest payments alone are likely to absorb almost one-third of the country's export proceeds (scenario 1). Under these conditions, it would be difficult for the Ivory Coast and also for other developing countries to service their foreign debt (principal and interest) and simultaneously to maintain the development efforts envisaged by the national authorities.

(iv)   Conclusion

The various simulations show that the evolution of the Ivory Coast's economic and financial situation will mainly depend on the international economic environment. The outlook will be favourable only if recovery is tangible.

Besides, it should be pointed out that simulations 1 to 4 do not take into account the serious deterioration of the terms of trade recorded these past years. If this deterioration was to persist for the remainder of the decade, the outlook for the country's development would be even gloomier than that reflected in scenarios 1 and 3, which assume stable terms of trade from 1983 to 1990. The same situation would arise if interest rates remained persistently high.

The results of the various projections suggest that economic recovery in developing countries that are wide open to the outside world, as is the Ivory Coast, cannot rely exclusively on internal measures but depend also on the conditions ruling in world markets. The results show moreover how greatly external factors, which have been particularly unfavourable since the second oil crisis, have aggravated the present difficult situation of the Ivory Coast.

Appendix

Tables

I.   Balance of payments, 1975-1983

II.   Imports in current dollars, 1975-1982

III.   Imports in constant prices, 1975-1982

III bis   Exports in constant 1975 prices, 1975-1982

IV.   Exports in current prices, 1975-1982

V.   Composition of exports, 1970-1982

VI.   Composition of exports, 1970-1983

VII.   Production and exports of cocoa, coffee and lumber, 1970-1982

VIII.   West African Monetary Union: Indices of international prices of the main agricultural export commodities, 1970-1982

IX.   Import unit values: 1970-1976 and 1977-1982

X.   Indices of export unit values, 1970-1982

XI.   Indices of export prices in current dollars, 1975-1982

XII.   Outstanding external debt and payments for factor services, 1975-1983

XIII.   Potential gross domestic output in current dollars, 1975-1983

XIV.   Gross domestic product in current dollars and in 1975 constant dollars, 1975-1983

XV.   Gross fixed investment at current and 1975 constant prices, 1975-1984

XVI.   Situation of the monetary institutions, 1974-1983

XVII.   Average yearly rates of the dollar to the CFA franc

XVIII.   Parameters of the economy

XIX.   Exogenous variables in 1983, which is the base year

XX.   Variables used in the simulation exercises

XXI.   Changes in GDP and in depreciation, 1970-1979

XXII.   Savings rates (s), 1975-1982

XXIII.   Output elasticity of employment

XXIV.   Potential export ratio (e)

Table I

IVORY COAST: BALANCE OF PAYMENTS, 1975-1983
(in thousands of dollars)

Balance-of-payments items	1975	1976	1977	1978	1979	1980	1981	1982	1983
GOODS AND SERVICES	- 242639.2	+ 10042.7	+ 124147.7	- 422806.8	- 810925.2	-1119314.7	- 684,364	- 639,664	- 388,436
. Trade balance	+ 227240.9	+ 574106.6	+ 814897.7	+ 571276.6	+ 489375.7	+ 398977.7	+ 674,062	+ 605,581	+ 795,244
- Exports (f.o.b.)	+1238859.6	+1734873.2	+2411722.1	+2616172.1	+2722358.0	+3012447.3	+2733,779	+2452,756	+2309,620
- Imports (f.o.b.)	-1011618.7	-1160766.6	-1596825.1	-2044895.3	-2232982.2	-2613469.6	-2059,716	-1847,174	-1514,376
. Services (net)	- 469880.1	- 564063.9	- 690750.0	- 994083.4	-1300300.9	-1518292.4	-1358,427	-1245,245	-1183,680
UNREQUITED TRANSFERS	- 141384.0	- 259017.5	- 299989.8	- 417931.6	- 567882.6	- 705665.2	- 496,716	- 447,339	- 380,562
. Of which workers' remittances/wages	- 183845.8	- 289564.0	- 344764.2	- 458262.2	- 572583.7				
CURRENT ACCOUNT	- 384023.2	- 248974.8	- 175842.1	- 840738.4	-1378807.8	-1824979.9	-1181,081	-1087,003	- 758,500
NON-MONETARY CAPITAL	+ 205776.7	+ 272407.7	+ 382212.3	+ 920956.4	+ 762034.6	+1063940.5	+ 636,533	+ 932,108	+ 417,306
. Private	+ 153049.3	+ 151058.7	+ 177063.2	+ 332281.6	+ 201203.5	+ 316626.4	+ 110381.4	+ 133897.3	+ 125,979
. Public	+ 52727.4	+ 121349.1	+ 205149.8	+ 587674.8	+ 560831.1	+ 747314.1	+ 526,251	+ 798,211	+ 172,856
ERRORS & OMISSIONS (NET)	+ 14465.0	+ 9205.8	- 24422.5	+ 8420.7	- 38078.2	+ 45908.4	+ 16,189	-	-
SURPLUS (+) DEFICIT (-)	- 16378L.5	+ 32638.7	- 181947.7	+ 88638.7	- 654851.4	- 806947.8	- 513,641	- 154,895	- 341,194

Table II

IVORY COAST: IMPORTS IN CURRENT DOLLARS, 1975-1982
(in thousands of dollars)

ITEMS	1975	1976	1977	1978	1979	1980	1981	1982
. Capital goods	343,591	420,316	651,784	894,063	836,377	836,102	500,350	504,100
. Machinery and electrical appliances	197,513	230,358	361,217	504,598	455,261	513,853	332,450	252,850
. Transport equipment	146,078	189,844	290,567	389,465	381,116	322,249	167,900	251,250
. Consumption goods and energy-related products	1,256,862	1,548,097	1,893,717	2,251,196	3,130,580	3,705,333	3,222,050	2,874,836
TOTAL IMPORTS	1,600,453	1,968,395	2,545,501	3,415,259	3,966,956	4,541,433	3,722,750	3,378,936
Of which energy-related products	156,726	167,550	199,674	220,857	362,773	557,215	530,370	405,260

Source: New tables and indices of foreign trade SSD/ETUDES.

Table III

IVORY COAST: IMPORTS IN CONSTANT PRICES, 1975-1982
(in thousands of dollars)

ITEMS	1975	1976	1977	1978	1979	1980	1981	1982
. Capital goods	343,000	390,000	566,000	625,000	493,000	546,000	331,000	292,000
- Machinery, electrical and other	197,000	223,000	333,000	389,000	294,000	351,000	220,000	177,000
- Transport equipment	146,000	167,000	233,000	237,999	198,000	195,000	111,000	115,000
. Consumer goods and energy-related products	1,257,000	1,527,000	1,825,000	2,175,000	2,210,000	2,473,337	2,436,853	2,167,272
- Energy-related products	157,000	168,000	196,000	195,000	260,000	241,000	207,000	203,000
- Consumer goods	1,100,136	1,359,000	1,629,000	1,980,000	1,950,000	2,232,337	2,229,853	1,964,272
TOTAL IMPORTS	1,600,000	1,917,000	2,391,000	2,800,000	2,703,000	2,972,927	2,738,010	2,477,071

Source: New tables and indices of foreign trade (Research Department).

Table III bis

IVORY COAST: EXPORTS IN CONSTANT 1975 PRICES, 1975-1982
(in thousands of dollars)

ITEMS	1975	1976	1977	1978	1979	1980	1981	1982
Cocoa beans	222,000	255,000	208,000	319,000	224,000	371,000	574,000	427,000
Green coffee	288,000	365,000	263,000	260,000	293,000	233,000	261,000	308,000
Lumber	213,000	283,000	294,000	245,000	248,000	274,000	211,000	217,000
Petroleum products	67,000	67,000	72,000	71,000	73,000	96,000	85,000	139,000
Others	449,000	395,000	474,000	613,000	540,000	396,000	511,000	700,000
TOTAL EXPORTS	1,239,000	1,365,000	1,311,000	1,508,000	1,378,000	1,370,000	1,642,000	1,791,000

Source: New tables and indices of foreign trade (Research Department).

Table IV

IVORY COAST: EXPORTS IN CURRENT PRICES, 1975-1982
(in thousands of dollars)

ITEMS	1975	1976	1977	1978	1979	1980	1981	1982
Cocoa beans	222,000	299,000	402,000	713,000	546,000	793,000	735,000	497,000
Green coffee	288,000	556,000	808,000	581,000	783,000	644,000	446,000	463,000
Lumber	212,000	328,000	354,000	316,000	401,000	586,000	359,000	298,000
Petroleum products	67,000	63,000	81,000	86,000	112,000	212,000	191,000	296,000
Others	449,000	489,000	766,000	920,000	880,000	777,000	804,000	865,000
TOTAL EXPORTS	1,238,000	1,735,000	2,411,000	2,616,000	2,722,000	3,012,000	2,535,000	2,419,000

Source: New tables and indices of foreign trade (Research Department).

Table V

IVORY COAST: COMPOSITION OF EXPORTS, 1970-1982

(Percentage of total value)

ITEMS	1970	1971	1972	1973	1974	1975	1976	1977	1978	1979	1980	1981	1982
Cocoa beans	20.5	17.1	16.2	14.6	21.4	18.7	18.2	18.7	30.7	21.7	25.2	29.0	1.8
Green coffee	33.2	33.3	26.5	22.9	21.9	24.2	33.8	37.5	25.0	31.1	20.5	17.6	20.4
Lumber	22.5	24.5	27.2	34.7	22.7	17.9	19.9	16.4	13.6	15.9	18.7	14.1	13.1
Petroleum products	0.8	0.6	2.1	2.3	3.7	5.7	3.9	3.8	3.7	4.5	6.7	7.5	13.0
Others	23.0	24.5	28.0	25.5	30.3	33.5	24.2	23.6	27.0	26.8	28.9	31.8	31.7
TOTAL	100.0	100.0	100.0	100.0	100.0	100.0	100.0	100.0	100.0	100.0	100.0	100.0	100.0

Source: Official statistics.

Table VI

IVORY COAST: COMPOSITION OF EXPORTS, 1970-1982

ITEMS	1970	1971	1972	1973	1974	1975	1976	1977	1978	1979	1980	1981	1982
					(thousands of tons)								
Cocoa beans	143.2	144.9	159.4	143.0	205.3	169.7	194.9	158.5	244.0	170.8	283.7	438.4	326.4
Green coffee	195.3	184.5	188.5	212.6	263.4	254.8	322.8	233.1	230.1	259.7	206.4	231.1	272.4
Lumber	2,097.5	2,259.3	2,566.5	2,882.1	2,578.6	2,075.8	2,787.1	2,850.7	2,300.5	2,442.1	2,706.5	2,031.1	2,047.8
Petroleum products	82.0	71.4	221.8	299.2	411.5	464.5	488.3	502.0	494.7	478.8	682.6	630.0	1,170.2
Others	483.0	442.2	573.3	645.5	835.7	824.7	765.1	737.3	771.8	747.5	972.3	1,118.3	1,097.1
TOTAL	3,001.0	3,102.6	3,709.5	4,182.4	4,294.5	3,789.5	4,558.2	4,481.6	4,041.1	4,098.9	4,851.5	4,448.9	4,913.9

Source: Official statistics of foreign trade (Customs Service).

Table VII

IVORY COAST: PRODUCTION AND EXPORTS OF COCOA, COFFEE AND LUMBER, 1970-82

(thousands of metric tons)

	1970	1971	1972	1973	1974	1975	1976	1977	1978	1979	1980	1981	1982
COFFEE													
Production (crop year) a/	279.6	239.7	269.0	301.8	195.2	271.0	308.1	291.3	195.7	277.0	248.7	336.8	246.8
Production (calendar year)	276.2	239.7	281.9	266.6	194.2	266.8	322.7						
Exports (calendar year)	195.3	184.8	188.5	212.6	263.4	254.8	322.8	233.1	230.1	259.7	206.4	231.1	272.4
COCOA													
Production (crop year) a/	183.0	182.2	227.8	182.8	214.0	245.0	234.6	235.8	306.0	311.8	379.4	418.3	471.7
Production (calendar year)	187.0	223.3	199.6	179.0	222.7	239.4	257.4						
Exports (calendar Year)	143.2	144.9	159.4	143.0	205.3	169.7	194.9	158.5	244.0	170.8	283.7	438.4	326.4
Production	3,548	3,919	4,168	5,169	4,629	3,690	5,096	5,223	4,580	4,980	4,844	4,059	106
Exports: logs	2,511	2,933	3,168	3,497	3,034	2,419		3,335	2,707	3,199	3,064	2,343	
Sawnwood and non-laminated	183	143	153	205	275	212	292	340	320	293	277	266	

Source: Official statistics: C.S.S.P.P.A; EEC; Ministère des Eaux et Forêts.

a/ The crop year runs from 1 October of the preceding year to 30 September of the year mentioned.

Table VIII

WEST AFRICAN MONETARY UNION: INDICES OF INTERNATIONAL PRICES OF THE MAIN AGRICULTURAL EXPORT COMMODITIES, 1970-1982
(1970 = 100)

	1970	1971	1972	1973	1974	1975	1976	1977	1978	1979	1980	1981	1982
Global index	100.0	98.3	99.2	136.4	180.7	146.2	237.4	371.7	301.7	300.6	274.7	288.6	306.7
of which:													
Coffee - Cocoa	100.0	91.6	93.7	113.9	158.8	128.2	267.0	489.5	346.9	340.1	282.1	271.1	313.4
Vegetable oil seeds and oils	100.0	107.4	93.5	132.2	237.8	146.7	153.3	195.5	218.0	189.2	177.0	254.7	191.4
Lumber	100.0	105.0	121.9	211.2	183.3	201.1	265.7	293.6	306.7	353.4	388.0	391.8	442.6

Source: B.C.E.A.O. Economic and Monetary Statistics.

Table IX

IVORY COAST: IMPORT UNIT VALUES: 1970-1976 AND 1977-1982
(CFA FRANCS PER TON)

ITEMS	1970	1971	1972	1973	1974	1975	1976
Petroleum products	5,861	7,272	6,239	7,948	20,793	22,029	24,453
Food products	45,110	51,996	53,447	57,600	84,366	94,017	9,484
of which cereals : rice	25,381	22,587	28,455	58,824	111,450	125,000	173,013
wheat	19,256	23,103	24,000	20,848	22,335	34,031	43,058
Plastic and chemical products	85,635	106,267	87,167	98,532	176,580	179,732	191,358
Yarn and textiles	475,728	440,191	429,319	396,694	572,139	520,737	505,338
Iron and steel products	76,033	85,651	81,967	94,203	135,478	159,242	142,434
Machinery and equipment	675,573	685,315	829,167	833,333	983,380	1,057,000	1,309,524
Others	69,895	71,615	64,520	73,485	82,356	91,902	111,728
TOTAL	51,655	58,071	46,558	54,395	71,498	77,204	89,376

ITEMS	1977	1978	1979	1980	1981	1982
Petroleum products	27,643	26,529	35,016	55,076	81,692	93,574
Food products	84,826	94,706	96,054	100,065	125,722	136,482
of which cereals : rice	70,840	74,426	68,826	95,614	104,682	96,159
wheat	36,987	36,550	41,169	49,073	52,128	63,406
Plastic and chemical products	213,423	268,378	229,645	190,951	321,029	337,728
Yarn and textiles	704,641	762,791	778,846	729,258	822,642	1,117,647
Iron and steel products	174,388	188,435	192,869	233,090	262,338	289,975
Machinery and equipment	1,383,775	1,529,570	1,753,623	1,297,491	2,232,099	2,613,208
Others	113,549	124,829	115,623	136,709	127,540	188,826
TOTAL	100,855	112,914	103,795	126,877	140,684	171,618

Source: Official trade statistics (Customs Service).

Table X

IVORY COAST: INDICES OF EXPORT UNIT VALUES, 1970-1982
(1973 = 100)

ITEMS	1970	1971	1972	1973	1974	1975	1976	1977	1978	1979	1980	1981	1982
Cocoa beans	95.9	77.0	72.9	100.0	156.1	144.3	188.4	320.6	339.2	350.0	303.9	234.3	257.2
Green coffee	107.4	110.8	95.0	100.0	117.6	117.5	199.7	413.5	276.6	311.2	320.1	254.4	271.2
Lumber	60.7	59.6	64.2	100.0	111.4	95.3	122.1	130.6	134.7	151.7	198.8	208.9	207.6
Petroleum products	91.2	66.7	88.9	100.0	180.1	210.8	211.7	270.9	266.7	339.4	446.3	561.3	566.0
Others	82.2	93.1	90.8	100.0	141.0	137.5	164.6	225.0	243.9	254.1	261.7	260.0	286.8
TOTAL	95.1	89.4	82.4	100.0	148.9	147.2	188.7	258.7	284.3	285.9	299.8	339.4	333.3

Table XI

IVORY COAST: INDICES OF EXPORT PRICES IN CURRENT DOLLARS, 1975-1982
(1975 = 100)

ITEMS \ YEARS	1975	1976	1977	1978	1979	1980	1981	1982
GLOBAL INDEX of which	100	119	184	173	197	220	154	135
- cocoa	100	117	194	223	244	213	128	116
- coffee	100	152	307	223	267	276	171	150
- lumber	100	115	120	131	160	213	168	136
- energy-related products	100	95	113	122	157	222	225	213

IVORY COAST: INDICES OF IMPORT PRICES IN CURRENT DOLLARS, 1975-1982
(1975 = 100)

ITEMS \ YEARS	1975	1976	1977	1978	1979	1980	1981	1982
GLOBAL INDEX of which	100	103	106	122	147	168	163	161
- capital goods	100	118	118	137	163	167	166	163
- energy-related products	100	99	106	110	151	243	280	269
- consumer goods	100	96	100	116	137	150	132	133

TABLE XII

IVORY COAST: OUTSTANDING EXTERNAL DEBT AND NET PAYMENTS DUE
TO INTEREST ON EXTERNAL DEBT AND INCOME ON FOREIGN DIRECT
INVESTMENTS, 1975-1983
(in thousands of dollars)

YEARS	OUTSTANDING DEBT	NET PAYMENTS[a]
1975	926,107.5	136,783.2
1976	1,111,877.6	158,389.8
1977	1,350,040.1	193,654.2
1978	2,423,367.8	312,247.7
1979	3,796,249.5	387,923.1
1980	4,986,350.5	477,542.7[b]
1981	4,534,930.2	445,572.8[b]
1982	3,838,187.2	441,252.5[b]
1983	3,963,121.0	554,500.0[b]

Source: Public Finances and balance of payments.

a/   Interest and income on foreign direct investments.

b/   Estimates.

TABLE XIII

Y* : POTENTIAL GROSS DOMESTIC OUTPUT IN CURRENT DOLLARS,
1975-1983 a/
(in thousands of dollars)

1975	4,218,347
1976	4,793,485
1977	6,519,825
1978	7,902,178
1979	9,448,063
1980	10,209,357
1981	9,115,716
1982	8,933,146
1983	9,077,585

a/ At average exchange rate for the year.

TABLE XIV

IVORY COAST: GROSS DOMESTIC PRODUCT IN CURRENT DOLLARS AND
IN 1975 CONSTANT DOLLARS, 1975-1983

YEAR	GDP IN CURRENT DOLLARS		GDP IN 1975 CONSTANT DOLLARS	
	IN THOUSANDS OF DOLLARS	PERCENTAGE CHANGE	IN THOUSANDS OF DOLLARS	PERCENTAGE CHANGE
1975	3,894,102.0	-	3,894,102	-
1976	4,661,298.0	+19.7	4,361,392	+12.0
1977	6,265,452.3	+34.4	4,566,381	+4.7
1978	7,902,178.3	+26.1	5,018,450	+9.9
1979	9,141,904.9	+15.7	5,113,802	+1.9
1980	10,175,048.5	+11.3	5,507,564	+7.7
1981	8,548,301.0	-16.0	5,518,576	+0.2
1982	7,586,805.0 a/	+4.8	5,297,834	-4.0
1983	6,953,007.1 a/	-15.9	5,064,799	-4.4

Source: National Accounts, Department of Statistics, Ministry of
            Planning and Industry;   B.C.E.A.O.

xx)   These figures correspond to the changes of GDP in volume
            terms in the years in question.

a/   Figures modified in January 1984.

TABLE XV

IVORY COAST: GROSS FIXED INVESTMENT AT CURRENT AND 1975
CONSTANT PRICES, 1975-1984

	GROSS FIXED INVESTMENT AT CURRENT PRICES[a]		GROSS FIXED INVESTMENT AT 1975 CONSTANT PRICES[b]	
	Value ($ 1000)	Variation (%)	Value ($ 1000)	Variation(%)[c]
1975	858,317	–	858,317	–
1976	1,034,317	+20.5	1,050,581	+22.4
1977	1,618,520	+56.5	1,499,179	+42.7
1978	2,344,676	+44.9	1,833,494	+22.3
1979	2,476,105	+5.6	1,657,478	-9.6
1980	2,478,134	+0.1	1,524,880	-8.0
1981	2,118,954	-14.5	1,351,043	-11.4
1982	1,721,798	-18.7	1,171,355	-13.3
1983	1,310,972	-23.9	934,739	-20.2
1984	501,200	-61.8	868,372	-7.1

Source: National accounts, Department of Statistics, Ministry of
Planning and Industry, Budgets Economiques; B.C.E.A.O.

a/ Figures corrected in January 1984.

b/ Figures converted to the average yearly rates of the dollar to
the CFA franc, see table XVII.

c/ These figures correspond to the variations in volume of gross
fixed investment in the years in question.

TABLE XVI

IVORY COAST: SITUATION OF THE MONETARY INSTITUTIONS, 1974-1983
(in millions of dollars)

As of 31 December

ITEMS	1974	1975	1976	1977	1978	1979	1980	1981	1982	1982
Foreign assets (net)	85.8	-53.7	-75.3	70.8	107.7	-324.4	-1,152.9	-1,434.2	-1,316.4	-1,664.5
Domestic credit	881.1	1,246.8	1,549.9	2,155.3	2,609.5	3,186.4	3,951.9	3,782.0	3,341.9	3,450.0
- Net Government position	-162.8	-118.0	-90.0	-309.3	-476.4	-535.4	-263.6	225.9	234.3	561.1
Credits	1,043.9	1,364.8	1,639.9	2,464.6	3,085.9	3,271.8	4,215.5	3,556.1	3,107.6	2,888.9
Rural credits	217.2	244.0	292.5	399.7	370.9	427.3	596.8	688.8	524.9	429.4
Other credits	826.7	1,120.8	1,347.4	2,064.9	2,715.0	3,294.5	3,618.7	2,867.3	2,582.7	2,459.5
ASSETS = LIABILITIES	956.9	1,193.1	1,474.6	2,226.1	2,717.2	2,862.0	2,799.0	2,347.8	2,025.5	1,785.5
Money supply	956.1	1,141.3	1,463.7	2,134.9	2,577.6	2,661.7	2,753.6	2,353.3	2,009.4	1,825.1
Fiduciary circulation	332.0	418.1	446.9	558.9	729.1	910.6	998.1	845.5	666.8	608.6
Deposits in Post Office checking accounts	10.7	10.7	6.7	9.7	11.5	-	-	-	8.8	11.8
Deposits in banks	613.4	712.5	1,010.1	1,566.3	1,837.0	1,751.1	1,755.4	1,507.8	1,333.8	1,204.7
Public agencies institutions	284.4	410.6	416.3	775.8	704.7	346.5	209.7	208.2	148.8	141.5
Others	329.0	301.9	593.8	790.5	1,132.3	1,404.7	1,545.7	1,299.6	1,185.0	1,063.2
Other items (net)	0.8	51.8	10.9	91.2	139.6	200.3	45.4	-5.5.	16.1	-39.6

TABLE XVII

AVERAGE YEARLY RATES OF THE DOLLAR TO THE CFA FRANC

1975 : 1 dollar	214.31 CFA F.
1976 : " "	238.98 " "
1977 : " "	245.675 " "
1978 : " "	225.635 " "
1979 : " "	212.72 " "
1980 : " "	211.29 " "
1981 : " "	271.785 " "
1982 : " "	328.61 " "
1983 : " "	381.015 " "

TABLE XVIII

IVORY COAST: PARAMETERS OF THE ECONOMY

Annual depreciation rate	5.083 %
Incremental output - capital ratio	0.4932
Output elasticity of employment	0.5742
Share of capital goods imports in total supply	0.0791
Share of non-capital goods imports in total supply	0.3300
Maximum saving rate	0.2575
Maximum annual growth of real consumption	7 %
Potential export ratio	0.3137
Real dollar value of capital goods imports is given by	$- 73 + jk.I(t)$
Real dollar value of non-capital goods imports is given by	$+ 948 + jy.Z(t)$
Real dollar value of consumption is given by	

$$681 + (1 - 1) \; {}^{(P}y_{(t)} \cdot {}^{Z}(+) - V_{(t)} - R_{(t)}) \quad {}^{P}c \; (t)$$

TABLE XIX

IVORY COAST: EXOGENOUS VARIABLES IN 1983, WHICH IS THE BASE YEAR
(in millions of dollars)

X (1983)	= 2,310
D (1983)	= 759
R (1983)	= 611
V (1983)	= 555
NF (1983)	= 3,963
Z* (1983)	= 9,078
I (1983)	= 1,311

TABLE XX

VARIABLES USED IN THE SIMULATION EXERCISES

D   Current deficit in current dollars

M   Total imports in current dollars

M_K Capital goods imports in current dollars

M_j Non-capital goods imports in current dollars

J_k Capital goods imports in base year dollars

J_y Non-capital goods imports in base year dollars

E   Exports of goods and non-factor services in current dollars

X   Exports of goods and non-factor services in base year dollars

X*   Potential exports in base year dollars

Y   Gross domestic product (or output) in current dollars

Y*   Potential GDP in current dollars

Z*   Potential domestic output in base year dollars

Z   Domestic output in base year dollars

I   Fixed investment in base year dollars

C   Sum of private consumption, government consumption and inventory changes in base year dollars

A   Domestic absorption in base year dollars

NF   Net foreign capital (or external debt) stock in current dollars at the end of the year

R   Remittances in current dollars

N   Level of employment

PARAMETERS

j_y Non-capital goods imports coefficient

j_k Capital goods imports coefficient

r   Rate of return on capital

s	Marginal saving rate
a	Output-capital ratio
d	Annual depreciation rate
b	Share of non-capital goods imports in total supply
g	Share of capital goods imports in total supply
h	Output elasticity of employment
e	Potential export ratio
t	Calendar year

Prices (with base year = 1.0)

P_y	Implicit price deflator of GDP
P_k	dollar price index of capital goods imports
P_j	dollar price index of non-capital goods imports
P_x	dollar price index of exports
P_c	dollar price index of consumption
P_i	dollar price index of investment
P_a	dollar price index of absorption.

TABLE XXI

IVORY COAST: CHANGES IN GDP AND IN DEPRECIATION,
1970-1979

YEARS	GDP	Amortization	d (per cent)
1970	414,862	15,000	3.616
1971	439,777	19,000	4.320
1972	471,837	22,000	4.663
1973	566,194	25,000	4.415
1974	739,000	30,000	4.059
1975	834,545	40,000	4.793
1976	1,113,957	55,000	4.937
1977	1,539,265	82,000	5.327
1978	1,783,008	120,000	6.730
1979	1,944,666	155,000	7.970
d = 5.083			

d = $\frac{depreciation}{GDP}$

Source: National Accounts, 1970-1979.

TABLE XXII

IVORY COAST: SAVINGS RATES (s), 1975-1982

1975	0.1521
1976	0.1999
1977	0.2575
1978	0.2106
1979	0.1511
1980	0.0650
1981	0.0408
1982	0.0366

N.B. $C = (1-s) \ (Y - V - R)$

$s = 1 - \dfrac{Y - V - R}{C}$

Sources: National Accounts, Balance of Payments Reports.

TABLE XXIII

IVORY COAST: OUTPUT ELASTICITY OF EMPLOYMENT

YEARS	OUTPUT (Z)	EMPLOYMENT (N)	h
	(in 1980 millions of CFA francs)		
1980	2226.2	877,000	0.5632
1985	2976.7	1159,000	0.5728
1990	4300.5	1563,000	0.5866

N.B.: $N_t = Z_t^{h}$ ------------) $h = \dfrac{Log.N_t}{Log.Z_t}$

Source: Economic and Social Development Plan of the Ivory Coast 1981-1985.

TABLE XXIV

IVORY COAST: POTENTIAL EXPORT RATIO (e)

YEARS	Z^*	X^*	e
1980	2226.2	715.2	0.3213
1985	2976.7	942.3	0.3166
1990	4300.5	1304.0	0.3032

$$X_t^* = e \ Z_t^* \quad ===) \quad e = \frac{X_t^*}{Z_t^*}$$

$$\bar{e} = 0.3137$$

Source: Same as for table XXIII.

FOREIGN DEBT, BALANCE OF PAYMENTS, AND GROWTH PROSPECTS:
THE CASE OF THE REPUBLIC OF KOREA, 1965-1988

Yungchul Park*

1. INTRODUCTION

The rapid buildup in the external debt of the developing countries since 1973 has created serious economic and political difficulties that could frustrate the development efforts of these countries and threaten the international financial system. In terms of outstanding debt, the Republic of Korea ranks fourth among third world borrowers and has experienced a noticeable deterioration in its debt-servicing capacity. Yet at the same time, it is widely recognized that the country has successfully adjusted to a series of adverse external developments since 1973 and in the process has maintained growth momentum while avoiding the financial difficulties other countries now face. The exceptional performance of its economy in recent years supports this assessment.

The purpose of this study is twofold. The first is to analyze Korea's experience with debt accumulation and management over the past two decades with a view to identifying some of the factors that may explain its "successful" debt management. The second objective is to examine the prospects of the national economy for the 1984-1988 period. Section 2 discusses profiles of the country's external obligations and analyzes several aspects of the outstanding debt pertinent to the discussion. Section 3 is devoted to a discussion of the evolution and causes of the country's foreign debt accumulation. This discussion is followed by a review of its response to external and internal shocks in sections 4 and 5. Section 6 examines questions related to the efficiency and optimality of foreign borrowing. Section 7 investigates the prospects of the national economy for the next five years. For this purpose, this section highlights some of the target revisions made in 1983 for the remainder of the Fifth Five-Year Economic and Social Development Plan, 1982-1986, and the Government's macroeconomic projections through 1988. Comparisons are made with simulation exercises under a number of scenarios that generate projections for the economy until 1990. A summary and concluding remarks constitute the final section.

*The author is Professor of Economics at the Institute of Economic Development, Korea University.

2.   EVOLUTION   OF   KOREA'S   EXTERNAL   INDEBTEDNESS,   1960-1983:   AN
OVERVIEW.

At the end of 1983, Korea's total foreign debt including
short-term obligations amounted to $40.1 billion, and it was the fourth
largest borrower behind Brazil, Mexico, and Argentina in the third
world. 1/

The total debt rose to 53 per cent of nominal dollar GNP in 1983
from about 30 per cent five years earlier (see table 1 in Appendix 2).
Between 1979 and 1983, Korea's external indebtedness doubled, growing
on average 22.5 per cent per year.   Export earnings also rose, but at a
much slower rate.   As a consequence, Korea's debt service as a
proportion of exports climbed markedly.

Much of the increase in external debt has come from the short end
of the maturity distribution: short-term obligations with maturities
of less than one year accounted for over 36 per cent of the total in
1983 (see table 1).   Some concern has been voiced over the possibility
that such a large share of short-term debt could cause debt-servicing
difficulties when liquidity is not adequate.

Before the 1970s, foreign loans with variable interest rates
constituted less than 5 per cent of the total.   Since 1973, a growing
proportion of capital inflows has been contracted at floating interest
rates.   Between 1977 and 1983, more than 60 per cent of new loans were
subject to variable interest rates.   The persistence of high interest
rates has raised Korea's average interest cost to over 10 per cent in
recent years from less than 5 per cent in the early 1970s.   Coupled
with an increasingly large share of foreign debt with flexible interest
rates, these high interest rates have added to Korea's debt-servicing
burden.   Because of Korea's close trade relations with both the United
States and Japan, these two countries have been the two major sources
of loans, accounting for about 45 per cent of Korea's total debt at the
end of June 1983.   Multilateral sources account for 21.7 per cent, the
European Community for 17.1 per cent and others for 16.5 per cent.

The buildup of Korea's external debt has been closely associated
with chronic current account deficits and the need for holding larger
reserves to accommodate a growing volume of foreign transactions.   As
shown in table 2, throughout the 1970s the cumulative increases in
current account deficits and reserve holdings accounted for practically
all of the debt increase.   During the 1980-1983 period, there was a
sharp drop in the use of foreign funds for these purposes.   This was
related to a large increase in exports on credit financed by foreign
loans. 2/   Unlike the situation in some developing countries, private
claims on non-residents have been virtually non-existent.

The rapid growth of debt and accompanying debt service obligations
have raised serious questions as to whether Korea has borrowed too much

Table 1

Profile of Korea's External Debt
(in $ billion and as percentage of nominal dollar GDP)

	Gross External Debt	Net External Debt a/	Short-term Debt	Debt with Variable Interest Rates as Percent of Gross Debt	Average Cost of Foreign Borrowings e/
1965	0.18 (5.89) b/	0.05 (1.66) b/	– –		
1970	2.25 (28.17)	1.57 (19.66)	0.37 (16.61) b/		2.33
1973	4.26 (31.55)	2.76 (20.44)	0.70 (16.46)		4.39
1975	8.46 (40.57)	6.75 (32.37)	2.41 (28.49)		6.18
1977	12.65 (33.80)	7.60 (20.31)	3.72 (29.37)		4.65
1979	20.50 (32.87)	14.20 (22.77)	6.60 (32.20)	56.90 c/	7.01
1980	27.37 (44.72)	19.90 (32.51)	10.61 (38.78)	61.50	9.24
1981	32.49 (48.35)	24.30 (36.17)	11.76 (36.20)	63.20	10.28
1982	37.31 (52.70)	28.00 (39.55)	14.22 (38.10)	65.30	9.37
1983	40.10 (53.39)	30.80 (41.01)	14.50 (36.1b)	65.60	7.37

Source: Economic Planning Board, Korean Economic Indicators, 1983, and data provided by the Bank of Korea.

a/ Gross debt minus external assets which include foreign exchange reserves, exports on credit, foreign banks' "A" account loans to
    Korean banks' foreign branches by their head offices and others.
b/ As per cent of nominal dollar GNP
c/ As per cent of gross external debt
d/ Data provided by the Bank of Korea.
e/ Actual interest payments divided by the debt for the end of the previous year (per cent).

Table 2

External debt, current account deficits, and reserve holdings
($ million)

	1966-1970	1971-1975	1976-1980	1981-1983
I. Cumulative Increase in Gross External Debt	2,068.0	6,211.0	18,909.0	12,735.0
II. Cumulative Current Account Deficits	1,906.7	5,437.1	10,858.3	8,914.6
(Interest Payments)	(152.2)	(1,270.6)	(6,446.2)	(10,854.4)
III. Cumulative Increase in Foreign Reserves	463.4	940.5	5,021.2	338.3
IV. (II + III)/I (per cent)	114.6	102.7	84.0	72.7

Source: Economic Planning Board, Major Statistics of Korean Economy, 1983.

or whether it can manage its burgeoning debt. In some quarters, the very soundness of Korea's rapid growth over the past two decades has been challenged. At the abstract level, one could perhaps obtain a set of conditions that may help determine both the optimality and the sustainability of a given amount of debt. However, application of these criteria to reality encounters many difficulties and often provides little guidance for making practical judgements on issues related to debt-servicing capacity.

Several indicators purporting to gauge the country's debt service capacity have been calculated and their changes over time have been extensively analyzed. As shown in table 2 in Appendix 2, the various indicators, for what they are worth, seem to suggest that Korea is not likely to experience any difficulties in servicing its debt. For a debt situation to be sustainable, lenders must also view it as such. Several international lending organizations, including the IMF, have expressed their confidence in Korea's debt service capacity and its management of the economy. More than anything else, Korea's successful adjustment to the external shocks and the exceptional economic performance in recent years have added to the confidence of international lenders in its economic future.

Although the country's external debt difficulties are by no means serious and in fact quite mild compared to the predicament faced by other developing economies, several aspects of the structure of its debt and balance of payments other than the large share of short-term debt suggest potential risks. The sheer size of the debt and the surge in the debt-to-GNP ratio have become a cause for concern and constitute the most serious debt issue since Korea launched its debt financed development through export promotion in the early 1960s. 3/ In order to reduce the growth of external obligations the Government plans to raise domestic savings as a percentage of GNP to 28.6 per cent by 1986 from the 24 per cent level in 1983 and to sustain the real growth of export earnings at over 10 per cent for the remaining three years of the Fifth Five Year Development Plan period. 4/ To judge by the past savings record and the unfavourable trade environment, these targets may be overly ambitious.

Korea's vulnerability to any deterioration in the climate for lending to developing countries is widely recognized. Notwithstanding its exceptional economic performance, Korea's access to international financial markets could be severely limited if any major debtor developing country in South or South-East Asia should default on its debt service.

Economists have also drawn attention to the danger associated with the high degree of rigidity in the country's external payments. The sum of debt service and imports for such "essentials" as oil, cereals, and raw materials for exports may total up to 80 per cent of commodity exports.

In recent years, Korea's current account imbalances have been dominated by the deficit of the public sector that includes the Government and para-statal corporations (see table 3 in Appendix 2). By definition, the current account deficit is the sum of the private and public deficit, that is, the excess of investment over savings. According to Corden (1977), the private sector can take care of itself, and hence the current account deficit that originates in the private sector's deficit is not a problem and not a matter for public policy concern. In Corden's words,

"If private firms choose to increase their spending and finance by borrowing abroad, and so generate a current account deficit, this does not call for any public policy concern or intervention." (p.50).

By contrast with the case of the private sector, one does not assume that the decisions to incur a deficit in the public sector are optimal, and therefore the current account deficit caused by the public sector's investment in excess of its savings is a balance-of-payments problem and may indeed be a matter for policy concern. As can be seen in table 3 in Appendix 2, the public sector has accounted for a growing share of the current account deficit in recent years, mainly because of the huge deficit incurred by para-statal corporations. In 1982, the private sector produced a small surplus. Since para-statal corporations are relatively unresponsive to demand management policies and government efforts at export promotion or import substitution, one could argue that it is more difficult than before to reduce the size of the current account deficit.

3.   EVOLUTION AND CAUSES OF KOREA'S FOREIGN DEBT ACCUMULATION

As can be observed in table 1 in Appendix 2, Korea experienced a rapid buildup in its foreign debt during three periods. Between 1965 and 1969, there was a more than tenfold increase in debt to $1.8 billion. The second upsurge took place during the first oil crisis. In the 1974/75 period, the outstanding debt more than doubled. The third buildup occurred during the second oil crisis, 1979/80, when gross debt mounted by 38 and 33.5 per cent in successive years.

Looking over the evolution of this external debt, one could suggest a number of factors responsible for its rapid accumulation. Some of these factors were external shocks beyond the country's control. In the 1970s, three external factors - oil price increases, high interest rates, and the worldwide recession - accounted for a large part of the accumulation. The promotion of investment in heavy and chemical industries that began in the early 1970s also contributed to the debt increase and to the subsequent debt-service burden as it resulted in a significant distortion in the allocation of resources. The debt explosion in the latter part of the 1960s was entirely in response to a policy reform. In this section we examine some of the structural reasons for the debt growth. This will be followed by a review of the policy responses and adjustment to both internally and externally generated shocks.

(a)   Debt-financed development strategy

One of the major causes of the country's debt accumulation is closely associated with some of the characteristics of its long-term growth strategy, in particular, the way in which the five-year development plans have been formulated and executed. The formulation of a five-year development plan begins with a reasonable target rate of growth. Within the framework of the Harrod-Domar model with a given capital-output ratio, the target rate of growth determines the required investment. The marginal propensity to save is assumed to be exogenous, though changing over time. If the domestic savings expected to be available during the plan period cannot meet the required investment, then the shortfall is made up by foreign capital inflows, which are assumed to be available.

In actual planning, Korean planners have relied on an increasingly sophisticated input-output model with many constraints. However, the fundamental philosophy underlying the planning has not changed:

whenever necessary, the planners have always been prepared to borrow abroad in order to achieve a target rate of growth. A heavy reliance on foreign savings was regarded as unavoidable in the early stages of development, though certainly not desirable in the long run. Rapid growth through the promotion of exports would, it was argued, gradually raise the propensity to save and hence reduce dependence on foreign savings. The growth of domestic savings as a percentage of GNP during the latter part of the 1960s was impressive but not sufficient to support fully the investment required to sustain the rapid growth planned by the authorities.

By the early 1970s, the country's exceptional growth performance had been recognized, thus helping to establish its creditworthiness in international financial markets. Although the debt-service ratio reached a 20 per cent level in the early 1970s, the country did not experience any serious problems in lining up additional loans. The availability of foreign loans, more than anything else, appears to have encouraged the authorities to pursue an expansionary demand policy during the first oil crisis to maintain a high rate of growth. The planners were not prepared to sacrifice growth and employment in favour of a response to the balance-of-payments difficulties that might be the consequence of such a policy.

During the latter half of the 1970s the planners once again demonstrated their readiness to incur heavy debts in order to promote investment in heavy and chemical industries. Given the past record of domestic savings, it was clear that the huge investment in capital-intensive industries would aggravate a current account situation that was fragile at best. Again the planners were not overly concerned about the adverse balance-of-payments consequences. Investment promotion caused a sharp increase in the ratio of investment to GNP to over 30 per cent from a historical average of 23 per cent in 1978 and maintained it at that high level for the subsequent five years. This, of course, was accompanied by an equally large increase in the current account deficits (see table 4 in Appendix 2).

One of the serious drawbacks of the national development strategy is that it reduces the scope and effectiveness of stabilization policies. Monetary policy is shown to be ineffective under an export-oriented growth regime. 5/ As long as the rates of growth of exports and output are set and pursued, considerations of stability are likely to be subordinated to the twin objectives of growth and employment. Partly for this reason, the country has suffered from a high rate of inflation, which in turn has undermined the competitiveness of its exports, discouraged domestic saving, and consequently resulted in larger current account deficits.

In a development planning framework in which an investment target is given and foreign borrowing is the residual, movements in the current account deficits will largely be determined by fluctuations in domestic savings. The Korean data support this proposition. From 1966 to 1977, fixed investment as a proportion of GNP remained relatively stable and certainly more stable than the domestic savings ratio (see table 4 in Appendix 2). During this period, the average investment ratio was 23.8 per cent with a standard deviation of 2.02. Domestic savings as a proportion of GNP fluctuated between 11.4 and 25.1 per cent with a mean of 18.1 per cent and a standard deviation of 4.3 per cent. As can be seen in table 4 in Appendix 2, the sharp deterioration of the current account for the 1974-1975 period was clearly the result of a downward savings shift. The subsequent improvement followed an upward shift in the savings ratio.

The large current account deficits in 1978 and 1979 were clearly due to an investment shift, which was in turn the consequence of a large increase in investment in capital-intensive industries. What is striking is that the investment ratio remained at about the 30 per cent level for the next four years. As a result, the increase in the current account deficit over 1980-1981 was caused by a sharp decline in the savings ratio.

The preceding argument should not be interpreted as implying that the availability of foreign capital has made the authorities complacent about mobilizing domestic savings. It is true that the savings target has not been as vigorously pursued as the export target, but it would be unfair to say that the Government has not been trying. Korea's domestic savings rate, which was 22.4 per cent of GNP on average during 1979-1983, is one of the highest among developing countries and there is no evidence of a reduction in domestic savings following the influx of foreign capital.

(b) High import intensity of exports

It was in general expected that export expansion would raise domestic savings as it promotes output growth and employment and would also narrow the foreign exchange gap. Export expansion throughout the period has been phenomenal, but part of that expansion has been spurious as most exporters have used large quantities of imported intermediate goods in their production processes. In fact, the growth of imported raw materials and intermediate goods used directly and indirectly in export production has been faster than export growth itself. Krueger (1979) shows that imports for export rose even more rapidly than exports until 1970 on the basis of the direct import content of manufactured exports (p. 137).

Input-output data show that the direct and indirect import intensity of exports rose markedly during the 1980s (see table 3). In 1970, the import intensity was 0.26. Five years later it rose to 0.36. After a small drop in 1978, it went up again to 0.38. The figure for 1980 is somewhat biased in that it reflects in part a sharp deterioration in the terms of trade. The 1978 figure is not subject to such a bias because by then export prices had fully recovered relative to import prices after the first oil crisis.

Table 3

Import inducement ratio[a]

	1970	1973	1975	1978	1980	Japan (1975)
Consumption	0.13	0.17	0.19	0.17	0.23	0.11
Investment	0.39	0.45	0.48	0.48	0.42	0.12
Exports	0.26[b]	0.35	0.36	0.36	0.38	0.17
Total demand	0.20	0.26	0.29	0.28	0.3	0.12

Source: Bank of Korea, Summary Analysis of 1980 Input-Output Tables, December, 1982

a/ Import inducement ratio is defined as the direct and indirect increase in imports per unit increase in a final demand component.

b/ One minus the import inducement ratio may be defined as the value-added share of exports.

Why has the import intensity of the country's exports been so high and, in fact, even rising? There are several reasons and they are all related to the characteristics of the nation's export incentive system. Exporters have had literally unlimited access to imported inputs and have paid neither tariffs nor indirect taxes on them (the tariff exemption system was changed to a drawback system in 1975). During the 1960s and in the early 1970s, wastage allowances were granted on imported duty-free raw materials over and above the actual requirements of export production, although they have since been pared down to the actual requirements. These incentive features combined with the fact that the exchange rate was overvalued throughout the 1970s have increased the relative attractiveness of imported intermediate goods compared to what would have been most efficient. According to a recent study, the nominal exchange rate (vis-à-vis the U.S. dollar) was overvalued by as much as 16 per cent on average during the latter part of the 1970s in terms of a real effective exchange rate against a basket of currencies of the country's major trading partners (Cha, 1983, p. 58).

The export financing system, which supplies subsidized short-term credit tied to export volume, is biased in favour of short-term investment which could produce exports soon after plant operations begin. Financial incentives also encourage the use of a relatively capital-intensive production technology in export production. 6/ Because of these incentive features it has been more profitable to export goods that require mostly assembly of imported parts and components than to develop and export these intermediate inputs themselves. Largely because of this investment bias, exporters have neglected investing in skill and technology development, manpower training, and the development of new export products. During the latter part of the 1970s, it was not uncommon in some industries such as machinery to import capital goods to acquire technology that was otherwise unavailable.

Since 1965, export incentives have been extended to domestic producers of intermediate goods used in export production. However, many of these import substitution activities were not profitable because of the limited domestic market. The incentive system definitely favoured exports over import substitution and positive import substitution was a response to economic development rather than a result of deliberate protectionist policies. The limited degree of import substitution may be inferred from the contribution of import substitution to output growth. According to Kim and Roemer (1979) and Kim (1979), the contribution of import substitution to GDP growth during 1963-1973 was about 16 per cent, or less than half that of export expansion.

Beginning in the early 1970s, Korean planners launched a massive investment programme that was envisaged to restructure industries. The new development strategy was basically designed to promote both import substitution and export promotion in heavy and chemical industries. As will be discussed later, the import substitution efforts stimulate the growth of imports of capital goods and intermediate goods, contributing to a growing current account imbalance.

(c)   Preference of debt financing over foreign direct investment

Compared with the case of other developing countries, foreign direct investment has played a minor role in this country's development. As presented in table 5 in Appendix 2, foreign direct investment accounted for less than 5 per cent of total foreign capital inflows between 1955 and 1980, except for the 1972-1976 period during which the share rose to 10 per cent. A greater reliance on foreign direct investment as a source of capital financing and as a channel for technology transfer could have alleviated Korea's foreign debt burden.

One could entertain several reasons for the insignificance of foreign direct investment. With its poor resource endowment, Korea lacks one of the most important inducements for foreign investment. The lack of natural resources has been further compounded by the country's national security problems. During the 1960s, it was clear that the Government preferred foreign loans so as to minimize Japanese ownership and control of Korean businesses. Even in the 1970s, feelings toward foreign direct investment were adverse, especially toward Japanese investors. Having demonstrated its ability to penetrate world export markets and its growth potential in the 1960s, Korea has since had relatively easier access to foreign loans on favourable terms and hence has not until recently had to solicit direct investment for foreign capital financing.

Until the mid-1970s, the country's exports consisted mostly of products of labour-intensive industries, since it did not require sophisticated technology to sustain the rapid expansion of exports. The standardized products such as textiles, clothing, footwear, and simple electronics that constituted the bulk of exports do not require sophisticated marketing in terms of an overseas network and servicing. For these products, the entire marketing effort from design to sales has often been carried out by the foreign importers. For these reasons, Korean planners and businesses did not seek foreign partners to gain marketing expertise.

Perhaps the most important reason why overseas borrowing has been emphasized more than direct foreign investment has been that foreign debt financing has been much more attractive than equity financing. As shown in table 4, throughout the 1970s the real interest rate on foreign loans was consistently negative, largely because of an overvalued exchange rate in an inflationary environment. However, in the case of foreign direct investment, the implicit subsidies associated with the negative real interest rate are repatriated in the form of investment earnings.

(d) **Interest rate differential between home and international financial markets**

From 1965 to 1979, the real interest rate Korean borrowers paid on foreign loans was mostly negative except in those years when large currency devaluations were undertaken (see table 4). During the 1966-1970 period, the foreign rate of interest (London inter-bank offered rate, LIBOR) adjusted for an exchange rate change was lower than the rate paid on domestic borrowing by as much as 15 percentage points, depending on how expected exchange rate changes are estimated. Even during 1971-1979, the foreign borrowing rate was consistently lower than the domestic rate, though the differential narrowed considerably. 7/

Much of the differential could be explained by the artificially low level of domestic interest rates and the overvaluation of the exchange rate while inflation was accelerating. In the 1970s, the high rate of inflation which induced an upward adjustment in the expected rate of inflation encouraged domestic firms to anticipate negative real interest rates on their foreign borrowing.

Table 4

Cost of foreign capital (annual averages)
(percentages)

	1966/70	1971/75	1976/80	1981/83
I. Domestic bank lending rate a/	24.4	17.0	18.0	12.5
(Curb market interest rate)	(54.2)	(40.1)	(41.3)	(30.6)
II. Foreign interest rate b/	6.4	7.9	11.5	11.1
III. Foreign inflation rate (GNP deflator) c/	4.9	8.4	5.9	4.1
IV. Exchange rate depreciation d/	5.1	7.8	5.5	10.1
V. GDP deflator (Rate of change): Korea e/	14.6	19.8	20.7	9.8
VI. Real foreign interest rate (II-III)	1.5	-0.5	5.6	7.0
VII. Interest rate differential between home and foreign markets (I-II-IV)	12.9	1.3	1.0	-8.7
VIII. Real private cost of borrowing abroad (II + IV - V)	-3.1	-4.1	-3.7	11.4

Source: Bank of Korea, Monthly Bulletin, various issues.

a/   Discounts on bills of deposit money banks (three-year moving averages).
b/   LIBOR (90 days).
c/   Average of Japan and the United States.
d/   Bank of Korea standard concentration rate (three-year moving averages).
e/   Three-year moving averages.

The interest rate differential was no doubt one of the powerful incentives to Korean firms to borrow abroad. During the latter part of the 1960s, the enormous influx was certainly induced by the interest rate differential. Although the differential fell considerably during the 1970s, the fall did not make much impact on actual foreign borrowing. Won currency lending by domestic banks was tightly controlled and rationed out to industries and sectors in a rigid manner. The costs of obtaining funds from other sources were at times prohibitively high.

Under these circumstances, domestic firms turned to foreign borrowing as an alternative source of credit. In particular, exporters who were allowed to import intermediate and capital goods used in export production borrowed heavily in the form of trade credits and borrowed much more than they would have done if the availability of domestic credit had been adequate. Thus, low interest rates combined with tight credit rationing and the import privileges given to exporters resulted in a strong demand for foreign loans that was difficult to control.

4. ADJUSTMENT TO INTERNAL SHOCKS AND DEBT ACCUMULATION

(a) Interest rate reform and foreign loan guarantees, 1965-1970

For more than a decade before the monetary reform of 1965, foreign capital inflows consisted mostly of foreign aid. Private capital flows were very small and as such could not play a significant role in resource allocation. It is partly true that Korea could not have begun to attract significant non-concessionary private capital until its creditworthiness in international capital markets had been established. However, what was more important was the fact that depressed domestic financial markets combined with an overvalued exchange rate and political uncertainties simply discouraged lending to Korea.

The military government that came to power in 1961 was determined to create an environment more conducive to capital inflows. In 1962, the Government enacted two supplements to the Foreign Capital Inducement Law promulgated a year earlier. One of the two supplements established procedures for granting repayment guarantees on foreign loans, a step which prepared for a massive inflow of foreign capital. In September of 1965, a monetary reform was undertaken by which deposit and lending rates at the banking institutions were more than doubled. In 1966, a number of amendments were made in the law which were designed to increase the attractiveness of lending and investing in Korea. These changes led to a flood of foreign capital inflows for the next several years. To foreign lenders, the interest rate differentials and the loan guarantee system which eliminated the risks of default and exchange rate depreciation were strong incentives to lend to Korea. Domestic borrowers were encouraged by the cost differentials between domestic and foreign interest rates (see table 4), and according to Frank, Kim and Westphal (1975), they did not expect that the exchange rate would change as much as it did during the late 1960s (p. 117). The divergence between the domestic and foreign borrowing rates ranged from 4.4 to 18 percentage points during the 1965-1970 period (see table 5).

Foreign debt increased from less than $60 million in 1962 to $2.25 billion by the end of 1970. The increased availability of foreign exchange enabled Korean firms to import capital goods, raw materials, and intermediate goods on a much bigger scale than before and set the stage for rapid growth. Exports began to surge, but so did imports. Since imports increased from a much larger base, there followed a sharp deterioration in the current account. Despite the continuing imbalances, capital inflows were large enough to enable the central bank to accumulate foreign reserves at a faster pace than before, and beyond a desirable level.

The most difficult problem the Korean authorities were faced with at that time was domestic liquidity management owing to a rapid buildup of reserves and the subsequent increase in the money supply. The authorities had four policy options. They could let the exchange rate float and appreciate until the appreciation narrowed the interest rate gap between home and abroad. Although the won was floating within a limited range, this option was not acceptable for fear that such an action would impair export earnings. As a result, during 1969/70 exchange rate policy was primarily directed to maintaining the real effective exchange rate on exports. As shown in table 5, the real exchange rate without the subsidies displayed considerable fluctuations, but the rate with subsidies was considerably more stable.

Another option was import liberalization which would soak up the excess liquidity of the economy. This course was again seriously considered; however, imports were already rising rapidly, and more important, there was intense opposition from protected domestic manufacturers. They were concerned that any further liberalization would reduce the profits on sales in the domestic market which enabled manufacturers to recoup their losses on exports. The third option was to impose direct controls or an interest equalization tax on capital inflows, but it was only recently that the guarantee scheme to attract foreign capital had been introduced, and it was obviously premature to shut off this flow of foreign credit and foreign exchange.

The fourth policy option, which was applied during 1966-1970, was to accumulate foreign reserves, squeeze the supply of domestic credit, and, in time, reduce the deposit interest rates. To offset the expansion of the supply of money originating in the reserve accumulations, the authorities attempted to reduce the rate of expansion of domestic credit by means of raising the reserve requirements of the banking sector. Thus, the monetary authorities found themselves pursuing two contradictory policies simultaneously.

Table 5

Macroeconomic development, 1965-1972 (annual averages)
($ million and percentages)

	1965/66	1967/68	1969/70	1971/72
I. Gross foreign debt	264.5	922.5	2,022.5	3,255.5
II. Foreign exchange holdings	187.1	376.8	566.5	614.2
III. Export earnings	212.7	387.8	728.9	1,345.9
IV. Debt service as per cent of export earnings	5.4	10.7	23.2	28.7
V. Current account deficit as per cent of GNP	1.4	6.5	8.0	6.3
VI. Real exchange rate a/	482.2	406.0	370.3	394.1
VII. Real effective exchange rate b/	305.0	298.0	303.5	337.0
VIII. Foreign interest rate	5.7	6.0	7.1	6.3
IX. Real foreign interest rate	2.6	1.4	1.4	1.3
X. Change in nominal exchange rate	13.9	1.0	6.0	12.5
XI. GDP deflator (rate of change)	10.3	16.2	15.1	15.0
XII. Domestic bank lending rate	24.0	25.0	24.3	18.8
XIII. Real domestic bank lending rate (XII-XI)	13.7	8.8	9.3	3.8

a/   From Table 7 in Appendix 2.

b/   Purchasing power effective (including subsidies) exchange rate on
exports from Krueger (1979), pp. 122-123.
Figures for 1965 are from Frank, Kim and Westphal (1975), pp.
70-71.

On the one hand, they raised the deposit interest rates to expand the real demand for bank liabilities and used these resources to augment the real supply of loans. On the other, because of the unexpectedly large increase in the foreign supply of loans, they had to squeeze the supply of domestic credit. As a result, they were mobilizing domestic financing savings (and real savings also) at a high rate of interest, converting them into foreign reserve assets, and in so doing lending to foreign borrowers at a low interest rate. The liquidity management policies amounted to subsidizing foreign savers at the expense of domestic savers.

As the monetary authorities continued to restrict the growth of the supply of domestic credit in order to moderate monetary expansion, the credit available to some sectors of the economy suffered a relative reduction. Not every Korean firm could borrow from abroad; to qualify for foreign loans, the prospective borrower had to have political connections and be engaged in favoured industries, especially in producing exports. The tightening of the domestic credit supply and the inflow of foreign capital therefore led to imbalances in sectoral credit allocation that discriminated against the non-tradeable or domestic-market-oriented sectors. These sectors were faced with a relative credit squeeze, whereas others, notably exporters and those who had access to foreign loans and could bring in cash loans, had a large amount of liquidity.

This situation would not pose serious problems in an economy with a sophisticated financial structure. If there had been organized short-term credit markets in Korea at that time, the excess liquidity of the export sector would have been channelled to those in need of credit which the banking system could not supply. There were no such secondary credit markets to take up this role, except the unregulated money market.

Controls on foreign borrowing had been in effect since 1962. However, in practice, foreign loan applications for financing investment in priority sectors were generally encouraged and no strict limits on foreign borrowing were enforced. The rapid increase in debt, and accompanying debt-service obligations, resulted in a sharp increase in the debt-service ratio in the late 1960s despite the rapid growth of exports. By 1971, the ratio had shot up to over 30 per cent.

Concerned with the apparent deterioration in Korea's debt-service capacity, the IMF required the Korean Government in a standby agreement to issue letters of intent to limit foreign capital movements to one to three-year loans, while very long-term loans were given liberal treatment (Frank, Kim and Westphal, 1975, p. 122). The effect of the IMF pressure was clearly visible. The growth of total debt slowed to 25 per cent in 1970 and 30 per cent in the following year. This deceleration brought about a sharp decrease in the growth of imports, particularly capital goods.

In 1970, it looked as though the economy was cooling off, as there was an appreciable drop in investment demand, caused mostly by the decline in capital inflows and in part by the tight monetary policy pursued over the preceding three years. The growth of export demand was also declining from its previous very high levels. The reduction in the growth of aggregate demand continued throughout 1971 and into most of 1972. Some expansionary measures were called for to stimulate the economy.

The high rate of growth of output and exports during 1965-1969 had bred an expectation in the business community that the expansion would continue for a considerable period. This optimism in turn led Korean firms to maintain a high rate of investment with funds obtained from domestic financial institutions and foreign sources, supplemented when necessary by short-term funds from the curb market. The average cost of capital in real terms was relatively low so long as prices kept rising and depreciation of the exchange rate was gradual. However, the major devaluation in 1971 that was designed mainly to stimulate exports also caused a sudden jump in the won cost of foreign debt servicing. This created severe short-run financial problems for those firms that had borrowed abroad most heavily, which was particularly the case for larger firms. As an increasing number of these firms found themselves unable to meet the principal and interest payments to their foreign creditors, the guaranteeing banks were forced to make good on their commitments. Korea was faced with an impending debt management crisis. To cope with the deteriorating situation, the Government could have let these debt-ridden firms go bankrupt and weathered the painful consequences. This alternative, however, was not acceptable because it was feared that the poor performance of the economy and an increasing number of business failures would undermine the nation's credit standing in the international capital markets and would thus hamper the inflow of much needed foreign loans. This option would also have involved a considerable sacrifice of growth and the risk of a high unemployment rate. As a result, to manage the debt crisis a more costly but less painful alternative was chosen; it was simply to bail out these troubled firms and exporters.

The Presidential Emergency Decree announced on 3 August 1972 initiated the Government's rescue effort. 8/ The Decree had two purposes. In the first place, it was intended to stimulate economic activity by reviving investment demand, which was a short-run objective. Secondly, it was designed to alleviate the interest burden of business firms by abrogating by fiat the existing informal loan contracts.

The two important features of the Decree pertinent to our discussion were:

(i) All the loan agreements between business firms with a business licence and lenders in the curb market as of 2 August 1972 were nullified and replaced by new ones. The borrowers would have to repay their informal loans over a five-year period after a three-year grace period at a 1.35 per cent monthly interest rate. The lenders had the alternative option to transform their loans into shares of the borrowing firms.

(ii) An overall reduction in the interest rates of banking institutions: the time deposit rate was lowered from 17.4 per cent to 12.6 per cent and that for general loans up to one year from 19 per cent to 15.5 per cent.

As from the fourth quarter of 1972, partly in response to a sharp depreciation of the real exchange rate, exports skyrocketed, and in 1973 expanded by 90 per cent. The economy grew by 16.5 per cent in 1973, the highest rate of growth in the nation's history. The sudden increase in exports lifted the economy out of the mild slowdown in 1971 and 1972 and, more important from our point of view, rescued Korea from its first debt crisis.

(b) Promotion of capital-intensive industries, and debt accumulation, 1975-1979

After a decade of promoting the export of labour-intensive manufactures, the Korean authorities began in the early 1970s to promote skill and technology-intensive industries, which are known in Korea as the heavy and chemical industries. 9/ A massive investment programme in these industries financed largely by foreign loans and central bank credit was put into effect in 1973 and pursued vigorously until 1979. To the dismay of policy-makers who had conceived this industrial restructuring, the development strategy ran into a host of financing, engineering, quality, and marketing difficulties. This section analyzes the effects of the industrial restructuring policy on inflation and the balance of payments. The effect of this investment policy on resource allocation is discussed in section 6(c).

Much of the investment in the heavy and chemical industries, which was by and large induced by distorted incentives, took place during the 1977-1979 period when the economy was already experiencing a high rate of inflation. To support this large increase in investment, the Government allocated $4.66 billion of foreign loans to these industries, which accounted for more than 30 per cent of total foreign loans approved and for almost 80 per cent of the loans absorbed by manufacturing between 1976 and 1980 (see table 6 in Appendix 2). Although the estimates vary, the loan figure represented anywhere from 40 to 50 per cent of nominal fixed investment undertaken in these industries during the period. A large part of the foreign loans allocated to the social overhead capital sectors was earmarked for augmenting infrastructure facilities such as the industrial sites and roads needed to promote these industries. Therefore, the actual infusion of foreign resources into the heavy and chemical industries was much greater than the amount of foreign loans used for investment in these industries.

As a result of the large investment, the ratio of fixed investment to GNP shot up to 33 per cent in 1979 from a historical average of about 25 per cent. Since the domestic savings-GNP ratio did not rise in tandem, the high rate of investment expanded aggregate demand and put pressure on the external balance. To make matters worse, the investment programme entailed serious supply-side problems that intensified inflationary pressures emanating from the demand side. During 1977-1979, more than 70 per cent of manufacturing investment was undertaken in heavy and chemical industries (see Section 6(c)). This lopsided allocation of investment resources generated severe sectoral imbalances between the tradable and nontradable sectors and within the tradeable sector. The lack of investment in light manufacturing - the traditional export sector - had adverse effects on Korea's export performance, while sluggish investment in the nontradeable sector caused a supply shortage and rapid price increases.

Since the one-shot devaluation in 1974, the nominal exchange rate had been kept at 480 won per U.S. dollar. The high rate of domestic inflation relative to the rates of inflation in major trading partners - Japan and the United States - resulted in an 18 per cent real appreciation of the won currency between 1974 and 1979 (see table 7 in Appendix 2). Other things being equal, such a real appreciation results in a shift of aggregate demand in favour of traded goods that include exportables and importables whose prices in a small open economy are greatly influenced by conditions prevailing in world markets. The real appreciation, on the supply side, induces a shift of domestic resources to the more profitable nontraded goods sector. These demand and supply shifts would in general slow down price increases and would be reflected in a deterioration in the current account.

Despite these market forces operating in the economy, the expected resource shift did not take place. On the contrary, a large share of resources was channelled to the tradeable goods, in particular the heavy and chemical sectors, through the Government's directed resource allocation. As a consequence, the excess demand for nontradables remained unabated and their prices went up further. To complicate matters further, this forced allocation of resources to heavy and chemical industries did not help meet the domestic demand for tradeables. One reason was that a large increase in the domestic demand for tradeables was accounted for by demand for consumer goods such as high quality and processed food products and consumer durables. Since the bulk of investment resources was allocated to the capital goods producing sector, an excess demand for these consumer goods had to be satisfied by imports. Another reason was that Korean firms continued to import machinery and petrochemicals - which were expected to be supplied by producers of domestic import substitutes - because of suspected low quality and the difficulty of securing domestic financing for purchases in the domestic market.

Although most of the heavy and chemical industries - shipbuilding, basic metals, and power generating equipment in particular - were from the beginning developed for export, they were not in the short run able to generate export earnings. As a result, while the tradeable goods sector was saddled with huge idle capacity, the import demand for tradeables rose sharply. The combined effect of these developments was a widening trade deficit and runaway inflation. From 1975 to 1979, the price of imports increased less than 1 per cent a year and export prices about 8 per cent, whereas the deflator for social overhead capital and services, which may be used as a proxy for a price index for nontradables, rose by 22 per cent on average per annum (see table 6). The current account deficit rose to 7.2 per cent of GNP in 1979 from a small surplus in 1977.

The heavy and chemical industry investment programme also produced a cost-push effect. Production inefficiencies and underutilized capacity reduced labour productivity considerably. Despite the decline in productivity, nominal wages and hence unit labour costs, soared as skilled workers, who were in short supply, were bid up by firms in heavy and chemical industries and construction workers were sent to the Middle East. Between 1975 and 1979, the unit labour cost index (1975 = 100) more than doubled (see table 8 in Appendix 2). This cost-push effect was validated through money expansion and subsequently undermined Korea's international competitiveness, leading to the need for larger foreign borrowings.

5.   POLICY RESPONSE AND ADJUSTMENT TO EXTERNAL SHOCKS

(a)   Policy response and adjustment to the first oil crisis, 1973-1977

The oil price increases of late 1973 and 1974 dealt a severe blow to the Korean economy. Because the country was entirely dependent on imported oil, the price increase caused a 23 per cent deterioration in its terms of trade, and the ensuing world recession and trade protectionism triggered by the oil crisis precipitated a sharp drop in world demand for exports which suddenly dampened Korea's growth prospects. These adverse developments coupled with the excessive credit expansion of the previous two years provoked a steep increase in the rate of inflation for the next several years.

Korea's policy response to the oil crisis was to adjust gradually to the adverse shock by resorting to foreign borrowing. To facilitate this protracted adjustment, the Bank of Korea, the Central Bank, approached international financial markets for bank loans to finance the imports needed to sustain the rapid growth Korea had been accustomed to. To mitigate the current account deterioration, heavy taxes were imposed on oil products to minimize their use, the predeposit requirement for imports was raised, more export credit with a lower interest rate was made available, and finally the exchange rate was devalued by almost 22 per cent towards the end of 1974. These measures were clearly designed to alleviate the worst effects of the price increases and to maintain overall growth.

Table 6

Changes in sectoral GNP deflators, 1960-1983 (annual averages)
(percentages)

	Mining & manufacturing	Social overhead capital & other sectors	Agriculture forestry fishery	GNP
1960-64	17.3	14.1	28.9	18.7
1965-69	9.2	17.7	9.3	13.4
1970-74	13.1	17.0	21.3	17.7
1975-79	16.7	22.8	22.4	21.0
1980-83	12.5	14.9	7.2	12.9

Source: Bank of Korea, National Income in Korea, 1982. Bank of
Korea, Monthly Bulletin, 1984.2.

Little effort was made to hold down domestic price increases. On
the assumption that Korea's export competitors would suffer equally,
policy-makers decided early on to absorb fully the oil price
increases. Bank credit was expanded by nearly 50 per cent to help
finance the needed imports. As a result, wholesale prices rose by 42
per cent in 1974. The current account deficit widened to 11.2 per cent
of GNP in 1974 - the highest ever in Korea's history - and almost half
of this huge deficit was financed by bank borrowing and the depletion
of foreign reserve holdings, which fell by 3.5 per cent in the course
of a year.

In 1975, the growth of imports tumbled to 6 per cent from 60 per
cent a year earlier, largely owing to a marked decrease in the import
demand for capital goods. On the other hand, export expansion was
respectable at 14 per cent, and this helped to reduce the current
account deficit to 9 per cent of GNP. Unlike the situation in the
preceding year, much of the deficit was financed by private borrowing.
As a result, the overall account deficit amounted to one-seventh of the
level a year earlier. Because of the heavy foreign borrowing, Korea's
external debt more than doubled to $8.5 billion in the 1974/75 period.
Nevertheless, debt service as a percentage of current earnings remained
virtually unchanged, largely thanks to a strong export performance.

Export earnings began to surge in 1976 with a worldwide recovery
and rich construction opportunities for Korea in the Middle East, while
import growth was moderate (see table 7). These favourable

Table 9

Macroeconomic developments, 1979-1983

	1979/80[a]	1981	1982	1983
GNP Growth rate (per cent)	0.7	6.2	5.6	9.3
Fixed investment (rate of change, per cent)	-1.0	-3.3	13.1	16.6
(as per cent of GNP)	(32.3)	(28.9)	(30.3)	(31.8)
Current account deficits (billion U.S. dollars)	4.7	4.6	2.6	1.6
(as per cent of GNP)	(7.7)	(6.9)	(3.7)	(2.2)
Exports (billion U.S. dollars)	16.3	21.3	21.9	24.4
(rate of change, per cent)	(17.4)	(21.7)	(2.8)	(11.4)
Oil payments (billion U.S. dollars)	4.4	6.4	6.1	5.6
Interest payments (billion U.S. dollars)	2.1	3.6	3.8	3.4
Buildup in gross external debt	6.2	5.1	4.8	2.8
Terms of trade (1975 = 100)	114.6	101.6	105.7	107.0
Nominal exchange rate	545.7	681.0	731.1	
Real exchange rate	430.5	438.7	423.1	
Unit labour cost (1975 = 100)	213.3	232.8	254.8	269.6
Inflation rate (GNP deflator, per cent)	23.4	15.9	7.1	2.9
M_1 growth rate (per cent)	33.9	4.6	45.6	17.0
M_2 growth rate (per cent)	25.8	25.0	27.0	15.2
Unified budget deficit (billion Won)	807.0	2,110.9	2,222.0	2,073.3
(as per cent of GNP)	(2.4)	(4.6)	(4.3)	(3.6)

Source: Bank of Korea, National Income in Korea, 1982.

        Bank of Korea, Monthly Bulletin, various issues.

        Economic Planning Board, Major Statistics of Korean Economy, 1983.

a/ Annual average.

developments led to a dramatic improvement in the current account to the point where a small surplus was recorded in 1977. Although the current account was improving, there was little slowdown in capital inflows. Induced by a substantial interest rate differential adjusted for changes in expected exchange rates and by the promotion of investment in heavy and chemical industries, private foreign borrowing continued to swell, resulting in a huge overall account surplus and hence domestic liquidity expansion in 1976 and 1977.

The expansionary policy response to the oil price shock seemed to have paid off handsomely as far as growth and employment were concerned. While many non-oil producing countries experienced a negative rate of growth, Korea managed to grow by 8 per cent and 7.1 per cent in 1974 and 1975 respectively. The growth-first response was, however, not without costs. It seriously undermined the stability of the economy and made it increasingly difficult to implement anti-inflationary policies.

Alarmed by the two years of high inflation following the oil crisis, the authorities began to pay more attention to restraining price increases. In 1976, they began to tighten the supply of credit and money, but given the automatic credit expansion associated with export growth, there was a clear limit to which they could squeeze credit supply. To complement the restrictive monetary policy, a comprehensive incomes policy was put into effect that included strong price control measures covering a wide range of consumer and producer goods. These measures seemed to slowdown the pace of inflation for a while. In 1976 and 1977, inflation showed a sharp deceleration, but in 1978 prices began to soar again to rise by more than 20 per cent in terms of the GNP deflator. The sudden upsurge was not unexpected and to some extent attributable to the growth-first response to the oil crisis.

An important question, in the light of Korea's response to the first oil shock, is to what extent it was appropriate to postpone the required adjustment by resorting to foreign borrowing. Krueger (1979) argues that if Korea had been forced to curtail imports abruptly because of the unavailability of foreign credit, the resulting dislocations would have prevented the rapid resumption of export growth. Korea's ability to borrow allowed it to weather the oil price increase and gave policy-makers the time to alter domestic policy and adapt to a hostile environment (p. 152). This view is widely shared, and in theory, given real world rigidities, lengthening the adjustment period could reduce the costs of adjustment (Martin and Selowsky, 1981).

Citing the opposite policy response to the oil shock of Taiwan, Province of China, many critics have pointed out that debt-financed growth was uncalled for, or at least excessive. They argue that the resumption of rapid growth would have been realized even if restrictive policies had been adopted. In retrospect, the critics argue, the expansionary policy made adjustment costs higher than they would otherwise have been, as it added to the inflationary pressures that were building up.

In 1974, that other economy grew by 1.1 per cent. After moderate growth in the following year, the economy picked up and registered 13.5 per cent growth in 1976. For the next three years rapid growth was accompanied by stable prices. The annual rate of increase of the wholesale price index (WPI) was about 3 per cent on average, whereas it was almost 11 per cent in Korea. This continuing inflation erased much of the gains from the expansionary policy in Korea. In hindsight, the critics may have been right, but one cannot fault policy-makers for not having predicted the future accurately. If they had expected a rapid worldwide economic recovery, they might have adopted a more conservative policy.

In order to analyze the evolution of the current account during the first oil crisis, we have decomposed the current account identity and then estimated its changes over time (see Appendix 1). This exercise is presented in table 8. Compared to the 1972/73 base period, the current account deficit as a proportion of nominal potential GDP in U.S. dollars was higher by more than 7 percentage points (i.e., + deteriorated) in 1974. As expected, much of the deterioration could be traced to the terms of trade loss (almost 5 percentage points). A surprising development during the crisis was that the increase in imports of capital goods and others excluding oil in relation to fixed investment and GDP (9.7 percentage points) was larger than the actual increase in the ratio of the current account to potential GDP. This relative increase reflected the lagged effect on import demand of the monetary expansion that had occurred in the preceding two years and in part supports those criticizing the growth-first policy. Luckily for Korea, much of this import expansion effect was offset by export growth (8.7 percentage points).

Beginning in 1975, the current account improved continuously for three years before going into deficit again in 1978. During this period, the improvement came mostly from changes in the terms of trade and from export growth.

(b) **Policy response and adjustment to the second oil crisis and high interest rates, 1979-1983**

As noted before, after two years of relative price stability, there occurred a steep rise in prices in 1978 as the rapid monetary expansion in the preceding three years built up strong domestic demand. This rise, combined with a slowdown in export growth due to weakening competitiveness, produced a deficit in the current account. The situation called for anti-inflationary measures. However, it was only in April of 1979 that the Government was able to direct its efforts to restoring domestic stability. The comprehensive programme announced in April 1979 consisted of tight fiscal and monetary policies, readjustment of investment in heavy and chemical industries, and clamping down on the real estate speculation that had been heating up for several years.

Table 8

Decomposition of change in the current account between each year and the 1972/73 base period[a]

(All variables are represented as ratios to potential GDP)

		1974[b]	1975	1976	1977
I.	Actual change in the ratio of current account imbalances to potential output	7.258	5.351	-1.782	-3.476
II.	Terms of trade effect	4.893	4.284	1.183	-0.254
	(i) Import price changes	-0.462	-1.573	-6.772	-11.495
	(a) Capital goods	-1.816	-1.621	-2.605	-3.048
	(b) Oil	3.064	3.302	2.954	2.608
	(c) Other	-1.710	-3.255	-7.121	-11.055
	(ii) Export price changes	5.355	5.858	7.956	11.242
III.	Interest rate effect	0.167	0.458	0.023	0.040
IV.	Accumulated debt effect	-0.142	0.134	0.210	0.170
V.	Import adjustment	9.528	7.621	10.727	14.769
	(i) Import substitution for capital goods	3.385	2.150	2.742	1.907
	(ii) Import substitution for non-capital goods	6.358	5.312	7.546	12.364
	(iii) Oil conservation efforts	-0.215	0.159	0.439	0.498
VI.	Export promotion (Construction services)	-7.883 (-0.031)	-7.791 (-0.098)	-15.932 (-1.632)	-21.667 (-3.954)
VII.	Aggregate demand adjustment	1.183	1.123	2.532	4.067
	i) Change in investment spending	0.680	0.736	1.292	2.463
	(ii) Change in aggregate demand policy	0.503	0.387	1.241	1.604
VIII.	Total effect (II+III+IV+V+VI+VII)	7.747	5.829	-1.256	-2.874
IX.	Interaction effects and adding-up errors (I-VIII)	-0.489	-0.478	-0.526	-0.602

a/ See Appendix 1 for a description of and data used for the decomposition.
b/ The decomposition factors were calculated using an average of current year and base period weights.

Note: Negative sign indicates a balance-of-payments improvement.

Already feeling strong inflationary pressures, Korea was hit by the second oil crisis that doubled the price of oil in the course of a year. The immediate impact of the oil price increase together with the removal of price controls on a large number of commodities 10/ was a sharp acceleration of inflation. The uncertainties generated by the oil price increase, the over-investment in heavy and chemical industries, and the Government's plan to readjust sectoral investment in these industries clouded the business climate further and induced businesses to cut back their investment spending.

Externally, commodity exports suffered from the deepening world recession and the loss of competitiveness associated with a steep increase in unit labour costs. Adjusted for price increases, real exports actually declined by 2.5 per cent in 1979. The current account deficit rose to 7.2 per cent of GNP (see table 9). While Korea was beset by these adverse developments, it had at the same time to confront the social and political uncertainties and turmoil which followed the death of President Park in October 1979 and which complicated the management of the economy further. To stop a further haemorrhaging of the economy and to cope with the unfavourable external and internal environment, strong policy measures had to be taken. Although a rise in unemployment would pose a serious threat to an already shaky social stability, it was evident to policy-makers that, by contrast with the situation in 1974, the growth-first policy was simply not a viable alternative. The foremost reason was the questionable availability of the external finance needed to lengthen the adjustment period. Indeed, it was obvious that any further deterioration in the current account might seriously undermine Korea's credit standing in international financial markets and cripple its ability to borrow.

Unlike what had happened during the first oil crisis, it was inconceivable that exports would grow as fast as they had done during the 1976/77 period. This pessimism of course reflected the rise in trade protectionism and expectations of deepening world recession. Persistently high interest rates and the diminished availability of external finance also raised the cost of borrowing abroad. Given the continuous requirement for external borrowing, the best policy alternative was to pursue stabilization policies in the hope of reducing the size of the current account deficit. To these considerations was added the argument that it would be relatively easier for a caretaker Government to implement unpopular stabilization measures.

In January 1980, the caretaker Government introduced a policy package clearly aimed at improving the current account. It included a 20 per cent devaluation of the won currency vis-à-vis the dollar, an upward adjustment of bank deposit and lending rates by 5-6 percentage points, and a 60 per cent increase in energy prices for end-users. 11/

The exchange rate devaluation was indeed much overdue. As pointed out in an earlier section, the won-dollar exchange rate had been kept

Table 9

Macroeconomic developments, 1979-1983

	1979/80a/	1981	1982	1983
GNP Growth rate (per cent)	0.7	6.2	5.6	9.3
Fixed investment (rate of change, per cent)	-1.0	-3.3	13.1	16.6
(as per cent of GNP)	(32.3)	(28.9)	(30.3)	(31.8)
Current account deficits (billion U.S. dollars)	4.7	4.6	2.6	1.6
(as per cent of GNP)	(7.7)	(6.9)	(3.7)	(2.2)
Exports (billion U.S. dollars)	16.3	21.3	21.9	24.4
(rate of change, per cent)	(17.4)	(21.7)	(2.8)	(11.4)
Oil payments (billion U.S. dollars)	4.4	6.4	6.1	5.6
Interest payments (billion U.S. dollars)	2.1	3.6	3.8	3.4
Buildup in gross external debt	6.2	5.1	4.8	2.8
Terms of trade (1975 = 100)	114.6	101.6	105.7	107.0
Nominal exchange rate	545.7	681.0	731.1	
Real exchange rate	430.5	438.7	423.1	
Unit labour cost (1975 = 100)	213.3	232.8	254.8	269.6
Inflation rate (GNP deflator, per cent)	23.4	15.9	7.1	2.9
M_1 growth rate (per cent)	33.9	4.6	45.6	17.0
M_2 growth rate (per cent)	25.8	25.0	27.0	15.2
Unified budget deficit (billion Won)	807.0	2,110.9	2,222.0	2,073.3
(as per cent of GNP)	(2.4)	(4.6)	(4.3)	(3.6)

Source: Bank of Korea, National Income in Korea, 1982.

Bank of Korea, Monthly Bulletin, various issues.

Economic Planning Board, Major Statistics of Korean Economy, 1983.

a/ Annual average.

at 480 won per dollar since 1975. Because of the high rate of domestic inflation relative to price increases in Korea's major trading partners, the real exchange rate had appreciated by more than 18 per cent. Over the years, exchange rate devaluation had become a politically unpopular and increasingly difficult measure to carry out. Given real wage rigidity, it was argued that devaluation would simply be dissipated into price rises without improving export competitiveness. Understandably, domestic-market-oriented firms always resisted devaluations. In the 1970s, the opposition was joined by exporters who had accumulated large amounts of foreign loan liabilities.

Exporters were concerned about possible large losses in their net real foreign asset positions associated with discontinuous and unexpected devaluations. 12/ While resisting devaluation, exporters demanded, and the Government often acquiesced in, continuous increases in export subsidies - mostly financial - to compensate for the loss in competitiveness resulting from the overvalued currency. It was therefore not surprising that Nam (1981) found that the real effective exchange rate inclusive of export subsidies was much more stable than the rate without the subsidies (p. 194).

In announcing the stabilization package, the Government also reaffirmed its determination to continue to apply a tight fiscal and monetary policy. By January 1980, however, the economy had already begun to slow down, and in succeeding months the overall performance of the economy deteriorated further. Concerned with this development, the Government eased its restrictive policy during the latter half of the year. However, the gradual relaxation did not have much impact on the level of economic activity. The rice crop failure and political uncertainties together with the deepening world recession contributed to a decline of GNP by 6.2 per cent, while prices shot up by almost 40 per cent and the current account deficit rose to $5.3 billion, equal to 9.4 per cent of GNP, in 1980.

In early 1981, economic recovery remained as elusive as before despite a strong surge in export orders. The Government took a further reflationary measure in April and official interest rates were lowered on three occasions during the last two months of 1981. The nominal dollar exchange rate was devalued by about 12 per cent, but because of the rapid domestic inflation, the real exchange rate appreciated by 3 per cent for the year as a whole.

Overall policy during the year may be described as a strategy of muddling through; at best it was moderately expansionary. However, aided by the relative stability of import and food prices, the rate of inflation slowed to about 20 per cent for the year. There was a small reduction in the current account deficit which was the result of an upturn in export growth and a slowdown in domestic demand. Investment demand was particularly sluggish, declining 6 per cent from the previous year's level.

The moderately expansionary policy pursued throughout 1981 gave way to an actively reflationary policy in 1982 partly by design, but mostly in response to a financial scandal that broke out in May of that year which required a substantial infusion of fresh credit into the economy. In January, the Government implemented a number of measures aimed at stimulating investment in housing construction and exports. These measures were followed by a reduction of bank interest rates on both deposits and loans by an average of 4 percentage points. This adjustment, together with the financial scandal and a proposal that would have imposed greater regulatory oversight on the unofficial financial sector, contributed to a sharp increase in the supply of money. At year-end, M_2 had grown by 27 per cent and M_1 by almost 46 per cent. Nevertheless, the rapid liquidity expansion did not have much impact either on inflation or on the current account. Wholesale prices rose by less than 5 per cent for the year as a whole, and the current account deficit was about one half of the level a year before. Some of the causes of the marked decline in the rate of inflation could be traced to a substantial decline in import prices, a good harvest, wage restraint, and considerable unused capacity in many sectors of manufacturing. In 1982, the actual output of the non-primary sector was 79 per cent below its potential output.

With the expectation of an imminent recovery of the world economy, policy-makers placed domestic price stability ahead of all other objectives in 1983. Accordingly, they reversed the policy stance from moderately expansionary to restrictive. In 1983, the expansion of the money supply was limited to 17 (M_1) and 15.2 per cent (M_2) respectively. A substantial increase in private consumption and private construction induced by the large liquidity increase of the previous year and a strong recovery in export earnings during the latter part of 1983 paved the way for 9.3 per cent growth in GNP. What was so remarkable about the economic performance of 1983 was that despite the impressive growth, prices (WPI) remained virtually unchanged and the current account deficit narrowed to $1.6 billion, a little over 2 per cent of GNP. Several factors contributed to the price stability. Food prices remained stable, oil prices declined, and, most of all, the capacity utilization rate in the non-primary sector was still less than 85 per cent.

The decomposition exercise in table 10 shows that the deterioration in the current account in 1979 was entirely the result of a fall in real exports. The worsening in the terms of trade and a surge in real import demand combined to widen the current account imbalances, despite impressive export growth in 1980. This was followed in 1981 and 1982 by a current account improvement caused by a reduction in domestic spending and export growth. A substantial improvement in the terms of trade was one of the major factors behind the smaller current account deficit in 1982. Export growth and a further gain in the terms of trade helped reduce the deficit to 2.2 per cent of GNP in 1983. From 1980 to 1983, the accumulation of foreign debt added to the change in the ratio of the current account deficit to potential GDP by about one percentage point on average per year.

Table 10

Decomposition of change in the current account between each year and 1977/78 base year[a]

(All variables are represented as ratios to potential GDP)

		1979[b]	1980	1981	1982	1983
I.	Actual change in the ratio of current account imbalances to potential output	4.838	6.099	4.398	1.675	0.607
II.	Terms of trade effect	-1.581	6.186	8.014	4.860	4.015
	(i) Import price changes	-2.846	6.490	8.666	3.719	3.142
	(a) Capital goods	-1.507	-0.645	-0.331	-0.139	0.216
	(b) Oil	0.389	3.892	4.472	3.973	3.274
	(c) Other	-1.728	3.242	4.524	-0.114	-0.348
	(ii) Export price changes	1.265	-0.303	-0.651	1.141	0.873
III.	Interest rate effect	0.586	1.308	1.746	1.534	0.945
IV.	Accumulated debt effect	-0.324	0.082	0.457	0.653	0.886
V.	Import adjustment	2.143	-0.641	-1.192	-0.724	-0.842
	(i) Import substitution for capital goods	1.003	-0.278	0.644	-0.246	0.061
	(ii) Import substitution for non-capital goods	1.666	-0.284	-1.095	0.310	0.271
	(iii) Oil conservation efforts	-0.526	-0.079	-0.741	-0.788	-1.174
VI.	Export promotion (Construction services)	5.106 (0.789)	4.309 (1.464)	2.753 (1.272)	2.216 (0.986)	0.123 (1.674)
VII.	Aggregate demand adjustment	-1.213	-5.269	-7.538	-7.012	-4.771
	(i) Change in investment spending	0.228	-1.154	-2.281	-1.778	-0.981
	(ii) Change in aggregate demand policy	-1.442	-4.114	-5.257	-5.234	-3.790
VIII.	Total effect (II+III+IV+V+VI+VII)	4.715	5.977	4.240	1.527	0.455
IX.	Interaction effects and adding-up errors (I-VIII)	0.123	0.122	0.158	0.148	0.152

a/ See Appendix 1 for a description of and data used for the decomposition.
b/ The decomposition factors were calculated using an average of current year and base period weights.

Note: Negative sign indicates a change for a balance of payment improvement.

6.   EFFICIENCY AND OPTIMALITY OF FOREIGN BORROWING IN KOREA

(a)   Growth and foreign borrowing

At an abstract theoretical level, it is possible to create a set of conditions that govern the optimality or efficiency of foreign borrowing. The actual application of these conditions to a fast-growing economy like Korea involves many difficulties, and it is not easy to assess the allocative efficiency or optimality of foreign borrowing. Our analysis in this section contains more informed speculation than hard facts, because hard facts are hard to obtain, and when it comes to allocative efficiency, economics does not tell us much. Hence, our conclusions are no more than strong impressions.

Has foreign borrowing been extended beyond or kept below the point which would optimize the long-run growth of the country's GNP? While there do not seem to be universally-accepted criteria for judging the optimality of foreign borrowing, several pieces of evidence suggest that Korea has not borrowed over and above what may be regarded as an optimal or prudent level.

At a macroeconomic level, Sachs (1981) argues that the buildup in external debt should not pose a problem if it reflects increased investment in the context of rising or stable, but not declining, saving rates. The growth in debt might be a cause of concern if borrowing reflected an attempt to maintain consumption at unsustainable levels. Judging by this criterion, Korea has not borrowed beyond its debt-service capacity. 13/ As pointed out earlier, the Korean Government exercises almost complete control over the allocation of foreign loans between industries and sectors. Because of the strict supervision, the degree of diversion of loans to uses other than designated ones appears to be relatively low (Park, 1984). Furthermore, private claims on non-residents have been practically non-existent. Although subject to considerable fluctuations, domestic savings as a proportion of GNP have been rising in recent years (see table 4 in Appendix 2).

During the first three Five-Year Plan periods, the actual rates of growth consistently exceeded the target rates set by the planners, and did so during the second Plan period by as much as 3 percentage points. Despite the rapid growth in foreign debt, consumption as a percentage of GNP declined during this period. Frank, Kim and Westphal (1975) show that, assuming a gross capital-output ratio of 2.5, about 4 percentage points of Korea's growth rate could be attributed to foreign savings during the 1960s (p. 107). Using actual incremental capital-output ratios, the Bank of Korea (1984) has also estimated the contribution of foreign savings to growth. During the 1970s, the estimates show that the contribution declined with the rapid rise in the capital intensity of the economy. Nevertheless, foreign savings during the 1972-1982 period accounted for an average of 1.8 percentage points of Korea's actual annual growth. The same study shows that between 1967 and 1982 foreign savings contributed to employment growth by as much as 36 per cent of the actual increase in employed workers over the period. These estimates are no more than rough calculations and certainly overstate the actual contribution, as they ignore other factors that contribute to growth. Nevertheless, they point to the important role foreign capital has played in the country's economic development.

(b) Efficiency of foreign loan allocation in the 1960s

Few firms in Korea can expect to borrow from abroad without payment guarantees issued by the domestic financial institutions controlled by the Government. Mainly through the guarantee system, the Government regulates access to international capital markets, the sectoral destination of foreign capital, and the types of investment projects to be financed by foreign loans. Table 6 in Appendix 2 presents a breakdown of the sectoral destination of both commercial and public loans since 1966. As can be seen from that table, except for the 1980-1982 period, the social overhead capital sectors received almost as much from both commercial and public sources as did manufacturing. Within manufacturing, heavy and chemical industries have received a growing share of foreign capital inflows. Krueger (1975) has little doubt that the social rate of return on capital exceeded the foreign borrowing rate which means that foreign loans were effectively used during the 1960s (p. 199). 14/ However, there were incentives for excessive borrowing and hence misallocation of resources in the latter part of the 1960s because of the large discrepancy between the actual foreign interest rate adjusted for exchange rate depreciation and a domestic financing cost which was more than 15 percentage points in favour of foreign borrowing (see table 4).

During the 1966-1970 period, the foreign interest rate adjusted for foreign inflation was about 1.5 per cent, whereas the real cost of foreign borrowing faced by Korean borrowers was negative (about -3 per cent). Since borrowers expected a stable exchange rate, 15/ this expectation understated the true cost of borrowing and induced Korean firms to borrow more than they otherwise would have done.

If Korean borrowers had been allowed to borrow up to the level at which the real rate of return to capital equals the cost of borrowing, given the rate differential between the home and international capital markets, the aggregate level of borrowing would have been too high to be absorbed in an efficient manner. 16/ Such a large inflow would have distorted sectoral resource allocation because the negative real interest rates on foreign borrowing would have induced local borrowers to use capital-intensive techniques and to invest in more capital-intensive industries. In addition, there would have been sectoral inefficiencies because some sectors were relatively favoured and some were disadvantaged, in contrast with what would have happened had all been free to borrow at the true social cost. In particular, foreign commercial loans were often tied to imports of capital goods. As a result, low-cost foreign loans favoured those sectors that were relatively heavy users of imported capital equipment (Frank, Kim and Westphal, 1975, p. 117).

In practice, however, the Government approved foreign loans on the basis of their investment priority ranking and profitability. This rationing constrained the level of foreign borrowing well below the level that would have been realized in the absence of Government control. In most cases, foreign loans financed only a fraction of the total cost of the projects undertaken. The remainder had to be obtained from domestic sources at much higher rates (Krueger, 1979, p. 200).

Although an excess of foreign borrowing occurred during the latter part of the 1960s because of distorted incentives, Krueger (1975) argues that the low cost of foreign borrowing did not constitute a major distortion in resource allocation. The reason was that much of the foreign borrowing was allocated to efficient export-oriented industries which were labour-intensive in their factor uses and enjoyed comparative advantage (p. 201).

(c)   Efficiency of foreign loan allocation in the 1970s

During the 1970s, the real interest rates on foreign borrowing continued to be negative, though the differential between domestic and foreign borrowing costs (row VII in table 4) was almost negligible. This suggests that, unlike the situation in the 1960s, foreign borrowing certainly constituted a major distortion in resource allocation, if it did not exceed an optimal level, in the 1970s.

Korean firms have used increasingly more capital-intensive techniques and invested in capital-intensive industries. Using the manufacturing census data, Hong (1979) shows that the capital intensity in manufacturing rose steadily between 1966 and 1976. Over the decade, the intensity - capital stock per worker - more than doubled (p. 26). Our calculation shows that the capital intensity in 1980 was almost four times as high as it was in 1968. Reflecting this rising trend, the aggregate capital intensity of exports has risen rapidly since 1960, and by 1975, it had increased to 3.1 from 0.6 in 1960. Although we do not have any recent data, it very probably rose at a faster rate in the latter part of the 1970s.

Although it is difficult to associate changes in factor intensity with those in the wage-rental ratio, the subsidies on credit including foreign loans could in part be held responsible for the rise. In particular, it was probably true in the case of the rise of the capital intensity of exports since exporters have been by far the most favoured borrowers. More important, however, the Government has allocated a growing share of domestic and foreign resources through credit rationing to capital-intensive heavy and chemical industries in the process of restructuring the manufacturing sector of the economy.

As presented in table 11, the actual amount of investment undertaken in the heavy and chemical industries between 1977 and 1979

Table 11

Investment in manufacturing*
(billions of won at 1975 prices)

	Plan 1977/81 (A)	1977	1978	1979 (P)	1977/79 (B)	Achievement (B)/(A) (%)
Investment in						
Heavy industry	2,893	588	1,024	1,194	2,806	97
Basic metals	731	263	357	331	951	130
MES a/	1,145	139	309	379	827	72
Chemical & others	1,017	186	358	484	1,028	101
Light industry	1,621	193	252	304	749	46
Textiles	900	152	140	155	447	50
Others	721	41	112	149	302	42
Total	4,515	781	1,276	1,498	3,555	78

Source: Economic Planning Board (EPB).

*   This table is also quoted by Balassa (1980).

a/   MES stands for machinery, electronics and ships.

was enormous and larger than the actually planned level which was, in
retrospect, ambitious to begin with. It was excessive in that much of
the investment in these industries turned into idle capacity. To be
sure, some industries - iron and steel, shipbuilding, and electronics -
have been successful in improving their efficiency and in expanding
their export markets. Largely, thanks to the good performance of these
industries, the share of heavy industrial exports in total manufactured
exports has been rising (see table 9 in Appendix 2). During 1980-1982,
the share was 45 per cent, twice the level of the early 1970s.

However, chemicals, including petroleum and petroleum products,
non-ferrous metals, and machinery have failed to achieve efficiency in
terms of international competitiveness and largely remain high-cost

industries with unpromising future export prospects. 17/ A large part of the investment - in some cases as much as 50 per cent - of these inefficient industries has been financed by foreign borrowing. As presented in table 9 in Appendix 2, during 1970-1974 the three high-cost industries received more than 60 per cent of the total foreign loans allocated to heavy and chemical industries, and that share has not declined. Policy-makers in Korea often argue that the three sectors are primarily developed for domestic import substitution in most developing countries, and hence a certain degree of inefficiency is to be expected. In the case of Korea, they have been promoted not only for purposes of import substitution, but also as future exporters exploiting the economies of scale. This strategy has resulted in higher resource costs than would have been incurred if they had been developed only for import substitution. 18/

7.   ECONOMIC PROSPECTS AND MACRO-SIMULATIONS FOR 1984-1988

(a) Revision of the Fifth Five-Year Development Plan, 1982-1986, and macro-projections through 1988

Two years into the Fifth Five-Year Development Plan, the Government undertook an overall revision of the target levels for major macro-variables for the remaining plan period and also produced projections through 1988. 19/ The revision was predicated on the marked changes which had occurred in the world economic environment in recent years. The initial plan had been formulated during 1980/81 when the economy was suffering from the oil price increases, higher foreign interest rates and political uncertainties caused by the death of President Park. The expectations of high rates of inflation throughout the world, rising interest rates in the international financial market and widespread trade protectionism convinced the planners that Korea would be quite successful in managing economic policy if it could hold down the rate of inflation to about 10 per cent and maintain a current account deficit of $4 billion on average per year during the plan period.

As shown in section 6, after decades of double-digit inflation, price increases tumbled to 4.7 per cent, while the economy recovered from the recession and grew by more than 9 per cent in 1982. This was followed by another year of price stability in 1983 when wholesale prices rose by less than one per cent. Resumption of rapid growth did not cause any deterioration in the balance of payments. In fact, the current account improved considerably and recorded a deficit of $2.65 billion in 1982 and $1.6 billion in 1983, well below the target level.

In the early months of 1983, the future prospects of the world economy looked much brighter than before. Prices of raw materials including oil were expected to remain stable, foreign interest rates fell sharply, and the country's major trading partners were slowly recovering from the recession. The Korean planners have also become more confident about their ability to maintain price stability with rapid growth. These internal and external developments led to a mid-period adjustment of the plan and to setting more ambitious macro-economic targets.

According to the revised plan summarized in table 12, it is projected that the Korean economy will maintain the momentum of rapid growth without running into either inflation or balance-of-payments difficulties. The new plan envisages an economy that will be growing at an annual rate of 7.5 per cent with an annual rate of inflation of 2 per cent for the next five years beginning in 1984. What is so impressive about the revised plan is that the current account will continue to improve and register a surplus in 1986 and thereafter. As presented in table 13 the invisible trade account is expected to be in deficit for the next five years, but a marked improvement in the trade balance will more than offset the deficit on invisibles and generate a current account surplus. The driving forces behind this remarkable performance of the economy are a sustained rise in the domestic propensity to save and a real export growth of over 10 per cent for the next five years. Domestic savings as a percentage of GNP are assumed to rise to over 31 per cent in 1988 from less than 25 per cent in 1983. Many people have expressed their skepticism about these assumptions as being too optimistic, although a series of studies undertaken for the plan revision support these projections. 20/

The expected improvement in the current account will reduce Korea's foreign borrowing requirements substantially below the level initially projected. The total requirements for the Fifth Five-year Plan period were originally placed at $46.5 billion. The revision brought down this figure to $31.7 billion. At the end of 1988, total foreign debt outstanding will be about $49.3 billion, an increase of 22 per cent over the 1983 level as opposed to the initial figure of more than $60 billion (see table 14). Indeed, if the economy follows the growth path mapped out by the planners, Korea is not going to experience any debt-service problem. In fact, debt-service payments as a proportion of total current earnings (total exports and transfer receipts) are expected to fall below 15 per cent in 1986 and to about 14 per cent in 1988 (see table 15).

This section is not concerned with the question whether the assumptions underlying the plan are realistic or whether the planned targets are attainable. Instead, it attempts to investigate, utilizing a simulation model developed by Bacha (1983) that is quite different from the Korean government model, the types of problems the Korean economy is likely to encounter in the course of promoting rapid growth through export expansion on alternative sets of assumptions concerning prospects of the world economy.

(b)   A simulation model for Korea

We reproduce below Bacha's model for simulation exercises, in which output is demand-determined subject to a foreign exchange

Table 12

Expenditure on gross national product in 1980 Prices
(billions of won)

	1983	1984a/	1985	1986	1987	1988	'84 – '88 Annual rate of increase (per cent)
Gross national product	45,634.6	48,994.7	52,669.3	56,619.5	60,865.9	65,430.9	7.5
Consumption	33,318.9	35,031.2	36,934.2	38,940.6	41,056.2	43,286.9	5.3
Government	4,636.5	4,742.8	4,979.9	5,228.9	5,490.4	5,764.9	4.4
Private	28,682.4	39,288.4	31,954.2	33,711.7	35,565.9	37,522.0	5.5
Gross investment	14,217.3	15,013.2	16,744.6	18,368.6	20,142.4	22,079.4	10.3
Fixed capital formation	15,136.4	15,748.1	17,007.9	18,368.6	19,838.0	21,425.1	8.0
Incremental capital-output ratio	3.80	4.61	4.63	4.65	4.67	4.69	
Increase in stocks	-919.1	-734.9	-263.3	–	304.3	654.3	
Total exports	19,286.5	21,759.1	24,002.2	26,272.3	28,460.8	30,558.9	9.4
Merchandise	14,749.1	16,661.4	18,497.5	20,353.2	22,125.2	23,792.7	9.6
Invisible	4,537.4	5,097.7	5,504.7	5,919.0	6,335.6	6,766.2	8.4
Total imports	21,126.5	22,848.6	24,627.2	26,481.8	28,346.3	30,358.0	7.7
Merchandise	16,467.8	17,507.3	18,790.4	20,262.5	21,737.7	23,345.4	7.4
Invisible	4,658.7	5,341.3	5,836.8	6,219.3	6,608.6	7,012.6	8.4
Foreign saving	1,840.0	1,089.4	625.0	209.5	-114.5	-200.9	
Domestic saving	12,315.6	13,963.5	15,735.1	17,678.8	19,809.7	22,144.0	
(Average propensity to save)	(0.242)	(0.259)	(0.273)	(0.286)	(0.299)	(0.312)	
(Marginal propensity to save)	(0.385)	(0.463)	(0.414)	(0.424)	(0.435)	(0.445)	
GNP deflator (rate of increase)	2.9	0.9	2.0	2.0	2.0	2.0	1.8

Source: Bank of Korea, *Economic Statistics Yearbook, 1984* and data provided by Economic Planning Board.

a/ Figures for 1984-1988 are government projections.

Table 13

Balance of payments
(in hundreds of $ million)

	1979	1980	1981	1982	1983	1984a/	1985	1986	1987	1988
Current balance	-42	-53	-46	-26	-16	-10	-3	4	10	12
Trade balance	-44	-44	-36	-26	-17	-10	-1	6	12	14
Exports	147	172	207	209	231	265	309	357	404	452
Imports	191	216	243	235	248	275	310	351	392	438
Invisible trade balance	-2	-14	-15	-6	-6	-6	-8	-8	-8	-8
Receipts	48	54	66	75	71	82	93	105	117	130
Payments	50	67	81	80	77	88	101	113	125	138
Unrequited transfers (Net)	4	5	5	5	6	6	6	6	6	6
Long-term capital (Net)	27	19	28	12	13	12	7	2	-3	-7
Basic balance	-15	-35	-18	-14	-3	2	4	6	7	5
Short-term capital (Net)	8	19	-1	0	9	-2	-	-	-	-
Errors and omissions	-3	-4	-4	-13	-10	-6	-6	-3	-	-
Overall balance	-10	-19	-23	-27	-4	-6	-2	3	7	5
Bank borrowings (Net)	19	29	27	33	3	10	6	4	-	3
Change in foreign exchange reserves	8	9	3	1	-1	4	4	7	7	8
Foreign exchange reserves	57	66	69	70	69	73	78	85	92	100

Source: Bank of Korea, *Economic Statistics Yearbook*, 1984, and data provided by Economic Planning Board.

a/ Figures for 1984-1988 are government projections.

Table 14

The uses and sources of foreign capital
($ million)

	1983	1984a/	1985	1986	1987	1988	'84 – '88 Amount	'84 – '88 Composition (%)
Uses of foreign capital								
I. Current account deficit	1,607	1,000	300	-400	-1,000	-1,200	-1,300	-4.2
II. Increase in foreign exchange holdings	-73	400	400	700	700	800	3,000	9.8
III. Debt service	2,760	3,010	3,560	4,030	4,630	5,000	20,230	66.2
IV. Exports on credit and others	1,620	1,620	1,850	1,700	1,600	1,850	8,620	28.2
Total (I + II + III + IV)	5,914	6,030	6,110	6,030	5,930	6,450	30,550	100.0
Sources of foreign capital								
I. Long-term capital	5,597	5,830	5,760	5,530	5,530	5,950	28,600	93.6
II. Short-term capital	122	-200	-	-	-	-	-200	-0.6
III. Foreign banks "A" account	94	200	100	200	-	-	500	1.6
IV. Foreign direct investment	101	200	250	300	400	500	1,650	5.4
External debts outstanding	40,448	43,410	45,710	47,410	48,310	49,260		
External asset holdings	9,330	11,285	12,685	14,485	46,435	18,685		
Net external debts	31,118	32,125	33,025	32,925	31,875	30,575		

Source: Bank of Korea, Economic Statistics Yearbook, 1984, and data provided by Economic Planning Board.

a/ Figures for 1984–1988 are government projections and minus sign means a surplus.

Table 15

Debt service as percent of GNP
(in hundreds of $ million, and percentages)

	1979	1980	1981	1982	1983	1984a/	1985	1986	1987	1988
Long-term debt service (A)	26	29	38	45	47	54	63	69	77	81
Total debt service including short-term interest payment (B)	31	41	56	60	58	66	74	80	88	92
Nominal GNP (C)	624	612	672	708	751	801	887	973	1,088	1,217
Total exports plus transfer receipts (D)	195	226	273	284	302	347	402	462	521	582
A/C (per cent)	4.2	4.7	5.7	6.4	6.3	6.7	7.1	7.1	7.1	6.7
B/C (per cent)	5.0	6.7	8.3	8.5	7.7	8.2	8.3	8.2	8.1	7.6
A/D (per cent)	13.3	13.0	13.8	15.9	15.4	15.7	15.6	15.0	14.7	14.0
B/D (per cent)	16.3	18.5	20.7	21.0	19.3	19.0	18.4	17.4	16.9	15.9

Source   Bank of Korea, Economic Statistics Yearbook, 1984, and data provided by Economic Planning Board.

a/ Figures for 1984-1988 are government projections.

constraint. One might question the applicability of the Bacha model to the Korean economy, where it is widely accepted that domestic saving, not the foreign exchange, is the constraining variable. It would nevertheless be instructive to compare the Government's projections with our simulation results and to observe how the Korean economy would behave in a foreign exchange-constrained regime.

(1)   Import functions

Imports (M_t) consist of current and capital goods. The former (J_{yt}) depend on the level of domestic output, Z_t, and the latter (J_{kt}) on gross fixed investment (I_t).

$$M_t = P_t \cdot J_{yt} + P_t \cdot J_{kt}$$

$$J_{yt} = 1.27 \ Z_t$$

$$J_{kt} = 1.28 \ I_t$$

where the coefficients are derived by averaging the actual figures for the past few years, and P_t is the dollar price level.

(2)   Export function

The foreign export demand for Korean goods and services is exogenous except when the economy is operating at capacity. In that case, exports (X_t) are determined as a residual between total supply and domestic absorption.

$$E_t = P_t \cdot X_t$$

$$X_t = X_0 \ (1 + x)^t \ X_{Max,t}$$

where x is the rate of growth of real export demand. In our simulation exercises, we will alter x to generate different profiles of economic growth.

(3)   Balance of payments

In this model both foreign capital inflows and reserve accumulation are given exogenously, so that the current account deficit (D_t) is also exogenous.

$$D_t = M_t + V_t - E_t$$

$$V_t = r_t \cdot F_{t-1}$$

$$F_t = F_{t-1} + D_t$$

where V_t is factor services in dollars, r_t is the rate of return to foreign capital, and F_t is net stock of foreign capital.

(4) Consumption, investment and domestic absorption

Domestic consumption (C_t), which includes inventory changes, is related to national income, and fixed investment is generated by the availability of foreign exchange. By definition, domestic absorption is equal to the sum of national output and the current account deficits (or supluses) net of factor services.

$$P_t \cdot C_t = 0.76 (Z_t - V_t/P_t + R_t/P_t) - 4,350$$

$$P_t \cdot I_t = P_t \cdot A_t - P_t \cdot C_t$$

$$P_t \cdot A_t = P_t \cdot Z_t + D_t - V_t$$

where R_t is remittances and A_t is domestic absorption.

(5) Potential output and exports

$$Z_t^* = (1 - a) Z_{t-1}^* + 0.38 I_{t-1} \, ,$$

where 0.38 is an estimate for the ratio of potential output to capital stock.

Actual exports cannot surpass the value of potential exports :

$$X_t \quad X_t^*$$

Where X^* is given by

$$X_t^* = e \cdot Z_t^*$$

and e is the potential export ratio.

(6) Dollar price level

$$P_t = P_0 (1 + a)^t \, ,$$

where $P_0 = 1$ and a is the rate of increase of P.

(7) Employment

$$N_t = h \cdot Z_t$$

where β is the income elasticity of employment and $N_0 = 100$.

(c) Simulation scenarios and exercises

For our simulation exercises, we have used the following values for the exogenous variables in 1983 in dollars million.

$Z^* = 83,000,$ $X = 29,807,$ $V = 3,400,$

$D = 1,600,$ $F = 30,800$

The value for Z^* was calculated on the assumption of full capacity utilization in 1978. The values for the subsequent years were then obtained from the potential output equation. The implied capacity utilization rate, the ratio of actual to potential output, in 1983 was about 87 per cent.

In the following scenarios, it is assumed that terms of trade remain constant and that dollar inflation will be running at 5 per cent per annum. At this stage, it is very difficult to forecast the behaviour of world interest rates. Although they have risen recently and may go up further, many experts believe that they would come down to about 12 per cent and remain at that level. We assume that throughout the 1984-1990 period, Korea will continue to pay the average dollar interest rate (the rate of return to capital) of 10 per cent. The income elasticity of employment is estimated to be 0.5 on the basis of past actual figures.

In all our simulation exercises, it is assumed that the marginal propensity to save will rise to 30 per cent by 1986, starting from 24 per cent in 1983, and remain at that level. The implied average propensity to save from the consumption function will then rise to 35 per cent in 1986 before falling to 34 per cent. The figures for the marginal propensity to save aresubstantially lower than those estimated for the revised plan that range from 38.5 per cent in 1983 to 42.4 per cent in 1986 (see table 12). The current account is assumed to record a deficit of $1 billion in 1984 and $0.6 billion in the following year. Thereafter, the current account is assumed to be in balance. We have assumed different rates of growth of real export demand for different simulations, all of which are lower than the rate assumed by the Korean planners. The first simulation sets it at 8.2 per cent for the 1984-86 period and then 8 per cent for the remaining years. The other three simulations are the same as the first except that the real growth rate of export demand for 1987-90 is set at 7 per cent in the second simulation, 6 per cent in the third, and 5 per cent in the fourth.

In summarizing the results of these simulations, the following five points require emphasis.

(1) The revised plan targets and projections through 1988 for major macro variables do not appear to be unrealistic and could in fact be easily attained if no dramatic disturbances in the world economy are foreseen. With the assumptions of a real rate of growth of exports between 8 and 10 per cent per year and the dollar interest rate of about 12 per cent, it is not difficult to duplicate the growth path of the economy envisioned in Korea's revised Fifth Five-Year Plan. That is, if the assumptions concerning the export growth rate and foreign interest rates are reasonable, Korea could continue to grow at 7.5 per cent per year without experiencing any balance-of-payments problems.

(2) In all our simulations, it is shown that the Korean economy will fall short of utilizing fully its productive capacity. Even when the economy is growing at 8 per cent as in simulation 2, the capacity utilization rate does not rise above 86 per cent on average. This implies that domestic austerity emphasized in the revised plan may not be called for to maintain a 7.5 per cent annual growth. However, the utilization rate could rise sharply if we assumed a higher rate of real export growth and higher marginal propensity to save as indicated by simulation 1. As noted before, the Korean planners do not consider the availability of foreign exchange as a crucial constraint on future growth and stability. They are confident about eliminating the current account deficit within a couple of years. Even if they fail to do so, they believe that the foreign financing needed will be forthcoming.

(3) The relatively low rate of capacity utilization may suggest some room for further growth that could be facilitated by a relaxation of external constraints. However, it should be pointed out that the low rate of capacity utilization reflects in part the idle capacities caused by the excessive investment undertaken in some of the heavy and chemical industries during the latter part of the 1970s. The recent experience does not necessarily support the proposition that these idle capacities could be utilized to meet any future increase in the demand for these industries' products.

(4) Export promotion does not appear to be the only way of alleviating the foreign exchange constraint. Import coefficients are relatively high in Korea. This means that, along with energy substitution, import replacement - in particular of capital goods - could help ease the foreign exchange constraint. This observation should not be interpreted as supporting a policy shift to a more inward-looking development strategy. It merely emphasizes the need for removing the biases against import substitution of capital goods.

(5) We have also experimented with higher dollar rates of interest up to 12.5 per cent. Because of the substantial improvement in the current account assumed in our simulation, the increase of the interest rate by two percentage points could be absorbed and would not hurt the growth performance of the Korean economy.

Table 16.   Simulations for 1984-1990

Economy parameters

Incremental output-capital ratio	0.38
Annual depreciation rate	3.33
Output elasticity of employment	0.50
Share of non-capital goods in total supply in base year	1.00
Share of capital goods imports in gross investment in base year	1.00
Maximum annual growth of real consumption	20.00
Maximum marginal savings rate	0.35
Real dollar value of capital goods imports given by	$0 + JK \times I(T)$
Real dollar value of non-capital goods imports given by	$0 + JY \times Z(T)$
Real dollar value of consumption	$-4,350 + (1-S) \times (PY(T) \times Z(T) - V(T) + R(T)/PC(T)$

8.   SUMMARY AND CONCLUDING REMARKS

The purpose of this study has been to analyze Korea's experience with foreign debt accumulation and management over the past two decades, 1965-1983. Although this study does not address the debt-servicing capacity, several studies and some of the conclusions of this study suggest that Korea is not likely to experience any debt-servicing difficulties in the near future. This assessment has been reinforced by the remarkable performance of the economy for the last two years. With the continuing world economic recovery, Korean planners forecast that the current account deficit, which has been declining, will turn into a surplus by 1986. Thereafter, Korea's gross debt will fall as a proportion of GNP. These rosy projections are somewhat dampened by several aspects of the structure of debt that suggest potential risks. One such aspect is that the accumulation of current account deficits and hence foreign debt has been mostly the result of investment in excess of savings in the public sector, in particular by para-statal corporations. Another aspect that may be of some concern is that during the two oil crisis periods adjustment to the external shocks was greatly facilitated by the improvement of the external environment. Except for export promotion, the authorities were not able to make other adjustments that might be of greater significance if the trade environment deteriorates.

In summarizing this study, one could hazard several tentative conclusions which are not necessarily backed by strong evidence or hard facts.

(1) The accumulation of external debt in Korea has been closely associated with chronic current account deficits and the need for holding larger foreign exchange reserves. Capital account transactions have by and large been accommodating and have financed the current account deficits. 21/ Under these circumstances, policy efforts aimed at slowing down the growth of external debt have been concentrated on eliminating the current account imbalances.

(2) With a limited number of policy tools whose effectiveness is at best uncertain, it has not been possible to achieve simultaneously all three objectives of growth, price stability, and external (current account) balance. Whenever any conflicts have arisen between the growth target and the management of external debt, Korean planners have not hestitated to sacrifice the balance-of-payments and price stability objectives. They have been able to pursue this growth-first policy because of the availability of foreign finance. The availability has not been fortuitous, but is the result of Korea's exceptional economic performance.

(3) Rapid growth through the promotion of exports is expected to reduce gradually Korea's dependence on foreign resources. While the growth of exports and output was impressive, the current account

remained persistently in deficit throughout the 1970s. Korea experienced a foreign debt crisis - or more properly a balance-of-payments crisis - during 1970/71 and the first and second oil crisis periods. The country's policy response to the debt crisis and to the first oil crisis was to step up export promotion by engineering a substantial real exchange rate (including export subsidies) depreciation. Each time exports grew rapidly - in part thanks to the depreciation - and rescued Korea from the crisis.

During the second oil crisis, however, Korea shifted its policy to a more classical prescription. Monetary and fiscal policies were tightened and the real exchange rate was depreciated to move resources to the tradeable goods sector. Once again, exports have responded (of course with the help of the world economic recovery) and spared Korea from potentially embarrassing debt-servicing problems.

(4) In the absence of the second oil crisis and the subsequent high interest rates and world economic recession, Korea could have maintained external balance and certainly avoided the doubling of the debt between 1979-83. Our counterfactual analyses, for what they are worth, indicate that Korea's current account deficits could have been lower by about 3 per cent of potential real GDP in 1973 if there had been no oil price increases. The adverse impact of external shocks on Korea's external position was more dramatic during the second oil crisis. In the absence of the shocks, Korea would have accumulated a significant surplus since 1981, and achieved near balance in 1980. These exercises also show roughly the magnitude of the debt accumulation Korea could have avoided but for external disruptions. In fact, with 1978 oil prices and foreign interest rates, the debt potential GDP ratio would not have increased at all since 1979 (see tables 17 and 18).

From the pattern of policy adjustment to external shocks in the 1970s, one can infer that Korean planners did not have any view on an appropriate level or flow of foreign capital. Since 1979, mounting debt and the debt-service burden in an uncertain international financial environment have made policy-makers aware of the magnitude of Korea's debt problem. The revised Fifth Five-Year Development Plan reflects this growing concern and determination on the part of the Government to reduce the rate of growth of the debt, but the revised document does not indicate the level of debt the authorities consider optimal, though it is clear that they are trying to eliminate the current account deficit as soon as possible. In view of the growing debt, the Government has been actively encouraging foreign direct investment and has begun since 1982 to implement a number of measures that have relaxed restrictions imposed on foreign investment and to simplify the processing of foreign investment project proposals.

(5) In order to examine the prospects of the Korean economy until 1990, we have undertaken simulation exercises under different scenarios of the future course of the world economy. We have compared the projections generated by the simulation model with those made by the

Foreign Debt, Balance of Payments, Growth Prospects: Korean Case

Table 17

Counterfactual analysis a/
(percentages)

	1972	1973	1974	1975	1976	1977
I. Actual ratio of current account deficit to potential output	4.61	3.52	11.35	9.43	2.26	0.56
II. Hypothetical ratio with oil prices fixed at 1973 level (I - II)	—	—	8.10 (3.24)	5.68 (3.75)	-1.60 (3.85)	-3.19 (3.75)
III. Hypothetical ratio with interest rates fixed at 1973 level (I - III)	—	—	11.16 (0.18)	8.92 (0.51)	2.20 (0.06)	0.49 (0.07)
IV. Hypothetical ratio with fixed oil prices and interest rates (I - IV)	—	—	7.92 (3.43)	5.17 (4.26)	-1.65 (3.91)	-3.26 (3.82)
V. Hypothetical ratio with 1973 level construction service exports (I - V)	—	—	11.37 (-0.03)	9.52 (-0.09)	3.68 (-1.42)	3.82 (-3.26)
VI. Hypothetical ratio with 1973 oil prices, interest rates and construction service exports (I - VI)	—	—	7.95 (3.40)	5.26 (4.17)	-0.24 (2.49)	-0.01 (0.57)

a/ Based on the decomposition exercise in Appendix 1.

Table 18

Counterfactual analysis[a]
(percentages)

	1977	1978	1979	1980	1981	1982	1983
I. Actual ratio of current account deficit to potential output	0.5	3.16	6.72	7.96	6.33	3.56	2.48
II. Hypothetical ratio with oil prices fixed at 1973 level (I - II)	-	-	5.49 (1.23)	3.51 (4.45)	-1.67 (4.66)	-0.62 (4.18)	-0.96 (3.44)
III. Hypothetical ratio with interest rates fixed at 1973 level (I - III)	-	-	6.21 (0.51)	6.65 (1.31)	4.42 (1.91)	1.83 (1.73)	1.36 (1.12)
IV. Hypothetical ratio with fixed oil prices and interest rates (I - IV)	-	-	4.98 (1.73)	2.20 (5.76)	-0.24 (6.57)	-2.35 (5.91)	-2.07 (4.55)
V. Hypothetical ratio with 1973 level construction service exports (I - V)	-	-	5.95 (0.77)	6.73 (1.23)	5.65 (0.68)	3.37 (0.19)	1.72 (0.76)
VI. Hypothetical ratio with 1973 oil prices, interest rates and construction service exports (I - VI)	-	-	4.21 (2.50)	0.97 (6.99)	-0.91 (7.24)	-2.55 (6.11)	-2.83 (5.31)

a/ Based on the decomposition exercise in Appendix 1.

Korean Government. Our simulation shows that the Korean economy could easily grow at an annual rate of 7.5 per cent without running balance-of-payments problems, provided that the demand for real exports grows at 8 to 10 per cent per year and that foreign interest rates do not rise above 12.5 per cent.

Even when the economy is growing at 8 per cent per year, it is expected that the rate of capacity utilization will fall below 87 per cent. An important question is whether this result means that the saving mobilization efforts currently mounted by the authorities are misguided. The Korean planners believe that the future growth of the economy will be constrained by domestic savings, not by the availability of foreign exchange. The relatively low rate of capacity utilization reflects the idle capacities caused by the excessive investment undertaken in heavy and chemical industries during the latter part of the 1970s. It is not altogether clear at this stage whether the existing idle capacities in some of the heavy and chemical industries could be utilized to meet the future increase in both the domestic and foreign demand for these industries' products.

Appendix 1

Decomposition exercise

$$\frac{D_t}{Y_t^*} = J_{kt}\left(\frac{P_{kt}}{P_{yt}}\right)\left(\frac{I_t}{Z_t^*}\right) + J_{0t}\left(\frac{P_{0t}}{P_{yt}}\right)\left(\frac{Z_t}{Z_t^*}\right) + J_{yt}\left(\frac{P_{jt}}{P_{yt}}\right)\left(\frac{Z_t}{Z_t^*}\right) + r_t\left(\frac{NF_{t-1}}{Y_t^*}\right)$$

$$\left(\frac{-P_{xt}}{P_{yt}}\right)\left(\frac{X_t}{Z_t^*}\right) \text{1/}$$

D	=	Current account deficit in current dollars;
Y^*	=	Potential domestic output in current dollars;
Z^*	=	Potential domestic output in 1975 dollars;
Z	=	Actual domestic output in 1975 dollars;
I	=	Fixed investment in 1975 dollars;
NF_{t-1}	=	Gross foreign debt in current dollars at the end of previous year;
X	=	Exports of goods and non-factor services in 1975 dollars;
J_k	=	Ratio of capital goods imports in 1975 dollars to fixed investment in 1975 dollars;
P_0	=	Dollar price index of crude oil imports with 1975 = 1.0;
P_k	=	Dollar price index of capital goods imports with 1975 = 1.0;
P_y	=	Implicit price deflator of GDP (with 1975 = 1.0) divided by the dollars/domestic currency exchange rate (with 1975 = 1.0);
J_y	=	Ratio of non-capital-goods imports in 1975 dollars to domestic output in 1975 dollars;
J_0	=	Ratio of crude oil imports in 1975 dollars to domestic output in 1975 dollars;
P_j	=	Dollar price index of non-capital-goods imports (with 1975 = 1.0);

1/ This decomposition of the current account is suggested by Bacha (1983).

r   =   Rate of return on foreign capital, expressed as the ratio of factor payments abroad in dollars in the current year to the dollar value of gross foreign debt at the end of previous year;

P_x =   Dollar price index of exports with (1975 = 1.0);

t   =   Calendar year.

$$\Delta\left(\frac{D_t}{Y_t^*}\right) = [J_{ko}\left(\frac{I_o}{Z_o^*}\right)\Delta\left(\frac{P_{kt}}{P_{yt}}\right) + J_{yo}\left(\frac{Z_o}{Z_o^*}\right)\Delta\left(\frac{P_{jt}}{P_{yt}}\right) + J_{oo}\left(\frac{Z_o}{Z_o^*}\right)\Delta\left(\frac{P_{ot}}{P_{yt}}\right)$$

$$- \left(\frac{X_o}{Z_o^*}\right)\Delta\left(\frac{P_{xt}}{P_{yt}}\right)] + \left(\frac{NF_{t-1}}{Y_o^*}\Delta\, r_t\right) - \left(\frac{P_{xo}}{P_{yo}}\right)\Delta\left(\frac{X_t}{Z_t^*}\right)$$

$$+ [\left(\frac{P_{ko}}{P_{yo}}\right)\left(\frac{I_o}{Z_o^*}\right)\Delta J_{kt} + \left(\frac{P_{jo}}{P_{yo}}\right)\left(\frac{Z_o}{Z_o^*}\right)\Delta J_{yt} + \left(\frac{P_{oo}}{P_{yo}}\right)\left(\frac{Z_o}{Z_o^*}\right)\Delta J_{ot}]$$

$$+ [J_{ko}\left(\frac{P_{ko}}{P_{yo}}\right)\Delta\left(\frac{I_t}{Z_t^*}\right) + J_{yo}\left(\frac{P_{jo}}{P_{yo}}\right)\Delta\left(\frac{Z_t}{Z_t^*}\right) + J_{oo}\left(\frac{P_{oo}}{P_{yo}}\right)\Delta\left(\frac{Z_t}{Z_t^*}\right)]$$

$$+ r_o\Delta\left(\frac{NF_{t-1}}{Y_t^*}\right) + \text{2nd and 3rd order terms.}$$

1. $\Delta\left(\dfrac{D_t}{Y_t}\right)$ = Actual change in the ratio of current account imbalances to potential output;

2. $J_{ko}\left(\dfrac{Z_o}{Z_o^*}\right)\Delta\left(\dfrac{P_{kt}}{P_{yt}}\right)$ = Change in the relative price of imported capital goods;

3. $J_{oo}\left(\dfrac{Z_o}{Z_o^*}\right)\Delta\left(\dfrac{P_{ot}}{P_{yt}}\right)$ = Change in the relative price of crude oil;

4. $J_{yo}\left(\dfrac{Z_o}{Z_o^*}\right)\Delta\left(\dfrac{P_{jt}}{P_{yt}}\right)$ = Change in the relative price of other imported goods;

5. $\left(\dfrac{X_o}{Z_o}\right)\Delta\left(\dfrac{P_x}{P_y}\right)$ = Relative export price changes;

<u>Terms of trade effect</u> = 2 + 3 + 4 - 5

6. $\left(\dfrac{NF_o}{Y_o}\right)\Delta\, r_t$ = Interest rate effect;

7. $r_o\Delta\left(\dfrac{NF_{t-1}}{Y_t}\right)$ = Accumulated debt effect;

8. $(\frac{P_{ko}}{P_{yo}})$ $(\frac{I_o}{Z_o^*})$ Δ J_{kt} = Import adjustment for capital goods;

9. $(\frac{P_{jo}}{P_{yo}})$ $(\frac{Z_o}{Z_o^*})$ Δ J_{yt} = Import adjustment for non-capital goods;

10. $(\frac{P_{0o}}{P_{yo}})$ $(\frac{Z_o}{Z_o^*})$ Δ J_{0t} = Oil conservation efforts;

Import adjustment = 8 + 9 + 10

11. $(\frac{P_{xo}}{P_{yo}})$ Δ $(\frac{X_t}{Z_t^*})$ = Export promotion;

12. $J_{ko}(\frac{P_{ko}}{P_{yo}})$ Δ $(\frac{I_t}{Z_t^*})$ = Change in investment spending;

13. $J_{yo}(\frac{P_{jo}}{P_{yo}})$ Δ $(\frac{Z_t}{Z_t^*})$ + $J_{0o}(\frac{P_{0o}}{P_{yo}})$ Δ $(\frac{Z_t}{Z_t^*})$

= Change in aggregate demand policy;

Demand adjustment = 12 + 13.

Appendix 2

Table

1. Korea's external debt, 1960-1983

2. Indicators of Korea's debt-servicing capacity

3. Sources of current account imbalances in current market prices

4. Domestic savings, gross fixed investment, and current account as percent of GNP, 1965-1983

5. Foreign loans and investment

6. Foreign loans by destination

7. Indices of nominal and real exchange rate

8. Wages, productivity, and unit labour cost in manufacturing

9. Foreign loans allocation and export performance in heavy and chemical industries

Table 1   Korea's external debt, 1960-1983   ($ million)

	1961	1962	1963	1964	1965	1966	1967	1968	1969	1970	1971	1972
I. Long-term	4 (18.2) b/	10 (17.2)	52 (49.5)	78 (56.5)	121 (68.4)	285 (81.0)	487 (75.4)	893 (74.5)	1,376 (76.4)	1,702 (75.8)	2,332 (78.8)	2,833 (78.9)
(1) Long-term loans	4	10	52	78	112	276	474	808	1,261	1,594	2,116	2,670
Public	4	10	33	42	52	114	191	301	446	588	906	1,320
Private	-	-	19	36	60	162	282	506	815	1,006	1,210	1,350
(2) Bank loans	-	-	-	-	-	-	-	40	70	75	153	155
(3) Bonds outstanding	-	-	-	-	-	-	-	-	-	-	-	-
(4) IMF facilities	-	-	-	-	9	9	13	45	45	33	63	8
II. Medium-term	18 (81.8)	48 (82.8)	53 (50.5)	59 (43.5)	56 (31.6)	62 (17.6)	93 (14.4)	218 (18.2)	230 (12.8)	170 (7.6)	111 (3.8)	116 (3.2)
(1) Trade credits	19	48	53	59	56	62	93	218	230	170	111	114
(2) Cash loans	-	-	-	-	-	-	-	-	-	-	-	2
III. Short-term c/	- (-)	- (-)	- (-)	- (-)	- (-)	6 (1.7)	66 (10.2)	89 (7.4)	186 (10.3)	357 (15.9)	450 (15.4)	600 (16.7)
(1) Private	-	-	-	-	-	-	60	72	114	193	246	397
(2) Banks	-	-	-	-	-	6	6	17	72	164	204	203
IV. Foreign banks "A" account d/	- (-)	- (-)	- (-)	- (-)	- (-)	- (-)	- (-)	- (-)	8 (0.6)	16 (75.8)	29 (1.0)	40 (1.1)
V. Total foreign debt	22	58	105	138	177	352	646	1,199	1,800	2,245	2,922	3,589
VI. Foreign direct investment	-	1	3	6	17	17	29	44	51	76	112	170
VII. GNP in nominal US dollar	2,103	2,315	2,718	2,876	3,006	3,671	4,274	5,226	6,625	7,834	9,370	10,570
VIII. Foreign Debt/GNP = V/VII (%)	1.0	2.5	6.0	4.8	5.9	9.6	15.1	22.9	27.2	28.7	31.2	34.0
IX. Foreign Debt plus direct investment/GNP = V+VI/VII (%)	1.0	2.5	6.1	5.0	6.4	10.0	15.8	23.8	27.9	29.6	32.4	35.6

Table 1 (cont'd)

Korea's external debt, 1960-1983
($ million)

	1973	1974	1975	1976	1977	1978	1979	1980	1981	1982	1983[a]
I. Long-term	3,420 (80.3)	4,545 (76.6)	5,745 (68.0)	7080 (67.2)	8,583 (67.9)	10,533 (70.8)	13,337 (65.1)	16,137 (58.9)	20,127 (61.9)	22,611 (60.6)	25,000 (62.3)
(1) Long-term loans	3,294	3,995	4,999	6,145	7,477	9,399	10,977	12,827	14,349	15,689	16,500
Public	1,688	2,028	2,470	3,114	3,640	4,320	5,270	6,531	7,899	9,374	–
Private	1,606	1,967	2,529	3,031	3,637	5,079	5,707	6,296	6,450	6,315	–
(2) Bank loans	126	399	465	483	602	620	1,980	2,309	4,174	5,322	6,500
(3) Bonds outstanding	–	19	19	93	163	251	242	288	358	341	600
(4) IMF facilities	–	132	262	359	341	263	138	713	1,246	1,259	1,400
II. Medium-term	139 (3.3)	153 (2.6)	302 (3.6)	408 (3.9)	350 (2.8)	483 (3.2)	561 (2.7)	617 (2.3)	602 (1.9)	488 (1.3)	600 (1.5)
(1) Trade credits	136	150	285	386	335	480	522	576	564	462	–
(2) Cash loans	3	3	17	22	15	3	39	41	38	26	–
III. Short-term[c]	612 (14.4)	1,136 (19.1)	2,167 (25.6)	2,681 (25.4)	2,923 (23.1)	2,593 (17.4)	4,651 (22.7)	7,575 (20.3)	8,486 (26.1)	10,307 (27.6)	10,500 (26.2)
(1) Private	489	413	1,158	1,499	1,828	1,041	2,251	4,158	4,110	4,020	–
(2) Banks	123	723	1,009	1,182	1,095	1,552	2,400	3,417	4,376	6,287	–
IV. Foreign banks "A" account[d]	89 (2.1)	103 (1.7)	242 (2.9)	364 (3.5)	792 (6.3)	1,262 (8.5)	1,951 (9.5)	3,036 (11.1)	3,275 (10.1)	3,908 (10.5)	4,000 (10.0)
V. Total foreign debt	4,260	5,937	8,456	10,533	12,648	14,871	20,500	27,365	32,490	37,314	40,100
VI. Foreign direct investment	325	481	544	646	737	826	953	1,023	1,128	1,228	1,596
VII. GNP in nominal US dollar	13,500	18,550	20,850	28,680	37,430	51,960	62,370	61,200	67,190	70,800	74,900
VIII. Foreign Debt/GNP = V/VII (%)	31.6	32.0	40.6	36.7	33.8	28.6	32.9	44.7	48.4	52.7	53.5
IX. Foreign Debt plus direct investment/GNP = V+VI/VII (%)	34.0	34.6	43.2	39.0	35.8	30.2	34.4	46.4	50.0	54.4	55.7

Source: Economic Planning Board, *Economic Indicators of Korea*, March 1983 and Bank of Korea, internal sources.

a/ Preliminary figures.
b/ Percentage of total foreign debt (V).
c/ Include trade credit and bank refinance.
d/ Foreign currency funds borrowed by the foreign bank branch offices from their headquarters or other branches for paid-in-capital and other operational uses.

Table 2

Indicators of Korea's debt-servicing capacity
(percentages)

	(I) Total Foreign debt GNP	(II) Debt service GNP	(III) Debt service ratio (Long-term only)	(IV) Debt service ratio (including interest on short-term	(V) Rescheduling probability a/	(VI) Real net interest payments as a percentage of of exports b/
1961	1.0	0.0	0.4	0.4	-	-
1962	2.5	0.1	0.7	0.8	9.5	-
1963	6.0	0.1	1.0	1.0	18.0	-
1964	4.8	0.2	2.6	2.6	22.3	-
1965	5.9	0.5	5.0	5.0	11.5	-
1966	9.6	0.4	3.0	3.2	7.4	-
1967	15.1	0.8	5.2	5.4	6.7	-
1968	22.9	0.9	5.2	5.4	8.0	-
1969	27.2	1.5	7.8	8.6	9.4	-
1970	28.7	3.3	18.2	18.5	10.9	-
1971	31.2	3.6	19.8	21.0	14.2	-
1972	34.0	3.9	18.4	18.7	9.8	-
1973	31.6	4.5	14.2	14.8	2.0	-
1974	32.0	3.8	12.4	14.4	2.3	-0.8
1975	40.6	4.1	12.0	14.4	2.9	-0.6
1976	36.7	4.0	10.6	12.1	2.0	2.0
1977	33.8	4.2	10.2	11.1	1.3	0.6
1978	28.6	4.6	12.3	13.9	1.3	0.1
1979	32.9	5.1	13.3	16.3	1.2	-1.1
1980	44.7	6.9	13.0	18.5	1.2	-1.6
1981	48.4	8.4	13.8	20.7	1.2	3.0
1982	52.7	8.4	15.9	21.0	1.6	6.9
1983	53.5	7.9	15.4	19.3	-	-

Source: Various tables in Appendix 2.

a/ Probability figures are from Kim (1983).
b/ Data obtained from Dooley, Helkie, Tryon, and Underwood (1983).

Table 3 — Sources of current account imbalances in current market prices (in billion won)

Year	Private Sector Individual (A)	Private Corporations (B)	Financial Institutions (C)	Sub-total (D=A+B+C)	Public Sector Government (E)	Para-statal Corporations (F)	Sub-total (G)	Statistical Errors (H)	Current Account Deficits & Surpluses (I)	A/GNP (%)	B/GNP (%)	C/GNP (%)	D/GNP (%)	E/GNP (%)	F/GNP (%)	G/GNP (%)	H/GNP (%)	I/GNP (%)
1963	7.3	-9.5	-3.1	-5.3	7.4	-15.8	-8.4	-4.9	-18.6	1.5	-1.9	-0.6	-1.1	1.5	-3.1	-1.7	-1.0	-3.7
1964	12.4	-7.3	0.4	5.5	12.4	-12.5	-0.1	-11.2	-5.8	1.7	-1.0	0.1	0.8	1.7	-1.7	-0.0	-1.6	-0.8
1965	17.6	-31.1	1.0	-12.5	19.7	-11.4	8.3	10.0	5.7	2.2	-3.9	0.1	-1.6	2.4	-1.4	1.0	1.2	0.7
1966	31.3	-69.8	1.7	-36.8	7.7	-12.4	-4.7	13.5	-28.1	3.0	-6.7	0.2	-3.5	0.7	-1.2	-0.5	1.3	-2.7
1967	26.3	-72.5	-0.6	-46.9	21.7	-48.8	-27.1	22.1	-51.9	2.1	-5.7	-0.1	-3.7	1.7	-3.8	-2.1	1.7	-4.1
1968	36.9	-133.1	-5.8	-102.1	21.0	-34.7	-13.7	-6.0	-121.8	2.2	-8.1	-0.4	-6.2	1.3	-2.1	-0.8	-0.4	-7.4
1969	76.4	-139.7	-0.0	-63.3	-20.0	-61.3	-81.3	-13.6	-158.2	3.5	-6.5	-0.0	-2.9	-0.9	-2.8	-3.7	-0.6	-7.3
1970	34.0	-188.8	-3.8	-158.6	19.7	-58.9	-39.2	4.3	-193.5	1.2	-6.9	-0.1	-5.8	0.7	-2.2	-1.4	0.2	-7.1
1971	57.0	-188.7	-3.4	-135.1	-6.1	-125.5	-131.6	-28.0	-294.7	1.6	-5.6	-0.1	-4.0	-0.2	-3.7	-3.9	-0.8	-8.7
1972	146.5	-39.1	-5.1	102.3	-80.9	-195.2	-276.1	29.2	-144.6	3.5	-0.9	-0.1	2.5	-1.9	-4.7	-6.6	0.7	-3.5
1973	370.9	-238.8	5.1	137.2	-64.6	-104.4	-169.0	-91.4	-123.2	6.9	-4.4	0.1	2.6	-1.2	-1.9	-3.1	-1.7	-2.3
1974	263.0	-582.4	33.5	-285.9	-183.1	-213.1	-396.2	-138.3	-820.4	3.5	-7.8	0.4	-3.8	-2.4	-2.8	-5.3	-1.8	-10.9
1975	167.7	-394.1	5.8	-220.6	-265.0	-463.2	-728.2	35.5	-913.3	1.7	-3.9	0.1	-2.2	-2.6	-4.6	-7.2	0.4	-9.0
1976	513.8	-438.7	54.3	129.4	162.0	-438.5	-276.5	-4.6	-151.8	3.7	-3.2	0.4	0.9	1.2	-3.2	-2.0	-0.0	-1.1
1977	1,063.0	-518.8	108.0	652.2	-175.7	-735.4	-911.1	264.7	6.0	5.9	-2.9	0.6	3.6	-1.0	-4.1	-5.0	1.5	0.0
1978	1,306.9	-1,439.5	172.8	40.2	110.1	-1,015.5	-905.4	339.9	-525.3	5.4	-5.9	0.7	0.2	0.5	-4.2	-3.7	1.4	-2.2
1979	1,286.8	-2,812.0	217.8	-1,307.4	99.9	-1,145.1	-1,045.2	343.4	-2,009.2	4.1	-9.0	0.7	-4.2	0.3	-3.7	-3.3	1.1	-6.4
1980	561.0	-2,737.5	218.1	-1,958.4	-444.4	-1,302.3	-1,746.7	480.8	-3,224.3	1.5	-7.4	0.6	-5.3	-1.2	-3.5	-4.7	1.3	-8.7
1981	521.5	-1,562.4	88.2	-952.7	-562.7	-1,861.4	-2,424.1	358.5	-3,018.4	1.1	-3.4	0.2	-2.1	-1.2	-4.1	-5.3	0.6	-6.6
1982	1,618.6	-578.1	-581.6	458.9	-66.5	-2,287.2	-2,353.7	-59.2	-1,954.0	3.1	-1.1	-1.1	0.9	-0.1	-4.4	-4.5	-0.1	-3.8
1983	1,711.2	-2,105.1	-481.6	-875.5	1,153.4	-1,674.0	-520.6	174.5	-1,221.6	2.9	-3.6	-0.8	-1.5	2.0	-2.9	-0.9	0.3	-2.1

Source: Bank of Korea, Economic Statistics Yearbook, various issues.

a/ A, B and C refer to the difference between savings minus investment in each sector.
b/ Figures for savings and investment of government invested corporations include non-financial operations of Federations of Agricultural and Fisheries Corporations.

Table 4

Domestic savings, gross fixed investment, and current
account as percent of GNP, 1965-1983
(percentages)

	Gross fixed investment/GNP	Saving/GNP	Current account/GNP
1965	14.8	7.4	0.3
1966	20.2	11.8	-2.8
1967	21.4	11.4	-4.5
1968	25.0	15.1	-8.4
1969	25.8	18.8	-8.3
1970	22.9	15.7	-7.8
1971	21.5	14.6	-9.0
1972	20.0	16.5	-3.5
1973	23.4	22.8	-2.3
1974	25.3	19.9	-10.9
1975	25.5	19.1	-9.0
1976	24.1	23.9	-1.1
1977	26.7	27.5	0.0
1978	30.8	28.5	-2.1
1979	32.8	28.1	-6.7
1980	31.9	21.9	-8.7
1981	28.9	21.7	-6.9
1982	30.3	22.4	-3.7
1983	31.8	24.5	-2.2

Source: Economic Planning Board, Korean Economic Indicators, 1983.

Table 5

Foreign loans and investment a/
($ million)

| | Total
I = II + III | Loans (II) | | (III)
Direct
Foreign
Investment |
		Public	Commercial	
1959–61	4.4	4.4	–	–
1962–66	307.9	115.6 (37.5)[b/]	175.6 (57.0)[b/]	16.7 (5.4)[b/]
1967–71	2,261.8	810.8 (35.8)	1,354.7 (59.9)	96.4 (4.3)
1972–76	5,988.8	2,388.9 (39.9)	3,043.9 (50.8)	556.0 (9.3)
1977–79	7,652.0	2,529.5 (33.1)	4,793.7 (62.6)	328.8 (4.3)
1980–83	11,084.7	6,246.5 (56.4)	4,434.1 (40.0)	404.1 (3.6)

Source:　Economic Planning Board, Handbook of Korean Economy, 1983.

a/　Arrival basis.

b/　As percent of total.

Table 6

Foreign loans by destination
($ million)

	1966-1970	1971-1975	1976-1980	1981/82
Total	1,693.2 (100.0)	4,523.2 (100.0)	11,810.5 (100.0)	5,734.1 (100.0)
Agriculture, Forestry and Fisheries	193.5 (11.4)	588.9 (13.0)	795.8 (6.7)	528.2 (9.2)
Mining	17.6 (1.0)	– –	10.2 (0.1)	13.8 (0.2)
Manufacturing	674.1 (39.8)	1,753.0 (38.8)	4,658.7 (39.4)	873.9 (15.2)
Heavy & Chemical	384.1 (57.0)a/	1,191.1 (67.9)	3,649.4 (78.3)	734.6 (84.1)
Light	290.1 (43.0)a/	561.9 (32.1)	1,009.3 (21.7)	139.3 (15.9)
Social overhead	668.8 (39.5)	1,348.7 (29.8)	4,581.9 (38.8)	3,183.9 (55.5)
Services	110.3 (6.5)	603.9 (13.4)	1,718.3 (14.5)	828.3 (14.4)
Others	29.9 (1.8)	228.4 (5.0)	38.9 (0.3)	306.0 (5.3)

Source: Economic Planning Board, Economic Indicators of Korea, 1983.

a/ As percent of manufacturing.

Table 7

Indices of nominal and real exchange rate

	1962	1963	1964	1965	1966	1967	1968	1969	1970	1971	1972
Nominal exchange rate a/	372.31 (130.00) e/	372.31 (130.00)	226.33 (213.85)	181.77 (266.27)	178.38 (271.33)	178.92 (270.51)	174.96 (276.64)	167.81 (288.42)	155.56 (311.13)	137.97 (350.80)	122.85 (393.97)
Effective nominal exchange rate(ENE) b/	410.13	410.78	251.09	202.55	196.32	201.57	198.67	188.94	174.17	151.04	125.03
Purchasing power Parity(PPP) c/	310.56	258.86	198.92	185.45	173.42	155.03	141.90	130.55	117.03	106.87	104.88
Real effective exchange rate(REER) d/	119.88 (430.73) e/	143.83 (336.51)	113.78 (425.39)	98.01 (493.80)	102.86 (470.54)	115.41 (419.37)	123.29 (392.56)	128.54 (376.54)	132.92 (364.12)	129.10 (374.90)	117.13 (413.21)

	1973	1974	1975	1976	1977	1978	1979	1980	1981	1982
Nominal exchange rate a/	121.51 (398.32)	100.00 (405.97)	100.00 (484.00)	100.00 (484.00)	100.00 (484.00)	100.00 (484.00)	100.00 (484.00)	79.68 (607.43)	71.07 (681.03)	66.20 (731.13)
Effective nominal exchange rate(ENE) b/	116.23	118.40	100.00	101.04	96.58	85.01	86.24	69.97	63.55	63.24
Purchasing power Parity(PPP) c/	122.92	119.08	100.00	90.42	89.92	92.53	84.45	74.48	64.42	57.87
Real effective exchange rate(REER) d/	98.85 (489.61)	100.12 (483.41)	100.00 (484.00)	110.60 (437.62)	111.21 (435.22)	108.08 (447.83)	118.47 (408.55)	106.98 (452.43)	110.32 (438.72)	114.39 (423.11)

Source: IMF, International Financial Statistics, various issues.

a/ Monthly average.

b/ Effective nominal exchange rate is calculated as a weighted average of the won prices of the currencies of Korea's four major trading partners, where the weights are given by the four countries' trade share.

c/ Trade weighted.

d/ REER = $e_k = \sum_{i=1}^{4} w_i \cdot WPI_i \cdot e_i / CPI_k$, where e_k : the won-dollar exchange rate, w_i : the trade weight for country i.

WPI_i : WPI for country currency-dollar exchange rate, CPI_k : CPI for Korea.

e/ Figures in parenthesis are the levels of nominal and real exchange rates.

Table 8

Wages, productivity, and unit labour cost in manufacturing

	Nominal Wages			Consumer Price Index 1975 = 100	Real Wages			Labour Productivity a/		Unit Labour Cost	
	Amount (Won)	Index 1975=100	Change (%)		Amount (Won)	Index 1975=100	Change (%)	Index(B) 1975=100	Change (%)	(A/B) 1975=100	Change (%)
1960	2,330	6.1	-	14.1*	16,525	43.1	-	19.0	-	32.1	-
1961	2,610	6.8	11.5	15.3*	17,059	44.4	3.0	21.3	12.1	31.9	-0.6
1962	2,780	7.2	5.9	16.3*	17,055	44.4	0.0	21.8	2.3	33.0	3.4
1963	3,180	8.3	15.3	19.6*	16,224	42.3	-4.7	23.2	6.4	35.8	8.5
1964	3,880	10.1	21.7	25.5*	15,216	39.6	-6.4	25.3	9.1	39.9	11.5
1965	4,600	12.0	18.8	27.6	16,667	43.4	9.6	29.7	17.4	40.4	1.3
1966	5,420	14.1	17.5	30.7	17,655	46.0	6.0	30.9	4.0	45.6	12.9
1967	6,640	17.3	22.7	33.9	19,587	51.0	10.9	36.3	17.5	47.7	4.6
1968	8,400	21.9	26.6	37.6	22,340	58.2	14.1	43.6	20.1	50.2	5.2
1969	11,270	29.4	34.2	42.3	26,643	69.4	19.2	55.1	26.4	53.4	6.4
1970	14,301	37.3	26.9	49.1	29,126	75.9	9.4	62.1	12.7	60.1	12.5
1971	16,611	43.3	16.2	55.7	29,822	77.7	2.4	68.0	9.5	63.7	6.0
1972	18,923	49.3	13.9	62.2	30,423	79.3	2.0	73.9	8.7	66.7	4.7
1973	22,330	58.2	18.0	64.2	34,782	90.6	14.3	80.4	8.8	72.4	8.5
1974	30,209	78.7	35.3	79.8	37,856	98.6	8.8	89.6	11.4	87.8	21.3
1975	38,378	100.0	27.0	100.0	38,378	100.0	1.4	100.0	11.6	100.0	13.9
1976	51,685	134.7	34.7	115.3	44,827	116.8	16.8	107.5	7.5	125.3	25.3
1977	69,168	180.2	33.8	127.0	54,463	141.9	21.5	118.7	10.4	151.8	21.1
1978	92,907	242.1	34.3	145.3	63,942	166.6	17.4	132.9	12.0	182.2	20.0
1979	119,515	311.4	28.6	171.9	69,526	181.2	8.7	153.9	15.8	202.3	11.0
1980	146,684	382.2	22.7	221.3	66,283	172.7	-4.7	170.4	10.7	224.3	10.9
1981	176,176	459.1	20.1	272.9	64,557	168.2	-2.6	197.2	15.7	232.8	3.8
1982	202,117	526.6	14.7	292.8	69,029	179.9	6.9	206.7	4.8	254.8	9.5

Source: Economic Planning Board, Monthly Statistics of Korea, various issues.
Ministry of Labour, Report on Monthly Labour Survey, various issues.
Office of Labour Affairs, Yearbook of Labour Statistics, 1971.

*   CPI in Seoul City.
a/   Labour productivity = output index/labour input index.

Table 9

Foreign loans allocation and export performance in heavy and chemical industries
($ million)

	1975-76		1977-78		1979-80		1981-82	
	Foreign Loans	Exports	Foreign Loans	Exports	Foreign Loans	Exports	Foreign Loans	Exports
I. Manufacturing	1,224.5	10,968.7	2,268.1	19,958.5	1,743.3	29,443.5	873.9	38,952.9
1. Heavy & Chemical Industries	868.6a/ (70.9)b/	3,587.4 (32.7)	1,829.8 (80.7)	7,501.0 (37.6)	1,400.7 (80.3)	12,705.2 (43.2)	734.6 (84.1)	19,397.0 (49.8)
(i) Chemicals	268.3 (30.9)c/	422.1c/ (11.8)	648.2 (35.4)	697.2 (9.3)	268.5 (19.2)	1,356.2 (10.7)	347.4 (47.3)	1,863.7 (9.6)
(ii) Metal & Nonferrous Metals	368.4 (42.4)c/	977.3 (27.2)	870.7 (47.6)	2,136.7 (28.5)	865.7 (61.8)	4,269.9 (33.6)	91.8 (12.5)	6,164.6 (31.8)
Iron & Steel	351.7 (40.5)c/	600.0 (16.7)	835.5 (45.7)	969.0 (12.9)	778.0 (55.5)	2,572.9 (21.7)		3,744.4 (19.3)
(iii) Transport Equipment	142.6 (16.4)c/	526.0 (14.7)	142.6 (7.8)	1,798.3 (24.0)	91.4 (6.5)	2,250.6 (17.7)	98.6 (13.4)	5,422.2 (28.0)
Shipbuilding	36.0 (4.1)c/	414.5 (11.6)	125.3 (6.8)	1,317.7 (17.7)	41.8 (3.0)	1,132.5 (8.9)		4,243.1 (21.9)
(iv) General Machinery	55.3 (6.4)c/	414.5e/ (11.6)	112.4 (6.1)	697.9 (9.3)	165.2 (11.8)	1,233.5 (9.7)	137.9 (18.8)	1,616.0 (8.3)
(v) Electrical Machinery	33.9 (3.9)c/	1,247.5 (34.8)	55.7 (3.0)	2,170.9 (28.9)	9.6 (0.7)	3,595.0 (28.3)	58.9 (8.0)	4,330.5 (22.3)
2. Light Industries	355.9 (29.1)b/	7,381.3 (67.3)	438.3 (19.3)	12,457.5 (62.4)	342.6 (19.7)	16,738.3 (56.8)	139.3 (15.9)	19,555.9 (50.2)

Source: Bank of Korea, Economic Statistics Yearbook, various issues and data provided by the Bank of Korea.

a/ SITC, 33, 5, 67, 68, 69, 7 and 86.
b/ As percent of manufacturing.
c/ As percent of heavy and chemical industries.
d/ Including petroleum and petroleum products (SITC 33).
e/ Including professional, scientific and controlling instruments, photographic and optical goods, watches and clocks (SITC 86).

FOOTNOTES

1. The official figures do not include the actual or contingent foreign exchange liabilities incurred by Korean companies' overseas construction and trading subsidiaries and by Korean banks' foreign offices. It is not clear whether these liabilities should be included in the official tally. When they are, it is estimated that Korea's external debt would amount to anywhere from $46 to $48 billion.

2. During 1966-1975, the cumulative increase in debt was smaller than the cumulative increase in current account deficits and reserves. It appears likely that some of the loans secured for military procurement were not included in the total debt. Definitional changes as well as errors and omissions may also explain some of the discrepancies.

3. Korea experienced a sharp rise in its debt-service ratio in the 1970-1972 period. However, the major concern at that time was not debt management problems but the growing current account deficits. On this point, see Krueger (1979), p. 148.

4. Government of the Republic of Korea (1983).

5. See Cole and Park (1983), Chapter 8.

6. See Park (1983).

7. The foreign interest rate in table 4 does not include the spread, fees and other costs, but then domestic lending rates also do not take account of other hidden costs. The level of the curb market rate indicates that the domestic lending rate was kept below a realistic level and thus the actual differentials to Korean borrowers were much higher than those shown in table 4.

8. For a detailed discussion see Cole and Park (1983), Chapter 5.

9. According to the Bank of Korea's definition based on KSIC (Korean Standard Industrial Classification), heavy and chemical industries include: 351 (Industrial Chemicals); 353 (Petroleum Products); 369 (Other Non-metallic Mineral Products); 371 (Iron and Steel); 372 (Non-ferrous Metals); 381 (Fabricated Metal Products except Machinery and Equipment); 382 (Non-electric Machinery); 383 (Electrical Machinery, Apparatus, and Appliances); 384 (Transport Equipment); and 385 (Professional and Scientific Measuring and Controlling Equipment, Photographic and Optical Products).

10. The removal was part of the move towards overall economic liberalization.

11. For an excellent analysis of the Government's stabilization policies, see Nam (1984).

12. According to Frank, Kim and Westphal (1975), similar problems were interfering with the conduct of exchange rate policy in the 1960s (p. 120).

13. This conclusion is also backed by other indicators of debt-servicing capacity.

14. From 1954 to 1971, the real rate of return to capital in manufacturing rose steadily from about 12 per cent to 26 per cent. Although these estimates overstate the actual return, they suggest that even after adjusting for risks the rate of return to capital in Korea was far higher than the real borrowing cost. See Hong (1979), pp. 180-181. The real rate of return in Hong's study is defined as the ratio of incremental value added to investment. It therefore represents the non-labour rate of return.

15. See Frank, Kim and Westpnal (1975), p.117,

16. The large accumulation of foreign reserves above a prudent level indicates the country's limited absorptive capacity during the 1960s.

17. This conclusion is based on a series of studies analyzing the cost of production and the international competitiveness of Korea's capital goods industries published by the Bank of Korea (1983).

18. The causes of excessive investment and the inefficiency of some of the heavy and chemical industries are discussed in detail by Park (1983).

19. For the details of the revised plan, see Government of the Republic of Korea (1984).

20. See Korea Development Institute (1983).

21. Commercial foreign loans, and public loans as well, are often tied to purchases of capital and intermediate goods abroad. Short-term private capital inflows have been essentially a financing item.

REFERENCES

Bacha, E.L., "Foreign Debt, Balance of Payments, and Growth Prospects of Developing Countries", 1983 (Mimeo).

Balassa, B., "Korea during the Fifth Five Year Development Plan: An Advisory Report", 1980 (Mimeo).

Cha, T.S., Park, S.Y., and Park, N.K., A Comparative Study of Export Competitiveness in Korea, Japan and Taiwan, KIET, Seoul, 1983 (Korean).

Cole, D.C., and Park, Y.C., Financial Development in Korea, 1945-78, Studies in the Modernization of the Republic of Korea, 1945-75, Council on East Asian Studies, Harvard University, 1983.

Corden, W.M., Inflation, Exchange Rates and the World Economy, (University of Chicago Press, 1977).

Dooley, M., Helkie, W., Tyron, R., and Underwood, J., "An Analysis of External Positions of Eight Developing Countries through 1990", International Financial Discussion Paper No. 227, August 1983, FRB.

Frank, C., Kim, K.S., and Westphal, L., Foreign Trade Regimes and Economic Development: South Korea, National Bureau of Economic Research, New York, 1975.

Government of Korea, A Revision of the Fifth Five Year Development Plan, Seoul, Korea, April 1984 (Korean).

Hong, W.T., Trade Distortions, and Employment Growth in Korea, Korea Development Institute, Seoul, Korea, 1979.

Kim, I.C., "Models of Foreign Debt Accumulation and Korea's Debt Management", KDI Review, Fall, 1983.

Kim, K.S., "The Pattern and Sources of Korea's Industrialization", KDI Working Paper, 1979.

Kim, K.S., and Roemer, M., Growth and Structural Transformation, Studies in the Modernization of the Republic of Korea, 1945-75, Council on East Asian Studies, Harvard University, 1979.

Korea Development Institute, Studies for a Revision of the Fifth Five-Year Development Plan, 1982-86: A collection of essays, November 1983, Seoul, Korea.

Krueger, A., The Developmental Role of the Foreign Sector and Aid, Studies in the Modernization of the Republic of Korea, 1945-75, Council on East Asian Studies, Harvard University, 1979.

Martin, R. and Selowsky, M., "Energy Prices, Substitution, and Optimal Borrowing in the Short-run", World Bank Staff Working Paper No. 466, July 1981.

Nam, C.H., "Trade, Industrial Policies, and Structure of Protection in Korea", in W.T. Hong and L. Krause (eds), Trade and Growth of the Advanced Developing Countries in the Pacific Basin, pp. 187-211. Seoul: Korean Development Institute, 1981.

Nam, Sang Woo, "Korea's Stabilization Efforts since the Late 1970's, KDI, 1984 (Mimeo).

Park, Y.C., "South Korea's Experience with Industrial Adjustment in the 1970's", ILO-ARTEP Working Paper, August 1983.

Park, Y.C., "Resource Allocation and Government Intervention", East-West Center, Honolulu, Hawaii, February 1984 (Mimeo).

Sachs, J., "Current Account and Macroeconomic Adjustment in the 1970's", Brookings Papers on Economic Activity 1, 1981.

The Bank of Korea, Summary Report of the 1980 Input-Output Table, Research Department, December 1982.

The Bank of Korea, Current State of Korea's Industries, Series No. 83-1 to 9, 1983.

The Bank of Korea, Foreign Debt and Domestic Savings, March 1984.

MEXICO'S RECENT BALANCE-OF-PAYMENTS EXPERIENCE
AND PROSPECTS FOR GROWTH

Ernesto Zedillo Ponce de León*

1. Introduction 1/

The evolution of Mexico's balance of payments since 1973 has been markedly different from what it had been during several decades. A single fact vividly illustrates this phenomenon: the net flow of the foreign public debt, which had averaged around $200 million a year throughout the previous two decades, increased to more than $1.6 billion in 1973 alone, and from then on, kept growing rapidly. Thus the stock of the foreign public debt, which was $6.8 billion at the end of 1972, reached almost $21 billion by the end of the Echeverría administration (1976), and soared to $58 billion by the time President López Portillo left office (1982). Taking into account the foreign debt of commercial banks and of private sector firms, the country's total external debt had reached $27.5 billion by late 1976, and stood at $84.1 billion six years later. Not surprisingly, the last two financial crises experienced by Mexico (1976 and 1982) have been closely linked to the size of its external debt.

It is the purpose of this study to analyse some aspects of the evolution of the country's balance of payments during the last decade, according to the framework suggested by Bacha. 2/ It is necessary for this purpose not only to look with some care at the possible impacts of external phenomena on this evolution, but also to review - albeit informally - the most relevant aspects of domestic macro-economic policy during the same period. After this recapitulation of the events of the period 1973-1983 an analysis of prospects is undertaken; again, this analysis is carried out, to the extent possible, within the framework suggested for all the country studies in this series.

In reviewing past events, it will prove very convenient to divide the analysis into three sub-periods: 1973-1977, 1978-1981 and developments since 1982. This analysis proceeds in three stages: first, it looks at the current account and its driving forces; second, it brings the capital account into the picture, which leads us to offer a few considerations on foreign-debt management; and, third, some comments are made on domestic macro policy.

*The author is Director, Banco de México. August 1985.

2.   The period 1973-1977

(a) The current account

The deficit in the current account averaged $750 million in the period 1966-1970, and had expanded to about $1 billion by 1972. Thereafter it rose rapidly to $4.4 billion in 1975, and fell back to $1.6 billion in 1977. Until 1976, the greater current account deficit was the result of the simultaneous occurrence of higher (and increasing) average import propensities, a somewhat overheated economy during 1973-1975, and a higher nominal interest rate on the foreign debt interacting with a larger size of this debt. Thus, the import content of real investment, which was 13.6 per cent in 1972, reached as much as 17.2 per cent in 1974, while the ratio of current imports to real output rose from 4 per cent to more than 6 per cent during the period. The implicit interest rate on the external debt exceeded 9 per cent during 1974-1975, having been around 6 per cent earlier in the period.

A more complete story can be told by decomposing the changes in the current balance into its various constituent parts, as suggested by Bacha. The decomposition used is given by the following expression. 3/

(1) $d(D/ZQD) =$ Deficit increase

$[(M2/ZD)_o d(PM2/PYD) + (M1/ZD)_o d(PM1/PYD)$ Terms of trade shock
$+ (M3/ZD)_o d(PM2/PYD)] - [(X1/ZD)_o$
$d(PX1/PYD) + (X2/ZD)_o d(PX2/PYD) + X3/ZD)_o$
$d(PX3/PYD) + (X4/ZD)_o d(PX4/PYD) + (X5/ZD)_o$
$d(PX5/PYD)]$

$+ (F_{-1}/ZQD)_o d(TAS)$ Interest rate shock

$-[(PX1/PYD)_o (X1/XW1)_o d(XW1/ZD)$ World recession shock
$+ (PX2/PYD)_o (X2/XW2)_o d(XW2/ZD)$
$+ (PX3/PYD)_o (X3/XW3)_o d(XW3/ZD) + (PX4/PYD)_o$
$(X4/XW4)_o d(XW4/ZD)]$

$+ (TAS)_o d(F_{-1}/ZQD)$ Burden of accumulated
                                                       debt

$+ (M2/ID)_o (PM2/PYD)_o d(ID/ZD)$ Fixed investment cuts

$+ (M1/YD)_o (PM1/PYD)_o d(YD/ZD) + (M3/YD)_o$
$(PM3/PYD)_o d(YD/ZD)$

Domestic output
contraction

$+ (PM2/PYD)_o (ID/ZD)_o d(M2/ID) + PM1/PYD)_o$
$(YD/ZD)_o d(M1/YD) + (PM3/PYD)_o (YD/ZD)_o$
$d(M3/YD)$

Import replacement

$- (PX1/PYD)_o (XW1/ZD)_o d(X1/XW1)$

$- (PX2/PYD)_o (XW2/ZD)_o d(X2/XW2)$

Export deepening

$- (PX3/PYD)_o (XW3/ZD)_o d(X3/XW3)$

$- (PX4/PYD)_o (XW4/ZD)_o d(X4/XW4)$

$- (PX5/PYD)_o d(X5/ZD)$

Effect of other
exports of services

$-d(V1/ZQD)$

Effect of interest
from abroad

$+d(V2/ZQD)$

Effect of profit
remittances

$+2$nd and 3rd order effects

In undertaking the decomposition, peso-measured variables were
translated into dollar figures by means of an "equilibrium" exchange
rate determined by a calculation of purchasing power parity. These
peso-measured variables were expressed in units of constant purchasing
power, a procedure that is most appropriate for studies that imply
international comparisons such as the present one. More particulars
concerning this rate can be found in the Appendix. The base year used
in the exercise was 1972, a year during which there was favourable GDP
growth, a moderate current account deficit, and a relatively stable
external environment.

As may be seen from table 1, a first interesting result is the
fact that the ratio of the current account deficit to potential GDP
deteriorated far beyond what was warranted by external shocks. The
latter, if not negligible, fall quite short of explaining the increased
external disequilibrium. In fact, the net impact of the terms of trade
and world recession shocks accounts for a rather low proportion of such
disequilibrium. This contrasts with the case of other developing
countries, where the manifold rise in the price of oil of 1973-1974 had
a very negative impact on the terms of trade. Mexico, being a marginal
importer of crude during those years, did not experience such a
deterioration (in three of the five years, the terms-of-trade shock has
a negative sign).

The picture corresponds rather to an economy trying to run at a pace faster than its historical trend, and where the realities of the external environment were ignored. Except in 1977, the values of the "domestic-recession" factor are positive. It would seem more correct to talk of "import-desubstitution", as suggested by the relevant coefficients, and the only positive policy response can be seen in the expansion of a few export categories with respect to world trade performance. Since the increase of the external debt was the "slack variable" of the system, it is not surprising to see its burden systematically augmenting the deficit ratio.

(i) The foreign debt

Table 2 shows how the current account deficit referred to above was financed. It is evident that the increased external disequilibrium was accompanied by an even bigger accumulation of external financial liabilities. If not nil, the net flow derived from direct foreign investment was quite modest. Consequently, the bulk of the balance-of-payments compensation had to rely on the growth of the external debt, expecially in the public sector component.

The same figures highlight a remarkable fact: increased indebtedness went far beyond what was demanded by the current deficit alone. As from 1973, the item "other capital flows and errors and omissions" started to have pronounced negative values, suggesting capital flight of considerable dimensions. 4/ As will be argued below, such outflows were very much related to the way in which domestic economic policy was conducted during the period.

By far the largest contributor to the capital account was the net flow of the foreign public debt. The evolution of this debt is shown in table 3. During 1970-1972, the net flow of the foreign public debt averaged only 1 per cent of GDP. The proportion more than tripled in 1973 and averaged 5.4 per cent in 1974-1976. Equally dramatic was the increase in the ratio of net flow to current account income - a proxy that more accurately depicts the growth of the debt with respect to the economy's capacity to service it. This ratio - of 11.6 per cent in 1971, the first year of the Echeverría administration - rose to more than 60 per cent in 1975 and 1976. It can also be seen that the increase in the foreign public debt far exceeded the increase in public expenditure and fiscal deficits during those years. Thus, the ratio of the net flow to public expenditure, which was normally around 6 per cent - see for example the figures for 1970-1971 - doubled in 1973 and tripled in 1976. As a proportion of the public sector's deficit, the aggregate average 60 per cent in the second half of the Echeverría administration (1974-1976), whereas it had averaged less than 40 per cent during the first half.

The spectacular growth of the foreign debt from 1973 onwards was accompanied by significant changes in several aspects of debt management that seem worth mentioning. 5/ First, let us look at the sources of credit. During the 1950s and early 1960s, credits granted by official entities - bilateral or multilateral institutions - were the main source of foreign public borrowing. This predominance of offical lending started to decline rather rapidly in the mid-1960s, so much so that by 1967 private financal flows were the main source of public external financing. This trend accelerated with the expansion of Mexican borrowing. Thus, by 1973, 55 per cent of the total stock of foreign public debt was owed to private financial institutions; three years later the proportion had increased to 75 per cent. Also during the same period, loans raised through syndications in the Eurocurrency market became the most popular instrument for tapping financial markets. Previously, direct bank loans had constituted the usual instrument. In turn, the greater reliance on syndicated Eurocredits allowed Mexico's foreign public debt to become much more diversified with respect to the number and nationalities of lending institutions. It also permitted a modest degree of diversification in the currencies in which the debt was denominated.

Relying on external financing was doubtless further encouraged by the relatively low cost of foreign savings. The nominal implicit interest rate paid on the foreign debt averaged somewhat less than 9 per cent during 1973-1976; however, when allowance is made for international inflation, the real rate was actually negative for the same period. This helps to explain why, in spite of the manifold increases in borrowing, the ratio of interest payments to total current account income did not rise very much until 1975-1976, as shown in the last column of table 3. Of course, as the debt mushroomed, lending conditions began to harden.

Although not as fast as its public sector counterpart, the foreign private debt increased at an average rate of almost $1 billion per year between 1972 and 1977.

(ii) Domestic economic policy

The foregoing shows that external shocks account for only part of the increased external disequilibrium and indebtedness during the period. As indicated by the analysis of table 1, internal "shocks" are also to be blamed for what happened in the economy's external sector. It is important, therefore, to describe - at least in very general terms - the main features of domestic economic policy during those years.

There is little doubt that the worsening of the country's external disequilibrium was a consequence of the abandonment of the "stabilized development" model that had been applied since the mid-1950s. 6/ The shift in policy is shown by the indicators of table 4.

Clearly, the active pursuit of financial stability, which had still commanded a great deal of respect in 1971, started to taper off in 1972. For one thing, GDP growth in 1971 had been the smallest for 18 years. Secondly, a mounting current of opinion at the highest government level felt that the economic policy model in effect since the mid-1950s had been "exhausted" and that, therefore, a change in priorities and in courses of action were long overdue. Consequently, public expenditure began to expand.

Although the new strategy had an immediate negative impact on the public sector deficit and on monetary expansion, it seemed to work well in many other important respects: GDP growth surged to 8.5 per cent, inflation was slightly higher than 5 per cent, and the current account deficit was not very different from the levels recorded in the two previous years - around $1 billion. These results reaffirmed the stance of those advocating a more active government involvement in the solution of social and economic problems through the expansion of public expenditure.

The "new medicine" was applied vigorously in 1973: public expenditure as a proportion of GDP, which had averaged 21 per cent during 1966-1970, reached 27 per cent; whereas the overall public sector's deficit relative to GDP (historically less than 2.5 per cent) soared to 6.9 per cent. This time, however, the "magic of 1972" worked rather imperfectly. Inflation climbed to a double-digit figure for the first time in almost two decades and the current account deficit jumped to $1.5 billion. Yet, GDP growth was sustained at the very respectable rate of 8.4 per cent and, furthermore, the financing of the enlarged external disequilibrium did not give rise to serious difficulties. As stated before, the net flow of the foreign public debt was easily increased many times over its trend value.

In spite of the noticeable acceleration of inflation and the financial and current account disequilibria of 1973 and the following years, economic policy was kept on the same track until the end of the administration. The early warning signals did little to induce a change of course. Undoubtedly, there was a marked change in the priorities of policy-makers during those years, partly provoked by the past accumulation of social and political demands, but also as a result of the very peculiar way in which President Echeverría exercised his governmental authority. Yet, it should be noticed that the main justification for the economic policy that prevailed at the time came from conditions abroad. For example, inflation was explained, not as a phenomenon caused by internal factors, but rather as a consequence of the worldwide rise in inflation. This was a most powerful argument for neglecting the urgency of pursuing an anti-inflationary policy. In turn, the recession in the industrial countries served as an argument for increasing domestic expenditure to compensate for the fall in external demand. The latter, because of its impact on Mexican exports, was also blamed for worsening the current account disequilibrium. As already seen, while these external factors were used to justify the economic policy, it was quite another external phenomenon that made such a policy sustainable over several years: the ample availability of foreign financing.

It is evident from table 4 that the seemingly smooth working of the "public-expenditure-led-growth model" did not last very long. In 1974, the rate of inflation - 12 per cent in 1973 - almost doubled, whereas GDP growth - though still high - fell by more than two percentage points compared to the previous year's rate. Economic growth further decreased in 1975 and 1976. At the same time, public finances continued to deteriorate and other economic policy instruments - such as the exchange rate 7/ and domestic interest rates - continued to be applied inflexibly, leading to a process of financial disintermediation that, together with the effective crowding out induced by public expenditure and other factors, produced stagnation in private investment. The explosive mixture of phenomena - mounting fiscal deficits, high rates of inflation, a fixed exchange rate, negative real rates of interests and bitter exchanges between the public and the private sectors about their respective roles in the economic and political life of the country - was bound to provoke the capital flight of which the evidence is given in the figures in table 2.

The situation became openly worrisome by late 1975; yet, only minor adjustments were made. After all, 1976 was an election year and foreign financing, if more expensive, was still available. Yet, during July and August, capital outflows became unbearable and on the eve of the last Presidential address - on 31 August - the crash occurred. The 22-year era of fixed parity was terminated and the peso was allowed to float against the dollar. By then, foreign sources of credit had shrunk and it became only a matter of days before a stand-by agreement had to be signed with the IMF as a precondition to avoid a complete exhaustion of external financing.

In short, the greater external disequilibrium of the Mexican economy until 1976 was provoked less by external shocks than by internal ones. The adoption of a broader range of economic and social objectives on the part of the government was not accompanied by more and better policy instruments. 8/ A sharply increased aggregate demand implied not only greater demand for imports, but also a reduced availability of surpluses to be exported. Such effects were further reinforced by the acceleration of domestic inflation vis-à-vis external rates. The latter phenomenon, interacting with a rather inflexible interest rate policy, implied a significant reduction in real yields of liabilities offered by domestic financial intermediaries. As a consequence, the rate of real growth of financial savings started to decline very rapidly, dropping to only one-sixth of what it had been during 1965-1970. As inflation continued - thus overvaluing the real exchange rate - and the external disequilibrium persisted, expectations about a peso devaluation rose sharply. The consequence was an avalanche of capital flight that was countered only by means of contracting more foreign loans and draining off foreign-exchange reserves.

The Echeverría administration, sincerely or not, tried to achieve more political and economic objectives than the administrations that had preceded it in the previous 40 years. Such efforts, however, demanded much more than an unbridled expansion of public expenditure and external borrowing. The final result was bound to be nothing less than a financial crisis, in the midst of which the López-Portillo administration took over in December of 1976.

Using the standard IMF recipe, 1977 can be qualified as truly a year of adjustment. Total real investment fell sharply, and GDP growth was the lowest in more than two decades. The average nominal exchange rate was   80 per cent higher than the rate that had been kept fixed during more than two decades. These adjustments formed the basis of the correction in the ratio of the current account deficit to potential GDP referred to previously.

Sacrifice as a guideline, however, did not last very long. As corrective remedies were being applied drastically, an important recovery-propelling factor materialized. It was revealed that the country's petroleum reserves were much larger than previously thought. Thus, proven hydrocarbon reserves, which were 6.4 billion barrels by end-1975, suddenly jumped to 11.2 billion by end 1976, and to 16 billion by late 1977. Undoubtedly, the fortunate discovery induced the earlier-than-expected recovery of the economy in 1978.

3.   The period 1978-1981

(a)   The current account during the boom years

The improvement in the ratio of the current account deficit to potential GDP achieved in 1977 was partially reversed in 1978 and the ratio continued to worsen rapidly, reaching in 1981 a value higher than the one registered in the "worst" years of the 1970s. The internal factors explaining the deterioration of the current account during the previous period intensified once again immediately after 1977. The economy's average propensity to import, as measured by the ratios of imports of capital goods to investment and imports of current goods and services to GDP, rose to record high values. Accelerated GDP growth also explains the external sector's performance.

A lack of export dynamism in important categories such as manufactures and tourism income also became more apparent than in the previous years. The deterioration of the ratio of the deficit to GDP is indeed striking when the impressive rise in exports of crude petroleum and the manifold increase in the price of this product are considered. Oil exports in current dollars rose from slightly more than $1 billion in 1977 to $14.6 billion in 1981. Again, a more thoughtful story can be told with the help of the decomposition analysis of table 5. On average, only 40 per cent of the increased deficit ratio can be accounted for by external shocks during 1979-1981. The sizeable interest rate shock was practically offset by the favourable evolution of the terms of trade, a fact that is not surprising in the light of the oil price explosion of 1979-1982. Nor, for that matter, was world recession a very powerful deficit-propelling factor.

If any generalization is allowed by the figures in table 5, it is that the Mexican economy was hit by diverse "internal shocks" during the period. The process of import "desubstitution" continued at an even faster pace than before. During 1980-1981, for example, the import coefficient is almost twice the change in the deficit ratio. The booming growth rates also worsened the disequilibrium and, as mentioned previously, frank export retardation in important items such as manufactures also played a role. Of course, the dramatic increase in oil exports - much larger than the expansion registered in the corresponding world market - was a most significant "positive" policy response. (Some analysts would go so far as to claim, however, that it was not a response but a cause of the crisis).

(b) The foreign debt, 1978-1981

A rough answer to the question as to how the current account imbalance was financed during 1978-1981 is also provided by table 2. Again, it was the net flow of the external debt that filled the gap, although the inflow of direct foreign investment also became significant during the period.

Tables 6 and 7 contain more detailed information on the evolution of the external debt. It can be seen from the data given there that the stock of foreign public debt grew rather conservatively during 1978-1980. The net flow of the aggregate averaged only $3.3 billion during that period - less than the average of more than $4 billion recorded in the last three years of the Echeverría term. Yet, other components of the country's external debt grew more dynamically. The private sector's foreign debt - including the debt of both firms and banks - which had amounted to $6.8 billion at year-end 1977, reached almost $17 billion by late 1980. Still, the total external debt, when measured against the size of the economy, consistently decreased through 1980. The ratio of total debt to GDP fell from 35.8 per cent in 1977 to 31.3 per cent in 1980. It should be noticed, however, that when the net flow of the total external debt is measured against total fixed investment and current account income, it begins to take on considerable importance immediately after 1978, as shown in table 7.

In any case, the foreign public debt, which had produced panic in 1976, evolved very reasonably through 1980. Its net flow, with respect to several relevant macroeconomic aggregates after the initial adjustment of 1977, was kept in rather modest proportions during two-thirds of the term of the López-Portillo administration. 9/ Thus, with respect to GDP, public expenditure and the public sector deficit, the net flow averaged 2.5 per cent, 7.5 per cent and 35.1 per cent respectively during 1978-1980.

The relative adjustment in the size of the foreign public debt during that period - together with the expectations created by the new oil wealth - should help to explain the tremendous upgrading of Mexico's credit in international capital markets. Fierce competition

among foreign lenders to grant new loans to the Mexican government and
to public enterprises was an everyday event during the booming years.
There was always an excess demand of lending institutions willing to
subscribe new Eurocredit syndications or credit lines for Mexican
public debtors. Undoubtedly, the frustration of many foreign lenders
to place new loans in the public sector was not unrelated to the ease
with which the Mexican private sector was able to finance itself abroad
during the same period.

Needless to say, Mexican negotiations took full advantage of the
"bullishness" of the market to improve on the maturity profile and cost
of the country's debt. Whereas the maturity of credits obtained by
Mexican public agencies in the Eurocurrency market was, on average, a
bit less than five years during 1975-1976, the average maturity
lengthened to eight years or more by 1978 and 1979. Equally important
was the improvement in the spreads over LIBOR charged for Eurocurrency
credits. In fact, what had been a very expensive debt with maturities
heavily concentrated in the medium term in 1976 had become a nicely
scheduled debt two years later, carrying very low spreads, and only
comparable to those paid by prime customers in Western industrialized
countries.

Up to 1980, foreign borrowing continued to be relatively cheap.
The   implicit   interest   rate   obtained   from   the   relevant
balance-of-payments figures show nominal rates averaging 10 per cent
during 1977-1980; after discounting for inflation in import prices, the
average real rate proves to be practically zero for the same period.

The whole foreign-debt scenario changed dramatically in just one
year. By year-end 1981, the country's total external debt had
surpassed the $74 billion mark - a nominal increase of 46 per cent with
respect to the figure registered the previous year. Not only had the
level of the debt changed significantly, but so had its maturity
profile and its cost.

As shown in table 2, the expansion in the external debt - and, in
the inflow of direct foreign investment - was much larger than required
by the current account deficit. The explanation of this situation can
again be found in the evolution of the other "capital flows and error
and omissions" item. Obviously, the existence of capital flight can be
detected as early as 1979, but the real stampede took place in 1981.

(c) The domestic environment

As stated above, expectations about Mexico's economic prospects
were very encouraging already by late 1977 and sharply contrasted with
what they had been a year earlier. Although several other
circumstances - such as the reconciliation of the public and private
sectors and the early successes of the economic stabilization programme
- contributed, the announcements about oil reserves and plans to export

crude were undoubtedly the main factors in explaining the speedy recovery of the economy in 1978. This recovery marked the beginning of the four-year period of unprecedented prosperity that, paradoxically enough, preceded the worst economic crisis in half a century of Mexican economic history.

The rough figures of table 8 highlight the oil boom. During 1978-1981, the rate of GDP growth averaged 8.4 per cent. Unlike what happened under the previous administration, not only did public investment soar but so did private investment. Thus, aggregate fixed investment, which had been less than 20 per cent of GDP in 1977, reached a proportion of almost 25 per cent of the same variable in 1981. By any measure, many segments of the labour market became, indeed, a supplier's market. Furthermore, the bet on oil was a winning one. Proven reserves consistently kept growing, and their exploitation proceeded at a rapid pace. Crude exports, which had been only 0.2 million barrels a day in 1977, surpassed the one-million-barrel-a-day mark by late 1980. The timing for tapping the oil wealth seemed even more fortunate: crude prices more than doubled between late 1975 and late 1980.

Although the sharp worsening in the country's foreign indebtedness situation occurred in 1981, the internal phenomena behind it started to materialize a few years earlier. Even though the traumatic events of the mid-1970s were so recent that they could hardly be forgotten, the public-expenditure-led growth model was already revived by 1978 with as much vigour as it had during the peak Echeverría years. What was supposed to be a three-year programme to correct fiscal disequilibrium was overridden after only one year. The overall public sector deficit (the "financial" deficit of table 9) as a proportion of GDP could not be lowered beyond the initial adjustment of 1977.

Although the emphasis on public expenditure in order to achieve high GDP growth was pretty obvious a year after the López-Portillo administration took office, not many people expressed concern. It was claimed at the time that the failed model was being revived in a form very different from that utilized in the previous administration. First, it was said, the resources for financing the development of Mexico in a non-inflationary fashion were going to be provided by the new oil wealth. Furthemore, taking advantage of such wealth would require the expansion of public investment at any event. Second, it was affirmed that the government was going to use more actively other policy instruments that had been practically unused before. In this respect, there were some encouraging symptoms at the beginning. A financial reform was undertaken by which the banking system was restructured and the instruments of monetary control were modernized. Interest rate policy became much more flexible and attentive to real yields and to developments in foreign financial markets, and Treasury Certificates (CETES) were introduced as a more rational way to finance the public sector's deficit. On the fiscal side, a far-reaching reform was announced with the introduction of the value-added tax. With respect to industrial and commercial policy, there were some early attempts to rationalize the whole structure of relative prices through the elimination (never achieved) of quantitative restrictions on imports and the simplification of fiscal incentives for industrial activities. And third, this time the public sector was not going to be alone in enhancing the country's stock of capital. Private investment was to be encouraged so that the pattern of growth would be more balanced.

As mentioned before, the results of this strategy in terms of investment and GDP growth, as well as job creation, were very impressive during four years. At the same time, however, some fundamental disequilibria in the Mexican economy made themselves felt with renewed force and reached huge proportions.

The external disequilibrium was analyzed in the previous two sections. It will suffice to recall that early efforts to adjust the current account deficit of 1977-1978 had frankly subsided by 1979, when the deficit reached $4.0 billion, in spite of the fact that the value of oil exports had increased almost four times in just a couple of years and non-oil exports had also been growing very dynamically. By 1980 the current account deficit exceeded $7.2 billion, which seemed inconceivable for an oil-endowed developing country.

Actually, this external disequilibrium was just the tip of the iceberg. It was purely a consequence of many other disarrays in the Mexican economy - most notably, the unchecked expansion in aggregate demand, led by the growth in public expenditure. Table 9 tells the story of the public finances during the López-Portillo years. Public expenditure as a proportion of GDP had peaked at 33.6 per cent during the previous administration. In spite of the early rhetoric, this proportion was reached again in 1979, and was surpassed by two percentage points in 1980. The reason was not only the need for increasing PEMEX investment: non-PEMEX public expenditure as a share of GDP consistently augmented from 1977 on. Although the public income derived from the oil sector almost doubled as a proportion of GDP between 1977 and 1980, the overall deficit could never be reduced to the levels contemplated at the beginning of the López-Portillo administration.

What happened was just the opposite, and the deterioration actually began after 1978. The monetary impact of the public sector's financial disequilibrium is better assessed by looking at a concept that in Mexican public finances is called the "internal" deficit. 10/ As shown in table 9 the deterioration of this factor was more acute than that registered by the overall financial deficit. The government's retreat from early intentions of increasing the relative size of fiscal and public-enterprise revenues explains this disequilibrium as much as the overflow in all categories of public expenditure. In view of the size of the public sector's disequilibrium and the consequential expansion in domestic credit, it is not surprising that money-supply growth averaged more than 30 per cent during 1977-1981.

The impact of the fiscal deficit on the domestic market's disequilibrium was reinforced by the rapid expansion of private demand, both in consumption and investment. In spite of the rather precipitate and unplanned opening of the economy to foreign imports, the strong demand-pull was bound to have a significant effect on domestic inflation. As shown by the figures of table 8, inflation could not be lowered even to the levels of 1975-1976, and it started to accelerate again in 1979. Yet, during more than four years - and well into 1981 - the exchange rate was kept practically fixed. Obviously, this situation had to lead to a growing overvaluation of the Mexican peso, as shown by the index of the real exchange rate of table 8.

Considering the overheating of the economy and the exchange-rate policy followed at the time, it is not surprising at all that the external sector disequilibrium worsened to the degree it did, despite increased oil revenues. These phenomena explain the adverse effect of domestic policy actions on the current account deficit discussed earlier.

The economic balance of 1980 should have sufficed to alert policy-makers of the risks ahead. At this point, measures far short of an overall adjustment would have been needed. A mild clean-up of public finances to stop the worsening trend of the fiscal deficit, plus some adjustments - especially, in exchange-rate policy, with possibly a more active "crawl" - would have sufficed. Admittedly, the budget approved for fiscal year 1981 explicitly incorporated the objective of not allowing the overall deficit to rise further in nominal terms. Unfortunately, this was just a formality. In practice, even a timid gradualistic approach on fiscal matters and exchange-rate policy sounded like heresy - even an insult to the reasoning of the time.

The inertia of the public-expenditure-led growth model proved to be overwhelming. The warning voices of the more prudent members of the cabinet were completely ineffective in provoking a change of course. This explains why the 1981 budget overlooked not only internal bottlenecks but also conditions abroad. Perhaps the most dramatic example of this miscalculation is provided by the projections of the value of crude exports for 1981. The budget assumed that Mexico could export a volume 75 per cent higher at a price 10 per cent above what was recorded in 1980, when oil prices were already above $30 a barrel and the world economy had started to enter into a deep recession.

The official scenario still had some credibility during the first half of 1981. The beginning of the debacle took place in June when it became clear that PEMEX had to lower sale prices in order to continue to secure orders of crude abroad. This was too hard to swallow. Instead of facing the signals given by the market - as naturally as had been done two years before, when oil prices started their upward swing - the Secretariat of National Properties and Industry (SEPAFIN) designed a "new" marketing strategy whereby those buyers unwilling to pay the Mexican prices would be struck off PEMEX's customer list. 11/ As a consequence of the "small-country" reality, a good percentage of

Mexican oil exports was left out of the international crude market for the space of several weeks. Although Mexican owners of wealth had started to read the basic economic statistics in a less complacent way, the possibility of a sharp exchange-rate devaluation still looked somewhat academic just before the oil affair. Such a possibility became an open threat by mid-June, however, leading to a tremendous capital flight and to the "dollarization" of deposits in the Mexican banking system.

The seriousness of the situation demanded bold actions, but once again these were not taken or were postponed. Even though the peso was under heavy attack, little effort was made, beyond rhetorical pronouncements, to face what had started to be a financial crisis. The exchange rate continued to be depreciated daily at an annual rate of only 9 per cent. An across-the-board cut of 4 per cent in public expenditure was decreed, but the cut applied with respect to the already higher-than-budgeted level. And, as it turned out, not even this timid adjustment was made.

By late July, the targeted overall deficit had been revised upward to 540 billion pesos (from less than 415 billion pesos in the original budget). Yet, when the year was over, the deficit reached 865 billion pesos. This outcome was not caused by a relative fall in public income, as was officially argued at the time, since the proportion of this income to GDP remained the same. Actually, the underlying factor was the tremendous increase in public expenditure. As can be verified in table 9, the latter aggregate rose from 35.6 per cent of GDP in 1980 to 42.4 per cent in 1981. As a consequence, the overall deficit reached almost 15 per cent of GDP (it had been 10 per cent in the "worst" Echeverría year). Such an imbalance was bound to produce a profound disequilibrium in the money market which, sooner or later, had to be settled either via prices or the balance of payments or a combination of both.

As indicated before, the balance-of-payments effect was the dominant one in the Mexican economy during 1981. The current account deficit soared to $12.5 billion (see Table 2), with the import bill reaching $24 billion. Admittedly, oil exprts did not reach the level officially forecast, but they did reach a value of $14.6 billion – 47.5 per cent more than during the previous year. Equally impressive was the drain via capital account, as mentioned earlier.

Needless to say, recourse to external borrowing on the scale on which Mexico did so during 1981 was bound to produce profound and adverse consequences. Immediately, there was a sharp deterioration in terms of lending to Mexico. At the close of 1980, the short-term foreign public debt was only $1.5 billion. A year later, the same aggregate jumped to $10.8 billion, not counting the amounts obtained through Mexican commercial banks. The enviable spreads of a few months earlier had also started to vanish and were superseded by new ones that were considerably higher.

4.   The events since 1982

(a) The disorderly and involuntary adjustment of 1982

        Despite some final and very costly resistance, it was announced
that the peso was being devalued on the night of 17 February -
initially by 40 per cent; some days later an overall stabilization
package - of a rather orthodox shape - was announced. For a few days,
it seemed possible that the Mexican economy could pass from a booming
situation to an orderly adjustment. Far from true: the initial
adjustment programme was soon overridden by measures that were clearly
inconsistent with it. For example, the programme called for a maximum
emergency wage increase of 10 per cent. Instead, and just a few weeks
after the devaluation, wage rises of up to 30 per cent were decreed by
the government. It also called for immediate increases in the prices
charged for services and goods produced by public enterprises: several
months elapsed, however, before the first significant rise was
announced; instead, an "emergency" plan to support productive firms was
implemented. By providing fiscal relief and granting outright
subsidies, this plan partially undid the adjustment sought by the
devaluation and constituted another clear signal that it would take a
while before public finances could indeed be improved. Pressures to
finish projects already started made it very difficult to control the
nominal expansion in public expenditure.

        Meanwhile, the clashes between the government and the private
sector spokesmen - reminiscent of those that occurred six years
previously - became more frequent and fiery. Not surprisingly, as soon
as early April 1982, there were signs that capital flight had started
again. Another major devaluation was avoided for several months, but
only at the expense of exhausting foreign exchange reserves and using
the last "voluntary" foreign credit available to Mexico. Renewing
short-term credits that had been obtained during 1981 became
increasingly difficult. Renewal periods became shorter and shorter,
while spreads climbed higher and higher.

        In order to alleviate an impressive piling-up of short-term
credits inherited from 1981, three important medium-term syndications
were arranged during the first semester of 1982. The first, placed by
PEMEX in February, 12/ raised $2 billion. NAFINSA was the borrowing
agency in the second, which took place in March; this provided an
additional $1.2 billion. The last syndication consisted of a "jumbo"
of $2.5 billion, with the Mexican federal government as debtor, and was
arranged during May/June. In many ways, this credit was a turning
point. As the facility was being put together, it became clear that
market perception concerning Mexico's credit-worthiness had completely
deteriorated. Even though the pricing of the loan to lenders was very
attractive compared to previous deals, it took an enormous effort on
the part of Mexican negotiators to gather the necessary
commitments.13/ To their dismay, only 75 banks out of 650 that were
invited agreed to subscribe to the facility. In view of the enormous
difficulties that had to be faced before signing the loan on 30 June,

it became clear that the only debt-management expedient left was to continue rolling over short-term credit - at any price, and at any maturity. This, of course, could not last.

The peso continued to be under heavy speculative pressure during July. Too late, it was decided to apply some of the measures that had been included in the Economic Adjustment Programme but had not been put into effect. Accordingly, at the beginning of August 1982, it was announced that the prices of some basic products would be raised. After this announcement was made, pressure on the central bank's reserves became unbearable. On 6 August 1982, a new two-tier-foreign-exchange system was set up. Still speculation continued, and just one week later, dollar-denominated deposits in the Mexican banking system were made payable in domestic currency only. Banks were ordered to suspend foreign exchange transactions temporarily. In the face of these events, it became evident that foreign creditors had been totally scared away, and that the resumption of any kind of normal credit conditions could not be expected for a long time.

At this moment, the financial authorities could either wait for foreign creditors to publicize the country's insolvency or confront the facts and declare unilaterally that the country was not able to keep up with payments of principal. Wisely, the second approach was followed. On 20 August, the Secretary of Finance, Jesús Silva-Herzog, met representatives of a large number of creditor banks and requested a three-month moratorium on payments of principal, as well as the formation of an "advisory group" of creditors to negotiate the restructuring of the foreign public debt. A few days earlier, the Mexican government had obtained important financial backing from its United States counterpart in the form of credits from the Commodity Credit Corporation and the Treasury Department. Negotiations with the Bank for International Settlements, with a view to obtaining a dollar credit of almost $1.9 billion from several of its members, were initiated in the last days of August. Early that month, formal talks about a stand-by agreement had been started with an IMF mission.

The realism of August comforted Mexico's creditors only for a short while. On 1 September, President López-Portillo announced that private banks were being nationalized, and that blanket foreign exchange controls were being instituted. The international banking community must have panicked at the idea that such a radical stance could also spread to the management of the foreign-debt problem - a possibility that, indeed, was very real for a few weeks.

When President López-Portillo left office on 1 December 1982, the Mexican economy was experiencing a crisis even more profound than that of six years earlier - something inconceivable for a country that earned $47 billion in oil revenues and had gone through a rapid process of capital formation during the previous five years. Thus, by year-end 1982, real GDP had fallen 0.5 per cent; inflation had reached almost 100 per cent (consumer-price-index growth, December/December); the monetary authorities had completely lost control of the foreign exchange market - so much so that the black market rate was more than double the average official rates; 14/ capital flight continued practically unchecked in spite of the supposedly blanket foreign exchange controls; the public sector's financial deficit had reached 17.9 per cent of GDP during the year; the domestic financial system was shrinking; and, for practical purposes, the country was in moratorium with respect to its foreign-debt obligations. The forced and somehow involuntary adjustment of the current account is reflected in the relevant coefficients of table 1.

In fact, during the last four months of 1982, the country made only payments of interest and a minor percentage of payments on the principal of the foreign public debt. All payments corresponding to the private foreign debt had been suspended. The country's overall external debt picture was dismal. The public sector had arrears of $8.1 billion in payments of principal already; another $14.3 billion were going to fall due in 1984 and 1985. Relatively speaking, the situation of the private sector was worse. It owed $18 billion to foreign financial institutions, two-thirds of which had repayment periods that went no further than 1984. In addition, liabilities of $4 billion outstanding with foreign suppliers were declared when a register of such debts was opened at the Secretariat of Commerce (not included in the debt figures of tables 6 and 7).

(b) The economic adjustment programme of 1983

The new administration opted for a drastic macroeconomic adjustment policy. The core of the stabilization programme was the correction of the public finance disequilibrium, the main target being the reduction of the overall deficit to 8.5 per cent of GDP in 1983. As a consequence, in addition to important across-the-board real cuts in public expenditure, stiff action on the income side was taken at once. The latter comprised significant increases both in the value-added tax and in income tax rates for upper-income brackets, as well as major revisions in the prices charged by public enterprises, for example, gasoline and electricity. Important rectifications were also made in the exchange rate and financial policies. The blanket system of exchange controls was replaced by a rather standard dual system consisting of a controlled market (covering all merchandise exports, the majority of merchandise imports and all foreign-related flows) and a "free" market (for remaining transactions). The initial level of the exchange rate for the free market was set pretty close to the rate prevailing on the black market, and as a result the volume of black market transactions shrank considerably. In the controlled market, an opening rate was offered that overshot the value considered to be equilibrium rate as measured by a purchasing-power-parity criterion. A daily crawl in this rate also followed. In the financial sphere, domestic interest rates were increased and strict monetary targeting, consistent with the desired adjustment in public finances, was implemented.

A number of these measures were mentioned in the letter of intent submitted to the IMF Board of Directors in November 1982. This was ratified as soon as the new administration took office. 15/

(c) Foreign debt management

The agreement reached with the technical mission of the IMF called for a net flow of foreign lending to the public sector provided by private banks of $5 billion in 1983. To the creditors' surprise, the IMF's Managing Director let everybody know that he would "not recommend the approval of the IMF agreement to the Executive Board of the IMF without assurances from both official sources and commercial banks that adequate external financing was in place for the success of the Mexican Adjustment Programme and the IMF Agreement, and that the principles of the realistic restructuring scheme of the Mexican debt would be favourably considered by the community". 16/ The telex from which this passage is quoted contained the principles of the strategy followed by the Mexican Government for dealing with both the borrowing of net resources and the restructuring of the foreign public debt in 1983.

The essence of the approach to obtaining the additional financing required for 1983 was to invite an unprecedented number of banks to subscribe to a "mammoth" loan ($5 billion). Each creditor's relative participation in the deal was defined on the basis of the claims of each on the country, as of August 1982. It implied that every bank with assets in Mexico was requested - and, somehow, subtly forced - to underwrite the facility. This element of "fairness" explains, to a great extent, the enthusiasm with which the largest banks joined in the efforts to raise the needed resources. The attractive pricing also helped to close the deal. Creditors were offered, at their own option, a spread of 2 1/2 over LIBOR or 2 1/8 over Prime. The maturity requested did not punish lenders either; it consisted of only six years, including a three-year grace period. Furthermore, attractive commitment and facility fees were offered as well. With the assistance of the "advisory group" and of top officials from the IMF and several central banks - including the Federal Reserve - the credit was granted practically on time, an impressive total of 526 banks having participated in this syndication.

As regards the restructuring of the foreign public debt, the objective was to reschedule all payments to fall due between 23 August 1982 and 31 December 1984, with the exception of payments due on "excluded" debt. The latter comprised, besides other minor categories, credits granted or guaranteed by official entities, whether governmental or multilateral. Consequently, the rescheduling was basically applied to the debt owed to private financial institutions. Mexican negotiators asked for a period of eight years for the repayment of principal, including a four-year grace period. In exchange, creditors were to be paid, at their own election, a rate of LIBOR plus 1 7/8 or Prime plus 1 3/4. They were also offered a 1 per cent restructuring fee. The rescheduling exercise was also quite successful. Only a year after the original request had been made, the first set of restructuring contracts were signed. By the end of 1983, 27 restructuring agreements between Mexican public sector entities and their foreign creditors had been concluded, representing liabilities of some $23 billion.

The problem of the private sector's foreign debt proved to be as challenging as that of the public sector. Arrears in interest that had accrued during the last four months of 1982 and early 1983 (almost $0.9 billion) had to be dealt with first. Debtor firms were asked to constitute - through a peso payment and at the controlled rate of exchange - dollar-denominated deposits in favour of their foreign creditors. These deposits earned interest at a commercial rate (LIBOR plus 1.0) and were transferred by the central bank in several instalments until complete settlement by the end of 1983.

It was clear, however, that an overall renegotiation of the private sector's debt was unavoidable. From the start, two important decisions were taken by the Mexican financial authorities. First, the government was not going to assume the private sector's debt - that is, foreign lenders would have to retain the commercial risk inherent in their credits, with debt renegotiations having to take place individually between lenders and borrowers; and, second, debtors would receive no subsidy to settle their foreign obligations.

In order to encourage the restructuring process, it was decided to offer exchange-risk coverage of principal and interest for debt that could be rescheduled according to the guidelines issued by the financial authorities. In plain terms, firms able to swap their dollar obligations into peso-denominated liabilities, as long as the latter could be restructured at long term. Accordingly, firms were able to transfer the foreign exchange risk of their liabilities to the public sector. This mechanism was also successful, and by the time the deadline arrived (late October 1983), private liabilities amounting to almost $12 billion had been covered by the facility. Almost 100 per cent of the amount corresponding to obligations renegotiated to mature on the expiry of eight or more years, including a four-year grace period. Nearly 300 different financial institutions agreed to the mechanism, in addition to 200 foreign suppliers. 17/

The private foreign debt not comprised in that programme was settled or restructured through other mechanisms. More than $800 million of debt owed to foreign suppliers were repaid through two other programmes, which were made public by the central bank on 28 February and 3 August 1983. Basically, these programmes allowed firms - through a peso payment - to constitute dollar-denominated deposits, whose ownership could be transferred in payment to foreign suppliers. In addition, up to 100 per cent of income from exports of debtor firms was permitted to be used to discharge debt of the same type. Another segment of private foreign debt - involving some $2 billion - was already long-term, and covered foreign exchange risks by virtue of another system of foreign currency swaps offered by Banco de Mexico since 1977. Loans guaranteed by agencies of foreign governments are to be settled through bilateral agreements that are in the process of negotiation. The remainder was largely that of firms in excellent financial condition whose liabilities are automatically rolled over and which have good export prospects and hence automatically enjoy protection against fluctuations in the exchange rate.

(d) The performance in 1983 and 1984

As was to be expected in response to this kind of adjustment real economic activity fell significantly in 1983. Gross fixed investment and GDP fell by 25.3 per cent and 4.7 per cent in real terms, respectively. These were the sharpest contractions in such variables since the early 1930s. At the sectoral level, the output of two key sectors, manufacturing and construction, fell sharply by 7.3 and 14.3 per cent respectively. By mid-1984, however, there was evidence that a mild recovery might be under way and the current trend of leading production indicators points to the GDP growth of around 3 per cent during 1984.

The 1983 target of reducing the public sector's overall financial deficit to 8.5 per cent of GDP was practically achieved (see table 4). But even more striking, was the adjustment in the balance of payments: the trade surplus amounted to $13.7 billion, while that of the current account was $5.6 billion.

Admittedly, a good part of the balance-of-payments adjustment was achieved by the drastic reduction (47 per cent) in imports. During 1983, the Mexican economy imported merchandise at a nominal value less than the corresponding figure recorded five years earlier. In any case, the current account adjustment permitted a very satisfactory restoration of international reserves, and an important liquidation of private foreign debt - especially debt owed to foreign suppliers.

At the time of writing (November 1984) it seems that an impressive balance-of-payments performance will have been repeated during 1984. Preliminary data show a current account surplus of $2.8 billion accumulated up to May 1984, in spite of the fact that imports - experiencing a healthy recovery - increased at an annual rate of 30 per cent. This was made possible by a remarkable rise in the exports of manufactures, growing at an annual nominal rate of around 40 per cent. These results have made it possible to reconstitute foreign-exchange reserves that had been practically exhausted during the last four months of 1982. It was reported that international reserves stood at $7.3 billion on the last day of August 1984.

Apart from some pressures experienced during February-March, due to the uncertainties of the international oil market, the foreign exchange market was rather calm during 1983. The controlled rate kept crawling at a decreasing percentage rate (13 peso-cents a day) throughout the year; the overshot free rate was practically fixed until September, when it began also to be depreciated at a daily rate of 13 peso-cents. Triggered by adverse expectations concerning foreign interest rates, there was another episode of mild speculation against the peso during May-June of 1984. It moderated after a few weeks; throughout most of 1984 the rate observed in the peso wholesale market in the United States is not significantly different from the so-called free rate ruling in the market operated by Mexican banks.

As usually happens in the early stages of most stabilization programmes, little progress was made on the inflation front. The consumer price index grew 81 per cent during 1983 and continued its upward trend at rather high monthly rates in the first third of 1984. But, by May of that year, the trend of inflation seemed to be headed significantly downward. The average monthly inflation rate was 5.1 per cent in 1983, and again 5.1 per cent during January-April of 1984, but only 3.2 per cent during May-August. Thanks to a slowdown in the monthly rate of inflation during the second and third quarters, the rate for the year is thought to be 58 per cent.

(e) More recent developments on the debt front

In December 1983, a general agreement was reached with the "advisory group", defining the conditions for the money to be lent to the Mexican government by commercial banks during 1984. The package comprised $3.8 billion. Lending banks were again asked to participate on the basis of their pro rata exposure to Mexico in August, 1982. This time, however, conditions were softened significantly, with creditors being offered 1 1/2 per cent over LIBOR or 1 1/8 over Prime, at their own election. Instead of the six-year maturity obtained in the previous deal, the new credit carries a ten-year term, including a five-and-a-half-year grace period. Commitment and facility fees were also reduced. Another encouraging fact was the relatively quiet way in which a PEMEX acceptances facility of around $4.5 billion was renewed for two more years in mid-1983.

It was foreseeable earlier that another and more comprehensive round of restructuring would have to be undertaken sooner or later. The policy actions of 1982 and 1983 concerning the foreign public debt were basically of an emergency nature, intended to deal with the problem until the end of 1984. It was obvious that new actions would be needed, for current maturity schedules of the foreign public debt owed to commercial banks imply repayments of $8.6 billion in 1985 and $36.6 more billion during 1986-1989. Obviously, under no internal macroeconomic scenario would the country be able to comply with such a repayment schedule, nor would present market conditions permit a normal refinancing of the maturities involved.

At the time when the $3.8 billion package was being put together in late 1983, the Mexican authorities spoke, for the first time, of the need for a "multi-year restructuring programme", an idea that initially did not receive a warm welcome on the part of the "advisory group". It took another semester before the banks' negotiating committee publicly accepted that it was ready to discuss a deal of that kind.

By June 1984, the main creditor banks were leaning towards a package comprising only liabilities falling due during 1985-1987. The Mexican side, however, called for a more far-reaching arrangement. Negotiations with the "advisory group" were quite intense during the summer of 1984, finally culminating on 8 September 1984, when the general principles for implementing the new arrangement were made public. 18/

The package comprises liabilities of more than $45 billion, and the restructuring would be organized around three different segments of the public debt: first, the $5-billion jumbo of 1983; second, the debt originally contracted to be repaid during 1985-1990, which consists of around $20 billion; and third, the $23.6 billion of liabilities that were restructured mostly in 1983. Each segment has its own repayment schedule, but the overall programme would consist of a total repayment period of 14 years, starting in 1985, when no amortization payments would be due. Repayment would start in 1986, but with rather minor amounts. Regarding interest rates, each segment would also have its own pricing. Typically, however, the average rate would be around 1 1/8 over LIBOR. An important innovation regarding pricing is introduced in this deal, to the extent that the United States prime rate has been eliminated as a reference rate. Other domestic reference rates such as an adjusted C.D. (certificate of deposit) rate, in the case of United States dollars, would be used instead. Another amendment to current contracts would arise from the stipulation of the right of creditor banks to switch to their respective home currencies for up to 50 per cent of their Mexican public sector assets.

Table 10 shows the effect of the proposed rescheduling on the amortization profile of the foreign public debt owed to commercial banks. As mentioned above, current agreements imply payments of principal in the amount of $36.3 billion within the next four years; if the restructuring gets underway, only $3.3 billion would be due during the same period.

An attempt to depict the repayment profile of the total foreign debt is made in table 11. It is shown by types of debtors (public debt is also broken down by different types of creditors).

Although the public sector would still have to make repayments of more than $6.5 billion during 1985-1987, the figure appears quite manageable if it is borne in mind that almost 45 per cent of that amount is owed to the World Bank, the Inter-American Development Bank, and bilateral institutions such as EXIMBANK. Presumably, it should not be very difficult to obtain gross lending from these official sources that would more than compensate for the amounts falling due. The so-called inter-bank debt owed by commercial banks (likewise almost

$6.5 billion), consisting of short-term liabilities that are assumed to be rolled over indefinitely, is more worrisome. Adverse market developments could possibly trigger a funding crisis that could force the Mexican Government to seek an explicit restructuring of those liabilities. As regards the foreign debt of the private sector, there is also the expectation that a process of voluntary, market-determined refinancing will start sooner or later. If this does not happen, another round of restructuring will inevitably have to be arranged.

5.   Prospects

Even granted that a major foreign debt crisis was avoided, that the future refinancing of the current stock of debt -- if not warranted -- seems feasible and that the macroeconomic stabilization programme has been successful in most -- if not all -- respects, it must nevertheless be admitted that any attempt to inquire into the medium and long-term prospects for Mexico's economic growth, and the role to be played by external savings in achieving such growth, still constitutes a hazardous and difficult undertaking. There is still a great deal of uncertainty about many variables -- both of an internal and of an external nature. With the acknowledgement of these difficulties, a simple prognosis exercise is attempted below.

It is focused on the question whether the Mexican economy can resume growth in spite of the depressed conditions of foreign capital supply. In seeking the answer to this question, Bacha (1983) and (1984) has suggested utilizing a simple "two-gap" simulation model. By using such a framework, it can be shown that a marginal real inflow of foreign capital can have a relatively large positive effect on domestic output, as long as the economy is subject to the foreign exchange constraint. The impact is greatly reduced as "full employment" is achieved. From then on, GDP growth has to evolve pari-passu with the expansion of the aggregate capital stock. Considering that many of the economies that are nowadays analyzed within this framework have been undergoing austerity programmes for long periods of time, it is not surprising that they are proved to be foreign exchange constrained. Consequently, applying the two-gap model has necessarily to produce a picture of immediate fast growth if the restriction is sufficiently relaxed. This kind of result is perfectly logical for cases in which a strong contractionary policy is being applied to correct a balance-of-payments disequilibrium caused chiefly by external shocks. Ex ante, however, it is known that such an outcome is an impossibility in the Mexican case. The control of inflation, the stabilization of the real exchange rate, the adjustment in the public sector's participation in the economy, the reduction of the national (internal and external) debt are only a few of the objectives the achievement of which could not possibly be attempted simultaneously with a strong drive to eliminate the slack in productive capacity. Yet, it was shown above that Mexico's current problems were not caused by adverse external conditions, but rather by internal imbalances rooted in poor economic management.

In the light of these considerations, the analysis of the Mexican case is instead carried out by means of a two-stage approach. First, a simple growth-cum-debt model, in which the overall savings constraint is binding all the way, is posed and solved. In this stage, the emphasis is on the following problem: what is the required trajectory of foreign savings in the context of a model in which GDP is driven by investment, the real exchange rate is kept fixed so that import elasticities do not explode, and external conditions prove to be no worse than they are at present? Once the model is solved, a judgement can be made as to whether the required savings are indeed realizable under the present conditions of international capital markets.

In the second stage, the impact of a few external shocks on GDP growth are analysed. This is done by transforming the model used in the first stage into a gap model in which the foreign exchange constraint is binding. For this purpose, the requirements of foreign savings, solved endogenously in the first stage, are imposed exogenously in the second model.

FORECASTING MODELS

Model I.

Let:

Y_t Real GDP.

P_t Price level (1984 = 1.0).

              Reciprocal of ICOR.

I_t Real gross fixed investment.

              Depreciation rate.

C_t Real consumption including inventory changes.

X_t Total real exports.

M_t Total real imports.

D_t Net flow of total external debt in current dollars.

V_t Net factor payments in current dollars.

v_t^1 Interest from abroad in current dollars.

v_t^2 Profit remittances in current dollars.

v_t^3 Interest payments on the external debt in current dollars.

s Savings rate.

F_t Total external debt in current dollars.

M_t^1 Real imports of current goods.

M_t^2 Real imports of investment goods.

M_t^3 Real imports of non-factorial services.

x_t^1 Real exports of non-oil primary products.

x_t^2 Real exports of manufactures.

x_t^3 Real exports of oil and derivatives.

x_t^4 Real "other" exports.

j Rate of real growth of exports of group j.

i_t Nominal interest rate on the external debt.

t International inflation rate.

r_t Real rate of interest.

Equations

(2) $Y_t = \sigma\, I_t + (1-\delta)\, Y_{t-1}$

(3) $P_t Y_t = P_t\, C_t + P_t\, I_t + P_t^x\, X_t - P_t M_t$

(4) $P_t C_t = (1-s)\ (P_t Y_t - V_t)$

(5) $D_t = P_t M_t + V_t - P_t^x\, X_t$

(6) $M_t^1 = \alpha_1 + \beta_1\, Y_t$

(7) $M_t^2 = \alpha_2 + \beta_2\, I_t$

(8) $M_t^3 = \alpha_3 + \beta_3\, Y_t$

(9) $M_t = M_t^1 + M_t^2 + M_t^3$

(10) $x_t^1 = x_{t-1}^1\ (1 + \gamma_1)$

(11) $x_t^2 = x_{t-1}^2\ (1 + \gamma_2)$

(12) $x_t^3 = x_{t-1}^3\ (1 + \gamma_3)$

(13) $\quad x_t^4 = x_{t-1}^4 (1 + \gamma_4)$

(14) $\quad x_t = x_t^1 + x_t^2 + x_t^3 + x_t^4$

(15) $\quad P_t = P_o (1 + \Pi)^t$

(16) $\quad \dfrac{x_t^1}{P_t} = P_t \dfrac{x_t^2}{P_t} = P_t \dfrac{x_t^4}{P_t} = P_t$

(17) $\quad \dfrac{x_t^3}{P_t} = P_o (1 + \theta)^t \quad ; \quad P_o = 1.0$

(18) $\quad v_t^1 = v_{t-1}^1 (P_t / P_{t-1})$

(19) $\quad v_t^2 = v_{t-1}^2 (P_t / P_{t-1})$

(20) $\quad v_t^3 = r_t F_{t-1}$

(21) $\quad V_t = v_t^2 - v_t^1 + v_t^3$

(22) $\quad F_t = F_{t-1} + D_t$

(23) $\quad r_t = (1 + i_t) (1 + \Pi_t) - 1$

From equations (2)-(4), it is clear that GDP growth is driven by overall savings and investment; the net flow of the total debt (D_t) is endogenous given equations (5)-(14). Equation (6) denotes the simplifying assumptions that the combined balance-of-payments effect of international reserves changes and direct foreign investment and capital flight (or repatriation) would be zero during the forecasting period. Equally simplistic -- but harmless -- is the assumed behaviour of profit remittances and interest earned on assets abroad suggested by equations (18) and (19).

Assuming initially that the relative price of oil is also constant, the solution of the model is provided in very simple terms by:

$$(24) \quad I_t = [P_t^X X_t - W_o P_t - (1-s) V_t - (W+s) \; (1-\delta) P_t Y_{t-1}] / (W+s) \sigma + \beta_2 - 1) P_t$$

$$(25) \quad D_t = (\sigma W + \beta_2) P_t I_t + W_o P_t + (1-\delta) W \; P_t Y_{t-1} + V_t - P_t^X X_t$$

Where:

$$W_o = \alpha_1 + \alpha_2 + \alpha_3$$

$$W = \beta_1 + \beta_3$$

The base period is 1984, whose relevant figures -- shown in tables 12 and 13 -- were constructed by assuming that the trends suggested by actual data of the first half of the year would continue on the same track during the second half. Accordingly, GDP growth of 3.3 per cent is forecast. It translates into a GDP valued in current dollars at $179.5 billion. It is assumed that, from 1985 onwards, the real exchange rate is pegged at its 1984 average value. It allows for forecasting the relevant national accounts variables directly in dollar terms. In the current account of the balance of payments a surplus of at least $2.7 billion is expected, in spite of higher interest rates abroad, thanks to a trade surplus of $13 billion. A net increase of the foreign debt of $3.6 billion is foreseen by year-end.

In order to simulate the model, the value of the structural parameters and s were assumed to be equal to their observed average values during 1961-1981, as calculated from the Mexican national accounts (σ = .40   s = .40). Rather arbitrarily, δ was given a value of 3 per cent. For the import functions, the following values were used:

$$
\begin{array}{lll}
\alpha_1 = 12.31 & \alpha_2 = -0.6 & \alpha_3 = -8.2086 \\
(26) & & \\
\beta_1 = 0.11204 & \beta_2 = 0.16 & \beta_3 = 0.0747
\end{array}
$$

The marginal propensities, although smaller than those suggested by the experience of the last decade, are attainable as long as the real exchange rate is kept constant at its current level, and the economy is not overheated. In fact, the assumed elasticities are higher than those recorded during the "stabilizing-development" period.

Model II

If equation (2) is eliminated and the value of D_t is imposed exogenously, Model I becomes a gap model with the foreign exchange constraint binding. Instead of (24), the solution of I_t is given by:

(27) $\quad I_t = [s(P_tM_t-W_oP_t) + W(D_t-sV_t)]/P_t(W+s\,\beta_2)$

whereas the trajectory of GDP is determined by:

(28) $\quad Y_t = [s(P_tM_t-W_oP_t)/(W+s\,\beta_2)+D_t-sV_t)(W-s\,\beta_2)/$

$$(W+s\,\beta_2)]/sP_t$$

This formulation is used to study the impact of external shocks on the results reported above. It is done by fixing the level of foreign savings (D_t) at the level determined by Model I, and varying a few of the underlying assumptions to reflect the following phenomena:[20]

(a)   The real rate of interest further increases to 10 per cent;

(b)   The real price of oil, instead of moving with world inflation, falls at a real rate of 2.4 per cent yearly;

(c)   Exports of manufactures grow at a real rate of 4.5 per cent -- that is, only half of the rate assumed before;

(d)   The combined effect of all the above.

The results of this exercise are summarized in Figures (1)-(3), where the evolution of real GDP, the debt-to-GDP ratio and the net transfer as a proportion of GDP are shown for five alternative scenarios. The base case refers to the results of Model I. Clearly, the most damaging of the three individual shocks considered is the increase in the real rate of interest on the foreign debt. A permanent rise of two percentage points in this variable would make the accumulated value of real GDP 3.9 per cent lower than the value obtained in Model I for 1985-1989. Thus, the average rate of GDP growth would fall to 5.1 per cent, and the net transfer, instead of averaging 3.6 per cent of GDP as in the base scenario, would amount to 4.6 per cent.

At least as threatening is the shock derived from a fall in the real price of oil. In the light of recent events, it is conceivable that petroleum prices could drop much faster than is assumed in the simulations reported here. In the absence of other cushioning factors -- such as additional foreign savings -- an event of this kind would modify the Mexican economy's prospects for growth substantially.

In spite of the above indicators, it should be obvious that obtaining access to the required net foreign lending ($6.1 billion during 1985-1989) will not be an easy task. According to the figures in table 24 there will still be amortizations of $28.4 billion falling due during the same period. 19/ That puts the gross borrowing effort at almost $35 billion for the next five years. As was mentioned before, some of this finance might be obtained voluntarily; the rest would have to come from new restructuring exercises.

Model II

If equation (3) is eliminated and the value of D_t is imposed exogenously, Model I becomes a gap model with the foreign exchange constraint binding. Instead of (25), the solution of I_t is given by:

$$(27) \quad I_t = [s(P_tM_t - W_oP_t) + W(D_t - sV_t)]/P_t(W + s\beta_2)$$

whereas the trajectory of GDP is determined by:

$$(28) \quad Y_t = [s(P_tM_t - W_oP_t)/(W + s\beta_2) + D_t - sV_t)(W - s\beta_2)/$$
$$(W + s\beta_2)]/sP_t$$

This formulation is used to study the impact of external shocks on the results reported above. It is done by fixing the level of foreign savings (D_t) at the level determined by Model I, and varying a few of the underlying assumptions to reflect the following phenomena:[20]

(a) The real rate of interest further increases to 10 per cent;

(b) The real price of oil, instead of moving with world inflation, falls at a real rate of 2.4 per cent yearly;

(c) Exports of manufactures grow at a real rate of 4.5 per cent -- that is, only half of the rate assumed before;

(d) The combined effect of all the above.

The results of this exercise are summarized in Figures (1)-(3), where the evolution of real GDP, the debt-to-GDP ratio and the net transfer as a proportion of GDP are shown for five alternative scenarios. The base case refers to the results of Model I. Clearly, the most damaging of the three individual shocks considered is the increase in the real rate of interest on the foreign debt. A permanent rise of two percentage points in this variable would make the accumulated value of real GDP 3.9 per cent lower than the value obtained in Model I for 1985-1989. Thus, the average rate of GDP growth would fall to 5.1 per cent, and the net transfer, instead of averaging 3.6 per cent of GDP as in the base scenario, would amount to 4.6 per cent.

At least as threatening is the shock derived from a fall in the real price of oil. In the light of recent events, it is conceivable that petroleum prices could drop much faster than is assumed in the simulations reported here. In the absence of other cushioning factors -- such as additional foreign savings -- an event of this kind would modify the Mexican economy's prospects for growth substantially.

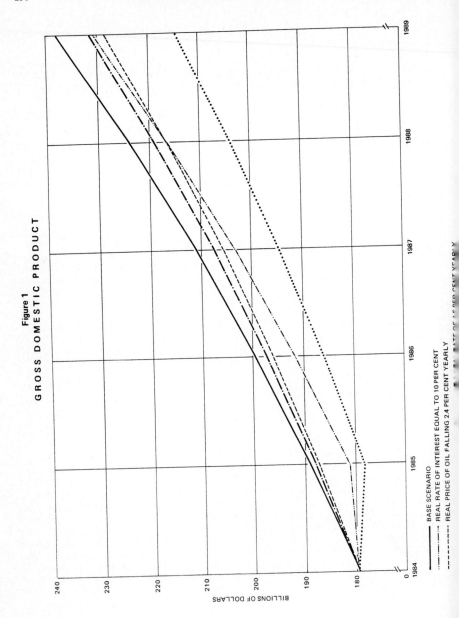

Figure 1
GROSS DOMESTIC PRODUCT

BASE SCENARIO
REAL RATE OF INTEREST EQUAL TO 10 PER CENT
REAL PRICE OF OIL FALLING 2.4 PER CENT YEARLY

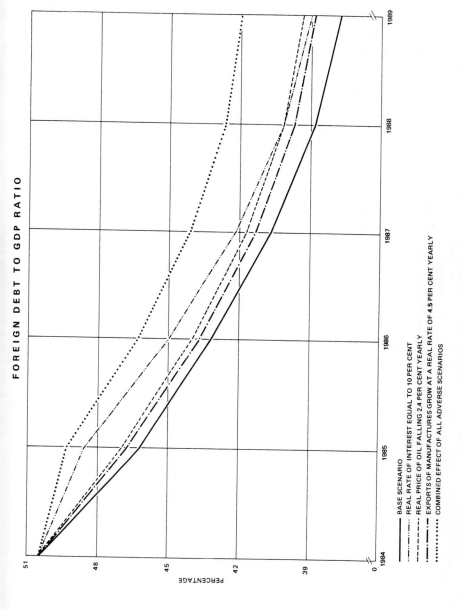

FOREIGN DEBT TO GDP RATIO

PERCENTAGE

—————— BASE SCENARIO
—·—·— REAL RATE OF INTEREST EQUAL TO 10 PER CENT
— — — REAL PRICE OF OIL FALLING 2.4 PER CENT YEARLY
—·—!— EXPORTS OF MANUFACTURES GROW AT A REAL RATE OF 4.5 PER CENT YEARLY
············ COMBINED EFFECT OF ALL ADVERSE SCENARIOS

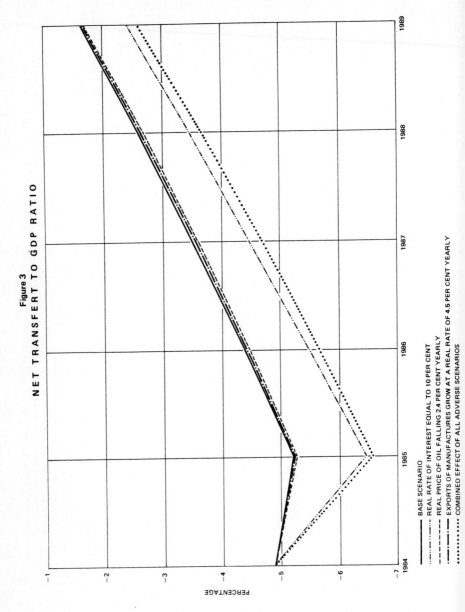

Figure 3
NET TRANSFER TO GDP RATIO

Table 1

MEXICO: DECOMPOSITION OF THE CURRENT ACCOUNT CHANGES
DURING 1973-1977 WITH RESPECT TO 1972. CALCULATIONS
WITH EQUILIBRIUM EXCHANGE RATES

EXPLANATORY FACTORS a/	1973	1974	1975	1976	1977
1. EXTERNAL SHOCKS	.0058	.0109	.0220	.0126	.0058
Terms of trade shock	.0017	-.0007	.0008	-.0032	-.0079
Interest rate shock	.0032	.0055	.0068	.0042	.0021
World recession shock	.0009	.0061	.0144	.0116	.0116
2. BURDEN OF ACCUMULATED DEBT	-.0014	-.0010	-.0000	.0033	.0074
3. DOMESTIC POLICY ACTIONS	.0077	.0210	.0100	.0007	-.0282
Domestic Recession	.0050	.0067	.0054	.0024	-.0020
Fixed investment cuts	.0026	.0034	.0038	.0022	-.0012
Domestic output contraction	.0024	.0033	.0016	.0002	-.0008
Increased Tradeability	.0027	.0143	.0046	-.0017	-.0262
Import replacement	.0090	.0264	.0162	.0042	-.0182
Export deepening	-.0063	-.0122	-.0115	-.0059	-.0080
Non-oil primary	-.0005	.0015	.0023	.0067	.0091
Manufacturers	-.0039	-.0112	-.0123	-.0100	-.0113
Oil	.0002	-.0001	-.0019	-.0016	-.0025
Tourism	-.0021	-.0023	.0003	-.0009	-.0034
4. EFFECT OF OTHER EXPORT OF SERVICES	-.0043	-.0042	.0017	.0008	.0084
5. EFFECT OF INTEREST FROM ABROAD	-.0015	-.0020	-.0006	-.0003	-.0009
6. EFFECT OF PROFIT REMITTANCES	-.0001	-.0004	-.0008	.0006	-.0013
CALCULATED DEFICIT INCREASE b/	.0076	.0253	.0324	.0145	-.0161

a/ Factors with a positive sign contributed to increase the relative size of the current account deficit. For example, if the "domestic recession" factor shows a positive sign it should rather be interpreted as "domestic expansion".

b/ Obtained by adding all the explanatory factors. The difference between this calculation and the observed deficit change is due to interaction and second-order effects as well as adding-up errors.

Calculations made according to equation (1).

Table 2

MEXICO: THE BALANCE OF PAYMENTS
1972 - 1983

(Millic of US dollars)

	CURRENT ACCOUNT	NET FLOW OF TOTAL EXTERNAL DEBT	DIRECT FOREIGN INVESTMENT	LOANS ABROAD	SPECIAL DRAWING RIGHTS	OTHER CAPITAL FLOWS AND ERRORS AND OMISSIONS	CHANGE IN RESERVES a/
1972	- 1 005.7	415.9	146.2	- 4.5	39.2	673.6	264.7
1973	- 1 528.8	2 488.0	199.5	- 5.1	-	- 1 031.3	122.3
1974	- 3 226.6	4 031.7	288.8	- 3.7	-	- 1 053.3	36.9
1975	- 4 442.6	5 865.9	168.2	16.7	-	- 1 443.1	165.1
1976	- 3 683.3	6 680.9	199.8	-47.1	-	- 4 154.3	-1 004.0
1977	- 1 596.4	3 300.0	326.0	-64.9	-	- 1 307.6	657.1
1978	- 2 693.0	2 988.8	364.5	-15.8	-	- 210.4	434.1
1979	- 4 870.5	6 634.7	742.6	17.6	70.0	- 2 175.5	418.9
1980	- 7 223.3	10 515.5	1 244.5	10.8	73.5	- 3 470.1	1 150.9
1981	-12 544.3	23 283.3	1 188.7	-359.7	69.6	-10 625.4	1 012.2
1982	- 4 878.5	10 089.6	708.7	-117.3	-	-10 468.7	-4 666.2
1983	5 545.7	3 486.6	373.8	-250.5	-	- 5 895.2	3 260.6

Source: Banco de México. *Indicadores Económicos.* Subdirección de Investigación Económica. Several issues.

a/ Positive sign indicates an increase in net reserves.

Table 3

MEXICO: THE EVOLUTION OF THE FOREIGN PUBLIC DEBT 1970-1977a/

YEAR	STOCKb/	FLOWb/	INTEREST PAYMENTS b/	NET FLOW GDP	NET FLOW FIXED INVESTMENT	NET FLOW CURRENT ACCOUNT INCOME	NET FLOW TOTAL PUBLIC EXPENDITURE	NET FLOW PUBLIC SECTOR'S DEFICIT	INTEREST PAYMENTS CURRENT ACCOUNT INCOME
1970	6 255.5	443.4	290.3	1.4	7.2	13.6	6.3	37.8	8.9
1971	6 666.7	411.2	306.2	1.2	6.7	11.6	5.8	48.8	8.7
1972	6 820.9	154.2	321.4	0.4	2.0	3.6	1.6	7.7	7.5
1973	8 448.8	1 627.9	442.1	3.2	16.8	30.1	12.0	47.3	8.2
1974	11 373.8	2 925.0	707.1	4.6	23.1	42.8	16.2	63.5	10.3
1975	15 705.1	4 331.3	1 031.5	5.5	25.8	60.7	16.7	55.2	14.5
1976	20 846.4	5 141.3	1 318.7	6.1	29.2	62.1	18.2	62.0	15.9
1977	23 833.7	2 987.3	1 542.3	5.1	18.5	32.5	11.3	51.8	16.8

Sources: Secretaría de Hacienda y Crédito Público (1983).   Estadísticas Hacendarias del Sector Público.   Dirección General de Informática y Evolución Hacendarias.

Zedillo E. (1981). "External Pubic Indebtedness in Mexico: Recent History and Future Oil Bounded Optimal Growth".   Ph.D. dissertation, Yale University.

Notes: a/   All comparisons between a dollar and a peso variable were made by means of an "equilibrium" exchange rate calculated as described in Appendix I.

 b/   Millions of US dollars.   All ratios are in percentage.

Table 4

MEXICO: SOME KEY MACROECONOMIC INDICATORS, 1966-1977

YEAR	REAL GDP GROWTH a/	INFLATION b/	PUBLIC SECTOR DEFICIT c/	PUBLIC EXPENDITURE d/	PUBLIC INCOME d/	MONEY SUPPLY GROWTH e/
1966-1970 f/	6.9	3.5	2.5	21.1	19.0	10.7
1971	4.2	5.3	2.5	20.9	18.2	8.3
1972	8.5	5.0	4.9	23.6	18.5	21.2
1973	8.4	12.0	6.9	27.0	19.8	24.2
1974	6.1	23.7	7.2	28.3	20.9	22.0
1975	5.6	15.1	10.0	33.2	23.0	21.3
1976	4.2	15.8	9.9	33.6	23.5	30.9
1977	3.4	27.2	6.7	30.9	24.2	26.6

Sources: Nacional Financiera, S.A. *La Economía Mexicana en Cifras*. Mexico, D.F., 1981.

Banco de México. *Indicadores Económicos*. Subdirección de Investigación Económica. Several issues.

Banco de México. *Indices de Precios*. Subdirección de Investigación Económica. Several issues.

Secretaría de Hacienda y Crédito Público (1983). *Estadísticas Hacendarias del Sector Público*. Dirección General de Evaluación Hacendaria.

Notes: a/ Notice that Mexico's Nactional Accounts were revised in 1980; as a consequence, GDP growth figures from 1970 onwards have been adjusted upwards.
　　　b/ For 1966-1977 the average annual percentage increase in the worker's cost of living was used; for 1971 onwards the average annual percentage increase in the consumer price index was taken.
　　　c/ The overall financial deficit as a percentage of GDP.
　　　d/ As a percentage of GDP.
　　　e/ Average annual increase.
　　　f/ Average for the period.

Table 5

MEXICO: DECOMPOSITION OF THE CURRENT ACCOUNT CHANGES
DURING 1979-1983 WITH RESPECT TO 1978. CALCULATIONS
WITH EQUILIBRIUM EXCHANGE RATES

EXPLANATORY FACTORS a/	1979	1980	1981	1982	1983
1. EXTERNAL SHOCKS	.0043	.0112	.0244	.0391	.0278
Terms of trade shock	-.0054	-.0155	-.0133	-.0007	-.0020
Interest rate shock	.0078	.0154	.0240	.0202	.0098
World recession shock	.0018	.0114	.0137	.0197	.0159
2. BURDEN OF ACCUMULATED DEBT	-.0025	-.0034	-.0014	.0068	.0124
3. DOMESTIC POLICY ACTIONS	.0183	.0318	.0290	-.1003	-.1578
Domestic Recession	.0045	.0072	.0102	.0000	-.0074
Fixed investment cuts	.0024	.0040	.0058	.0008	.0002
Domestic output contraction	.0021	.0032	.0044	-.0008	-.0076
Increased Tradeability	.0138	.0246	.0188	-.1003	-.1504
Import replacement	.0213	.0565	.0671	.0016	-.0447
Export deepening	-.0075	-.0318	-.0483	-.1019	-.1057
Non-oil primary	-.0014	-.0039	-.0004	-.0006	.0012
Manufacturers	.0006	.0038	.0059	-.0040	-.0027
Oil	-.0067	-.0326	-.0559	-.1058	-.1101
Tourism	.0000	.0009	.0021	.0006	.0005
4. EFFECT OF OTHER EXPORT OF SERVICES	-.0047	-.0100	-.0094	.0134	.0190
5. EFFECT OF INTEREST FROM ABROAD	-.0016	-.0026	-.0037	-.0028	-.0017
6. EFFECT OF PROFIT REMITTANCES	.0008	.0007	.0010	.0012	-.0011
CALCULATED DEFICIT INCREASE b/	.0170	.0313	.0413	-.0495	-.1138

a/ Factors with a positive sign contributed to increase the relative size of the current account deficit. For example, if the "domestic recession" factor shows a positive sign it should rather be interpreted as "domestic expansion".

b/ Obtained by adding all the explanatory factors. The difference between this calculation and the observed deficit change is due to interaction and second order effects as well as adding-up errors.

Calculations made according to equation (2).

Table 6

MEXICO: THE TOTAL EXTERNAL DEBT: 1978–1983

	STOCK OF FOREIGN PUBLIC DEBT a/	STOCK OF FOREIGN PRIVATE DEBT a/	STOCK OF FOREIGN DEBT OF COMMERCIAL BANKS a/	STOCK OF TOTAL FOREIGN DEBT a/	STOCK OF FOREIGN PUBLIC DEBT b/	STOCK OF TOTAL FOREIGN DEBT b/
1978	26 422.5	5 200.0	2 000.0	33 622.5	25.7	32.7
1979	29 757.2	7 900.0	2 600.0	40 257.2	23.2	31.4
1980	33 872.7	11 800.0	5 100.0	50 772.7	20.9	31.3
1981	52 156.0	14 900.0	7 000.0	74 056.0	27.6	39.1
1982	58 145.6	18 000.0	8 000.0	84 145.6	29.8	43.1
1983	64 279.0	17 500.0	8 000.0	89 779.0	37.2	51.9

Sources: Banco de México. Indicadores Económicos. Subdirección de Investigación Económica. Several issues.
Secretaría de Hacienda y Crédito Público. Mexico: Economic and Financial Statistics, December 1983.

Notes: a/ Millions of US dollars. Year-end value. These figures exclude direct supplier's credits.
b/ As percentage of GDP. This comparison was made by means of an "equilibrium" exchange rate calculated as described in the Appendix.

Table 7

MEXICO: FLOWS OF EXTERNAL DEBT: 1978-1983

	NET FLOW OF TOTAL EXTERNAL DEBT a/	NET FLOW OF FOREIGN PUBLIC DEBT a/	INTEREST PAYMENTS TOTAL EXTERNAL DEBT a/	INTEREST PAYMENTS FOREIGN PUBLIC DEBT a/	NET FLOW OF TOTAL EXTERNAL DEBT AS PERCENTAGE OF		NET FLOW OF FOREIGN PUBLIC DEBT AS A PERCENTAGE OF			INTEREST PAYMENTS ON EXTERNAL DEBT AS A PERCENTAGE OF	
					TOTAL FIXED INVESTMENT b/	CURRENT ACCOUNT INCOME	GDP b/	PUBLIC EXPENDITURE a/	PUBLIC SECTOR DEFICIT a/	MERCH. EXPORTS	CURRENT ACCOUNT INCOME
1978	2 988.8	2 588.8	2 571.6	2 031.1	13.8	25.6	2.5	7.8	37.8	42.4	22.1
1979	6 634.7	3 334.7	3 709.3	2 888.4	22.1	40.8	2.6	7.8	35.3	42.1	22.8
1980	10 515.5	4 115.5	5 476.7	3 957.6	26.9	42.2	2.5	7.1	32.3	36.2	22.0
1981	23 283.3	18 283.3	8 278.8	5 476.0	48.0	75.6	9.7	22.8	66.0	43.2	27.2
1982	10 089.6	5 929.6	11 264.0	8 400.4	23.2	32.8	3.1	6.4	17.4	51.8	35.4
1983	3 486.8	4 486.8	9 861.4	7 346.2	22.4	12.3	2.5	6.1	29.2	46.1	34.9

Sources: Banco de México. Indicadores Económicos. Subdirección de Investigación Económica. Several issues.

Secretaría de Programación y Presupuesto. Sistema de Cuentas Nacionales de México. Several issues.

Notes: a/ Millions of US dollars.

b/ All comparisons between a dollar and a peso variable were made by means of an "equilibrium" exchange rate calculated as described in the Appendix.

Table 8

MEXICO: SOME KEY VARIABLES DURING 1978-1983

| | GDP REAL GROWTH | INFLATION | | TOTAL INVESTMENT a/ b/ | | EXCHANGE RATE REAL (INDEX) c/ | OIL | |
		AVERAGE	DECEMBER TO DECEMBER				RESERVES d/	PRODUCTION e/
1978	8.2	17.5	16.2	15.2	20.0	99.1	40 194.0	1 212.6
1979	9.2	18.2	20.0	20.2	22.1	93.9	45 803.6	1 471.0
1980	8.3	26.3	29.8	14.9	23.4	83.9	60 126.3	1 936.0
1981	7.9	28.0	28.7	14.7	24.9	77.3	72 008.4	2 313.0
1982	- .5	58.9	98.9	-16.8	20.7	145.4	72 008.4	2 748.2
1983	-4.7	101.9	80.8	-25.3	16.5	115.4	n.a.	n.a.

Sources: Banco de México. *Indicadores Económicos*. Subdirección de Investigación Económica. Several issues.
Banco de México. *Índices de Precios*. Subdirección de Investigación Económica. Several issues.
Secretaría de Programación y Presupuesto. *Sistema de Cuentas Nacionales de México*. Several issues.
PEMEX (1983). *El sector Petrolero Mexicano, 1979-1982. Estadísticas Seleccionadas*. Gerencia de Análisis y Evaluación del Mercado Internacional, Coordinación de Comercio Internacional.

Notes: a/ Percentage change in real investment.
b/ Investment as percentage of GDP.
c/ Real exchange rate index calculated as described in the Appendix. Value at the closing of December of each year.
d/ In millions of barrels, includes oil and natural gas. Petroleum reserves had stood at 11.1 billion barrels in 1976.
e/ Daily production in thousands of barrels.

Table 9

MEXICO: PUBLIC FINANCE 1978–1983a/

	TOTAL PUBLIC EXPENDITURE	PUBLIC EXPENDITURE WITHOUT PEMEX	PEMEX EXPENDITURE	PUBLIC EXPENDITURE WITHOUT INTEREST PAYMENTS b/	TOTAL PUBLIC INCOME	INCOME OIL SECTOR	INCOME NON-OIL SECTOR	FINANCIAL DEFICIT	FINANCIAL DEFICIT	
									EXTERNAL	INTERNAL
1978	32.2	27.5	4.7	30.2	25.5	5.0	20.4	6.7	4.0	2.7
1979	33.6	28.3	5.3	31.4	26.2	6.1	20.1	7.4	4.5	2.9
1980	35.6	30.4	5.2	33.5	27.8	8.0	19.7	7.9	4.9	2.9
1981	42.4	35.0	7.5	40.0	27.7	8.0	19.7	14.7	6.2	8.5
1982	48.9	41.3	7.6	40.8	31.0	12.4	18.6	17.9	14.1	3.8
1983	41.7	35.6	6.1	29.3	33.9	16.2	17.7	8.7	-3.0	11.8

Sources: Secretaría de Hacienda y Crédito Público (1983). Estadísticas Hacendarias del Sector Público. Dirección General de Informática y Evaluación Hacendaria.

Secretaría de Hacienda y Crédito Público (1984). Estadísticas Hacendarias del Sector Público. Dirección General de Informática y Evaluación Hacendaria.

Notes: a/ All variables as percentages of GDP. Some sums may not check because of rounding.

b/ Paid by the public sector on its internal and foreign debts.

Table 10

MEXICO:　AMORTIZATION PROFILE OF PUBLIC DEBT OWED TO COMMERCIAL

BANKS BEFORE AND AFTER MULTI-YEAR RESTRUCTURING[a]

(Millions of dollars)

		BEFORE	AFTER
Stock[b]	1984	54,744	53,744
	1985	8,647	277
	1986	7,183	527
	1987	11,301	991
	1988	9,549	1,491
	1989	8,533	3,487
	1990	6,336	3,718
	1991 and after	3,195	43,253

Source:　Secretaría de Hacienda y Crédito Público.

Notes:　a/ Debt originally contracted before 1983 amounts to $45.1
billion.　All of this was to be included in the multi-year
restructuring programme.　Yet, the latter implies only a
total of $43.7 billion. The difference of $1.4 billion is
assumed to be due in even instalments during 1985-1989.

b/ Year-end.

Table 11

MEXICO: AMORTIZATION PROFILE OF THE FOREIGN DEBT[a]
(Millions of dollars)

	1984 (STOCK)	1985	1986	1987	1988	1989	1990	1991 md after
Public Sector	68,406	1,630	2,071	2,876	3,718	5,443	5,679	46,989
Commercial Banks	53,744	277	527	991	1,491	3,487	3,718	43,253
World Bank and IDB	4,871	388	372	444	506	551	628	1,982
Bilateral Loans	3,168	625	560	526	424	372	175	486
Private Placements	757	138	46	141	170	122	69	71
Bonds	3,412	202	466	474	627	111	335	1,197
IMF	2,454		100	300	500	800	754	
Nationalized Banks	7,949	713	640	191				6,405
Interbank Debt[b]	6,405							6,405
Commodity Credit Corp.	1,544	713	640	191				
Private Sector[c]	17,000	700	940	1,153	3,460	3,553	3,228	3,966
FICORCA	11,900		60	273	2,580	2,673	2,348	3,966
Other	5,100	700	880	880	880	880	880	
TOTAL	93,355	3,043	3,651	4,220	7,178	8,996	8,907	57,360

Sources: Secretaría de Hacienda y Crédito Público, "Mexico: Development Financing Strategy", and author's own estimations.

Notes: a/ Assuming multi-year restructuring programme is signed-up.

b/ The source above assumes that this short-term debt can be rolled-over indefinitely.

c/ This figure definitely differs from the official source cited above. The latter assumes that no private debt has been repaid or written-off during 1983-1984.

Mexico's Balance-of-Payments Experience

Table 12

MEXICO: FORECASTING MODEL, KEY MACROECONOMIC VARIABLES

AND RATIOS 1984-1989[a]

	Billions of Dollars						
	$P_t Y_t$	$P_t I_t$	$P_t C_t$	$P_t M_t$	$P_t^x X_t$	D_t	F_t
1984	179.5	26.9	140.7	15.7	29.5	3.6	93.3
1985	198.6	39.4	149.4	22.6	32.3	2.0	95.3
1986	220.1	44.6	166.5	26.4	35.4	3.0	98.3
1987	244.4	50.7	185.7	30.8	38.9	4.3	102.6
1988	272.2	58.2	207.5	36.0	42.7	6.2	108.9
1989	304.1	67.2	232.2	42.3	46.8	9.2	118.0

	Percentage						
	Real GDP Growth	I_t/Y_t	$D_t/P_t V_t$	$F_t/P_t Y_t$	$V_t^3/P_t^x X_t$	$(D_t-V_t^3)/P_t Y_t$	$(D_t-V_t^3)/P_t^x X_t$
1984	3.3	15.0	2.0	52.0	40.0	-4.6	-27.9
1985	5.3	19.8	1.0	48.0	38.7	-5.3	-32.4
1986	5.5	20.2	1.3	44.7	36.0	-4.5	-27.8
1987	5.7	20.8	1.8	42.0	33.9	-3.6	-22.8
1988	6.0	21.4	2.3	40.0	32.2	-2.7	-17.5
1989	6.4	22.1	3.0	38.8	31.2	-1.8	-11.7

[a] 1984 figures projected according to first semester trends. 1985 and onwards figures from forecasting model I.

Table 13

MEXICO: CURRENT ACCOUNT OF BALANCE OF PAYMENTS
1984-1989 a/

(Billions of dollars)

	1984	1985	1986	1987	1988	1989
CURRENT ACCOUNT	2.7	-2.0	-3.0	-4.3	-6.2	-9.2
Total exports	29.5	32.3	35.4	38.9	42.7	46.8
Non-oil primary products	2.0	2.1	2.3	2.5	2.6	2.8
Manufactures	5.0	5.7	6.5	7.5	8.6	9.8
Oil and derivatives	16.5	17.8	19.3	20.9	22.6	24.4
Total merchandise	23.5	25.6	28.1	30.9	33.8	37.0
Other exports	6.0	6.7	7.3	8.0	8.9	9.8
Interest on assets abroad	1.1	1.2	1.2	1.3	1.3	1.4
Total imports	-15.7	-22.6	-26.4	-30.8	-36.0	-42.3
Current goods	-7.7	-9.8	-11.6	-13.6	-16.1	-18.9
Capital goods	-2.8	-6.1	-6.9	-7.9	-9.1	-10.5
Total merchandise	-10.5	-15.9	-18.5	-21.5	-25.2	-29.4
Other exports	-5.2	-6.7	-7.9	-9.3	-10.8	-12.9
Profit remittances	-0.4	-0.4	-0.4	-0.5	-0.5	-0.5
Interest on foreign debt	-11.8	-12.5	-12.8	-13.2	-13.7	-14.6

a/   1984 figures projected on basis of actual data for the first
semester of the year.   1985-1989 figures come from forecasting
model.

Table 14

MEANING OF VARIABLES USED IN CURRENT ACCOUNT DECOMPOSITION

(Variables beginning with P stand for the price deflator
of the immediately preceding variable)

YQ   GDP in current pesos.

PY

Y   GDP in 1975 pesos.

YQD   GDP in current dollars.

PYD

YD   GDP in 1975 dollars.

ZQD   Potential GDP in current dollars.

ZD   Potential GDP in 1975 dollars.

IQ   Fixed investment in current pesos.

PI

ID   Fixed investment in 1975 dollars.

F   Total external debt in current dololars (year-end value).

D   Current account deficit in current dollars.

XQ1   Exports of non-oil primary products in current dollars.

PX1

XQ2   Exports of manufactures in current dollars.

PX2

XQ3   Exports of oil and derivatives in current dollars.

PX3

XQ12   Non-oil merchandise exports in current dollars.

PX12

XQ123   Merchandise exports in current dollars.

PX123

XQ4   Tourism "exports" in current dollars.

PX4

XQ5   Other exports of services in current dollars.

PX5

XQT   Total exports in current dollars.

PXT

X1   Exports of non-oil primary products in 1975 dollars.

X2   Exports of manufactures in 1975 dollars.

X3   Exports of oil and derivatives in 1975 dollars.

X4   Tourism exports in 1975 dollars.

X5   Other exports of services in 1975 dollars.

XWQ1 "World" exports of non-oil primary products in current dollars.

PXW1

XWQ2 "World" exports of manufactures in current dollars.

XWQ3 "World" exports of oil exports in current dollars.

PXW3

XWQ4 "World" exports of tourism.

PXW4

XW1   "World" exports of non-oil primary products in 1975 dollars.

XW2   "World" exports of manufactures in 1975 dollars.

XW3   "World" exports of oil in 1975 dollars.

XW4   "World" exports of tourism in 1975 dollars.

MQ1   Current goods imports in current dollars.

PM1

MQ2   Capital goods imports in current dollars.

PM2

MQ3   Imports of services in current dollars.

PM3

MQ12 Merchandise imports in current dollars.

PM12

MQT   Total imports in current dollars.

PMT

M1   Current goods imports in 1975 dollars.

M2   Capital goods imports in 1975 dollars.

M3   Imports of services in 1975 dollars.

M12   Imports of merchandise in 1975 dollars.

MT   Total imports in 1975 dollars.

V1   Interest from abroad.

V2   Profit remittances.

V3   Interest on the total external debt.

TAS Implicit interest rate on the total external debt.

EXR Exchange rate (average).

$\overline{\text{EXR}}$ "Equilibrium" exchange rate (average).

APPENDIX

Sources of data for the analysis of the decomposition of the current account.

1. National accounts and balance of payments figures obtained from: Secretaría de Programación y Presupuesto, Sistema de Cuentas Nacionales, various issues; and Banco de México, Indicadores Económicos, Subdirección de Investigación Económica, various issues.

2. Export price indices were estimated through several proxies. The index for the non-oil primary products group was constructed with quantum and value data of a large sample of products obtained from Banco de México, Indicadores de Comercio Exterior, Subdirección de Investigación Económica, various issues. The item "consumer goods (non-food) except automotive" of the U.S. general imports unit-value indices was used to construct a proxy for the price index of the manufactures group. The index for oil and derivatives was built from data in Petróleos Mexicanos, El Sector Petrolero Mexicano, 1977-1982: Estadísticas Seleccionadas, July 1983. The item "Hotels, restaurants, etc." of the National Consumer Price Index, adjusted by variations in the exchange rate, was used to estimate a proxy for the price index of exports of tourism services. Disaggregated Mexican price indices are reported in Banco de México, Indices Precios, Subdirección de Investigación Económica, various issues. Average inflation of industrialized countries as reported in International Monetary Fund, International Financial Statistics, various issues, was used to build a price index for the other exports group.

3. In the absence of more systematic and complete data, U.S. imports of each export group were used to estimate the behaviour of world exports. For merchandise, the relevant data came from U.S. Department of Commerce, Highlights of U.S. Export and Import Trade (FT 990), various issues. The item "travel expenses abroad of U.S. citizens" was used as a proxy for world exports of tourism services. The data came from the table "U.S. International Transactions" published in U.S. Department of Commerce, Survey of Current Business, various issues. The current dollar figures were deflated by consumer prices of industrialized countries as reported in the IMF publication cited above.

4. The item "consumer goods (non-food), except automotive" of the U.S. domestic exports unit-value indices was used to build the price index of current goods imports, whereas the item "capital goods except automotive" of the same indices was used to make a proxy of the price index of capital goods imports. Data from the U.S. Department of Commerce publication cited above. Inflation in industrialized countries was used for making the price index of other imports.

5. More because of the simplicity of its calculation and interpretation than because of its theoretical appeal, a purchasing power parity (PPP) method was chosen here to estimate the "equilibrium" exchange rate. Using the formulation suggested by Lipschitz (1979), an index of the real exchange rate (IRR) was computed with the following formula:

$$IRR = \sum_{i=1}^{n} (e_i \, P_i/P)^{w_i}$$

where e_i is an index of the domestic currency price of foreign currency; P_i, an index of the price level in country i; P, an index of the domestic price level; and w_i the weight of country i in the index

$$(\sum_{i=1}^{n} w_i = 1.0).$$

The wholesale price index of each country was used; $n=21$; w_i was determined according to each country's participation in Mexico's total merchandise trade; the base year is 1978 and was chosen for several - albeit arbitrary - reasons. Firstly, it was a year of high economic growth. Secondly, merchandise imports - excluding those by the oil sector - grew 15 per cent in real terms, not a very high income elasticity. Thirdly, non-oil merchandise exports grew 8 per cent in real terms; other exports such as "tourism" also grew very dynamically. And fourthly, the "errors and omissions" item of the balance of payments was negligible, a fact that suggests that capital flight and smuggling were insignificant. In short, even though 1978 was a year of rapid growth, the external sector was very much in "equilibrium". The fact that it is a rather recent year is convenient too. All relevant data were obtained from the International Financial Statistics of the IMF.

FOOTNOTES

1/ Some parts of this report rely on Zedillo (1984) and the author's contribution in L. Solis and E. Zedillo (1984).

2/ E. L. Bacha (1983).

3/ For the definition of variables used, see table 14.

4/ Admittedly, this item comprises other relevant phenomena such as smuggling. For the most part, however, it reflects unrecorded financial flows.

5/ These aspects of debt management are more extensively studied in E. Zedillo (1981), pp. 58-89.

6/ These considerations are not to be taken as praise for the "stabilized development" model. The dull and unimaginative modus operandi of such a model is much to blame for the inequalities and industrial retardation of the Mexican economy.

7/ Compare the observed and the equilibrium exchange rates of tables 3 and 4.

8/ For interesting studies of the period, see L. Solis (1981) and L. Solis and G. Ortiz (1979).

9/ It should be said, however, that a significant proportion - more than 50 per cent - of the debt contracted by commercial banks during 1979-1981 was re-lent to public sector agencies.

10/ Expenditure on domestic goods and services minus public sector's income denominated in pesos (non-foreign exchange earnings).

11/ See the New York Times (1981).

12/ The acronym of Nacional Financiera, S. A., the most important development bank in Mexico.

13/ As explained in E. Castro (1983).

14/ At the time, there were two official rates (50 to 70 pesos per dollar); the black-market rate fluctuated around 140 pesos to the dollar).

15/ As a matter of curiosity, it should be said that the programme submitted to the IMF Board contained basically the same targets - both in nominal figures and as a percent of GDP - that had been negotiated during August 1982. The latter programme, however, had been designed before the economy suffered further internal shocks during the last four months of 1982. These shocks totally invalidated the original 1983 forecasts of inflation, exchange rate, interest rates, nominal GDP, etc. Thus, the approved IMF programme and the 1983 fiscal budget were technically inaccurate. A few cynics credit this inaccuracy with the Mexican success of 1983.

16/ Quoted from a telex sent by the Secretary of Finance of Mexico to the international banking community on 8 December 1982, p. 4.

17/ A description of this mechanism is given in E. Zedillo (1983).

18/ The proposed restructuring is presented in Secretaría de Hacienda y Crédito Público (1984).

19/ On the assumption that none of the debt owed to commercial banks is repaid before 1991.

20/ The size of these shocks was chosen arbitrarily. Given the linearity of the model, however, the results can be extended to analyse shocks of other sizes.

BIBLIOGRAPHY

Bacha, E.L. and C. Díaz-Alejandro (1980). "Financial Markets: A view from the Periphery", mimeo, Rio de Janeiro, Brazil.

Bacha, E.L. (1983). "Foreign Debt, Balance of Payments, and Growth Prospects of Developing Countries", published as "Terms of reference" for this series of country studies and appended to G. Helleiner's synthesis paper (UNCTAD/MFD/TA/32).

_____ (1984). "External Shocks and Growth Prospects: The Case of Brazil, 1973-1988", published in this series of country studies as document UNCTAD/MFD/TA/32/Add.1.

Banco de México (1982). Informe Anual 1981, Mexico, D.F.

_____ (1984). Informe Anual 1983, Mexico, D.F.

Castro, E. (1983). "Algunas Consideraciones sobre el Financiamiento Externo de México en los añ 1980-1982", mimeo, Mexico, D.F.

Lipschitz, L. (1979). "Exchange Rate Policy for a Small Developing Country, and the Selection of an Appropriate Standard", IMF Staff Papers, 26: 423-449.

Secretaría de Hacienda y Crédito Público (1984). "The United Mexican States: Financing Principles for Mexican Public Sector Debt to Commercial Banks, Maturing 1985-1990", mimeo, New York.

Solís, L. (1981). Economic Policy Reform in Mexico, A Case Study for Developing Countries, Pergamon Press, New York.

_____ and G. Ortiz. "Financial Structure and Exchange Rate Experience, Mexico 1954-1977", Journal of Developing Economics, 6 (1979) 515-548.

_____ and E. Zedillo (1984). "A Few Considerations on the Foreign Debt of Mexico", mimeo, Mexico, D.F.

The New York Times (1981). "Mexico, in Switch, Will Lift Oil Price", 17 June.

Zedillo, E. (1981). "External Public Indebtedness in Mexico. Recent History and Future Oil Bounded Optimal Growth". Ph.D. dissertation, Yale University.

_____ (1983). "The Program for Coverage of Exchange Risks. A General Description and Financial Aspects", mimeo, Mexico, D.F.

_____ (1984). "The Mexican External Debt: The Last Decade" in Wionczek, M. (ed.). Politics and Economics of Latin American Indebtedness, Westview Press, Boulder, Co. Forthcoming, 1984.

FOREIGN DEBT, BALANCE OF PAYMENTS AND THE ECONOMIC
CRISIS OF THE PHILIPPINES IN 1983-84

E. Remolona, M. Mangahas and F. Pante Jr.*

1.   Introduction

The Philippines is now (August 1984) facing its worst balance-of-payments crisis since the end of the Second World War. Foreign exchange reserves were virtually depleted in the latter part of 1983, as international banking flows came to a standstill.   In October of that year, a 90-day moratorium on amortization of external debt was declared.   Since then, the moratorium has been extended thrice, pending the approval by the International Monetary Fund of a $635 million standby loan and the rescheduling of the country's debt with its other creditors.

This crisis is the culmination of mounting current account deficits for at least six years.   The worsening of the current account was due in part to a severe deterioration in the country's terms of trade and in part to a policy response that relied heavily on foreign borrowing to the neglect of other adjustment measures.   Not only did such borrowing finance the perceived investment requirements of the country's growth strategy;   it also financed an accumulation of exchange reserves that for a time prevented any real depreciation of the peso.

This paper provides an account of the Philippine macro-economic experience leading to the current difficulties, and pays special attention to the relationships between external shocks and domestic policy responses. With the aid of a simple forecasting model, the paper also makes a preliminary assessment of the country's medium-term growth prospects in the light of the short-term austerity measures being adopted to resolve the debt problem.

The next section presents an overview of the balance of payments as it evolved between 1971 and 1983 and broadly indicates the role of external shocks and domestic policies.   Section 3 subsequently focuses

*The authors are Assistant Professor, U.P. School of Economics, Vice-President, Research for Development Department, Development Academy of the Philippines, and President, Philippine Institute for Development Studies, respectively.

on the current account by applying a decomposition analysis. Section 4 inquires more deeply into the developments between 1979 and 1983 by conducting counterfactual exercises to isolate the effects of various external shocks and policy responses. Section 5 reports on the simulation of a simple forecasting model designed to evaluate the country's growth prospects, and Section 6 contains the concluding remarks.

2.   An overview of the Balance of Payments

   2.1 <u>Balance-of-payments experience, 1971-83</u>

   The striking feature of the balance-of-payments experience of the Philippines during 1971-1983 is the generally rapid increases in current account deficits after the oil price shocks of 1973-74 and 1979-80. Table 2.1 shows that, after posting a surplus of $536 million in 1973 which was due mainly to the world commodity boom, the current account turned into progressively larger deficits, so that in 1982 the deficit exceeded the $3 billion mark, accounting for 31.8 per cent of trade and 7.9 per cent of GNP (see also table 2.2).1/

   From 1973 to 1974, during which time oil prices quadrupled, import payments almost doubled, causing the 1973 current account surplus to become a deficit in 1974. However, the deficit was kept to only 4.6 per cent of trade and 1.2 per cent of GNP; while export volume fell, export prices increased by 66 per cent on the average, allowing export receipts to grow by a hefty 44 per cent and preventing larger deficits from being registered (table 2.3). Export prices collapsed subsequently in 1975 and 1976. Together with the continuing climb in imports, the current account deficit grew from $176 million in 1974 to $892 million in 1975 and $1,050 million in 1976. The ratio of the deficits to trade accordingly jumped from 4.6 per cent in 1974 to 23.4 per cent in 1975 and 25.6 per cent in 1976. The ratio of the deficit to GNP likewise increased from 1.2 per cent in 1974 to 5.7 per cent and 5.9 per cent in 1975 and 1976, respectively.

   An improvement in the current account balance occurred in 1977, though it fell far short of reversing the deficit. In 1978, the current account deficit worsened again, amounting to the equivalent of 19.6 per cent of trade and 4.6 per cent of GNP. As oil prices nearly tripled in 1979-80 and the worldwide recession made its impact, the current account further deteriorated, with the consequence that the deficits averaged 30 per cent and 8 per cent of trade and GNP, respectively, in 1982 and 1983. Until 1983, receipts from merchandise exports were not able to recover to the level they had reached in 1980. As compared to the recession that had followed the first oil shock, which had been relatively mild and short-lived, the recession which followed the second oil shock turned out to be deeper and longer in duration. Meanwhile, the growth of merchandise imports into the Philippines continued unchecked until 1982, and even then, the drop of less than 4 per cent per year in 1982 and 1983 was hardly enough to offset an already critical level of current account deficits.

Non-merchandise receipts and net transfers dampened trade deficits during the period 1974-1981, but only to a limited extent. Net inflows of these items averaged $107.6 million per year, as compared to trade deficits which averaged $942.8 million per year during this period. Starting in 1982, the non-merchandise trade and transfers components of the current account aggravated rather than mitigated current account deficits, largely as a result of the dramatic rise in interest payments reflecting both the impact of the Philippines' heavy borrowing from abroad since the first oil shock and the rise in world interest rates. In 1982, interest payments totalled $1.91 billion. This was more than three times the interest payments made in 1979 and accounted for 61.2 per cent of the total current account deficit incurred during the year. In 1983, the recorded interest payments declined by 6.7 per cent, partly because of the softening of international interest rates and partly because of the disruption of banking flows into the country towards the end of the year.

The interesting question to ask at this juncture is how the relatively large current account deficits experienced during most of the 1970s and the early 1980s were financed. As the capital account of the balance of payments shows, the Philippines relied heavily on foreign capital inflows to finance the current account deficits in 1974-1983. Net direct foreign investments during this period accounted for only 9.0 per cent of total net long-term capital inflows on the average; hence, it is quite clear that the larger portion of foreign capital inflows came in the form of foreign loans. From 1973 to 1982, capital inflows in the form of long-term and medium-term loans averaged $1.5 billion per year. This amount is twice as much as the combined long-term and medium-term loans incurred during the immediately preceding ten years (about $750 million).

Thus, despite huge current account deficits, the relatively large volume of external financing that was available to the monetary authorities enabled them not only to moderate overall balance-of-payments deficits but also to shore up the level of international reserves, at least until 1980. In 1980, gross reserves stood at $3.2 billion as compared to $1.0 billion in 1973. From 1973 to 1980, the Central Bank maintained a reserve level equivalent to an average of 4.3 months' imports. In contrast, the corresponding figure from 1960 to 1972 was 2.5 months' imports. In 1981 and 1982, the rate of external borrowing obviously could no longer match the increase in current account deficits, and as a result reserves were drawn down from a level equivalent to five months' imports to about four months' imports.

The real squeeze came in the second half of 1983 when unsettling political events led international banks, which were already nervous about the capability of developing countries to repay their mounting debt, to halt further lending to the Philippines and call their short-term loans. As regards the latter, it should be noted that the rapid build-up of short-term loans particularly after 1979, no doubt contributed to the balance-of-payments crisis in no small way. In 1982, the level of short-term capital inflows was nearly three times that in 1979, reaching $12.1 billion. From 1973 to 1978, the ratio of short-term capital inflows to inflows of long-term and medium-term loans averaged 1.86. The comparable ratio for 1978 to 1982 was 4.60. It is clear that as long-term and medium-term loans became more difficult to obtain in the international financial market, greater reliance was placed on short-term loans to cover the widening current account deficits.

The effect of the drastic drying up of external funds on the Philippines was swift and dramatic. The net inflows of foreign capital dropped from $1.4 billion in 1982 to $506 million in 1983. With a current account deficit of $2.7 billion, corresponding to 28.4 per cent of trade and 8 per cent of GNP, the situation very quickly turned into a full-blown debt and balance-of-payments crisis. International reserves were virtually depleted, with the end-December 1983 level being equivalent to only one and a half months' imports. In October 1983, the reserves were in fact down to less than one month's imports. As this paper was being written (August 1984), the Philippines was still awaiting the approval by the IMF of a $635 million stand-by agreement. Such approval will serve as the green light for the rescheduling of the country's debt, which will have to be negotiated with some 400 banks in so far as it is debt owed to private lenders. Official debt will be negotiated under the auspices of the Paris Club. Meanwhile, a moratorium on amortization of external debt has been agreed upon with the country's creditors. This was to have ended on 16 January 1984 but has been extended for three 90-day periods.

2.2 The role of external shocks

Any explanation of the balance-of-payments crisis will not be complete without a discussion of the effects of external shocks. Accordingly, this section will look more closely at the role of oil prices, the terms of trade and recession in the industrialized countries in the evolution of the crisis.

From 1971 to 1973, the Philippines was importing (in value terms) only an average of $142.5 million per year of crude oil (see table 2.4). This accounted for 10.7 per cent of total imports during this period. In 1974, the value of oil imports rose four times to $573.2 million, accounting for 18.2 per cent of total imports. The share of oil imports in the value of total imports peaked in 1981 at 26.2 per cent and settled at about 23.5 per cent in 1982 and 1983. The important observation to make about these developments is that while the country has been paying more and more for oil imports, it has been receiving a diminishing quantity of oil. In 1982, the country paid $1.8 billion for oil imports. This was more than ten times the value of oil imports in 1973, but 12 million barrels, or almost 20 per cent, less than the quantity of oil imported in 1973.

Table 2.5 shows terms of trade indicators for 1971-83. With 1972 as the base year, the terms-of-trade index for the Philippines was 58.7

in 1982 and 65.0 in 1983. The deterioration is less pronounced if only the prices of non-oil imports are compared to export prices (about 92.0 in 1982-83), but it is much more severe if the comparison is made in terms of oil import prices (about 16.1 in 1982-83). If 1973 is used as the base year, the terms of trade can be expected to be much worse for the country because of the high commodity prices which prevailed during the said year. As Power (1983) observes: "Few countries in the world have suffered as much from the movement of international prices." Quantifying the relative effects of the terms-of-trade deterioration and the reduced world demand for Philippine exports on the current account, he found that for the period 1973-1982, about 78 per cent of the total external shocks is accounted for by the deterioration in the terms of trade and only 22 per cent is accounted for by the effects of world recession or the so-called export volume effect. The terms of trade effect was higher during the first oil shock (1974-77: 83 per cent) than during the second oil shock (1979-82: 72 per cent). This is not surprising because the terms of trade deterioration was more severe during 1974-77 than during 1979-82. Moreover, traditional exports accounted for 83 per cent of total exports in 1974; in 1982, their share declined to about 40 per cent. As regards the export volume effect, the estimated impact is greater during the second oil shock (28 per cent) than during the first (17 per cent). This reflects the greater depth and length of the world recession after the second oil shock.

The latter point can be readily illustrated by comparing what happened to exports after the first with what happened after the second oil shocks. After the oil price escalation in 1973-74, exports dropped in 1975 by 16 per cent. However, exports quickly recovered and posted an annual growth rate of 20.7 per cent per year from 1976 to 1980. It was a different story thereafter, for exports declined every year from 1981 to 1983, clearly indicating the effects of the deepest and longest-lasting recession since the early 1930s.

The situation became more difficult for major debtor developing countries like the Philippines after the second oil shock, because as industrialized countries adopted restrictive domestic monetary policies to contain inflation, international interest rates rose and increased the debt service burden of borrowing countries. Thus, while these countries found it more difficult to earn more foreign exchange, they simultaneously found themselves saddled with greater debt servicing requirements. Under such circumstances, what happened to Mexico, Brazil, Argentina, Nigeria and other borrowing countries in Latin America and Africa was not unexpected. The emergence of the relatively widespread debt servicing problems aggravated the situation for many debtor countries, for the consequence was a drastic cut in the amount of new bank lending to non-oil developing countries, which fell from $51 billion in 1981 to only $25 billion in 1982 (William et al. 1983). The greater reliance of the Philippines on short-term capital inflows, particularly in 1982, can be explained by this development. Such a posture, however, only increased the vulnerability of the country to a major disruption of normal banking flows, which is a consequence of its heavy dependence on banking flows to finance current account deficits and service foreign debt.

2.3 The role of domestic policies

2.3.1 The growth strategy

The study by J. Power cited earlier is a good starting point. Aside from providing an idea of the relative importance of external shocks, it also broadly indicates how and to what extent Philippine domestic policies accommodated these shocks. In Power's analysis, the accommodation or adjustment process is decomposed into export expansion, import substitution and slower output growth. The difference between total shocks and total adjustments represents that part of external shocks which must be financed by additional external capital inflows. Power found that the Philippines adjusted in such a way as to accommodate only about one-fourth of the external shocks, leaving 75 per cent to be covered by additional external financing. In this adjustment process, export expansion was the most important element, followed by import substitution. The rate of growth of output had a negative accommodation effect; in other words, it took the form of an internal shock which necessitated the imbalances generated by external shocks.

Although the model employed by Power has many limitations, 2/ its results depict rather accurately the directions of Philippine domestic policies in the period following the two oil shocks. Rather than curtailing imports and holding down the overall growth rate, the Philippine Government decided to maintain the momentum of growth. This is clearly shown by the growth targets of successive Philippine Development Plans, which are as follows: 3/

Years	Growth target (% per year)
1972-1975	6.9
1974-1977	7.0
1978-1982	7.6
1983-1987	6.5
Actual growth rate:	
1960-1970	4.9

That this was in fact the strategy adopted can be further seen from table 2.6. Instead of tapering off as a result of the 1973-74 oil shock, the investment rate actually increased as from 1974, averaging 30 per cent from 1974 to 1982. The comparable ratio for the period 1960-1970 was only about 20 per cent. While the domestic savings rate also increased during the period, such increase was not enough to prevent a widening of the resource gap. Thus, the investment/saving gap as a percentage of GNP rose to an average of 6.0 per cent during 1974-1982 as compared to an average of only 1.7 per cent from 1960 to 1970. The government played a significant part in shoring up investments during the period. Government capital expenditures expanded by 25 per cent per year from 1974 to 1982. The comparable rate of expansion in the 1960s was 21.1 per cent annually. Moreover, total government spending increased by 24.7 per cent per year in 1974-1982, as compared to 13.4 per cent per year in the 1960s. However, while fiscal policy tended to be expansionary, the budgetary deficit as a percentage of GNP was kept below 2.0 per cent until 1980, primarily because of the increase in government savings up to that year.

There is also evidence of an expansionary monetary policy supporting the overall strategy. The growth in liquidity as measured by M3 from 1973 to 1982 averaged 23.6 per cent annually, as compared to the average growth of 13.6 per cent per year during 1960-1970 and 12.5 per cent per year in 1971-1972. Excluding the export boom year of 1973, the average growth in liquidity is still relatively high at 20.5 per cent annually.

The strategy described above appears to have succeeded at least until 1979. From 1973 to 1979, the Philippine economy grew by 7.0 per cent annually, much faster than the 4.9 per cent annual growth rate attained in the 1960s when world economic conditions were in general more favourable. Of course, this period of fast growth included 1973 when high export prices benefited not only traditional exports like sugar, copper and coconut, but also manufactured exports. In 1973, agricultural output increased by 6.1 per cent while that of industry grew by 12.3 per cent. Even without 1973, however, economic growth was a respectable 6.5 per cent per year.

After 1979, the economy began to falter. GNP growth in real terms progressively slowed down from 7.5 per cent in 1979 to 4.4 per cent in 1980, 3.7 per cent in 1981, 2.8 per cent in 1982 and 1.4 per cent in 1983. The latter is the lowest growth rate experienced by the Philippines since the country's independence in 1946. While the country continued to pursue its strategy of maintaining growth, at least two factors prevented a repetition of the favourable performance from 1973 to 1979. First, as mentioned above, the prolonged worldwide recession following the second oil shock had a double-edged effect on the Philippines: it increased the debt-service burden on an already high level of external debt 4/ and, at the same time, led to lower export receipts. Certainly, the rate of borrowing needed to sustain growth targets could no longer be realized. Secondly, the country was not able to translate large doses of investments into higher rates of economic growth because of the relative inefficiency of investments. This is indicated by the high incremental capital-output ratios shown in table 2.6.

Despite the unfavourable international economic environment which followed the second oil shock, the government continued to pursue its "countercyclical" strategy. The current account deficit continued to expand and budgetary deficits as a proportion of GNP rose to 4.0 per cent and 4.3 per cent in 1981 and 1982, respectively. It now seems that the length and depth of the recession were not anticipated, and it was believed that, as in the case of the recession following the first oil shock, the country would be able to get over the hump successfully. By 1981-1982, however, the difficulty of servicing an external debt that had grown too large relative to the country's ability to pay began to be felt. The politically unsettling events of August and September of 1983 clearly demonstrated the serious vulnerability of the country's balance-of-payments position at that particular time.

2.3.2 Management of the external debt

The immediate consequence of the strategy of maintaining growth through external financing is the concomitant build-up of external debt. The accumulation of the debt is evident from the figures in table 2.7 which shows the end-of-year levels of Philippine outstanding external debt of the non-monetary sector from 1971 to 1983, broken down into public and private debt. Total outstanding foreign debt exhibited a continuous upward trend in the last twelve years. In 1971, total external debt outstanding was only $2.1 billion. By 1983, this level had risen nine-fold. 5/ The trends in public and private outstanding external debt generally followed that of total outstanding foreign debt.

The annual average growth rates of outstanding external debt for different time periods are shown in table 2.8. The first period, 1963-1972, consists of the ten years before the energy crisis, while the second period, 1973-1982, refers to the ten-year period when the world was subjected to the oil shocks of 1973-74 and 1978-79. The second period is further subdivided into two sub-periods, namely: the two five-year periods which followed the oil shocks. The growth rates are shown in both nominal and real terms, the latter alternatively derived using import and export prices. Data are given for total public and private outstanding external debt.

The table shows that total external debt of the non-monetary sector grew more rapidly during the 1973-1982 period, although inflation has overstated this rate increase. This is particularly true when the growth rates are adjusted for changes in import prices. If one looks at the data for the two sub-periods, one can see that total external debt grew faster during 1973-1977 than during 1978-1982, reflecting the generally easy international financial situation after the first oil shock 6/ and the subsequent tightening up of international credit after the second oil shock.

The trends in public sector external debt generally follow that of total external debt. Public external debt grew more rapidly in 1973-1982 than during 1963-1972. It also expanded at a quicker pace after the first oil shock than after the second. The growth in private sector foreign borrowings during the periods exhibited a somewhat different trend. Private external debt grew less rapidly in 1973-1982 than in 1963-1972. However, private external debt, like total and public external debt, posted higher rates of growth after the first oil shock than after the second.

As regards the distribution of outstanding external debt between the public and private sectors, table 2.9 shows that public sector borrowings have accounted for a growing proportion of total foreign borrowings since 1971. In 1971, outstanding public sector debt accounted for only 39.9 per cent of the total external debt; by 1982, the public sector's share had risen to 57.8 per cent of the total debt.7/

What happened to the private sector's external debt is a mirror image of public external debt. The foreign borrowings of the private sector accounted for 60.1 per cent of total outstanding external debt in 1971. The share of private sector borrowings almost consistently tapered off, so that at the end of 1982 this proportion stood at only 42.7 per cent.

Philippine external debt has been composed mainly of long-term loans, as shown in table 2.10. From 1971 to 1978, the share of long-term loans in the total rose consistently. From 59.8 per cent in 1971, long-term loans as a share of the total increased to 78.6 per cent in 1978. The high share of long-term loans from 1974 to 1978 coincides perfectly with the period of easy credit in the international financial markets. From 1979, the share of long-term loans in the total began to decline as tightness in the international financial community set in.

When long-term loans as a proportion of the total started to fall, the share of short-term loans increased from an average of 13.3 per cent in 1973-77 to an average of 21.4 per cent in 1978-83. 8/ As noted earlier, because long-term loans became difficult to obtain in the tight international financial market, the country relied more on short-term borrowings to cover current account deficits. Medium-term loans probably also became difficult to secure since their share in the total declined from an average of 11.6 per cent in 1973-77 to 5.3 per cent in 1978-83.

The heavy reliance on short-term borrowings particularly in the late 1970s and early 1980s is likewise shown by the ratio of short-term debt to gross Central Bank international reserves. In 1971 and 1972, this ratio was high because reserve levels were low. In 1973, however, short-term debt was only 27.1 per cent of the Central Bank's gross reserves. The proportion went up to 72.1 per cent in 1978 and rose dramatically to 175.6 per cent in 1982. In 1983, the ratio reached 465.7 per cent, principally on account of the drop in international reserves towards the end of the year.

The effect of the build-up of the external debt on the country's debt burden is indicated by the magnitude of the debt service ratios shown in table 2.11. Alternative ratios are presented, namely: (1) the "official" debt-service ratio, i.e., the ratio of principal and interest amortization, or debt service for short, to total foreign exchange receipts, including foreign capital inflows lagged by one year 9/; (2) a ratio similar to the first, except that the numerator and denominator are contemporaneous; (3) the ratio of debt service to merchandise exports; and (4) the ratio of debt service to exports of goods and services exclusive of transfers. The marked differences among these ratios are immediately noticeable, but two features should be highlighted. First, the debt-service ratios using total foreign exchange receipts as the denominator are consistently lower than those based on exports of goods and exports of goods and services. By definition, this can be expected. Secondly, while the trends in the last two ratios are similar, they do not match those of the first two. In certain years, a decline in the former set of ratios is accompanied by an increase in the latter ones and vice versa. In 1982, the ratios based on exports indicated drastic increases, which should have caused some alarm. On the other hand, the official ratio hardly moved and the other ratio even declined. Obviously, the official debt-service ratio tends to understate the debt burden, because it partly depends on the ability to borrow abroad. Thus, it cannot and should not be employed as an indicator of whether or not the country can afford to borrow more without triggering a liquidity crisis, which seems to have been the case. While the other two ratios have limitations of their own, they are more reflective of the country's internal capacity to generate foreign exchange for debt-service payments.

2.3.3 Foreign exchange rate policy

The foreign exchange rate is one of the important policy instruments in balance-of-payments adjustment. Accordingly, it would be necessary to inquire into the nature of the foreign exchange rate policy applied by the government during the period under consideration. The Philippines adopted a flexible exchange rate system in early 1970 and has maintained it since then. 10/ Thus, in comparison with the previous period of fixed exchange rates, the monetary authorities had the flexibility to make adjustments in the price of foreign exchange as they saw fit at a given point of time. There is ample evidence, though, that exchange rate policy was not used effectively to adjust to the imbalances in the country's external accounts.

Table 2.12 shows exchange rate indices for Philippine nominal, effective and real effective exchange rates. 11/ From 1973 to 1980, nominal exchange rates exhibited a generally depreciating trend, but the rate of depreciation was kept at only 1.5 per cent per year. Effective exchange rates depreciated at roughly the same pace. Meanwhile, the Philippine inflation rate (GNP deflator) accelerated from 5.3 per cent per year in the 1960s to 13.9 per cent per year from 1973 to 1983 (table 2.13). While the Philippines' major trading partners also experienced high inflation rates after 1973-74, these were not as high as those in the Philippines. Thus, the limited nominal adjustments in the peso-dollar exchange rate led to real effective exchange rates that in fact appreciated after 1973 and hardly moved until 1981. Relatively larger nominal adjustments were made in 1982 and 1983, but these did not lead to any significant depreciation of the real effective exchange rate.

It will be difficult to appreciate this state of affairs if one were to look only at the current account. For certainly, given such large imbalances, the exchange rate ought to have depreciated more rapidly. The answer can be found in the capital account. Because the Philippines was able to obtain relatively large amounts of foreign loans, the monetary authorities were able to "hold the line" as far as the exchange rate was concerned. As noted above, the rate of foreign borrowing even allowed an increase in the Central Bank's international reserves. The shortcoming of this policy response is that the easy external financing led to the postponement of required adjustments in the exchange rates. Certainly, such large current account deficits as described earlier cannot be dismissed as symptoms of fundamental disequilibrium in the balance of payments, necessitating basic policy adjustments.

2.3.4 Trade and industrial policies

The balance-of-payments problem that the country is facing is not only financial but also structural in character and can be traced to the highly protective and biased trade and industrial policies which date back to the 1950s (Bautista, Power and Associates 1981). These policies strongly favoured the import-dependent manufacture of consumer goods for the domestic market at the expense of exports and agricultural production. Attempts were made towards the end of the 1960s to correct the situation through the grant of liberal fiscal incentives to exporters under the Industrial Incentives Act of 1967 and later in 1970, under the Export Incentives Act. Furthermore, the government embarked on a more active export promotion programme involving not only the expansion but also the diversification of exports in terms of commodities and markets. However, the effort remained as a balancing act, because the biases of the productive system were just the same kept in place. It was only in 1980 that a programme of trade and financial liberalization and rationalization of fiscal incentives was initiated with the World Bank providing "adjustment assistance" in the form of a structural adjustment loan. Essentially, this programme involves the reduction of effective rates of protection, the liberalization of imports, the correction of the capital-bias of fiscal incentives, the freeing of interest rate ceilings, and other institutional reforms in the financial sector. While these changes can be expected to improve the long-term prospects of the Philippine economy, the impact of these policy reforms can only be felt after a number of years, especially in view of current financial difficulties.

Nevertheless, as pointed out earlier, exports responded favourably in the 1970s. From 1970 to 1980, Philippine exports expanded by an average of 20.7 per cent per year, as compared to 7.1 per cent per year in the 1960s, with the share of non-traditional exports in the total increasing from 7.5 per cent in 1970 to 38.0 per cent in 1980. 12/ Leading the group of new exports were electronics and semi-conductor devices, garments, furniture and fixtures, handicrafts, food products, beverages, chemical products and footwear. The manufacturing sector also improved its performance in the 1970s, growing by 7.0 per cent per year as compared to 5.1 per cent in the 1960s. However, this growth was achieved at a high investment cost, as manifested by the relatively high incremental capital/output ratios mentioned earlier. Moreover, because of the capital bias of incentives, it was not able to expand employment in the sector, its share in total employment remaining at about 11 per cent throughout the 1970s.

3.   Analysis of the Current Account, 1971-1982

We can retell the history of the evolution of the current account of the Philippines between 1971 and 1982 by dividing it into three episodes leading to the 1983 crisis. There was an initial episode covering just three years when sustained improvements in the current account culminated in a surplus of over 4.9 per cent of potential domestic output in 1973. This was followed by another short episode but this one marked by a worsening of the current account. This worsening was so serious that by 1976 there was a deficit amounting to 5.8 per cent of potential domestic output. The third episode was a much longer period of deterioration following the single significant improvement in 1977. In this episode, the current account deficit climbed steadily from 3.6 per cent of potential output in 1977 to a record 8.0 per cent in 1982. In the passages which follow, we use Edmar Bacha's (1983) accounting framework (see Appendix) to dissect those episodes.

3.1 The 1971-73 episode

The improvement in the current account balance from a negligible deficit in 1971 to a surplus of over 4.9 per cent of potential domestic output in 1973 (see table 3.1) was due to some extent to falling imports of capital goods. The decomposition of capital-goods imports in table 3.2 shows that this trend can be attributed in part to import substitution and in part to a cyclical contraction of fixed domestic investment. In real terms, the ratio of those imports to fixed capital formation fell from 32.1 per cent in 1971 to 26.5 per cent in 1973 (table 3.2), while the ratio of such investment itself to potential domestic output declined from 17.3 per cent to 16.1 per cent.

With the onset of the first oil price shock in 1973, the oil import bill as a fraction of potential output nearly doubled (table 3.1). But this rise in the import bill was more than offset by a suddenly impressive export performance as the world commodity boom brought a 27 per cent hike in export prices for the Philippines and as the country took advantage of this development by expanding its exports (table 3.4). At the same time there was a drop in interest payments and a rise in inflows from factor payments and transfers. All these combined to produce the last current account surplus the Philippines has had.

3.2 The 1974-76 episode

The second episode bore the brunt of the oil price shock. The substantial 1973 surplus turned into a deficit of almost 1.2 per cent of potential output in 1974, then into deficits of 5.5 and 5.8 per cent in 1975 and 1976. While it is true that the relative price of oil imports tripled between 1973 and 1975, the contribution of capital-goods imports to the sharp deterioration of the current account was almost as significant as that of oil. The substitution away from oil imports was so successful that the ratio of those imports to actual output was no more than 4.5 per cent in 1975 compared to 8.2 per cent in 1973 (table 3.3). At the same time, the effort to reduce reliance on imported energy resulted in a surge of fixed investment from 16.1 per cent of potential output in 1973 to 23.7 per cent in 1975 (table 3.2). So heavily dependent on imports was such investment that capital-goods imports increased from 4.5 per cent of potential output in 1973 to 7.1 per cent in 1975.

However, the import bills for capital goods, oil, and other imports all fell between 1975 and 1976 (table 3.1) with a general decline in import prices. The relative price of oil imports hardly moved, while the relative price of other non-capital goods imports fell by 22.4 per cent, enough to offset the 14.2 per cent rise in the prices for capital-goods imports (tables 3.2 and 3.3). Yet the current account deficit worsened slightly. This was due to an increasingly disappointing export performance attributable entirely to a 20.0 per cent fall in export prices (table 3.4). A year after the oil price shock, it was weak exports rather than oil imports that were causing problems, and the global recession that followed the oil price shock was to blame.

3.3 The 1977-82 episode

The last improvement in the current account occurred in 1977. The improvement was due mainly to lower relative import prices for capital goods and oil as well as to import substitution for both these items. There was at the same time a slight drop in interest payments and a recovery in exports in spite of the continued decline in export prices. From then on, the current account steadily deteriorated. Starting with a deficit of 3.6 per cent of potential output in 1977, the deficit by 1982 was 8.0 per cent (table 3.1).

It was during this episode that interest payments on foreign debt figured prominently. The worsening of the current account was accompanied by incessant increases in interest payments from 1.1 per cent of potential output in 1977 to 4.6 per cent in 1982, or from less than a third to over half of the current account deficit (table 3.1). It was also during this period that import items other than capital goods and oil contributed to the deterioration in the current account. The ratio of such imports to actual domestic output increased from 10.3 per cent in 1977 to 15.8 per cent in 1982 (table 3.3).

After a setback in 1978, export performance improved until 1980 but not enough to narrow the gap between exports and imports. This gap was just over 3.6 per cent of potential output in 1977 and about 5.4 per cent in 1980. From then on, the onset of the world recession, deeper and more prolonged than the earlier one, precluded any reversal of that trend. Export revenues fell from 16.2 per cent of potential output in 1980 to just 12.0 per cent in 1982 as export prices dropped 22.4 per cent (table 3.4), and the gap between imports and exports widened to 6.3 per cent of potential output.

In the next section, we inquire more deeply into what happened to the current account between 1979 and 1983 in order to isolate the effects of the various external shocks and policy responses that presumably led to the crisis.

4.   Counterfactual scenarios, 1979-83

External developments almost certainly played a major part in the slide of the balance of payments into the 1983 crisis. The four years preceding the crisis were, after all, the years of the second oil price shock and the ensuing world recession. This oil price shock was not nearly as terrible as the first, but the recession this time was devastating. This time there was the added dimension of an international credit squeeze which shortened loan maturities and pushed interest rates up to record levels. Indeed, it was the interest rate shock that caused the initial deterioration of the current account of the Philippines. Only in 1981 did the terms of trade take a turn for the worse to make matters all but irredeemable.

The policy response was apparently causing damage from the outset. In 1979 and 1980, the real shift towards imports other than oil and capital goods together with the investment boom stimulated by the government apparently deepened the current account deficit more than did the terms of trade and international interest rates. Not until 1981 did the external shocks begin to dominate, and these shocks combined with the continued import bias in 1982 were perhaps the last straw. In 1983, no longer able to take the strain of both external shock and policy response, the system collapsed.

4.1 External shocks

Taking the average for 1976 to 1978 as the benchmark, the current account deficit in 1979 as a fraction of potential output was only 0.6 of a percentage point worse (table 4.1) and the external shocks from the terms of trade and international interest rates taken together would not account fully for this worsening. Indeed if the terms of trade had stayed where they were in 1976-78 and all the other variables had moved as they did, the deficit as a fraction of potential output would have been 2.1 percentage points smaller in 1979 and almost 0.6 of a percentage point smaller in 1980 (table 4.1). The relative prices of all imports other than oil were lower in both years than the 1976-78 levels (table 4.2). The rise in interest rates contributed at most 1.2 percentage points in 1979 (table 4.1) to the deterioration of the current account, not enough to offset the favourable effects of the terms of trade, unlike in 1980, when the former contributed 1.6 points and the latter contributed minus 0.6 points.

It was in 1981 that the terms of trade turned adverse. While prices for capital-goods imports continued their fall, their effect was swamped by that of the sudden surge in the prices of oil imports and of other non-capital goods imports. The effect altogether was to make the 1981 deficit as a fraction of potential output 4.6 percentage points larger than the 1976-78 average (table 4.1). During this year also, interest rates reached their peak, possibly aggravating the deficit by as much as 2.3 percentage points. More or less the same pattern was repeated in 1982, except that this time the prices of imports other than oil and capital goods and interest rates returned to more moderate levels. In 1983, the terms of trade remained poorer than the 1976-78 average only because of the high price of oil imports (table 4.2). In that year, before the advent of the world recovery could reverse those terms, the crisis came.

During this whole period, the effect of the recession was detrimental to the terms of trade but not to export volumes. Indeed, the increasing share of Philippine exports in the exports of Asian oil-importing developing countries may have contributed as much as 2.3 and 2.7 percentage points to alleviating the deficit in 1981 and 1982, respectively (table 4.1).

4.2 Policy responses

A significant part of the deterioration of the current account in 1979 and 1980 from the average of the 1976-78 levels can be attributed to the government's attempt to sustain the country's growth momentum by means of expansionary fiscal policy. In consequence of the government's spending spree in 1979 and 1980, fixed investment rose to 27.9 per cent of potential output and 26.9 per cent respectively, from an average of 24.6 in 1976-78 (table 3.2). The effect on the current account was to widen the deficit as a fraction of potential output by 0.9 of a percentage point in 1979 and by 0.6 in 1980 (table 4.1). Indeed but for this effect, the deficit in 1979 would have been no worse than the 1976-78 average, and the deficit in 1980 only 0.5 of a percentage point larger as a fraction of potential output.

From 1981 on, the impact of the recession was so devastating that even the continued expansion in government spending could not maintain the 1979-80 levels of fixed investment as a fraction of potential output. The effect of the slowdown was naturally to stem the growth in imports, so that during these years the counterfactual exercises do not attribute any of the continued deterioration of the current account to expansionary fiscal policy.

More telling during this period were the movements in import coefficients, particularly of items other than oil and capital goods, possibly engendered by the trade and industrial policies. While there was import substitution in the case of oil and capital goods, imports of other items took a larger share of actual output. The import coefficient of such items in relation to actual output increased in 1979 to 15.3 per cent from an average of 11.0 per cent between 1976 and 1978 (table 3.3). The effect was to worsen the deficit as a fraction of potential output by 3.6 percentage points (table 4.3), so that the deficit was four times larger than it otherwise would have been. In 1982 again, the same import shift accounted for 4.0 percentage points (table 4.3), and the deficit was twice what it would otherwise have been.

5.   Simulations with a Forecasting Model

5.1 The model

The model applied here is nearly recursive. The first part of the model involves the determination of the (dollar) price index of domestic output, P_y, on the basis of the "foreign" price indexes covering exports, P_x, and the imports of capital goods, petroleum, and other imports, denoted by P_k, P_p and P_j respectively. The simple correlations between P_y and the traded goods over 1979-83, which is used as the base period for the simulations, are:

$$
\begin{aligned}
P_k &\quad - .22 \\
P_p &\quad\ \ .70 \\
P_j &\quad\ \ .68 \\
P_x &\quad\ \ .14
\end{aligned}
$$

They indicate that the prices of petroleum and of "other" imports -- the bulk of which are intermediate goods used in production, rather than final consumer goods -- have a much stronger relationship to P_y than do the export prices or the prices of imported capital goods. Thus, instead of setting $P_y = P_x$, as suggested by Bacha, the model sets

(1) $P_y = P_p^h \, P_j^{(1-h)}$

with h = 0.33, the average actual exponential weight during 1979-83 13/ (for 1983 in particular the actual weight is 0.20).

The (dollar) price index for consumption goods is set by

$$(2) \qquad P_c = P_j^b \; P_y^{(1-b)}$$

where b = 0.10, the average during 1979-83 of

$$\frac{P_j j_y Z}{P_j j_y Z + P_y Z} \qquad \text{or} \qquad \frac{P_j j_y}{P_j j_y + P_y}$$

The (dollar) price index for investment goods is similarly determined:

$$(3) \qquad P_i = P_k^g \; P_y^{(1-g)}$$

where g = 0.19 is the average during 1979-83 of

$$\frac{P_k j_k \; I}{P_i \; I} \qquad \text{or} \qquad P_k \; j_k \; / \; P_i \; .$$

Equations (2) and (3) and the procedures for obtaining b and g are as suggested by Bacha. Thus (1) - (3) set the three domestic price indexes in terms of the three indexes of prices of imports; the export price is not involved. Note that (1) ; (3) are self-contained.

The model has three types of imports, capital goods (M_k), petroleum (M_p), and other imports or 'current goods' imports (M_j). The real level of M_k, M_k/P_k, is related to the real level of fixed investment, while the real levels of M_p and M_j, or M_p/P_p and M_j/P_j respectively, are related to the level of real output.

$$(4) \qquad M = M_k + M_p + M_j$$

$$(5) \qquad M_k = j_k P_k I$$

$$(6) \qquad M_p = j_p P_p Z$$

$$(7) \qquad M_j = j_y P_j Z$$

Equations (4) - (7) give

$$M = j_k P_k I + j_p P_p Z + j_y P_j Z$$

(8) $$M = j_k P_k I + (j_p P_p + j_y P_j) Z$$

In the simulations, exports $(P_x X)$, overseas workers' remittances (L), interest payments $(r\ NF_{-1})$, net other flows and transfers (T) and the current account deficit (D), are all predetermined variables; hence M is by accounting definition also predetermined.

(9) $$M = P_x X + L + T - rNF_{-1} + D.$$

Then (8) and (9) imply:

(10) $$P_x X + L + T - r\ NF_{-1} + D = j_k P_k I + (j_p P_p + j_y P_j)\ Z.$$

On the right-hand side, the coefficients of I and Z are also predetermined, and thus I and Z become the "unknown" in what may be called the trade-gap equation.

The current account deficit is also equal to aggregate domestic demand (fixed investment plus consumption) minus national income:

$$D = P_i I + P_c C - (P_y Z + L + T - r\ NF_{-1})$$

It is assumed that consumption is a fixed proportion (1-s), where s is the savings ratio, of the national income, and therefore

$$D = P_i I - s P_y Z - s (L + T - r\ NF_{-1})\ or$$

(11) $$s (L + T - rNF_{-1}) + D = P_i I - s P_y Z$$

in which all items except I and Z are predetermined. This may be called the investment-gap equation. Thus I and Z are jointly determined by reconciliation of the investment and the trade gaps. 14/

After (9) - (11) give M, I and Z, then (5) - (7) will give M_k, M_p and M_j. Furthermore,

$$(12) \qquad C = (P_y Z + L + T - r \, NF_{-1} - P_i \, I)/P_c.$$

The model is used to trace out a five-year time path corresponding to alternative sets of five-year projections for the predetermined variables. The only internal mechanism for generating changes over time in the endogenous variables is

$$(13) \qquad NF = NF_{-1} + D.$$

5.2 Predetermined variables

The assumptions regarding the predetermined variables for 1984-88 are summarized in table 5.1. The price assumptions are taken mainly from UNCTAD price projections. 15/ For crude petroleum, the UNCTAD price changes are 1.7 per cent in 1984, 3.7 per cent in 1985 and 5.0 per cent per year in 1985-1990; these assumptions have been applied to P_p. For manufactured exports, the UNCTAD price increases are, also 1.7 per cent for 1984, 3.7 per cent for 1985 and 5.0 per cent per year for 1985-1990; these assumptions have been applied to P_j and P_k.

For export prices, the UNCTAD secretariat has made the following projections for products which are found in the Philippine export mix:

	1984	1985	1986	1987	1988
	(Annual per cent changes in current dollar prices)				
Sugar	5.6	4.0	4.0	4.0	4.0
Bananas	-3.0	-1.2	2.3	3.6	3.3
Coconut oil	17.9	19.9	3.5	5.0	4.7
Copra	19.0	21.1	4.3	5.9	5.6
Lumber	6.0	7.8	4.4	6.0	5.7
Copper ore	9.1	10.4	5.1	7.7	7.2
Manufactured exports	1.7	3.7	5.0	5.0	5.0

The weights used for combining the commodities are based on the 19
distribution, namely: sugar, 10.78 per cent, bananas, 1.97 per cent, cocon
oil, 9.79 per cent, copra 0.82 per cent, lumber, 3.13 per cent, copper, 7.
per cent, and others, 65.9 per cent. The results of this procedure are giv
in the figures for P_x in table 5.1. They show an optimistic gain in expo
prices of 18 per cent in 1984, 7 per cent in 1985 and from 4 1/2 to 5 1/2 p
cent per year over 1986-1988.

The values of P_y, P_c, and P_i are obtained using equations (1),
and (3) earlier discussed.

The import coefficients for capital goods and for petroleum have fai
linear time trends over 1979-1983: for capital goods, r = -.82 with an ann
change of -1.68 percentage points; while for petroleum, r = -.91 with
annual change of -0.26 percentage points. These are fairly sharp tren
which it is hoped, may continue. The projections will have j_k and
falling from the 1983 level by 1.68 points per year and by 0.26 points
year respectively. For other imports the trend is very weak (r = -.002),
the projection will assume j_y = 13.72, which is the 1979-83 avera
constant throughout 1984-88.

For the real level of exports, the annual growth rate (logarithmic tre
over 1979-83 was 6.06 per cent (r = .89). One set of projections uses 6
cent annual growth while another set extrapolates from 1983 by only 4.0
cent per year. In the cases of workers' remittances and net other transfe
all projections will assume these unchanged from 1983 levels of $983 mill
and $603 million respectively.

For the interest rate, the simulations assume a constant level of 8.29
cent, which is derived as follows. The proportion of the external debt wh
carries floating interest rates is 43 per cent; it is assumed that
floating rate over the simulation period is 10 per cent. The remainder of
debt, or 57 per cent, carries an average fixed interest rate of 7 per cent
of 1982). It is assumed that the composition of the external debt in terms
fixed and variable interest rates remains unchanged.

The savings rate used in the simulations is computed from (11), the
vestment-gap equation, with all other variables set at their 1983 levels,
cept for P_i. The investment goods price index P_i is not available in
e data set, and so there is no ex-post 1983 value available for use in
1); a value was computed for 1983 from projection model equation (3), with
and P_y set at 1983 levels. The resulting computed savings rate for
83, which is maintained in the simulation for 1984-88, is 0.178.

In all cases, the simulations are made for four levels of D, namely $0.25,
.5, $1.0 and $2.0 billion dollars (current values) respectively. These are
l below the deficit of 1983, namely $2.7 billion (7 per cent of $P_y Z$),
ich is judged as no longer tenable. There could be several alternative
chanisms by which a given level of D could result; the simulation model
stracts from all these, however. Ideally, there could also be a capital
count sub-model which would be able to clarify the determination of D.
though there is a current moratorium on the repayments of debt principal,
e policy intention is to keep interest payments up to date; the current
ount model used here is consistent with this.

The level of the foreign debt as of the end of 1983 has been provisionally
umed to be $25.0 billion, for purposes of the simulations made in this
er.

5.3 Simulation results

Table 5.2 presents eight of the numerous simulations which were
ried out with the model. The table uses two alternative rates of
wth for real exports, namely 6.0 per cent and 4.0 per cent, and four
ernative levels of the trade deficits, namely, $250, $500, $1000 and
00 million. All these levels of D are below the 1983 level of over
7 billion, and show the different degrees of negative impact in 1984
ch are implied for the key variables I, Z M and C. The trade
icits, as a proportion of GNP, and the interest service, as a
portion of exports plus workers' remittances plus transfers, are
o given.

The simulations all show initial declines in the state of the
homy in 1984, with some rebounding in 1985-1988. The trade balances
slightly positive for the two smaller D assumptions, implying that

the current account deficit is entirely being used to service interest payments. They are significantly negative for the two higher D assumptions, though still smaller than in 1983, when the trade deficit was 6.3 per cent of GNP. The interest service ratio declines over time but remains substantial under all assumptions, taking up from one-fifth to one-fourth of current account revenues.

It could be emphasized, at the outset, that the simulations in table 5.2 are based on some assumptions that certain recent favourable trends would continue. In particular, these assumed trends include the continuation of the sharp improvements in efficiency in the use of petroleum imports and capital imports. The assumptions of 6 per cent and 4 per cent real export growth are also relatively favourable, especially in the light of UNCTAD projections of a significant recovery in export prices in 1984–1985. It is to be hoped that such expectations will materialize.

There were also other simulations in which all the exogenous variables were maintained at the levels of 1983, with only the current account deficit varying. All the simulations, as may be expected, show a continuous decline in GNP and other major variables, not only in 1984 but throughout the next five-year period. Given that there is no doubt that the past current account deficit levels can no longer be maintained, it is very clear that some countervailing forces are badly needed in order to shore up the economy. In particular, the steady growth of real exports, the recovery of export prices, and the increased efficiency in the use of imports are all essential in order to counteract the reduced availability of foreign resources.

It was recently reported that the current account deficit for the first semester of 1984, adjusted for debt service arrears, was $ 729 million. 16/. This figure strongly suggests that the deficit for the entire year 1984 may be upwards of $ 1 billion. The same source reported that the growth in the dollar value of exports was about 6 per cent (annualized) in the first half of the year. This export performance in current value terms is somewhat disappointing, and suggests that the increase in the real volume of exports has not been more than a few percentage points. In any case, the most pertinent among the simulations, given this recent information, seems to be simulation No. 5.3, under which real GNP declines by 4.3 per cent in 1984. Real investment declines by 22 per cent, imports by 11 per cent, and real consumption by 5 per cent. However, GNP would bounce back the following year, and investment after about three years, provided that the favourable assumptions in exports and in increased efficiency in the use of imports are valid. It is quite difficult at this time to judge whether or not such assumptions could be too optimistic. These assumptions are the extrapolations of past trends, and one can never be fully confident that the economic institutions in place will be able to facilitate these trends.

6. Concluding Remarks

The balance-of-payments crisis of 1983 was brought about by both internal and external factors. The counterfactual analysis indicates that, in the critical 1979-83 period, it was the internal factors, such as the government-led investment boom, which dominated in the first two years, while in the last three years it was the external factors which prevailed. By 1983, the balance-of-payments position had grown so fragile that political events in the latter part of the year were a shattering blow.

One can point to the increase in interest rates, the second oil shock, the world recession, and the drastic decline in terms of trade as extremely difficult conditions within which to operate. All that being granted, the key question, nevertheless, is how best to direct the economy. This study suggests that, in hindsight, the efforts of adjustment towards economic equilibrium should have been stronger and should have been made earlier. The foreign exchange rate could have been used more aggressively to promote exports of goods and services and to dampen imports. It would have been more realistic to tone down the rate of investment, particularly on large scale projects. Instead, a prodigious expansion of the external debt, with a substantial portion at floating rates of interest, was used in order to contend with the trade gap, with a minimal depreciation of the peso. The public sector could have exercised more restraint in incurring such debt, particularly short-term debt. The events of August and September of 1983 demonstrated the serious vulnerability of the country's balance-of-payments position to changes in the internal political environment.

At present, the dependence of the economy on the current account deficit is so great that, under conservative scenarios, there was bound to be a substantial shock to GDP, investments, and consumption in 1984. The economy's ability to halt a further decline and to start on the road to recovery in 1985 and thereafter depends crucially on its continuing past trends in the growth of export volume and in the improvement of efficiency in the use of imports. In particular, efforts are needed to produce a downward trend in the intensity of use of non-petroleum and non-capital goods imports, i.e., essentially the imports of intermediate goods. The severity of the initial shock depends on the extent to which the current account deficit is reduced; there appears to be no way of avoiding some cut in the deficit incurred in 1984. If only export prices could improve as much as projected by the UNCTAD secretariat, then the simulations show that the economy could bounce back within the five-year projection period.

In conclusion, it seems clear that certain mechanisms, including adjustment of the foreign exchange rate, which would work towards reducing the trade gap, should be put into operation. In particular, as normal banking flows are restored, it would be important to pursue the programme of trade, industrial and financial reforms which were

initiated   in   1981   but   were   somehow   sidetracked   by   the
balance-of-payments crisis.   Finally, it is now apparent that the
monitoring system has been too ineffective in giving early warnings
about an impending crisis.   The statutory limitation imposed on debt
service is obviously defective since additional debt automatimcally
loosens the limitation.   More reliable and regular monitoring is needed
for the external debt incurred by the monetary sector and by public
corporations, and for government guarantees of loans to the private
sector.

Appendix 1

Bacha's Decomposition of the Current Account

The only significant modifications we make in Edmar Bacha's decomposition of the current account deficit is to separate oil imports from capital goods and other imports and to separate worker remittances from other inflows. The resulting expression is

$$D/Y^* = j_k (P_k/P_y) I/Z^* + j_p (P_p/P_y) Z/Z^*$$

$$+ \; j_y (P_j/P_y) Z/Z^* + r \; NF_{-1}/Y^*$$

$$- \; L/Y^* - T/Y^* - (P_x/P_y)(X/W)(W/Z^*)$$

where

D = current account deficit in current dollars;

Y^* = potential domestic output in current dollars;

Z^* = potential domestic output in 1975 dollars;

Z = actual domestic output in 1975 dollars;

I = fixed investment in 1975 dollars;

L = worker remittances in current dollars;

T = net other flows and transfers in current dollars;

NF = net foreign debt in current dollars at the end of the year, with the subscript -1 indicating a one-year lag;

X = exports of goods and non-factor services in 1975 dollars;

W = index of exports of Asian oil-importing LDCs such that X/W in 1975 = 1.0;

P_k = price index of capital goods imports with 1975 = 1.0;

P_p = price index of oil imports with 1975 = 1.0;

P_j = price index of other imports with 1975 = 1.0;

P_x = price index of exports with 1975 = 1.0;

P_y = implicit GDP deflator (with 1975 = 1.0) times the dollar/peso exchange rate (with 1975 = 1.0);

r = interest rate on foreign debt, using the US price rate as a proxy;

j_k =   ratio of capital-goods imports in 1975 dollars to fixed investment in 1975 dollars;

j_p =   ratio of oil imports in 1975 dollars to domestic output in 1975 dollars; and

j_y =   ratio of all other imports in 1975 dollars to domestic output in 1975 dollars.

The counterfactual exercises divide the change in $D/Y*$ in 1979, 1980, 1981, 1982, and 1983 from the 1976-1978 average into the following terms:

(1) $j_{ko}(I/Z*)_o \Delta (P_k/P_y) + j_{po}(Z/Z*)_o \Delta (P_p/P_y)$

$+ j_{yo}(Z/Z*)_o \Delta (P_j/P_y) - (X/Z*)_o \Delta (P_x/P_y)$

(2) $-(P_x/P_y)_o (X/W)_o \Delta (W/Z*)$

(3) $(P_k/P_y)_o (I/Z*)_o \Delta j_k + (P_p/P_y)_o (Z/Z*)_o \Delta j_p$

$+ (P_j/P_y)_o (Z/Z*)_o \Delta j_y - (P_x P_y)_o (W/Z*)_o \Delta (Z/W)$

(4) $j_{ko}(P_k/P_y)_o \Delta (I/Z*) + j_{po}(P_p/P_y)_o \Delta (Z/Z*)$

$+ j_{yo}(P_j/P_y)_o \Delta (Z/Z*)$

(5) $(NF_{-1}/Y*)_o \Delta r$

(6) $r_o \Delta (NF_{-1}/Y*)$

(7) $\Delta (L/Y*)$

where the subscript o indicates the average value for the variable between 1976 and 1978, and Δ indicates the change in the variable from its average in 1976-1978 to the year in question.

Here we call (1) the terms-of-trade effect; (2) the world-recession effect; (3) the positive policy effect; (4) the negative policy effect; (5) the interest-rate shock; (6) increased borrowing effect; and (7) the worker-remittance effect. The difference between (D/Y*) and the sum of (1) to (7) we call the residual. Note that since not all of the Philippines' external debt is subject to floating interest rates and since NF_{-1} is simply taken here as the ratio of interest payments to an interest-rate variable, (5) will overstate the interest-rate shock and (6) will understate the effect of the accumulation of debt.

Appendix 2

Table

2.1   Balance of Payments 1971-73

2.2   Current Account Deficit and International Reserves

2.3   Exports and Imports: Quantum, Price and Value Indices

2.4   Oil Imports

2.5   Export Price and Terms-of-Trade Indicators

2.6   Selected Economic Indicators

2.7   Philippine Outstanding External Debt, 1971-1982

2.8   Growth of Philippine Outstanding External Debt: 1963-1982

2.9   Percentage Distribution of Philippine External Debt
        Outstanding: Public vs. Private, 1971-1983

2.10   Term Structure of Total Philippine Outstanding External Debt
        and Ratio of Short-Term Debt to Gross Central Bank Reserves,
        1971-1983

2.11   Debt Service Ratios, 1971-1983

2.12   Exchange Rate Indices, 1970-1983

2.13   Philippine Inflation Rates

3.1   Components of the Current Account, 1971-1982

3.2   Decomposition of Capital Goods Imports

3.3   Decomposition of Oil Imports and Other Non-Capital Goods
        Imports

3.4   Decomposition of Exports

4.1   Decomposition of Changes in the Current Account Deficit from
        1976-1978 Average

4.2   Decomposition of Terms-of-Trade Counterfactuals

4.3   Decomposition of Positive Policy Counterfactuals

5.1   Values of Predetermined Variables used in Simulations

5.2(a) Simulation Results based on Alternative Assumptions as to Real
        Export and (b) Growth

Table 2.1

BALANCE OF PAYMENTS 1971-1973
(In million US dollars)

	1971	1972	1973	1974	1975	1976	1977	1978	1979	1980	1981	1982	1983
A. Merchandise Trade	-50	-124	290	-418	-1165	-1060	-764	-1307	-1541	-1939	-2224	-2646	-2482
Exports	1136	1106	1886	2725	2294	2574	3151	3425	4601	5788	5722	5021	5005
Imports	1186	1230	1596	3143	3459	3634	3915	4732	6142	7727	7946	7667	7487
B. Net Non-Merchandise Trade	-87	-55	-	-34	-45	-259	-248	-107	-311	-399	-309	-1040	-747
of which interest payment	-93	-120	-125	-152	-234	-259	-236	-440	-626	-975	-1374	-1990	-1992
C. Net Transfers	134	188	246	276	318	269	260	312	355	434	472	486	472
Current Account Balance	-3	9	536	-176	-892	-1050	-752	-1102	-1497	-1904	-2061	-3200	-2757
D. Direct Investment (Net)	-4	-22	64	28	125	144	216	100	20	-102	175	17	112
E. Net Medium- and Long-Term Loans	35	140	71	145	357	1040	662	891	1151	1032	1332	1548	1392
of which inflow	285	372	380	456	677	1407	1242	1850	2110	1579	2072	2533	2336
F. Net Short-Term Capital	62	27	-73	-70	57	-380	-172	-90	-458	310	-219	-56	-836
of which inflow	453	579	657	1138	1283	1381	2475	3442	4265	7537	8767	12127	13429
Capital Account Balance	-19	145	62	243	539	804	706	901	713	1240	1288	1509	668
G. Errors and Omissions	-112	-83	66	43	-168	85	210	115	145	126	-214	-207	-168
H. Monetization of Gold	11	7	-	-	-	-	-	32	41	128	400	277	183
I. Allocation of SDRs	17	16	-	-	-	-	-	-	28	29	27	-	-
OVERALL BALANCE	6	94	664	100	-521	-161	164	-54	-570	-381	-560	-1621	-2074

Source: Central Bank of the Philipp

Table 2.2

CURRENT ACCOUNT DEFICIT AND INTERNATIONAL RESERVES

Year	Current Account Deficit		International Reserves[b]	
	As % of "Trade" a/	As % of GNP	Months of Imports equivalent c/	As % of "Trade" a/
1971	0.2	0.0	3.8	25.6
1972	-	-	5.4	35.7
1973	-	-	7.8	43.6
1974	4.6	1.2	5.7	39.8
1975	23.4	5.7	4.7	35.7
1976	25.6	5.9	5.4	40.0
1977	15.9	3.6	4.7	32.1
1978	19.6	4.6	4.8	33.7
1979	20.8	5.0	4.7	33.8
1980	20.7	5.4	4.9	34.5
1981	20.9	5.4	4.1	27.3
1982	31.8	7.9	3.8	24.8
1983	28.4	8.0	1.8	11.6

Sources: Central Bank, National Economic and Development Authority.

a/ Average of exports and imports (merchandise and non-merchandise).

b/ Refers to the year-end gross international reserves of the Central Bank.

c/ Central Bank year-end international reserves in terms of average monthly imports for the current year.

Table 2.3

EXPORTS AND IMPORTS - QUANTUM, PRICE AND VALUE INDICES
(1972 = 100)

Year	EXPORTS			IMPORTS		
	Quantum	Price	Value	Quantum	Price	Value
1970	88.0	111.1	97.8	92.6	93.5	86.6
1971	96.4	105.6	101.8	99.1	95.5	94.6
1972	100.0	100.0	100.0	100.0	100.0	100.0
1973	107.7	145.9	157.2	93.6	128.8	120.5
1974	96.2	242.3	233.2	110.3	211.6	233.5
1975	101.9	192.8	196.4	115.8	219.6	254.2
1976	130.5	168.8	220.3	122.6	217.2	266.2
1977	157.4	171.3	269.7	119.2	241.1	287.5
1978	152.6	192.1	293.1	140.9	245.8	346.3
1979	166.8	236.1	393.8	153.8	288.4	445.2
1980	201.3	246.0	495.4	155.8	358.6	558.5
1981	203.5	240.6	489.7	143.2	398.6	570.8
1982	215.0	199.9	429.8	163.4	340.5	556.4
1983	197.2	213.9	421.8	161.1	329.3	531.3

Source: Central Bank of the Philippines.

Table 2.4

OIL IMPORTS
1971-1973

Year	Volume (In million barrels)	Value (In million dollars)	As percent of total imports
1971	66.7	127.4	10.7
1972	64.9	134.0	10.9
1973	67.1	166.1	10.4
1974	61.8	573.2	18.2
1975	66.5	709.8	20.5
1976	69.6	801.2	22.0
1977	69.4	858.8	21.9
1978	72.2	907.3	19.2
1979	65.8	1,115.0	18.2
1980	63.9	1,857.0	24.0
1981	61.4	2,081.4	26.2
1982	54.4	1,784.1	23.3
1983	59.8	1,750.0	23.6

Source: Central Bank of the Philippines.

Table 2.5

EXPORT PRICE AND TERMS-OF-TRADE INDICATORS
(1972 = 100)

Index	Export Price	Export Price Overall Import Price	Export Price Non-oil Import Price	Export Price Oil Import Price
1971	105.6	110.6	–	–
1972	100.0	100.0	100.0	100.0
1973	145.9	113.3	112.7	115.8
1974	242.3	114.5	135.5	62.2
1975	192.8	87.8	107.5	42.9
1976	168.8	77.7	97.2	34.8
1977	171.3	71.0	92.4	32.9
1978	192.1	78.2	99.1	36.5
1979	236.1	81.6	111.1	33.0
1980	246.0	68.6	104.9	20.1
1981	240.6	60.4	99.1	17.2
1982	199.9	58.7	90.2	14.7
1983	213.9	65.0	94.6	17.5

Source: Central Bank of the Philippines.

Table 2.6

SELECTED ECONOMIC INDICATORS

	Gross Investment As % of GNP	Gross National Saving As % of GNP	Foreign Saving (I-S Gap) As % of GNP	Government Saving As % of GNP	Incremental Capital Output Ratio	Budget Deficit (Surplus) As % of GNP	Liquidity (M3) % Change	Real GNP Growth Rate (%)	Liquidity (M), Less Real GNP Growth (%)
1960-1970 Average	19.8	18.1	-1.7	1.6	3.26	1.1	13.6	4.8	8.8
1971	21.1	19.2	-1.8	2.7	3.46	(1.0)	11.8	5.8	6.0
1972	20.8	19.0	-1.8	1.7	3.46	0.7	13.1	4.9	8.2
1973	21.6	24.9	3.3	5.8	1.87	0.5	52.2	9.6	42.6
1974	26.8	24.0	-2.8	4.9	3.55	(0.7)	34.2	6.3	27.9
1975	31.2	24.1	-7.1	4.1	3.56	1.2	19.2	5.9	13.3
1976	30.9	23.5	-7.4	1.9	3.54	1.8	24.3	6.1	18.2
1977	29.5	25.2	-4.3	3.1	3.35	1.9	22.4	6.9	15.5
1978	29.5	23.5	-5.8	4.0	4.31	1.2	18.0	6.2	11.8
1979	31.2	25.9	-6.3	5.3	3.87	0.6	10.7	7.5	3.2
1980	30.7	24.8	-5.9	5.0	5.22	1.3	18.2	4.4	13.8
1981	30.7	24.7	-6.0	3.7	6.72	4.0	21.1	3.7	17.4
1982	28.9	20.7	-8.2	2.8	8.24	4.3	16.1	2.8	13.3
1983	26.9	19.5	-7.5	3.4	22.55	1.7	18.6	1.4	17.2

Source: National Economic and Development Authority, Central Bank of the Philippines and Ministry of Finance.

Table 2.7

PHILIPPINE OUTSTANDING EXTERNAL DEBT*, 1971-1982
(End of period, in millions of US dollars)

Year	TOTAL		PUBLIC		PRIVATE	
	Level	Growth Rate (%)	Level	Growth Rate (%)	Level	Growth Rate (%)
1971	2088	-	834	-	1254	-
1972	2210	5.8	956	14.6	1255	0.1
1973	2306	4.3	1003	4.9	1303	3.8
1974	2723	18.1	1190	18.6	1533	17.6
1975	3402	24.9	1582	32.9	1820	18.7
1976	5099	49.9	2719	71.9	2380	30.8
1977	6563	28.7	2951	8.5	3612	51.8
1978	8195	24.9	4168	41.2	4028	11.5
1979	9733	18.8	5341	28.1	4392	9.0
1980	12187	25.1	6731	26.0	5455	24.2
1981	14826	21.7	8443	25.4	6384	17.0
1982	17475	17.9	10015	18.6	7460	16.9
1983[a]	18864	7.9	10848	8.3	8016	7.4

Source: Central Bank of the Philippines.

* Refers to the outstanding external debt of the non-monetary sector. Inclusive of short-term debt, i.e., external debt with maturity of less than one year.

a/ Preliminary. Data for revolving credits are as of September 1983.

Table 2.8

GROWTH OF PHILIPPINE OUTSTANDING EXTERNAL DEBT*:   1963-1982
(Average Annual Growth Rates in Percent)

	At Current Prices	Deflated by Import Prices	Deflated by Export Prices
TOTAL			
1963-72	19.2	15.4	18.3
1973-82	23.4	11.3	19.2
1973-77	25.2	8.2	19.5
1978-82	21.7	14.4	18.9
PUBLIC			
1963-72	15.7	12.0	14.9
1973-82	27.6	15.4	23.6
1973-77	27.4	10.7	22.7
1978-82	27.9	20.2	24.4
PRIVATE			
1963-72	27.2	23.2	26.3
1973-82	20.1	8.0	15.8
1973-77	24.6	7.1	18.0
1978-82	15.7	8.9	13.5

Source: Central Bank of the Philippines.

*   Refers to outstanding external debt of the non-monetary sector.

Table 2.9

PERCENTAGE DISTRIBUTION OF PHILIPPINE EXTERNAL DEBT
OUTSTANDING: PUBLIC VS. PRIVATE, 1971-1983

Year	Public	Private
1971	39.9	60.1
1972	43.2	56.8
1973	43.5	56.5
1974	43.7	56.3
1975	46.5	53.5
1976	53.3	46.7
1977	45.0	55.0
1978	50.9	49.1
1979	54.9	45.1
1980	55.2	44.8
1981	56.9	43.1
1982	57.3	42.7
1983	57.5	42.5

Source: Central Bank of the Philippines.

Table 2.10

TERM STRUCTURE OF TOTAL PHILIPPINE OUTSTANDING
EXTERNAL DEBT AND RATIO OF SHORT-TERM DEBT TO
GROSS CENTRAL BANK RESERVES, 1971-1983
(In percent)

Year	Ratio to Total Debt			Ratio of Short-Term[a] Debt to Gross Central Bank International Reserves
	Long-Term	Medium-Term	Short-Term[a]	
1971	59.8	23.9	16.3	90.6
1972	64.3	21.2	14.5	58.3
1973	70.6	17.2	12.2	27.1
1974	74.8	13.0	12.2	22.0
1975	75.4	11.7	12.9	32.1
1976	77.0	9.0	14.0	43.5
1977	77.3	7.3	15.4	66.1
1978	78.6	4.8	16.6	72.1
1979	76.8	4.6	18.6	74.8
1980	73.1	6.0	20.9	80.8
1981	70.0	5.9	24.1	135.9
1982	69.5	4.9	25.6	183.9
1983	72.3	5.4	22.4	379.4

Source: Central Bank of the Philippines.

a/ Inclusive of revolving credits.

Table 2.11

DEBT SERVICE RATIOS, 1971-1983

Year	Debt Service pursuant to Republic Act No. 6142 a/	Debt Service FX from G,S,T & C b/	Debt Service FX from G c/	Debt Service FX from G & S c/
1971	24.0	26.0	44.2	35.8
1972	19.0	18.3	36.5	27.8
1973	20.0	12.4	22.9	17.1
1974	20.0	10.9	18.6	14.2
1975	16.2	10.9	21.7	15.6
1976	12.6	15.3	33.3	24.9
1977	13.7	10.2	23.1	17.2
1978	18.0	11.0	29.4	20.8
1979	18.6	11.1	27.2	20.3
1980	18.7	9.6	25.4	18.7
1981	19.1	10.1	30.7	21.2
1982	19.4	9.9	44.7	28.9
1983	18.2	n.a.	n.a.	n.a.

Source: Central Bank of the Philippines.

a/ Debt service burden including IMF loans divided by the total of for⟨ exchange (FX) receipts from exports of Goods (G) and Services Transfers (T), medium- and long-term loans, direct foreign investment short-term loans net of revolving credits (C), lagged one year.

b/ Same as the denominator in a/, but for the current year.

c/ Contemporaneous.

Table 2.12

EXCHANGE RATE INDICES, 1970-1983
(1973 = 100)

Year	Nominal Exchange Rate Index	Effective Exchange Rate Index	Real Effective Exchange Rate Index
1970	89.17	85.94	98.89
1971	95.20	92.44	103.64
1972	98.80	97.09	107.18
1973	100.00	100.00	100.00
1974	100.47	99.82	83.79
1975	107.28	104.87	92.34
1976	110.12	103.48	89.03
1977	109.58	101.68	86.86
1978	109.20	103.60	88.31
1979	109.19	105.46	85.84
1980	111.18	109.31	87.16
1981	116.92	111.05	87.17
1982	126.40	115.68	88.21
1983	164.44	145.95	92.66

Sources: Central Bank of the Philippines; IMF, International Financial Statistics; and OECD, Quarterly National Accounts No.2, 1983.

Table 2.13

PHILIPPINE INFLATION RATES
(In percent)

Year	Inflation Rate	
	GNP Deflator	CPI
1971	12.4	21.9
1972	6.7	8.2
1973	17.6	16.5
1974	31.3	34.2
1975	8.0	6.8
1976	9.5	9.2
1977	7.7	9.9
1978	9.5	7.3
1979	15.7	16.5
1980	15.0	17.6
1981	10.5	12.4
1982	7.7	10.2
1983	10.7	10.0

Sources: National Census and Statistics Office and National Economic
and Development Authority.

Table 3.1

COMPONENTS OF THE CURRENT ACCOUNT, 1971-1982
(Percent of Potential Domestic Output)

	1971	1972	1973	1974	1975	1976	1977	1978	1979	1980	1981	1982	1983
1. Exports	14.06	12.54	17.36	18.05	14.19	14.09	14.90	14.08	15.43	16.25	14.94	11.99	12.86
2. Imports	-14.68	-13.95	-14.69	-20.82	-21.40	-19.89	-18.51	-19.45	-20.60	-21.70	-20.06	-18.31	-19.31
Capital goods	-6.57	-6.10	-4.51	-5.46	-7.11	-6.70	-5.09	-5.76	-5.99	-5.58	-4.85	-3.51	-4.06
Petroleum	-1.60	-1.45	-2.67	-3.79	-4.39	-4.32	-4.05	-3.73	-3.75	-5.21	-5.26	-4.22	-4.63
Others	-6.51	-6.40	-7.51	-11.57	-9.90	-8.81	-9.37	-9.96	-10.86	-10.91	-9.95	-10.54	-10.62
3. Interest payments	-1.13	-1.30	-1.10	-0.97	-1.38	-1.35	-1.06	-1.81	-1.98	-2.37	-3.47	-4.56	-4.04
4. Worker Remittances a/	n.a.	n.a.	n.a.	n.a.	n.a.	n.a.	1.00	1.19	1.22	1.18	1.38	1.93	1.26
5. Net other payments and transfers	1.71	2.81	3.36	2.57	3.07	1.40	0.11	1.17	0.64	0.88	1.92	0.93	1.93
6. Current Account Balance	-0.04	0.10	4.93	-1.17	-5.52	-5.75	-3.56	-4.82	-5.29	-5.76	-5.29	-8.02	-7.30

a/ : Includes only seamen and contract workers.

n.a.: Not available

Source: National Economic and Development Authority and Central Bank of the Philippines.

Table 3.2

DECOMPOSITION OF CAPITAL GOODS IMPORTS

Year	M_k/Y^* (1)	J_k (2)	P_k/P_y (3)	I/Z^* (4)
1971	6.56	32.13	1.18	17.27
1972	6.10	41.39	0.89	16.57
1973	4.51	26.50	1.06	16.09
1974	5.46	31.73	0.90	19.03
1975	7.11	29.95	1.00	23.73
1976	6.70	24.18	1.14	24.29
1977	5.09	22.06	0.96	24.07
1978	5.76	26.20	0.87	25.41
1979	5.98	23.63	0.91	27.91
1980	5.58	25.13	0.82	26.91
1981	4.85	23.63	0.78	26.29
1982	3.51	17.81	0.77	25.48
1983	4.06	18.90	0.93	23.08

Note: Column (1) is the product of columns (2) to (4), where columns (1), (2) and (4) are in percentage terms, M_k/Y^* is the ratio of capital-goods imports to potential output, J_k is the ratio of capital-goods imports in 1975 units to fixed investment in 1975 units, P_k/P_y is the ratio of the dollar price index of capital-goods imports to the implicit GDP deflator times the dollar/peso exchange rate with 1975 = 1.0, and I/Z^* the ratio of fixed investment in 1975 units to potential output in 1975 units. Source of basic data: National Economic and Development Authority.

Table 3.3

DECOMPOSITION OF OIL IMPORTS AND OTHER
NON-CAPITAL GOODS IMPORTS

Year	Oil Imports			Other Non-Capital Goods			
	$M_p/Y*$ (1)	J_p (2)	P_p/P_y (3)	$M_j/Y*$ (4)	J_Y (5)	P_j/P_y (6)	$Z/Z*$ (7)
1971	1.60	6.91	0.24	6.51	10.08	0.67	96.45
1972	1.45	5.43	0.28	6.40	8.99	0.75	95.35
1973	2.67	8.18	0.33	7.51	8.58	0.89	97.82
1974	3.79	4.17	0.92	11.57	10.10	1.18	97.23
1975	4.39	4.48	1.00	9.90	10.13	1.00	97.82
1976	4.37	4.51	1.00	8.81	11.53	0.78	98.51
1977	4.05	4.11	0.99	9.37	10.31	0.91	99.40
1978	3.73	4.01	0.94	9.96	11.28	0.89	99.66
1979	3.75	3.46	1.08	10.86	15.33	0.71	100.32
1980	5.21	3.24	1.60	10.91	13.10	0.84	99.43
1981	5.26	3.09	1.75	9.95	10.40	0.98	97.38
1982	4.22	2.39	1.85	10.54	15.79	0.70	95.48
1983	11.63	2.61	1.97	10.62	13.97	0.84	90.37

Note: Column (1) is the product of columns (2), (3) and (7), (4) is
the product of (5), (6) and (7), all columns except (3) and (6)
are in percentage terms. $M_p/Y*$ is the ratio of oil imports to
potential output; J_p is the ratio of oil imports in 1975
units to actual domestic output in 1975 units; P_p/P_y is the
ratio of the dollar price index of oil imports to the implicit
GDP deflator times the dollar/peso exchange rate with 1975 =
1.0; $M_j/Y*$ is the ratio of other imports to potential
output; J_y is the ratio of other imports in 1975 units to
actual domestic output in 1975 units; P_j/P_y is the ratio of
the dollar price index of other imports to the implicit deflator
of GDP times the dollar/peso exchange rate with 1975 = 1.0, and
$Z/Z*$ is the ratio of actual domestic output in 1975 units to
potential output in 1975 units. Source of basic data: National
Economic and Development Authority.

Table 3.4

DECOMPOSITION OF EXPORTS

Year	X/Y^* (1)	P_x/P_y (2)	X/W (3)	W/Z^* (4)
1971	14.06	0.87	1.29	12.54
1972	12.54	0.80	1.11	14.14
1973	17.36	1.00	1.14	15.15
1974	18.05	1.27	1.01	14.04
1975	14.19	1.00	1.00	14.19
1976	14.09	0.82	1.07	16.07
1977	14.90	0.76	1.22	15.99
1978	14.08	0.79	1.07	16.57
1979	15.43	0.84	1.06	17.38
1980	16.25	0.77	1.14	18.40
1981	14.44	0.72	1.06	18.88
1982	11.99	0.60	1.04	19.21
1983	12.86	0.90	n.a	n.a

Table 4.1

DECOMPOSITION OF CHANGES IN THE
CURRENT ACCOUNT DEFICIT
FROM 1976-1978 AVERAGE
(Per cent of Potential Output)

Effects	1979	1980	1981	1982	1983
Terms of trade	-2.10	-0.59	4.61	3.92	1.69
World recession	-1.04	-1.94	-2.37	-2.66	n.a.
Positive policy	3.57	0.78	0.01	1.49	n.a.
Negative policy	0.94	0.58	-0.06	-0.44	-0.16
Interest rate shock	1.15	1.64	2.33	1.39	0.60
Increased borrowing	-0.32	-0.31	-0.10	0.89	0.79
Worker remittances	-0.12	-0.09	-0.28	-0.83	0.12
Residual	-1.50	0.98	-3.06	-0.45	_____
Change in deficit	0.58	1.05	1.08	3.31	0.96

Table 4.2

DECOMPOSITION OF TERMS-OF-TRADE COUNTERFACTUALS
(Changes from 1976-1978 average in per cent of potential output)

Price Effects	1979	1980	1981	1982	1983
Capital-goods imports	-0.05	-0.98	-1.24	-1.28	-0.35
Oil imports	0.41	0.26	3.18	3.41	4.09
Other imports	-1.67	-0.22	1.36	-1.68	-0.19
Exports	-0.79	0.35	1.31	3.47	-1.86
Total Terms of Trade	-2.10	-0.59	4.61	3.92	1.69

Table 4.3

DECOMPOSITION OF POSITIVE POLICY COUNTERFACTUALS
(Changes from 1976-1978 average in per cent of potential output)

Effects of Import Substitution and Export Inflows	1979	1980	1981	1982	1983
Capital-goods imports	-0.13	0.24	-0.13	-1.54	-1.28
Oil imports	-0.70	-0.91	-1.06	-2.02	-1.52
Other imports	3.65	1.75	0.54	4.04	2.49
Exports	0.75	-0.30	0.73	1.01	n.a.
Total positive policy response	3.57	0.78	0.08	1.49	

Table 5.1

VALUES OF PREDETERMINED VARIABLES USED IN SIMULATIONS

	1983	1984	1985	1986	1987	1988
P_k	139.0	141.4	146.6	153.9	161.6	169.7
P_p	294.4	299.4	310.5	326.0	342.3	359.4
P_j	125.8	127.9	132.7	139.3	146.9	153.6
P_x	100.1	117.9	126.0	131.7	138.1	145.5
P_y	166.5	169.3	175.7	184.4	194.2	203.3
P_c	161.9	164.7	170.8	179.3	188.9	197.7
P_i	160.9	163.6	169.7	178.2	187.6	196.5
j_k	18.90	17.22	15.54	13.86	12.18	10.50
j_p	2.61	2.35	2.09	1.83	1.57	1.31
j_y	13.97	13.72	13.72	13.72	13.72	13.72
L	953.00	953.00	953.00	953.00	953.00	953.00
T	603.00	603.00	603.00	603.00	603.00	603.00
r	8.80	8.29	8.29	8.29	8.29	8.29

Note: P_y, P_c and P_i are determined from P_k, P_p and P_j as per the text.

Table 5.2(a)

SIMULATION RESULTS BASED ON ALTERNATIVE ASSUMPTIONS
AS TO REAL EXPORT GROWTH

Simu-lation No.	Real Export Growth 6% per year		1984	1985	1986	1987	1988
			Growth Rates (%)				
4.1	D = 250	I	-35.2	13.9	10.3	10.6	12.0
		Z	-12.1	14.4	10.6	10.9	12.4
		M	-19.8	13.6	11.0	11.4	12.0
		C	-12.8	14.6	10.8	11.0	12.5
			Ratios (%)				
	Trade Balance		0.78	0.71	0.65	0.60	0.54
	Interest Service		26.9	24.5	22.8	21.0	19.3
			Growth Rates (%)				
4.2	D = 500	I	-30.3	12.5	9.2	9.7	11.2
		Z	-8.9	13.6	10.1	10.4	11.9
		M	-16.4	12.7	10.3	10.8	11.4
		C	-9.6	13.8	10.2	10.5	12.0
			Ratios (%)				
	Trade Balance		0.04	1.39	2.06	2.51	2.77
	Interest Service		26.9	24.8	23.2	21.6	20.0
			Growth Rates (%)				
4.3	D = 1000	I	-20.5	10.2	7.5	8.1	9.6
		Z	-2.5	12.3	9.0	9.5	11.1
		M	-9.6	11.1	9.1	9.7	10.5
		C	-3.1	12.3	9.1	9.5	11.2
			Ratios (%)				
	Trade Balance		-1.28	-0.91	-0.63	-0.40	-0.22
	Interest Service		26.9	25.3	24.1	22.9	21.5
			Growth Rates (%)				
4.4	D = 2000	I	-0.9	7.0	4.9	5.6	7.4
		Z	10.2	10.0	7.3	7.9	9.6
		M	4.0	8.6	7.1	7.9	8.8
		C	9.7	9.8	7.2	7.8	9.6
			Ratios (%)				
	Trade Balance		-3.46	-2.69	-2.09	-1.58	-1.14
	Interest Service		26.9	26.2	25.9	25.3	24.5

Note: Trade Deficit = $(P_x X - M)/P_y Z$

Interest Service = $rNF_{-1}/(P_x X + L + T)$

Table 5.2 (b)

SIMULATION RESULTS BASED ON ALTERNATIVE ASSUMPTIONS
AS TO REAL EXPORT GROWTH

Simu-lation No.	Real Export Growth 6% per year		1984	1985	1986	1987	1988
			Growth Rates (%)				
5.1	D = 250	I	-36.4	11.6	8.1	8.4	9.8
		Z	-13.9	12.1	8.4	8.6	10.1
		M	-21.4	11.3	8.8	9.2	9.7
		C	-14.6	12.3	8.5	8.8	10.3
			Ratios (%)				
	Trade Balance		0.80	0.74	0.70	0.65	0.60
	Interest Service		27.3	25.3	23.9	22.4	21.0
			Growth Rates (%)				
5.2	D = 500	I	-31.6	10.4	7.1	7.5	9.0
		Z	-10.7	11.4	7.9	8.2	9.7
		M	-18.0	10.5	8.2	8.6	9.2
		C	-11.4	11.5	8.0	8.3	9.8
			Ratios (%)				
	Trade Balance		0.04	0.14	0.22	0.27	0.31
	Interest Service		27.3	25.6	24.4	23.1	21.8
			Growth Rates (%)				
5.3	D = 1000	I	-21.8	8.3	5.6	6.1	7.6
		Z	-4.3	10.2	7.0	7.3	8.9
		M	-11.2	9.1	7.0	7.6	8.3
		C	-4.9	10.1	6.9	7.3	9.0
			Ratios (%)				
	Trade Balance		-1.30	-0.94	-0.67	-0.44	-0.25
	Interest Service		27.3	26.1	25.3	24.4	23.4
			Growth Rates (%)				
5.4	D = 2000	I	-2.2	5.4	3.2	3.8	5.4
		Z	8.4	8.1	5.4	5.8	7.5
		M	2.4	6.8	5.2	5.8	6.7
		C	7.9	7.9	5.2	5.7	7.4
			Ratios (%)				
	Trade Balance		-3.52	-2.79	-2.21	-1.69	-1.25
	Interest Service		27.3	27.1	27.2	27.0	26.6

Note: Trade Deficit = $(P_x X - M)/P_y Z$

Interest Service = $rNF_{-1}/P_x X + L + T)$

FOOTNOTES

1. "Trade" is defined as the simple average of both merchandise and non-merchandise exports and imports.

2. For instance, the model assumes given constant shares, given constant elasticities and given growth rates.

3. The 1983-1987 Philippine Development Plan has recently been revised; growth targets have been substantially scaled down.

4. Higher interest rates had to be paid on new debt as well as on outstanding debt that was subject to variable interest rates. At the end of 1979, the 33 largest borrowers among the developing countries had a total variable interest debt of about $180 billion. This is almost half of the total medium- and long-term debt of developing countries in 1979 (World Bank, World Development Report 1981 p.52). In 1981, about 41 per cent of Philippine outstanding external debt was subject to floating interest rates.

5. As of the end of 1982, Philippine outstanding external debt was reported to be $17.5 billion. Later in 1983, the figure cited was $25.0 billion. This apparent sudden increase needs some explanation. The standard reports on external debt include only the debt of the non-monetary sector. This is perhaps done for practical reasons rather than anything else. While the liabilities of the monetary sector are reported every now and then, the difficulties of obtaining comprehensive data on banking stocks and flows and of avoiding double counting make more regular reporting impracticable. Thus, the $17.5 billion refers to the debt of the non-monetary sector. The balance making up the total of $25 billion includes the liabilities of the monetary sector. The latter consist of obligations of commercial banks and the Central Bank, and so-called "contingent" liabilities (mainly guarantees and unconfirmed letters of credit). What seems to be a large jump in reported debt figures is therefore due to differences in coverage rather than to a real increase in foreign borrowings in 1983.

6. After computing real interest rates on long-term loans to the country, Intal (1983) found that the Philippines obtained external financing at a "bargain" in 1973-79. The catch is, of course, the stipulation of floating rates in loan agreements.

7. The public sector's share in the total outstanding external debt may be understated because the borrowings of a number of quasi-public corporations may have been aggregated with private sector debt.

8. Interestingly, the share of short-term debt in total external debt at the end of 1969 is roughly the same as at the end of 1982 (about 25 per cent). The Philippines rescheduled its external debt in early 1970.

9. Republic Act No. 6142 establishes a debt ratio of 20 per cent as the foreign borrowing ceiling.

10. See Pante (1983) for a discussion and evaluation of the flexible exchange rate system up to 1981.

11. The effective exchange rate (EER) is a weighted average of the exchange rates of the Philippines' trading partners. Thus,

$$EER = w_i r_i$$

where r_i denotes units of domestic currency per unit of the currency of trading partner i, and w_i represents the weights for trading partner i. The real EER is defined as:

$$Real\ EER = w_i r_i \frac{P_i}{P_0}$$

where w_i and r_i are as previously defined; P_i is the price or cost index in trading partner i, while P_0 is the price or cost index in the Philippines. The computed EER's and Real EER's are transformed into indices using 1973 as the base year. Bilateral trade shares covering seven major trading partners (United States, Japan, Germany, United Kingdom, Australia, France and Canada) are used as weights. Alternative weights could have been used, but earlier work (Intal, 1983) has shown that the use of different weights does not lead to substantial variation in the resulting indices.

12. The share of non-traditional exports rose further to 50 per cent in 1982.

13. In any reference year, the actual value of h is $(\ln P_y - \ln P_j)/(\ln P_p - \ln P_j)$. Computing $P_p^{0.33} P_j^{0.67}$ for actual values of P_p and P_j over 1979-83, the simple correlation with actual P_y of 1979-83 is .76, which is an improvement over the simple correlations of P_y with the two price indexes. The actual P_y mean of 1.66 (1975 = 1.0) compares with the computed mean of 1.62.

14. The solutions for I and Z are

$$I = \frac{M + a_2}{a_1} \quad and \quad Z = \frac{s R + D - P_i I}{-sP_y}$$

where $a_1 = j_k P_k + \frac{(j_p P_p + j_y P_j) P_i}{sP_y}$

$$a_2 = \frac{(J_p P_p + j_y P_j)(sR + D)}{sP_y} \quad and$$

$$R = L + T - rNF_{-1}$$

15. The UNCTAD secretariat has made projections using three growth scenarios for OECD countries. The scenario used here is the medium-growth scenario, which assumes that the GNP of OECD countries will grow by 3.2 per cent in 1984 and by 3.0 per cent annually over 1985-1990.

16. MBC Economic Papers, 3:12, 12 September 1984, p.5.

REFERENCES

Bacha, Edmar L., "Foreign Debt, Balance of Payments, and Growth Prospects of Developing Countries", see "Terms of reference" for this series of country studies, appended to G. Helleiner's synthesis paper UNCTAD/MFD/TA/32.

Balassa, B., "The Newly Industrializing Developing Countries After the Oil Crisis", World Bank Staff Working Paper No. 437, 1980.

Bautista, R.M., "The Balance of Payments Adjustment Process in the Philippines", paper presented at the UNCTAD/UNDP Second Expert Group Meeting on the Balance of Payments Adjustment Process in Developing Countries, 1978.

Bautista, R.M., J.H. Power and Associates, Industrial Promotion Policies in the Philippines, Philippine Institute for Development Studies, 1979.

Dell, S. and R. Lawrence, The Balance of Payments Adjustment Process in Developing Countries, Pergamon Press New York, 1980.

Intal, P. Jr., "Three Essays on the Philippine External Sector", Unpublished Ph.D. Dissertation, Yale University, 1983.

Naya, S., "Crisis Management of the Philippine Economy: Dimensions and Directions", paper presented at the 20th Annual Meeting of the Philippine Economic Society, Manila, December 1983.

Pante, F. Jr., "Exchange Rate Flexibility and Intervention Policy in the Philippines, 1973-1981", Yale University Economic Growth Centre Discussion Paper No. 412, July 1982.

Power, J., "Response to Balance of Payments Crises in the 1970's: Korea and the Philippines", Staff Paper Series No. 83-05, Philippine Institute for Development Studies, 1983.

Republic of the Philippines, Philippine Development Plans, 1972-1975, 1974-1977, 1978-1982, 1983-1987

Rhomberg, R.R., "Indices of Effective Exchange Rates", IMF Staff papers 23 (1976) pp. 88-112.

Williams, R., P. Keller, U. Lipsky and M. Mathieson, "International Capital Markets: Developments and Prospects, 1983", Occasional Paper No. 23, International Monetary Fund, July 1983.

World Bank, World Development Report, 1981.

ZIMBABWE: TRANSITION TO ECONOMIC CRISES 1981-1983
RETROSPECT AND PROSPECT

R.H. Green and X. Kadhani*

Government has produced this short-term plan designed
to provide perspective and serve as a guidepost during
the transition period...An average real economic growth
rate of 8 per cent ... target ... based on an assessment
of the economy's past performance, existing productive
capacity and estimated deliberate action by government...

> Minister of Finance, Economic and
> Development Planning, B.T.G. Chidzero
> Transitional National Development-
> Plan 1982/83 - 1984/85,
> November 1982

Weak world economic performance since 1979 and successive
droughts in Southern Africa since 1980 have sharply reduced
the rate of Zimbabwe's growth... The world economy, however,
turned sharply upwards in 1983... Growth prospects for
Zimbabwe's foreign trade sector - and through it for the
entire economy - are thus likely to be enhanced... But
the ability to capitalize upon them depends crucially upon
the extent to which output surplus to domestic requirements
can be generated for export... As the World Bank's Africa
Report concluded... a programme of policy reform can be
sustained only through increased flows of concessionary aid.

> Zimbank, Economic Review,
> March 1984

1.   Growth, Recession, Recovery and Imbalance: An Introduction

When in April 1980 Zimbabwe attained independence the country was
widely perceived - at home and abroad - as having good economic
prospects.   The end of sanctions was thought likely to improve both the
terms of trade and market access for exports.   More external finance -
including aid - would further augment import capacity, thus relieving

*Xavier Kadhani is Senior Executive, Zimbabwe Development Bank;
Reginald Herbold Green is a Professorial Fellow of the Institute of
Development Studies at the University of Sussex and a member of the
London Liaison Committee of the Southern African Development
Coordination Conference (SADCC).   July 1985.

the economy of the capacity utilization, capital stock maintenance and renewal and new investment constraints of the preceding Rhodesian era. Excess capacity existed to allow more production, and past and expected increases in grower prices and wages were likely to provide the markets for the greater output.

During 1980-81 most observers saw this scenario as coming close to reality. Real GDP and real imports rose by over a quarter. 1980 was a good and 1981 a record agricultural year. While the current account deficit rose, external borrowing was readily available to fill the gap. Only a few critics expressed caution about worsening terms of trade and declining export volume, a rising government borrowing requirement during a revenue boom, the quality of the external loans and the sharp rises in both inflation and interest rates.

In the period 1982-84 Zimbabwe's economy came to be seen as suffering from very serious imbalances. Inflation remained high, output and employment fell - as did exports in real terms through 1983. The current account deficit was compressed only at the price of re-idling capacity, and the quality of external finance deteriorated further. Budgetary stringency - at least as compared to 1980-82 - did not avoid further increases in borrowing requirements because with depression real revenue fell. Relations with the IMF became increasingly strained despite the Government's substantially orthodox policies concerning the interest rate, exchange rate and - up to a point - demand contraction .

What had happened? The answer depends in part on whether one takes the standard view that the causes of imbalance are basically endogenous (i.e. due to national policy) or whether one accepts the alternative argument that exogenous factors are often more decisive. More critically, it depends on an evaluation of the relative impact of shocks and policies on Zimbabwe's external balance since independence.

The standard analysis of the road to macro-economic and especially current external account imbalance starts by positing unsustainable increases in domestic consumption (and/or of investment not balanced by reduced domestic spending or long term capital inflows) and in imports. From this starting point it is relatively easy to prescribe cuts in both domestic consumption and in imports and - perhaps less uniformly - increased domestic investment and inflows of medium to long term foreign capital.

However, external and internal imbalances may be attributable wholly or mainly to other causes:

(a) a fall in the terms of trade that reduces earned import capacity (and real national command over resources);

(b) a rise in the real cost of external capital with similar consequences;

(c) real export declines or stagnation due to sluggish growth of world trade or of main export markets;

(d) sectoral or micro shocks, including especially weather, which sharply reduce production and exports (and/or increase imports);

(e) shifts from consumption to investment if the latter has a higher import content than the former and/or if attempts to compress consumption are strongly resisted.

Under these conditions it remains true that compression of GDP will reduce external current account deficits. It is however much less obvious:

(a) that such a restoration of balance can achieve a socio politically acceptable macro economic or distribution position;

(b) that reducing consumption in favour of investment affects primarily future GDP growth rather than present output levels; or

(c) that rigorous contraction is economically efficient in terms of future GDP growth and exports either as regards the economy concerned or as regards the growth of world trade and the global economy.

Zimbabwe - while clearly showing some signs of conventional overheating in 1981/1982 - would appear to fit the case of imbalances whose causes do not lie basically in rapid expansion. In 1981 real output per capita stood at 94 per cent of its 1974 peak (table 3). Over 1973-1983 real GDP growth averaged 1.6 per cent versus about 6 per cent over 1965-1973 with capacity utilization in the opening year 97 per cent, in the closing one 85 per cent and also 85 per cent for the eleven-year average. These performances hardly suggest sustained overheating or a dash for growth, nor do they offer any very unambiguous evidence that more fixed investment and potential output would have raised the growth rate as opposed to reducing capacity utilization, consumption and - perhaps - actual output.

A quick review of the Zimbabwean economic statistics for 1973-1983 (for 1973-79 stricto sensu Rhodesian statistics) strongly suggests that external events - especially as manifested in terms of trade and borrowing opportunities but also the weather - have dominated both domestic economic performance and, with a lag, domestic economic policy. Accordingly, the analysis of the Zimbabwean economy's performance during the past two decades and especially since 1973 can perhaps most usefully start with an examination of its international economic performance and parameters and then proceed to inquire into domestic economic structure, performance and policy. This is not to deny that there is a feedback from domestic to international policy and performance, but it is submitted that the basic causal relationships run in the opposite direction.

The combination of low savings rates, low actual output growth
(except in boom years), low capacity utilization and recurrent severe
problems in reducing external current account deficits to manageable
levels raises questions as to whether and how higher domestic savings
ratios would have raised actual output. Indeed given the higher ratio
of direct and indirect imports to gross fixed capital formation (GFCF)
than to other elements in GDP (Table 6), it is necessary to examine the
proposition that higher domestic savings ex ante would have reduced
both consumption and actual output, possibly to a degree resulting in
little change in ex post savings or capacity growth.

This proposition is not the same as support for recurrent deficits
of the government's budget - reducing such deficits and (pari passu)
private saving might be an appropriate policy response even when an
overall increase in the ex ante savings ratio target would be
undesirable.

2. Zimbabwe: Some aspects of the pre-1980 experience

Any economic analysis of Zimbabwe must take account of the very
special conditions arising out of the illegal unilateral declaration of
independence (Rhodesian rebellion) of 1965 and the country's accession
to independence in 1980. The former led to certain constraints on
external trade and financial flows while the latter had significant
positive effects on both counts. Further there are significant
discontinuities arising from the very different political and economic
points of view and priorities of the Rhodesian Front and of ZANU (PF),
the governing parties from 1965 to April 1980 and as from April 1980,
respectively.

However, there are also very substantial continuities in economic
constraints, parameters, performance and - to a not inconsiderable
extent - policies. Many of the constraints confronting the Smith
regime in 1973-75 and those facing Prime Minister Mugabe's government
since 1982 are remarkably alike, as are some, though by no means all,
of the policies seriously canvassed and/or adopted. It would be a
mistake to suppose that the response to economic structures, parameters
and constraints is totally independent of the political economic stance
of a State's leaders. The 1975-1979 pattern of moderate external
balance, falling real GDP per capita, recurrent budget balance, falling
real African wages and rural incomes, falling real fixed investment and
stable or rising European consumption per capita was a result quite
consonant with what the Smith regime saw as its dominant concerns but
would not be so today. It would be an even greater mistake to assume
that political and economic will has total freedom to override
international and domestic economic structures and parameters -
especially in the short or medium run.

In the period 1964-1973 Rhodesia (as it then was) attained a growth
rate of about 6 per cent a year. The initial shock of economic
sanctions 1/ and other costs of the illegal declaration of independence

were fairly rapidly overcome, and an altered pattern of sectoral growth actually produced a better performance than that of the late 1950s and early 1960s.

Rhodesia was very greatly affected by the economic events of 1973-74. Because they coincided with domestic overheating (97 - 98 per cent capacity utilization) and a highly import intensive expansion of GFCF, they led to a massive current account deficit. The domestic response was in a sense an ultra-orthodox demand-cutting strategy, albeit one concentrating on achieving a visible trade surplus and near balance on current account rather than on domestic demand management per se and one eschewing use of active interest or exchange rate policies. Its effects on GDP, GFCF, capacity utilization and income distribution in the period 1975-1979 have been noted above.

3.   The Structural Heritage: Rhodesia to Zimbabwe

The economic history of Zimbabwe's predecessors under colonial rule for about a century is relevant to the imbalance crises of the independent Zimbabwean economy because of the structural parameters, institutional framework and experience of policy instruments which were - and are - part of its colonial heritage.   Certain other historic events - e.g. Rhodesia's 1974-1979 experience in running an IMF type stabilization programme successfully on its own terms without the IMF - are of interest but only tangentially relevant to the present study.

Southern Rhodesia (as it then was) developed as a settler colony and as the centre of a three-colony grouping - the Central African Federation - whose other members were Northern Rhodesia (now Zambia) and Nyasaland (now Malawi). The core of the economy was large-scale settler farming, concentrated on tobacco, beef and maize, but manufacturing and services, for the regional as well as for the domestic market, were the main growth sectors.

Economic - like political - policy was designed to ensure white supremacy. Wage rates for blacks were very low. Zimbabwean Africans were limited to 'communal areas' mostly of low productivity and a substantial proportion of African workers were migrants from the poorest parts of rural Malawi. All services to Africans - including agricultural extension and access to credit, inputs and markets as well as health, education and water - were incomplete and of low standard, with the consequence that skills, productivity and income were sharply differentiated.

After the independence of Zambia and Malawi and the break-up of the Central African Federation and especially after the illegal declaration of independence in 1965, the economy and the economic policy instruments - previously infrastructure provision and subsidized transport in support of laissez faire - changed.

The central objective of economic policy was perceived as the achievement of the capability to finance a current account deficit by means of a trade surplus (a large visible goods surplus more than offsetting a moderate non-factor services deficit), limited factor payments and remittances and moderate external borrowing (largely from or via the Republic of South Africa)$\underline{2/}$. This strategy gave rise to:

(a) detailed balance-of-payments projections linked to macro-economic forecasts of potential levels of current account deficits;

(b) detailed foreign exchange allocation machinery to hold down import levels;

(c) fiscal, credit and wage policies designed to back up the foreign exchange allocation system by avoiding upsurges in demand;

(d) increasingly sophisticated parallel marketing (sanctions busting) to preserve global market access through intermediaries (albeit at a substantial cost - perhaps 15 per cent on imports and 20 per cent on exports by the late 1970s);

(e) severe constraints on factor payments and remittance outflows which both built up blocked balances (forced foreign reinvestment at the low interest rates then prevailing) and induced already present foreign firms to engage in substantial reinvestment because of the low opportunity cost of such programmes at a time when the funds were, in any event, not remittable and because domestic growth and parallel marketing of exports provided prospects for profits on these investments;

(f) increased power of the Reserve Bank and the Treasury to control use of foreign exchange, government recurrent account balance and specific interventions in prices taxes, financing and ownership of directly productive sectors, including those designed (successfully) to promote the development of the mineral sector and to shift the emphasis within agriculture from tobacco to maize, beef, sugar, tea and coffee.

Paradoxical as it may seem, therefore, sanctions both provided incentives for systematic import substitution and new export development and generated foreign funds (unremittable earnings) that could be used for promoting the expansion of manufacturing, the mineral sector and to a lesser extent agriculture. At the same time the regime's economic policy - including to a not inconsiderable extent ownership beyond infrastructure and public utilities - became much more pervasive and differentiated and was backed up with an increasing and increasingly professional set of institutions and personnel.

Through 1973 Rhodesia achieved rapid growth. Attempts to sustain or expand this by stepped up investment led to overheating and an external deficit which coincided with the 1973-74 oil price explosion. Radically restrictionist policies (within the framework cited above) were instituted. As a result, the current account came back into balance rapidly, but GDP per capita declined in each year through 1979,

Table 1

Gross domestic product, capital stock, potential output, capacity utilization
(millions of current Zimbabwean dollars)

	1973	1974	1975	1976	1977	1978	1979	1980	1981	1982	1983c/
Gross domestic product	1450	1790	1900	2060	2070	2170	2535	3205	3995	4465	4900
Capital stock	3720	4335	5175	6175	7020	8160	9580	10705	13050	15000	18815
Potential output a/,b/	1510	1835	2070	2400	2675	2885	3370	3835	4215	4810	5740
Capital utilization b/	97%	98%	92%	86%	77%	75%	76%	83%	95%	91%	85%

a/ Capital/output ratio rises in current dollars because GFCF deflator has risen 1.4 times as rapidly as GDP deflator and incremental C/O ratio has been held constant at 2.5 in 1975 $.

b/ Based on 1974 direct estimate, for other years 1973 potential output adjusted for change in fixed capital stock. Overheating present in 1973, 1974, 1981.

c/ Estimate.

Table 2

Factor shares in GDP
(millions of current Zimbabwean dollars)

	1973	1974	1975	1976	1977	1978	1979	1980	1981	1982
1. Labour										
Wages and salaries	781	904	1050	1154	1248	1333	1502	1881	2395	2916
+ Communal areas agricultural output	63	111	95	108	106	74	102	146	265	271
+ 20 per cent salary element in other unincorporated business surplus	19	25	26	27	27	10	15	24	17	16
Total	863	1040	1171	1290	1381	1417	1619	2051	2677	3203
per cent	59.5	58.6	61.6	62.5	66.7	65.4	63.6	64.0	67.5	71.7
2. Land										
Rent	56	60	61	65	68	62	62	61	70	71
– Improvement element	-38	-40	-40	-43	-45	-41	-40	-40	-47	-47
+ 20 per cent value added mining	21	27	26	30	30	31	45	57	50	49
+ 10 per cent gross output commercial agriculture	25	36	37	40	39	42	44	59	78	84
Total	64	83	84	92	92	94	101	137	151	157
per cent	4.4	4.1	4.4	4.5	4.6	4.3	4.3	.4.2	3.3	3.5
3. Capital										
Gross surpluses	613	827	791	845	753	773	983	1264	1530	1478
– Adjustments	-90	-159	-143	-165	-157	-116	-166	-246	-363	-373
Total	523	668	647	680	596	657	817	1018	1167	1105
per cent	36.1	37.3	34.0	33.0	28.7	30.3	32.1	31.8	29.2	24.8
Gross surplus as proportion of capital stock	14.1	15.4	12.5	11.0	8.5	8.1	8.5	9.5	8.9	7.4

Notes:
a/ Labour includes implicit working proprietor wage/salary income; rent is defined in Ricardian terms excluding "rent" on buildings and improvements.
b/ Adjustments based on National Accounts data.
c/ Gross Surplus/Capital stock ratio computed on basis of K. Stock in table 1.

the share of profits in GDP and the rate of return on capital fell sharply and capacity utilization dipped to 75 per cent (see tables 1, 2, 3 and 5).

Employment growth, which was moderately buoyant through 1975, thereafter turned negative. In view of a 3.5 per cent annual growth of population, unemployment increased substantially, especially because African "tribal lands" were increasingly incapable of providing even subsistence for a majority of the households assigned to them. The conditions prevailing in 1974-1979 exacerbated rather than created this state of affairs.

The political and economic viability of the 1974-79 "IMF programme without the IMF" depended on its distributional impact: real investment and real African consumption were cut but real white personal consumption and access to public services were maintained. This left a heritage of major African expectations of restored personal consumption capacity and expanded services, of badly deteriorated or obsolete capital stock and of a white community not at all used to economic austerity.

4.   Independence, Transition and Boom 1980-82

Zimbabwe became independent in April 1980 after a brief formal return to Crown colony status during the pre-independence electoral period and the formation of the independence government. Initially, the changes in economic policy took the form of a relaxation of restraint - on foreign exchange, incomes, borrowing - rather than of specific changes of direction and in government spending concentrated more on extending public services to Africans than on changing the structure of government activities.

Because with independence there was a once-for-all recovery in terms of trade (with the end of sanctions), plus access to external finance (both commercial and concessional) and because at independence there was 25 per cent unused capacity and a low external debt (a heritage of Rhodesia's lack of access to financial markets), GDP grew at a rate of more than 11 per cent in 1980 and more than 15 per cent in 1981, and capacity utilization rose again to 95 per cent (table 3). Gross fixed capital formation - made possible by greater access to foreign exchange and credit as well as by higher profits and encouraged by the rising profits and buoyant market - recovered from 13.7 per cent of GDP in 1979 to 14.8 per cent and 15.5 per cent in 1980 and 1981 peaking at 17.5 per cent in 1982. In constant price terms it grew at a rate of more than 60 per cent, albeit even then it was only barely over 80 per cent of its 1974-75 level. Capacity rose by a little over 1 per cent in 1980 (1979 investment) 1.5 per cent in 1981, and just under 3 per cent in 1982 and 1983 (tables 3 and 4).

Table 3

GDP, capital stock, potential output, fixed investment
(millions at 1975 prices)

	1973	1974	1975	1976	1977	1978	1979	1980	1981	1982	1983c/
Gross domestic product	1796	1912	1901	1876	1733	1718	1743	1936	2231	2189	2112
Index (1973 = 100)	100	106.5	105.8	104.5	96.5	95.7	97.0	107.8	124.2	121.8	117.6
Index population a/	100	103.6	107.3	111.2	115.2	119.3	123.7	128.2	132.8	137.6	142.5
Index per capita	100	102.8	98.6	94.0	83.8	80.2	78.4	84.1	94.3	88.5	82.5
Capital stock	4360	4875	5175	5460	5625	5725	5770	5810	5890	6040	6210
Potential output	1850	1950	2070	2185	2250	2290	2310	2325	2355	2415	2485
Index (1973 = 100)	100	105.3	111.8	117.7	121.5	123.7	124.7	125.5	127.3	130.5	134.4
Capacity utilization	97%	98%	92%	86%	77%	75%	76%	83%	95%	91%	85%
Gross fixed capital formation	410	471	467	353	300	245	239	285	355	383	347
Depreciation b/	162	171	181	191	197	200	202	203	206	211	217
Net fixed capital formation	248	300	286	162	103	45	37	82	149	172	130
Index (1973 = 100)	100	121.0	115.3	65.3	41.5	18.5	14.9	33.1	60.1	69.3	52.4

Notes:

a/ Estimated on basis of 3.6 per cent annual population growth.
b/ Estimated at 3.5 per cent opening fixed capital stock for year.
c/ Estimate.

Table 4

Savings, consumption and gross capital formation: shares in GDP
(per cent)

	1973	1974	1975	1976	1977	1978	1979	1980	1981	1982	1983*
Consumption	75.3	78.0	78.2	75.7	78.7	78.7	82.6	84.9	87.3	84.2	80.7
Domestic savings	21.6	18.7	18.4	20.7	17.7	17.2	12.7	11.5	9.0	9.6	10.5
Net external factor payments/remittances	3.1	3.3	3.4	3.6	3.6	4.1	4.7	3.6	3.7	6.2	8.8
Gross fixed capital formation	22.8	24.6	24.6	18.8	17.3	14.3	13.7	14.8	15.5	17.5	16.4

* Estimate.

Wages and salaries for Africans were sharply increased both by scale changes and by the removal of de facto restrictions on access to employment, while grower prices were raised sharply to provide incentives for both settler and African farmers. Although taxes were raised and recurrent revenue rose rapidly, expenditure on health and education, on demobilization and security and on increased wages grew so fast that - despite stated policy - the government's recurrent deficit was not only not closed but tended to grow.

Employment, which had fallen from 1.05 million in 1974 (when it was 40 per cent above its 1965 level) to 985,000 in 1979, grew by just under 3 per cent in 1980, 2.75 per cent in 1981 and by less than 1 per cent in 1982. This very low rate, despite the growth of GDP in 1980 and 1981, is probably explained by substantial increases in minimum and low wages - especially in agriculture where 1982 employment was 18 per cent below the 1979 level, contrasting with a 19 per cent increase in non-agricultural employment.

Taken together with rising capacity utilization these factors at first largely continued the 1979 surge in inflation - from 6 per cent in 1977 to 16 per cent in 1979 to 13 per cent in 1980, 9 per cent in 1981 and 11 per cent in 1982 as measured by the implicit GDP deflator. Since the Zimbabwean dollar actually appreciated against the US dollar in 1980, fell back to its 1980 rate in 1981 and was substantially devalued only in 1982, significant overvaluation built up which threatened the viability of much of the mining sector, deterred the growth of manufactured exports and gave rise to large government deficits in respect of steel and agricultural exports. On the basis of a 1975-1984 purchasing-power-parity ratio the Zimbabwean dollar was by late 1984 perhaps 15-20 per cent undervalued vis-à-vis the US dollar. However, as the latter is overvalued and the United States is not a leading trade partner, overall the Zimbabwean dollar is not self-evidently either overvalued or undervalued. Because of the collapse of the South African rand in 1983-84 (now clearly undervalued on a purchasing power parity basis), there are specific problems with respect to that currency. South Africa is a secondary export market and also a direct competitor with Zimbabwean manufacturing and agriculture not only in Zimbabwe but in key regional export markets, e.g. Botswana, Malawi, Mozambique, Swaziland and Zambia.

Net factor payments and remittances increased steeply from $Zim 114 million in 1979 to $Zim 72 million in 1980, $Zim 123 million in 1981 and $Zim 206 million in 1982 (table 5). In part this increase reflected higher emigrant and pension remittances which more than offset the revival of grant aid, but mainly it reflected higher interest and dividend payments. The higher interest payments were due to rising interest rates and debt levels, and the higher dividend payments to an unsuccessful attempt to increase foreign equity investment by reducing limitations on dividend remittances.

The cumulative effect of the boom which followed the post-independence relaxation was to cause the current account to move

Table 5

Current account balance of payments
(millions of current Zimbabwean dollars)

	1977	1978	1979	1980	1981	1982	1983[b/]
Exports	+624.1	+687.1	+816.3	+1062.1	+1125.5	+1169.3	+1300
Visible	520.3	579.2	667.5	813.7	925.6	857.7	1025
Gold	45.7	46.1	66.6	115.2	76.3	140.5	100
Invisible	58.1	61.8	82.2	133.2	133.6	171.1	175
Imports	-558.6	-594.0	-775.8	-1106.0	-1419.1	-1434.2	-1475
Visible	421.7	443.1	594.9	860.5	1059.4	1114.3	1130
Invisible	136.9	150.9	180.9	245.5	359.7	319.9	345
Factor payments (net)	-64.7	-76.1	-76.3	-72.4	-122.7	-206.4	-285
Transfers/ Remittances (net)	-9.6	-12.0	-38.0	-40.4	-23.0	-62.3	-75
Current-Account Deficit[a/]	8.8	(25.2)	73.9	156.7	439.2	532.8	535
Gold stock change [c/]	-8.5	+5.8	+14.3	+29.7	+41.7	-17.7	-88.7
Adjusted Current-Account Deficit [a/d/]	17.3	(31)	59.6	127.0	397.5	550.5	446.3
Adjusted Current-Account Deficit as Proportion of Potential output (%)	0.7	(-1.1)	1.8	3.3	9.4	11.4	7.8

Notes:

a/ ( ) = current account surplus.
b/ Estimate.
c/ Change in Reserve Bank holdings of domestic production to be exported. Changes largely represent short-term external asset/liability preferences and therefore arguably distort underlying current account deficit.
d/ Adjusted for Reserve Bank gold stock.

from a surplus of $Zim 25 million in 1978 to deficits of $Zim 74 million :
1979, $Zim 157 million in 1980, $Zim 439 million in 1981 and $Zim 533 millic
in 1982, or, if adjustment is made for changes in the gold holdings of th
Reserve Bank, from a surplus of $Zim 31 million in 1978 to deficits of $Zim ‹
million in 1979, $Zim 127 million in 1980, $Zim 398 million in 1981 and $Z:
551 million in 1982 (tables 5 and 7). Clearly, the immedia'
post-independence growth rate was unsustainable on government and extern:
balance accounts. Capacity expansion could not sustain it, nor - as th
droughts of 1982, 1983 and 1984 which followed 1981's record harvest ha'
shown - was the weather sufficiently reliable. However, it is important '
realize that these increases in deficits on current account came after
period in which GDP per capita and total GFCF had declined steadily since 19'
and in neither case did they even restore 1974 levels on the accession '
power of a government committed to improving African incomes and access '
services, but obliged not to reduce real consumption of Europeans rapid,
because their skills and enterprises were still crucial from a producti‹
viewpoint.

The government's economic strategy was not consolidated in comprehensi
form until November 1982 when it formulated the <u>Transitional Plan</u>. By th
time the current account deficit and the growth of the government recurre
domestic deficit had already forced retrenchment, but the Plan represents t
broad strategy initially partially outlined before independence and th
refined and consolidated during the first two years of independence. Th
strategy represents a clear break with that of the previous regime. Howeve
while it affected sectoral and spending policy in 1980-1982 (i.e. while t
Plan was under formal preparation), it did not have a comparable influence
macroeconomic - especially fiscal and monetary - policy. Planning was at th
time the responsibility of a separate Ministry and neither the policy of t
Treasury nor that of the Reserve Bank was based on or closely coordinated wi
the new strategy. Their macroeconomic strategy appears to have had growth a
allocation objectives very different from those embodied in the new strateg
The Plan's long-term commitment was to equity, socialism and improved livi
standards. The short-term macroeconomic targets were:

(a)   growth of GDP at an annual rate of 8 per cent, with production of goc
      to rise faster than that of services;

(b)   raising GFCF from 19 per cent of GDP in 1981/82 to 23 per cent in 1984/
      and domestic savings (net of stock changes) from 11 per cent of GDP
      1981/82 to 17 per cent in 1984/85;

(c)   raising wage employment by 3 per cent a year;

(d)   increasing the share of imports in GDP to 26 per cent and of exports
      23 per cent, implying a 10.4 per cent annual turnover growth and a slig
      trade deficit reduction over 1981/82 - 1984/85;

(e)   financing about 37.5 per cent of 1981/82 - 1984/85 gross capi'
      formation from net external borrowing, grants and investment;

(f)   an average inflation rate of 15 per cent a year.

These projections were broadly internally consistent. Given the steady inflation of GFCF prices relative to other GDP components there may be some doubt that, if GFCF were 23 per cent of GDP, it would lead to 8 per cent capacity expansion, and equally it is doubtful that the medium-term import elasticity of growth is as high as 1.3, but these are fairly secondary issues.

Broadly the Plan envisaged: over 5 per cent real annual consumption growth (allowing 5 per cent per capita for Africans consistent with no significant fall for Europeans); a sharp increase over 1974-1979 growth but only a moderate one over 1965-1973 backed by very high levels of GFCF and savings with a high - but by no means unique for low- and middle-income developing countries - ratio of net capital inflow to GFCF. The employment target - even with high growth - was actually below the population growth rate which is in the 3.3 to 3.6 per cent range. The external finance target seems to have been influenced by the level of pledges made at Zimcord (Zimbabwe's 1980 Aid Coordination Conference with External Donors) and the belief - subsequently found to be mistaken - that these represented bankable, rapidly disbursable commitments of concessional funds to which export credits and commercial finance would be additional.

Given the post-1973 economic slump, the target rates were not implausibly high technically with one exception - that for export growth. Here the projection was to break from approximate stagnation to over 10 per cent annual real growth - a target so high as to suggest that this figure was either a residual after computing maximum plausible domestic savings and necessary GFCF to sustain 8 per cent growth or the product of excessive microeconomic optimism not supported by sufficient evidence regarding sectors and products.

5. 1982-1984: The macroeconomics of crisis management

The Zimbabwean policy response to the 1982-1984 current account deficit crisis has basic elements quite similar to those of the Rhodesian regime in 1974-75, at least at the macro-economic level. In respect of distribution there are significant differences, in that lower-range real wages were cut less (e.g. increases to offset 1983 and 1984 food subsidy reductions), famine relief received top priority (running to about 10 per cent of recurrent spending by 1983/84) and education, health and service provided to African agriculture continued to expand rapidly.

At the macroeconomic level there are on closer examination two differences: the use from late 1982 of an active exchange rate policy starting with a large devaluation and followed by a downward float taking the rate of the Zimbabwean to the US dollar from 1.3 at the beginning of November 1982 to under 0.70 by the end of 1984; the institution of an interest rate policy which raised bank rate from 4.5 per cent to 9 per cent during 1981 and the Treasury bill rate from 3.3 per cent to over 8 per cent in the same period with a subsequent rise to 8.5 per cent, while minimum overdraft rates charged by the banks have risen from 7.5 per cent at the beginning of 1981 to 13 per cent since September of that year.

However, the basic instruments have remained foreign exchange allocation and attempts to restore the recurrent government budget to balance. The former has been bolstered by preferential credit and foreign exchange allocations to exporters (probably critical) together with devaluation, to sustaining mineral exports and allowing increases in non-traditional manufactured exports) and by a greater awareness on the part of government and business of the need to promote non-traditional exports especially to Zimbabwe's two regional markets (South Africa and SADCC/Preferential Trade Area) but also to other markets (e.g. beef to EEC). This more balanced approach to foreign exchange allocation in order to promote exports as well as constrain imports reflects in part the absence of the particular constraints confronting the predecessor regime, but also in part reflects a greater Treasury commitment to trying to restore balance by increasing supply and not only by cutting demand.

Recurrent budgetary balance has not been regained despite serious efforts partly because, owing to drought, externally backed insurgency in Zimbabwe and Mozambique (where Zimbabwe troops are deployed for transport protection), the expansion of basic services and subsidies to railways, steel and agricultural marketing, nominal recurrent spending has risen far more rapidly than recurrent revenue which has been hit by the real erosion of its import, manufacturing and profits bases.

The efforts made in 1982-83 to restore balance have been less successful than those of 1974-76. Real imports were cut by perhaps 10 per cent in 1982 and again in 1983, but the apparent current account deficit in current Zimbabwean dollars rose from $Zim 439 million to $Zim 533 million to $Zim 535 million over 1981-82-83 (table 5). However, adjusted for year-to-year swings in domestic gold holdings of the Reserve Bank the pattern becomes $Zim 398 to $Zim 551 to $Zim 446 million (table 7). If these figures are converted into current US dollars the resultant deficit was $575 million in 1981, $719 million in 1982 and $439 million in 1983, an indication that the 1982 restrictions did not bite fully until 1983, but then did have a significant impact reducing the deficit by about 40 per cent in US dollar terms. By 1984 the visible trade balance had returned to surplus (with exports expanding in volume as well as value) and the current account deficit was halved.

The apparent production - though, not through 1983 GFCF - cost of efforts to achieve external balance has been similar to the previous retrenchment, with a 2 per cent real decline in 1982, 3.5 per cent in 1983 and prospects for -2 per cent to +1 per cent in 1984 (table 3). However, in part this result reflects the droughts in three successive years (1982, 1983, 1984) which would have reduced GDP growth even had the external balance and import allocations been healthier.

Table 6

Imports, import ratios, exports
(millions of Zimbabwean dollars)

	1977	1978	1979	1980	1981	1982	1983 c/
Imports goods and non-factor services							
Total Current $Zim	559	594	776	1106	1419	1434	1475
1975 $Zim	448	419	420	521	679	663	610
% GDP	26.5	25.1	30.5	34.5	35.5	33.1	30.2
Capital goods							
Current $Zim a/	112	100	116	205	347	482	442
1975 $Zim	90	70	81	98	168	223	177
% Gross fixed capital formation	30.0	28.7	33.8	32.5	47.2	59.3	51.0
Exports goods and non-factor services							
Current $Zim	624	687	816	1062	1126	1169	1300
1975 $Zim	575	595	615	604	581	619	648
Price indices (1975 = 100) b/							
Imports	124.6	141.9	194.3	208.2	207.1	216.4	238.3
Exports	108.6	115.5	132.7	175.9	193.9	188.8	200.7

Notes:

a/ Non-factor services allocated to capital goods and other imports in same proportion as visible imports.

b/ Price data available for visible imports/exports only. Deflation based on assumption of parallel price movement of services.

c/ Estimate.

Employment is estimated to have fallen by about 2.5 per cent in
1983. Savings recovered slightly from a 1981 low of 9 per cent of GDP
to 9.6 per cent in 1982 and 10.5 per cent in 1983, but GFCF fell from
17.5 per cent in 1982 (up from 1981's 15.5 per cent) to 16.4 per cent
in 1983.

Measures were recently taken to limit or suspend remittances of
income, including dividends, profits, rents and emigrants' allowances.
In addition the government compulsorily acquired the trustee-held pool
of external securities, for which beneficiaries were paid compensation
in Zimbabwean dollars. The government also suspended remittance of
interest on blocked funds and instead introduced (for individuals and
companies, respectively) 12 and 20-year 4 per cent external bonds as a
phased remittance channel for these balances. These measures were
accompanied by a budget which sought to raise real recurrent revenue
and to hold real recurrent spending growth to nominal levels. However,
in nominal terms - though not in terms of constant prices - the
government's borrowing requirement was not reduced.

6. Current account deficit 1978/80 - 1981/83: A causal decomposition

Zimbabwe's current account deficit on the face of it ballooned
from 1.3 per cent of potential output in 1978-80[3/] to 8.1 per cent in
1981, 10.1 per cent in 1982 and 6.5 per cent in 1983 (table 7). This
movement greatly understates the underlying deterioration, because a 4
per cent gain could reasonably have been expected from the reversal of
the negative impact of sanctions/intermediation on the terms of trade.
In fact that gain was achieved but was submerged in negative
developments affecting terms of trade and other factors, and hence the
overall ratios to be explained are 12.1 per cent, 14.1 per cent and
10.5 per cent respectively (table 8).

External shock - initially dominated by the recession's impact on
trade growth but with equivalent terms-of-trade losses in 1982 and
larger in 1983 and interest rate impact significant and rising -
accounted for 28 per cent, 38 per cent and 59 per cent respectively of
the annual deteriorations. Debt burden was relatively insignificant
until 1983 and even then accounted for under 8 per cent of the widened
gap. Indeed, relaxation of profit remittances (basically a domestic
policy measure) was much more significant in 1981 and 1982 and of about
the same magnitude in 1983.

Domestic policy changes (including profit remittances) accounted
for 57 per cent, 30 per cent and 18 per cent of the annual
deteriorations. The main element of these changes was the attempt
(successful in 1981 and to a degree in 1982 and 1983) to operate the
economy nearer to capacity - a not unreasonable goal since the base
period utilization rate was about 75 per cent. The rise in the share
of GFCF - again the result of a deliberate policy to raise very low
rates in the base period and one which never led to regaining 1973-75
real GFCF levels (see table 3) - had only a small effect. In 1981
general import relaxation accounted for 14 per cent of the broadening

Table 7

Ratio of current account deficit (CAD) to potential output (PO)
(millions of current Zimbabwean dollars)

	1973	1974	1975	1976 b/	1977	1978 b/	1979	1980	1981	1982	1983 c/
CAD a/ 2.6	95.5	131.3	(13.2)	17.3	(31)	59.6	127.0	397.5	550.5	446.3	
PO	1509	1833	2070	2402	2676	2885	3370	3833	4217	4808	5738
CAD/PO	0.2	5.2	6.3	(0.5)	(0.7)	(1.1)	1.8	3.3	9.4	11.4	7.8
Capacity utilization (per cent)	97	98	92	86	77	75	76	83	95	91	85

Notes:

a/ Current-account deficit adjusted for changes in the gold stock. See Table 5.

b/ ( ) = current account surplus.

c/ Estimates.

of the gap between the deficit and output but in 1982 and 1983 import controls were if anything tighter than in the base period. Similarly, while allowing the Zimbabwean dollar to float up at a time when domestic inflation was above the global average accounted for perhaps 4 to 5 per cent of the 1981 and 1982 deterioration, by 1983 the Zimbabwean dollar measured on a purchasing power parity basis had been adjusted downward enough to increase <u>tradeability</u> marginally vis-à-vis the base period.

A special factor in Zimbabwean experience was the <u>capital rehabilitation shock</u>. At independence much of the plant, machinery and transport equipment portion of the capital stock was obsolete and/or beyond its useful life and in the case of another substantial portion maintenance had been deferred as a direct result of the intensity of foreign exchange restrictions after 1974. As a result the capital goods import share in GFCF rose from 31.7 per cent in the base period to 47.2 per cent, 59.3 per cent and 51.0 per cent in 1981, 1982 and 1983 respectively, accounting for 18 per cent, 27 per cent and 16 per cent of the respective increases in the annual ratios of current account deficit to potential output (tables 6, 8).

This decomposition suggests that regaining the ratios of 1978-80 without significant global economic changes would require not merely a once-for-all reduction in GDP but also negative "equilibrium" rates of growth of capacity and of achieved GDP. For example, if the following conditions were to be fulfilled:

(a) assuming no further terms-of-trade deterioration or interest rate rises;

(b) elimination of the negative recession impact;

(c) continued exchange rate adjustments to sustain tradeability;

(d) total reversal of the profit remittance relaxation (i.e. near blocking of non-interest factor payments); and

(e) return of the capital goods imports/GFCF ratio to 45 per cent;

then capacity utilization and investment shares would have to decline. For capacity utilization the fall would be about 5 per cent (of potential output) to 60 per cent capacity and for investment the decline would be to 8-10 per cent of GFCF. This is below the 11-15 per cent of share in constant price GDP for GFCF needed to maintain capacity at a constant level.

Such a scenario can hardly be deemed acceptable in political and economic terms since at least in the medium term real income increases for the African majority are socio-politically imperative while continued or accelerated decline in the white minority's real income will lead to a rate of exodus causing severe output losses (including export output losses) because of the Rhodesian heritage of inadequate training and experience for African managers, professionals, large scale farmers and skilled workers. <u>4</u>/.

Table 8

Causation of the 1981-83 increase in the ratio of current
account deficit to potential output

Decomposition of the increase in the current account deficit
as a percentage of potential output: 1981-1982-1983
compared with 1978-80 base

CAD/PO 1978-80 = 1.3 per cent			
1. Increase 1981 CAD/PO 8.1%	1982 10.1%	1983 6.5%	
2. Expected terms-of-trade gain from reversal of sanctions a/	4.0%	4.0%	4.0%
3. Total deterioration to be explained	12.1%	14.1%	10.5%
I. External shock	3.39%	5.40%	6.20%
Terms of trade a/	.82	2.45	2.55
Interest rate	.58	1.28	1.30
Recession	1.40	1.88	2.36
Weather b/	–	(-.41)	(-.09)
Transport c/	.58	.21	.09
II. Debt burden	0.02%	0.19%	0.80%
III. Domestic policy	6.93%	4.16%	1.92%
Output 3.61%	2.73%	1.48	
Investment	.11	.29	.20
Tradeability d/	.58	.62	(-.36)
Import relaxation e/	1.75	(-.41)	(-.18)
Profit remittance relaxation f/	.88	.92	.77
IV. Capital rehabilitation shock (Increase M/GFCF Ratio) g/	2.22%	3.74%	1.68%
V. Total calculated	12.6%	13.5%	10.6%
VI. Total 'Observed' h/	12.1%	14.1%	10.5%
Interaction effects/errors/ omissions i/	(-0.5)%	0.6%	(-0.1)%

Notes to table 8:

a/ Removal of sanctions allowed ending intermediation which had raised import prices perhaps 15 per cent and reduced export prices 20 per cent on average. In 1980 about 60 per cent of this gain was achieved but in 1981-1983 it was rapidly offset by terms-of-trade deterioration. These calculations compute the counterfactual 1981-83 terms of trade adjusted for sanctions reversal and take terms-of-trade loss from these levels.

b/ the 1981 weather-boosted harvest had a positive (deficit-decreasing) impact in 1982-1983. The 1982-84 weather stricken harvests will have severe negative impact in 1984 and 1985.

c/ In 1981 and to a lesser extent in 1982 and 1983 some potential exports (particularly steel) could not be exported because no transport to ports was available. Rough estimates of amount from Treasury sources.

d/ Estimated sector by sector effect of real exchange rate appreciation (depreciation) from base period level.

e/ Change in ratio of non-capital imports to GDP from base period.

f/ Change in ratio of profit remittances allowed to GDP.

g/ Change resulting from increased ratio of capital imports to GFCF. This was caused by making good deferred maintenance and restoring a more normal makeup of GFCF after 1976-1979 import constraints which had altered its composition as well as reducing its overall magnitude.

h/ 'Observed' including adjustment for 'lost' terms of trade improvement explained in note a/.

i/ The sectoral computations of loss of exports due to tradeability and impact of recession in certain cases probably posit exports beyond sub-sectoral capacity limits.

7. Political and economic policy: prospects and parameters

The preceding summary of economic events in 1980-83 and the decomposition of the current account deficit both indicate major policy components and their impact on the deficit. However, they do not - by themselves - either indicate the political and economic prospects and perceived parametric constraints within which the policies were formulated nor the main 1984 policy choices debated in Zimbabwe. These will be reviewed in this and the subsequent section.

In 1980-81 the main political and economic goals were: to raise (actually to restore) African per capita consumption; to launch a programme of rapid universal provision of basic services (defined as including health, primary and secondary education, pure water, and, less clearly, housing); to revitalize African agriculture and begin reversal of the land access patterns created by the colonial period; to achieve a growth of wage employment comparable to that of the population; to retain the services of professional, skilled and managerial (including farming) Europeans; to begin to scale down economic dependence on South Africa in the context of regional cooperation.

These goals were seen as requiring a rapid growth in GDP, which in turn required sharply increased GFCF and increased imports financed both by export growth and substantial external concessional, commercial and investment finance as well as a sharp increase in government expenditure - more than balanced on the recurrent account by revenue gains from growth.

The factors seen as offering scope for achieving these targets were: substantial generalized unused capacity; gains through better terms of trade and export market access expected from the ending of sanctions; substantial, apparently firm, pledges of concessional finance; a policy (including remittability of profits) intended to attract foreign investors; expected positive impact of grower price and favourable weather on agricultural output; potential for resettlement of African farmers on fairly readily purchasable European farms combined with increases of marketed output expected from the provision of services, inputs, credit and markets for African farmers.

The Transitional Plan was based on these goals and elements of the macroeconomic scenario. As noted its main weakness was its unrealistic assumptions about exports and, in the event, about concessional and investment finance.

On the fiscal side the strategy did not work well because the Treasury was unable to hold recurrent expenditure growth below or even at that of revenue, buoyant as the latter was. On the external balance, errors are visible in retrospect: far too rapid freeing of factor payment transfers, absence of a coherent external borrowing strategy and slow response to worsening external balance realities and probable future developments.

Both the Treasury and the Reserve Bank were far too sanguine about external investment - and indeed were to remain so at least until 1984.   Investors first held back to see what would happen and by 1982 saw little in the picture of falling profits, high inflation, weakening domestic demand and problematic export prospects to encourage them to choose Zimbabwe as an investment site except for special projects.   The main external investments, a new RTZ goldmine, the Heinz bean project, a chewing gum factory, the Holiday Inn and a food processing takeover were the rule - not the exceptions - in that all were special cases.

The growth achieved from the combination of planned expansion, a record 1981 harvest and the Treasury's and Reserve Bank's loosening of fiscal, monetary and exchange control discipline in 1980 and 1981 was well above planned levels.   Its price was a growing government borrowing requirement, inflation (partly cost-push via wage increases but much of its demand-pull), overvaluation of the domestic currency and a rapid rise in the current account deficit.

When the external shocks on terms of trade, quality of external finance and depressed markets hit in 1981-82, these weaknesses impeded adjustment.

Policy outlook - or at any rate perceptions of objective and political constraints - changed sharply and rapidly in 1982-83.   While IMF pressure and World Bank structural adjustment advice may have played a part, both the shift and its limitations were largely Zimbabwean.

Raising real personal incomes was dropped as a short-term goal. Wage restraint, grower price increases less than cost increases for large-scale farmers (though probably not for peasant producers), sharp increases in electric power rates (apparently with little analysis of the implications for the cost of production of export sectors), reductions in food subsidies (in principle - but doubtfully in practice - offset by income increases for low-income households[5/]) became repetitive policy themes which were acted on.   Monetary policy became restrictive (albeit as demand for credit except from the government fell the impact may have been marginal) and foreign exchange allocations for visible imports suffered draconian cuts in respect of goods financed out of export earnings (i.e. in practice inputs into production and maintenance rather than into new capacity creation).

However, despite tax increases, the recurrent budget was not brought nearer to balance.   The momentum of domestic spending proved too strong (albeit its rate of increase was sharply slowed) in the context of a stagnant tax base.   Until late 1982 no significant steps were taken to reverse the overvaluation of the Zimbabwean dollar resulting from inflation above the world average (and the rapid fall of the South African rand) and, somewhat oddly, foreign exchange allocations for invisible imports and factor payments remained liberal so that payments on these items rose sharply even as visible imports for use in production were cut back.

As the decomposition of the current account deficit (table 8) illustrates, these measures - despite their incompleteness and/or lagged nature - might have been adequate to restore balance but for the impact of the series of negative exogenous developments: deterioration of terms of trade, export market stagnation, continued near-absence of concessional finance, rising global interest rates, drought, South Africa's destabilization efforts (especially through their effect on transport costs). However, in the event they were not leading to further shifts of position in 1984.

In part the measures taken were much the same as those instituted in 1982-83 (including an "active" exchange rate policy to prevent a return to overvaluation). With respect to the recurrent budget deficit limited progress was made - while uneven constraint was achieved on basic expenditure: defence, drought relief (broadly defined), interest and subsidies (from 1981-83 rail, crop marketing and steel export losses). Clearly, there was a limit on the extent to which it was politically possible to raise taxes in a depression and in a pre-election budget. Hence there was a reduction in constant prices but not in nominal prices.

In respect of external payments sharp changes were made. These radically reduced the remittability of factor payments - of dividends on pre-1979 investment, rents, interest on blocked balances - probably by $Zim 200 million a year. In parallel about $Zim 200 million of privately held external securities were acquired for local currency and liquidated. These shifts - which appear to have been delayed more by differences of priority and judgement within the financial and economic wings of the public sector than by any general political constraint - were made possible by four factors:

(a) a growing realization that further cuts of visible imports would lead to accelerated falls of output;

(b) parallelled by increasing disbelief in the value of a general liberal policy for factor payments as a means of attracting either equity or inflows of loan capital;

(c) a shift toward either selective or radically reduced use of external credit (in its extreme form a call for current account surpluses by 1986) and

(d) projected requirements of grain imports to the value of $Zim 300-400 million 1984/85 as a result of a third consecutive drought year.

In the event 1984 exports performed better than expected and a higher than forecast crop reduced grain import requirements. As a result of the policy, and the good luck, by mid-1984 it became possible to halt the erosion of visible inputs into production.

The critical political and economic macro policy questions as of late 1984 turned on the continued political acceptability of austerity. Real production per capita had fallen to 82.5 per cent of its 1973 level by 1983 (table 3) and probably below 80 per cent in 1984. In late 1984 the Standard and Chartered Bank (Zimbabwe) estimated that it was back to 1968 levels. In terms of more recent years only 1978 was worse (table 3). While these data overstate the decline suffered by wage-earning Africans and African small farmers, they do constitute a political barrier to more severe or indefinitely continued austerity.

However, to date there are no signs that the government intends to revert to relaxed monetary or budgetary policies. These would, given the import constraint, lead to more inflation and - depending on the initial recipients of increased incomes - perhaps some export reduction through shifts from export to local market sales. The only 'reflationary' measures taken in 1984 were grower price increases for 1985 harvests - still below the real levels for the 1981 harvest. The only proposed reflation was that concerning visible imports for production and maintenance use as soon as foreign exchange availability allowed.

If exports - whether in response to better terms of trade or because volume expands - rise from 1985 on by at least 5 per cent a year and if 1985-90 harvests are average to good, and if a current account deficit approximating that of 1983 in nominal US dollar terms can be financed, then a continuation of austerity phasing into gradual renewal of growth is seen as politically practicable. However, Zimbabwe is a clear case illustrating the aptness of the World Bank's recent warnings that policy reforms aimed at stabilization and structural adjustment have high initial production and political costs before gains are achieved. These may be unsustainable if the external setting is unfavourable in the absence of substantially increased external resource inflows on concessional terms or at least on terms granting longer than commercial grace and repayment periods. Unfortunately, Zimbabwe also illustrates the Bank's point that, unless bilateral and multilateral institutions act promptly, net capital account transfers to Africa may fall by 50 per cent before the end of the decade.

8.   Zimbabwe 1984: Macro policy issues

Zimbabwe is, and until 1990 almost certain to remain, foreign exchange constrained, not capacity constrained. Prolonged living with foreign exchange constraints (including low capacity growth) is creating a situation in which both GDP and export responses to increased export demand and/or improved terms of trade will be crippled by the low capacity ceiling. That ceiling results from the import constraints that have prevailed almost continuously since 1973-74. While that ceiling was hit in some sectors in 1981, a recurrence of capacity constraints is not an immediate nor (unfortunately) even a likely constraint prior to 1990, with the possible exception of certain sectoral bottlenecks.

Raising domestic savings rates would increase GFCF and capacity growth, but reduce consumption by rather more and thus diminish GDP growth. The explanation lies not in the standard Keynesian thrift paradox, but in the fact that GFCF's direct and indirect import coefficient is at least .56 while that for operation of capacity (consumption) is under .21. As a result every Zimbabwean dollar diverted from consumption to savings can - without worsening the current account deficit - increase GFCF by only $0.375, with the other $0.625 either aborted GDP or increase in stocks of non-exportables. Thus while the current price potential future GDP multiplier of domestic savings is about .275 its immediate achieved GDP multiplier is -2.7 before adjustment for external interest saved and perhaps -2.4 after such adjustment.

The implications of the external balance constraint for GFCF and the perverse short and medium term GFCF/output trade-off are:

(a)   priority to GDP growth higher than population growth (i.e. at least 4 per cent);

(b)   subject to the constraint that GFCF must be adequate to sustain positive capacity growth;

(c)   investment should be concentrated on breaking bottlenecks not on raising capacity across the board. This implies concentration on export production/finance (foreign exchange bottleneck), land reform/resettlement/small farming sector support services (employment bottleneck), regional transport links (foreign exchange saving and earnings bottlenecks), regional energy sourcing (GFCF and foreign borrowing bottlenecks);

(d)   and investment should be restructured toward less capital-intensive and import-intensive approaches, e.g. continued redressing of balance in favour of small-scale agriculture, substitution of regional (e.g. Cabora Bassa generator capacity/transmission line) for national (e.g. additional coal-fired capacity) power generation;

(e)   reduction of import content of GFCF both by selecting technology and construction patterns with lower foreign exchange content (e.g. not highly mechanized/diesel pump irrigated agriculture) and by altering production mix to substitute domestic for imported plant and equipment (e.g. altering the integrated steel industry's output mix to help meet the requirements of the expansion of structural steel and engineering sectors).

The reduction of the Zimbabwe government's borrowing requirement by eliminating the recurrent deficit has been advocated as a way to increase savings, to reallocate investment from the public to the private sector, to reduce the disincentive effects of taxation and (assuming tax increases rather than cuts in services or food subsidies) to make after-tax income distribution more equitable. Raising savings by balancing the recurrent budget would have the same impact on output as any other method of raising savings. In fact, private investment has not been squeezed out by public investment on the credit front, and public investment is - on balance - less import-intensive. In practice recurrent budget balancing will require tax increases, selective reductions of subsidies for food and enterprises and a limit on the growth of public services. The case for that course is that it would reduce inflationary pressure, improve income distribution (on the assumption that income tax and amenity consumer goods are the main sources of additional revenue and that food subsidy reductions are offset by income increases for lower income households) and avoid an imbalance between significantly rising real public services and significantly falling real disposable income. In practice the likely impact of eliminating the recurrent deficit on savings would be low with private savings falling by a large fraction of the decrease in government dis-saving, unless a parallel expansion of the economy is possible.

The recurrent deficit, wage and employment and savings problems are interlinked. The rundown of output, savings and African consumption at the time of the Rhodesian regime in the years 1975-1978 was reversed as to consumption by the massive wage-salary increases during the Muzorewa administration in 1979-80. These were followed by another round of increases by the Zimbabwe government. Taken together with rapid advance of high level African cadres in the civil service, private employment and business, the rapid expansion of basic services and continued high war costs these had the effect of:

(a) reducing both the ratio of surplus to capital stock and that of saving to income;

(b) despite rises in nominal average income levels, sharply increasing income inequality among Africans and drought-related rural-urban inequality increases;

(c) generating increases in output (over 1980-81), the current account deficit and the government's recurrent deficit, adding demand-pull to cost-push inflation;

(d) causing a once for all reduction (over 1980-84) in the wage employment base on top of its existing labour shedding trend (at constant output levels);

(e) contributing to forcing a return of budgetary and foreign exchange policy toward stringency as from 1982 because no margin remained to accommodate negative external economic and weather shocks.

The options as regards <u>wage and employment</u> policy appear to be very limited. Reducing real wages – by holding increases below rises in cost of living - may be inevitable, but as for many workers they are already below Rhodesian levels a reduction imposes great political strain and human hardship. Unless and until the economy can be made more labour intensive or real GDP growth is restored to 9 per cent there seems no way to prevent a continued erosion of the ratio of wage employment to the potentially economically active population. Even the Transitional Plan provided for only a 3 per cent target (at 8 per cent real growth).

<u>Interest and exchange rate</u> policy options are not the subject of much discussion. While the real interest rate to savers and to most lenders is negative, there is already excess liquidity parallelling low GFCF and profit rates. That pattern hardly suggests that higher interest rates would have much impact except in a context of a viable policy package for substituting labour for capital in investment in replacement and expansion. Given the sensitivity of exports of mining and manufacturing products to the exchange rate and of large-scale farming to net income (and therefore either to the exchange rate or to government subsidies), there appears little reason for reversing the present policy of downward floating at least to the degree necessary to avoid a real appreciation of the Zimbabwean dollar[6].

<u>Price controls</u> (and, briefly, wage controls under the predecessor regime) have been used as a means to limit price increases during periods of scarcity and to deflect their incidence on basic consumer goods. They have on the whole been perceived as a necessary, marginal form of market management to limit abuses and/or protect vulnerable groups. Since 1983 they have been loosened as part of a process of subsidy limitation offset by minimum wage increases, but remain politically prominent (both for their advocates and for critics) even if, arguably, of negligible economic impact.

The controls have been introduced and are advocated to prevent creeping increases in production margins and – especially – distribution margins. This they probably do achieve so long as there is a moderate seller's market but not in times of extreme shortage[7]. In principle, when the controls are on a cost-plus basis they would appear likely to protect inefficient firms and render the domestic market more attractive than exports, but the delays in price revision largely cancel out this effect. Improved calculation (unit cost with efficient operation at levels likely to be possible given foreign exchange constraints - not actual or claimed cost-plus), a more limited range of products and speedier revision are plausible reforms. The abolition of controls would not seem to have a clear economic case in its favour and would have a high political and social cost because it would (perhaps wrongly under present market conditions) be seen as likely to raise the prices of basic consumer goods dramatically.

<u>Foreign exchange allocation</u> has been a central policy instrument ever since the time of the unilateral declaration of independence.

Zimbabwe inherited a very detailed, complex, tight allocation system oriented to the defence of the balance of payments and to the promotion of production. Initial loosening - especially as to invisibles - was reversed as from 1982 in respect of goods and goods-related invisibles as from 1984 in respect of factor payment transfers (except pensions). No Rhodesian or Zimbabwean government has ever seen abolition of foreign exchange controls as an acceptable policy option because - given purchasing power patterns - it would raise imports of consumer goods relative to imports of production input and investment goods, with a negative impact on output and future exports. The options have been seen in terms of more or less tight priorities in allocation, value of factor payment remittability as a means of securing new investment, promptness and efficiency (or otherwise) of the process, i.e. ways and means of implementing; the principle of foreign exchange allocation itself remains unquestioned.

The allocation system has been criticized on the grounds that it introduces rigidity, discourages exports, uses cumbersome and micro-inefficient procedures and is a poor substitute for market price allocation. The first and third criticisms are partly valid, but the remedy lies in administrative streamlining and economic (production impact) analysis, not major macro-policy changes. The alternative implied in the fourth criticism - unless presented as advocacy of an open general licence list for certain key spares and production inputs not readily divertible either to direct consumption or low priority production - seems as unworkable now as it seemed to the Rhodesian regime in 1965 and even more unworkable than it appeared to the incoming Zimbabwe cabinet in 1980.

The key question is whether foreign exchange allocation can be used to promote exports by preferential allocations to exporters and/or allowing exporters to retain a share of foreign exchange earnings for production, maintenance and capital imports related to their enterprises over and above their basic allocations. Given the pervasiveness of foreign exchange constraints on production (and the absence of severe overvaluation), this broadening of exchange control and allocation to enhancing foreign exchange availability as well as reducing use would appear to be both practicable and to deserve the priority attention it has been receiving since 1982.

External borrowing policy shifted sharply at independence and again in 1982. The first shift was very close to a "more the better" stance with relatively little attention either to interest rates or to maturities/repayment schedules. The bulk of the borrowing has been at best on quasi-concessional terms, and at least a third at full commercial floating rates, while the average grace and maturity periods seem to have been set at or below three and seven years respectively. In reaction, Zimbabwe has adopted a policy of accepting very few loans - with the ironic and major exception of the Reserve Bank's lines of credit at Libor plus - with interest rates above 10 per cent, grace periods of less than five years or repayment periods shorter than 10 years (for a total of 15). As the country's chances of obtaining concessional finance are limited and export credits (except for very long gestation projects) rarely meet the repayment standards, the only evident way of sustaining this policy is the rapid reduction of the current account deficit. Indeed elimination of the deficit has seriously been canvassed apparently without a clear realization that balancing by reducing imports would require a 25-40 per cent initial fall of GDP, negative subsequent capacity growth for several years and low output growth (significantly below that of population over at least 1980-90, continuing the 1974-79 trend for another decade). However, with debt service approaching 30 per cent of export earnings in 1983, a return to the unselective borrowing policy of the years 1980-82 is also patently an untenable proposition.

Within its present foreign-exchange-constrained parameters, GDP multipliers for Zimbabwe are very high for real export demand increases (about 4), net current account deficit financing (about 3.6 assuming a 10 per cent average interest rate) and reductions in the capital goods and current goods import coefficients (about 4). The capacity multipliers with a one to two year average lag would (in current price terms) be about .375 times the income ones assuming unchanged savings and GFCF to GDP ratios.

These constraints - combined with capacity utilization of 80 to 84 per cent in late 1984 - suggest that restoring the rate of output growth to 4 to 5 per cent (versus a 3.5 per cent population growth rate) while sustaining capacity growth at 2.5 per cent may be the least bad practicable option, in the absence of major improvements in the global economic environment as it confronts Zimbabwe or unless the production structure can be changed in such a way as to ensure rapid, substantial reductions in overall and especially capital goods import coefficients. General global economic recovery may not be enough since one key Zimbabwe export commodity (asbestos) faces a secularly declining market and another two (tobacco and sugar) secularly stagnant markets, and several (e.g. nickel, ferrochrome, steel) suffer from such severe global overcapacity as to make short-term price recovery and volume expansion problematic; the two national regional markets (for food and manufactures) - the Republic of South Africa and the States members of the SADCC/PTA (Preferential Trade Area) - are both depressed and foreign exchange constrained, while the former is reversing the preferential treatment (especially the informal preference) it accorded to Rhodesian products before the unilateral declaration of independence.

While a 5 per cent increase of output parallel to 2.5 per cent capacity growth is evidently not permanently sustainable, it would only raise capacity utilization to about 95 per cent by 1990. Over that period it would produce less political and economic tensions and more human welfare than 3 per cent growth of output and of capacity and buy time to take advantage of any external market opportunities or of possibilities of reducing import coefficients. More optimistic (or less constrained) scenarios would require substantially faster export growth, significant (say $US 200 million net a year) concessional external finance and/or very high (say 10 per cent) sustained rates of annual growth in small-farmer output. None of these would appear to be sufficiently likely to materialize to make their insertion in the parameters constraining the strategic option prudent.

9. Policy issues and perspectives: sectoral

Purely macroeconomic analysis has limitations for any economy, but is less subject to limitations in the case of large, highly integrated, flexible industrial economies. Zimbabwe is relatively small in population and productive forces. Integration within and among sectors is uneven - e.g. the basic steel plant is not well co-ordinated with the metal-working industry. Flexibility is limited, at least in the short run, particularly in the sense that reduced domestic use of many products does not, in practice, allow their diversion to bolster exports. While Zimbabwe's manufacturing sector does account for 25 per cent of GDP it has tended to be a responsive rather than a leading sector and, despite relatively low ratios of imported current inputs to output, it is both the sector most vulnerable to foreign exchange shortages and the sector less able than agriculture or mining to earn its own foreign exchange.

In addition, Zimbabwe's location, in the middle of a continent with relatively long, and physically as well as politically uncertain, access routes to the sea, creates both regional advantages and global disadvantages for most exports (and natural protection against most imports). Furthermore, because Zimbabwe is small, changes of parameter often imply decisions on one particular project, e.g. additional coal-fired electricity generation at Hwange or arrangements to import power from the Cabora Bassa hydroelectric plant; rehabilitating and expanding the steel mill to broaden its range of outputs so as to ensure better integration into the metal working and engineering industry (potentially lowering the capital goods imports/GFCF ratio) and to move partially upmarket in exports (where sheet and plate are less of a drag on the market than rod and billet) or limiting risks of further losses and investing elsewhere.

Agriculture is usually seen as Zimbabwe's most promising sector in the short and medium term. Because agriculture is crucial to increases of exports (including manufactures based on agricultural inputs) and to avoiding or reducing food imports, the sector is central to structural adjustment to external imbalance constraints. This view prevails despite an agricultural output growth trend of about 2 per cent in the decade 1970 to 1980. It turns to a usually unrecognized degree on the bumper 1981 harvest which was the joint product of sharply higher grower prices, serious attention to facilitating production and sales by African peasant farmers and abnormally favourable weather. As the three drought years since have shown, sustained large output increases - or even the absence of substantial setbacks - cannot be counted upon.

Unless the output growth trend can be raised to at least 4 to 4.5 per cent, industrial input and export-oriented production will be squeezed by the growing food demand associated with a 3.5 per cent rate of population increase. In constant prices agricultural and forestry output (1969 $Zim) was $177 million or 13 per cent below the 1980 level of $203 million. Thus, despite the $260 million of 1981 the trend growth rate for the decade and a half remains under 2 per cent.

Furthermore, agriculture is the only sector with the short to medium-term potential to solve the employment/productive self-employment conundrum. It is not now doing so. Wage employment in the large-scale farming sector fell from a 1975 peak of 365,000 to about 260,000 in 1983, while of the approximately 350,000 African peasant households not more than a tenth have incomes (including production for own use) comparable to those of lower wage earners. Output growth in the 1970s was based on increased capital and energy intensity - notably in irrigation and mechanization - which raised import intensity and reduced labour intensity. Independent Zimbabwe has begun to extend services, markets and credits to small farmers and has initiated a strategic programme for resettling half the peasant households, but progress to date - while already substantial, indeed surprisingly so given the short time span and absence of experience - is limited. The 50,000 tonne increase in 1984 cotton sales and the 300,000 tonne rise in 1984 maize sales by smallholders above pre-independence records are evidence of substantial potential and of rapid response even under unfavourable weather conditions.

The key to sectoral progress appears to be the five-sixths of large-scale farm arable (and some portion of large-scale farm ranching) land which almost all studies report as unutilized or underutilized. In general this represents a portion of virtually all large farms, it does not mean that one-sixth of units are wholly efficient and that five-sixths are inefficient or deserted. Buying whole farms is both a cost and output risk (other large farmers leaving, lower output in transitional period, inefficient means of land transfer).

What is needed is a means - a land tax on rated potential (not actual) output that would be offset against income tax and therefore would be chargeable only on unused or ill-used land - of encouraging large-scale farmers to sell their extra land at very low prices. By definition this should not reduce their actual output (on fully used land) more than marginally. Combined with a low initial capital input and a labour-intensive resettlement strategy this could achieve the aims of enabling most peasant households to earn a livelihood and meeting the Plan's 5 per cent sectoral and 8 per cent small farmer annual output growth targets.

This approach is grounded at least as much on economic structural constraints and possibilities as on income distribution or political economic considerations - positive as the latter are. It is a variant of the recent consensus that African peasant agriculture has received inadequate and often inappropriate policy attention and has been the victim of biases favouring the urban population and large-scale enterprises in resource allocation despite being - for most crops in most cases - both more cost efficient in market price terms and less capital and foreign exchange intensive than large-scale farming, public or private.[8/]

In the case of Zimbabwe, there are four special factors:

(a)   until   independence   African   peasants   were   very   markedly
      discriminated against as regards access to services, inputs,
      credit, markets, land and infrastructure;

(b)   while the partial redressing of the balance of access to the first
      four has led to dramatic increases of output (and especially of
      market output) by the sub-sector, the latter two constraints
      remain;

(c)   large and medium-scale agriculture is capital and import intensive
      to an extent preventing rapid expansion but holds large areas of
      underutilized or unutilized "reserve" land;

(d)   the resultant allocational inefficiency can be resolved or
      mitigated by increasing peasant access to surplus large and
      medium-scale farm land.

        Clearly this approach can neither be a panacea nor a permanent
structural   solution   to   the   employment/self-employment   constraint.
There is not an unlimited supply of land;   infrastructure costs for
peasant sector development (while below those for major large-scale
expansion) are not negligible;   over time capital intensity even in
small-scale agriculture is likely to rise.   However, for the purpose of
achieving short-term gains in output and employment and of making the
structural adjustment to foreign exchange and GFCF constraints, it is
vital to redress the economically inefficient allocation of land and of
the supporting infrastructure between large and small-scale agriculture.

        As is shown by the 32 per cent fall from the peak (good weather)
output in 1981 to the level of 1983 (second drought year), Zimbabwe's
agriculture is exposed to very high weather risks which bear most
heavily on small peasants (without reserves to ride out bad years) and
on food crops (tobacco and cotton are less vulnerable).   A strategic
approach may need to follow three lines:

(a)   fuller and more effective water use (total irrigation is not
      possible;   indeed present irrigation in many areas has to be
      curtailed in drought years);

(b)   larger national grain reserves to ensure domestic food and
      regional export security (1982 and 1983 were covered from the 1981
      crop, but storage costs were high and the reserves ran out early
      in 1984);

(c)   shifting cropping patterns in the most vulnerable areas (e.g.
      perhaps to millet and sorghum to replace maize as cattlefood and
      as emergency human food supply?).

        Finally agricultural pricing poses several problems.   First,
import and export prices are widely divergent because of transport
costs.   Thus, for crops which have a substantial local market and/or
which swing between imports and exports the choice of appropriate
prices may be a difficult problem.   Second, for some products - notably

meat and sugar exports to the EEC and other markets - prices received by Zimbabwe are not homogeneous. Average pricing creates marginal losses and intramarginal surpluses, differential price quotas (especially for small farmers) seem impracticable. The cost structures, product preferences, and price responsiveness - as well as the particular support services sought - vary sharply between the large and small-scale sectors. While Zimbabwe has a reputation for setting prices which are fair to farmers, it is doubtful whether they have risen as fast as the cost of living since 1981 - a particularly critical issue for the large-scale sector with high and rapidly rising cash production costs (and heavy debt from drought losses).

<u>Mining</u> in Zimbabwe faces a rather uncertain future. Gold production has risen to record levels and may continue to grow if gold prices remain at or about $US 400-450 an ounce. Base metal production has stabilized, thanks to the adjustment of the exchange rate and other State assistance. However, unless real prices rise by close to 50 per cent the incentive for developing new mines (except perhaps by the use of unremittable profits) would appear negligible - a serious medium-term factor as most of Zimbabwe's mines are relatively small and short life. Asbestos - for global health reasons - is clearly on the road to extinction.

Coal's prospects turn on acquiring access to the sea by a custom-built railway line to a major coal loading terminal - preferably vis Botswana and Namibia to Walvis Bay and via Mozambique to Nacala or Maputo. If such a line was built, it would become possible to export 10 million tonnes a year at some time in the 1990s (market forecasts disagree on the timing of global trade growth and the entry to new suppliers).

<u>Ferrochrome</u> and <u>steel</u> are both mining and manufacturing products. While the price of the former has recovered, it is still too low to justify major plant expansion or, indeed, full use of the existing plant (at least from the external owner's point of view). Steel faces poor market prospects globally (especially as the Republic of Korea and Brazil have more financial muscle and home market profits to subsidize exports), and greater regional and domestic sales would seem to depend partly on rehabilitation and expansion to lower unit costs and partly on building in a broader product range.

<u>Manufacturing</u> appears to have reached a plateau or crossroads:

(a)   all easy and much moderately hard import substitution has taken place;

(b)   this includes some aspects of metal working, engineering and capital goods production;

(c)   further broadening the range probably requires regionally oriented production (and access to regional markets);

(d) while the import content of production is - on average - relatively low this would - at present - be less true for new lines of production while the capital goods/GFCF ratio is very high (probably 55 per cent direct and indirect nationally and 65-75 per cent for manufacturing);

(e) many manufacturers now seek to (and do) export regionally and (peripherally) globally under the incentives of limited local demand and preferential foreign exchange availability for (or from) exports, but this move often seems to be seen as additional and peripheral to a basic national orientation and needs to be more integrated into company strategy if recent manufactured export growth - apparently over 25 per cent in volume terms in 1984 - is not to be reversed as soon as domestic market demand or general foreign exchange availability rises.

It is easier to raise than to answer the questions implicit in this position. On the face of it, cost efficiency and foreign exchange saving efficiency vary widely (and not necessarily in tandem), which suggests that a more selective policy than the de facto one of the past twenty years "if we use it protect it" is needed. Similarly, export incentives may need to be more selectively concentrated on product, local content and market than they are at present. It is fairly clear that several countries which achieved large and growing manufactured exports in the late 1960s and 1970s - e.g. Brazil, Republic of Korea - had earlier practiced fairly unselective protectionism and collective some very high cost plants before - contrary to all conventional wisdom at the time - they succeeded in breaking through into selected export lines to selected markets while maintaining high domestic protection (and prices). The problem is to discover how and why this policy worked and what elements are applicable to Zimbabwe.

As regards the supply of electric power, Zimbabwe must soon choose between a strategy of continued reliance on electricity from national coal-fired plants and a revised regional strategy of using hydroelectric energy. The former (going beyond committed units at Hwange) would probably cost $US 1,000 million (80 per cent import content) but have negligible operating import content. The latter (using additional generators at Cabora Bassa in Mozambique and at Zambian dams) might cost $300 million (same import content) shared with Mozambique and Zambia but involve $50-75 million annual power imports. Given the nature of Zimbabwe's foreign exchange and debt-service constraints, economic logic (albeit not nationalism and perhaps not security and certainly not the Anglo-American Group's coal and contracting lobby) would appear to favour the latter solution. An additional point is that Zambian and Mozambican imports of Zimbabwean manufactures are constrained not by price or demand levels but by ability to pay. Therefore the idea of regional comparative advantage in power and certain lines of manufacturing (e.g. steel, railway rolling stock?) respectively seems worth immediate serious analysis if Zimbabwe seriously wishes to adjust export structures and markets as a means to medium-term adjustment and medium to long-term parametric shifts in its present foreign exchange constrained position.

Transport is a problem to Zimbabwe in several senses. Use of far away South African ports and inefficiencies on routes through Mozambique cost about $US 40 million a year (which saved and redirected to goods imports would allow a 4 per cent increase in GDP at a constant current account deficit). South African-sponsored attacks on the Mozambique routes create severe uncertainties (and necessitate the deployment of security forces to protect routes) as does South Africa's use of delays and non-shipments as a means of exerting pressure on Zimbabwean policies. Clearly any solution must be regional and have several elements:

(a) the lines to Maputo, Beira and Ncala (the last partly in hand) must be rehabilitated and harbour facilities must be improved;

(b) the traffic requirements of Botswana, Zambia, Malawi, Mozambique and Swaziland, as well as of Zimbabwe, must be taken into account;

(c) the security problem posed by South Africa (which may be reduced by the Nkomati Accord) must be dealt with.

Again there are clear foreign exchange implications beyond cost savings: e.g. transit revenue gains from Botswana (partly offset by losses on Zambian cargo now routed through Zimbabwe to South Africa), potential export increases to Mozambique financed by the increase in its revenues from Zimbabwean transit traffic.

As the manufacturing, steel, power and transport sectoral issues suggest regional economic relations are critical to Zimbabwe. Its two regional markets - South Africa and SADCC/PTA (basically Ethiopia through Angola) - are both depressed; relations with the former are complicated by political hostility and those with the latter by payments arrears. For Zimbabwe the problem is not so much what it can sell to SADCC/PTA as how it can be paid. The method of concluding annual balanced trade agreements and of granting mutual credits may help to overcome this constraint, but only to the extent Zimbabwe can plan (at public sector and enterprise level) to import more (preferably in substitution for imports from outside the region) from these trading partners - whether industrial raw materials, selected manufactures (e.g. cloth, clothing), power and/or transport. How to articulate and act on that approach - which is gaining increasing acceptance - is a question that does not yet seem to have been tackled.

10. Prospects 1985-1990

In the period 1985 - 1990 Zimbabwe will continue to be foreign exchange constrained. If one assumes a 6 per cent rate of growth of world trade and a constant Zimbabwe share in that trade, constant terms of trade, a continuing $US 440 million current account deficit, 9 per cent interest on external debt, and pluses and minuses on weather averaging out, the following scenario is possible at least in macroeconomic terms:

(a)   5 per cent GDP growth;

(b)   2.5 per cent capacity growth (GFCF 18 per cent of GDP);

(c)   domestic savings financing two-thirds of GFCF;

(d)   wage employment growing by 1 per cent a year;

(e)   capacity utilization of the order of 90 per cent in 1990.

This scenario, while hardly very attractive, does represent a slow recovery from the conditions of 1982-84, even though in this scenario per capita GDP in 1990 would still be only about 85 per cent of what it was in 1975 and 110 per cent of its 1984 level. Hence, while the answers to the ultimately critical questions depend on what structural changes are possible to improve possible performance by reducing parametric constraints, the immediate questions concern the sectoral practicability of the scenario.

The key immediate questions are:

(a)   can real exports be raised 6 per cent a year?

(b)   is overall terms-of-trade stability plausible?

(c)   can net external finance of $US 440 million a year be raised?

The first question has been discussed in the sectoral notes above and can be answered in the affirmative if articulated policies in the key areas cited there can be agreed and implemented. The ability to implement them promptly turns in large measure on the answer to the second question.

The question whether and how net external finance of $US 440 million a year at 10 per cent average interest can be raised is a very real one:

(a)   with a per capita GDP of the order of $US 550, a severe foreign exchange constraint and 1984-84 emergency food needs Zimbabwe should be able to secure more concessional finance than it has obtained to date;

(b)   the larger projects in the lists for action by enterprises and government should be able to obtain official export credit finance at 10 per cent repayable after eight years following construction;

(c)   in principle it should be possible to negotiate World Bank sectoral funding (at Bank not IDA rates) in respect of production substantially or wholly directed to export and for medium term export finance (to promote capital goods exports), although increasing parallelism in Bank and Fund processing of projects/programmes is likely to delay rate of useability of Bank finance.

However, it is far from clear that these sources could be counted on for $US 440 million net per year. Recourse to loans at Libor rates plus short-term commercial bank finance - whether for enterprise projects, government programmes or Reserve Bank standbys (balance of payments cover) - is inherently risky (because of the need to roll over frequently) and may be prohibitively expensive at levels above $US 50-100 million net a year.

It is by no means clear that the financing requirement can be met. If it is to be met, a borrowing strategy with specific targets for both government and major enterprises will have to be formulated and implemented soon. Neither the early independence approach of taking whatever is to be had nor the extreme caution in borrowing at all (except the Reserve Bank's high interest, short duration standbys) of 1982-84 is consistent with economic stabilization and an early resumption of growth.

The areas in which structural/parametric changes might be achieved have to some extent been covered in the discussion of sectoral issues. They include:

(a)   a breakthrough in the matter of land utilization and small farmer production (the only likely way to loosen the wage employment/productive self-employment constraint in the next decade);

(b)   achievement of the status of a major coal exporter (and/or a coal-based chemical industry);

(c)   sub-sectoral development from the present steel - metal-working - engineering - transport equipment industries to a much more substantial capital goods sector (allowing reduction of the direct capital goods imports/GFCF ratio from .45 to .30);

(d)   a qualitative increase in regional exports balanced by a parallel growth of regional imports (at least in part substituting for extraregional imports);

(e)   achievement of significant reductions in transport costs (inter alia increasing global tradeability of a wider range of agricultural, mineral and heavier manufactured products).

With the partial exception of the first and last heads, these would appear to be changes which need to be worked for in the late 1980s so that in 1991-1996 constraints can be relaxed, in contrast to the situation in 1985-1990. These changes are urgent, not so much because of their short-term results - albeit in agriculture, transport and regional trade these could be significant - as because several years will necessarily elapse between initial decisions and actions and major results. Deferral of action - for whatever reasons - is likely to mean a continuation of the present parametric constraints up to 1990 and the very sluggish economic scenario they impose.

Turning to the international context, one can identify several policy changes which would improve Zimbabwe's prospects and are not, in principle, beyond the realm of negotiation through joint approaches by the Group of 24 and the Group of 77 in various forums:

1. IMF programmes more oriented to immediate output recovery and involving conditions more conducive to the expansion of production for export (as opposed to import or domestic use constriction) especially in cases - such as Zimbabwe over 1984-85 - when drought (or other reversible external shock) is the key cause of high current account and government recurrent deficits;

2. World Bank and bilateral structural import support and export sector support loans at sub-market rates (6 per cent?) to countries which are neither very poor nor in a state of complete external balance collapse and domestic economic disintegration;

3. Greater flexibility in use of official export credits so that they can be a more general source of capital goods, spares and imports for rehabilitation and less uniquely tied to single large projects or lumpy pieces of equipment (e.g. aircraft);

4. Reduction of average commercial real interest rates to 2 to 3 per cent (say 7 to 8 per cent nominal);

5. Reversal of the new protectionism of the industrialized countries (in Zimbabwe's case in particular against steel) and of dumping of subsidized surplus agricultural production (especially meat, sugar and grain);

6. Greater assistance to regional economic coordination projects including initial credits to promote intraregional trade by covering its extraregional import component and to cover the foreign exchange requirements of such projects with respect to transport, energy, agricultural inputs, and certain kinds of plant and equipment;

7. Enhanced international support for international, regional and national applied agricultural research in Sub-Saharan Africa which is gravely deficient in location-tested, economic-viability tested, producer-compatibility-tested seeds, inputs, implements and techniques, both absolutely and in comparison with South and South-East Asia.

None of these is uniquely a Zimbabwean concern. However, several, e.g. the second and third, relate specifically to lower middle-income countries falling outside the normal concessional aid category but also with limited access to or ability to service commercial bank borrowing. Similarly, the last two are of particular interest to

Sub-Saharan African economies (and perhaps most particularly in terms of present governmental concerns to those of Eastern and Southern Africa).

11. Conclusion

Zimbabwe's economic prospects are for the foreseeable future conditioned by foreign exchange constraints. In part this state of affairs is a heritage from the years of the earlier Rhodesian regime and in part attributable to the somewhat loose prioritization of the 1980-81 recovery years' policy framework. However, it is now mainly (see table 8) the result of adverse economic environment shifts.

The response to these changes should take the form of both short-term adjustment and medium to long-term structural adjustment. The latter needs to be articulated sectorally. In practice, the policy issues are very close to those of medium-term development in general, partly because external balance stability consistent with growth requires structural adjustment and is a sine qua non for development. Further, allocational efficiency and equity as well as political considerations make reallocation of land and productive services to the small-farming sub-sector critical. Similarly, the strategy concerning the current account deficit/external borrowing target is central to adjustment but also to broader development and resource allocation.

While options in each sector and policy area are bounded by parametric constraints - some of which are only alterable at international level - in most real policy options are open to Zimbabwe. However, to determine what they are one must pay careful attention to the true parametric constraints. For example, because investment has a higher import content than other sectors within the present foreign exchange constraint, a higher domestic savings rate would raise capacity and unutilized capacity but reduce possible output and, probably, exports. These interactions as well as the cost efficiency of different instruments with respect to external balance, output and distribution have only recently begun to be analyzed systematically - in retrospect, a failing of the strategy and policy formulated in 1980-82.

Medium-term strategy needs to encompass future needs to adjust reductions, i.e. to restructure and to phase in ways of making the economy less vulnerable to external shocks by cost reduction (e.g. regional versus South African external transport links), export diversification (including toward regional markets) and expansion, savings for investment for any given level of growth (e.g. electric power imports and greater emphasis on small-scale agriculture). These policy choices would require action in the period 1985-90 in order to ease external constraints on growth in the period 1991-2000, but this is not a case for deferral because substantial lags between decisions, input allocations and major returns will occur whenever the decisions are taken.

There is no reason to expect that Zimbabwe can achieve a breakthrough to 8-10 per cent a year growth in the foreseeable future. However, through 1990 a 5 per cent average annual rate appears to be a realistic target, and a higher post-1990 rate can be achieved if relevant medium-term policy decisions and resource allocations can be made as from 1985/86.

Notes

a.   The Current Account Deficit (CAD) figures used in this paper are adjusted for changes in domestic gold holdings of the Reserve Bank.

b.   The Domestic Savings Rate in this paper is defined as net of changes in stocks, i.e. as domestic savings' contribution to GFCF.

1.   For many products - especially fuel - South Africa was a high-cost source.

2.   Remittances to South Africa were largely restricted because Rhodesia had direct access to the South African capital market.

3.   No truly satisfactory base period exists. 1971-73 might be least bad but is too far in the past. 1976-78 is clearly unsuitable. 1978-80 on average can be viewed as normal involving as it does one slump, one bottoming out and one recovery year.

4.   The dangers of this pattern were luridly - if accidentally - underlined when the loss of foremen, fitters, engineers and artisans at Air Zimbabwe was described as necessitating a "crash training programme".

5.   The intention to offset food subsidy reduction for low-income groups exists. In the case of wage earners it was achieved. However, informal sector workers and food deficit peasant households are much harder to protect.

6.   Zimbabwe is in a position intermediate between low-income primary exporters and high-income industrial economies. Many - but not all - of its exports are sensitive to the exchange rate at least in the sense that overvaluation will deter them even though an exchange rate induced reduction of domestic demand will only very partially convert to additional exports. In addition, elimination of overvaluation reduces pressure on the foreign exchange allocation system and the need for the Treasury to engage in crosscancelling taxation/subsidy exercises. This is not an argument for predatory undervaluation - repetitive competitive devaluations by all mineral exporters would not raise their net

hard currency earnings unless hard currency producers (e.g. the United States), failed to protect their sectors and even for manufactured goods the net results would be modest. It is an argument for any one country dependent on mineral and manufactured exports avoiding overvaluation which erodes both financial viability of producers and saleability of products. That some other country may snap up the markets Zimbabwe loses and activate its idle capacity while Zimbabwe's grows is not a very relevant point against a flexible Zimbabwean exchange rate policy.

7. At least this was the experience in Tanzania over 1973-78 when the cost of price-controlled manufactures rose significantly less than either the import price or cost-of-living indexes and parallel marketing was limited. When shortages become extreme - as in Tanzania from 1979 - price control is markedly less effective.

8. Furthermore output per worker in Africa is lowest in relation to world levels (or other developing country levels) in agriculture, not in services or industry. While this phenomenon reflects in part the influence of the weather and resource endowments, in a number of cases greater spending on agriculture may be associated with high benefit/cost ratios.

THE WORLD DEBT PROBLEM: A DIAGNOSIS

Sidney Dell*

INTRODUCTION AND SUMMARY

More than three years have passed since the explosion of the debt crisis in August 1982, and still the international community has yet to address itself to the long-run implications of that crisis. While short-run crisis management has been successful in avoiding immediate threats to the international financial system, the outlook even for the immediate future and still more for the long run remains uncertain.

The debt problem did not begin in 1982. As long ago as 1961 the President of the World Bank felt it necessary to warn of the danger "that the machinery of economic development could be overloaded with foreign debt until it sputtered to a halt amid half-built projects and mountains of discarded plans".1/ The Secretary-General of UNCTAD, in reporting to the third Conference of that institution in 1972 - before the first oil shock - gave reasons for expecting that the debt problems of developing countries would assume "more serious dimensions" in the 1970s. 2/

The shortcomings of international treatment of the debt problem also antedate the crisis of 1982. The approach has almost invariably been short-term and ad hoc, has taken little or no account of the long-run dynamics of debt accumulation and management, and has been based on the presumption that responsibility for any difficulties associated with international lending lies mainly or wholly with the debtors. This is in spite of the fact that there is a long history of international debt crises exhibiting common features, in which the behaviour of debtors interacted with external factors in the international environment such as recession or financial stringency in major markets, accompanied by insistence of creditors on unduly high rates of return and excessive reliance on short and medium-term debt. These characteristics of the international environment have continued in the 1980s and are broadly typical of the problems faced by all debtor countries, whether their debts originated mainly from commercial or official sources.

*The author is Project Director of UNDP/UNCTAD Project INT/84/021. January 1986.

Crisis management since 1982, as in earlier years, has consisted essentially of the postponement of debt amortization and the introduction of severe programs of austerity by the debtor countries. Nevertheless debt service ratios, though stabilized for the time being in the major debtor countries, have generally continued to deteriorate elsewhere. The advantages of multi-year rescheduling and other improvements in terms gained by some of the larger debtors have not been extended to other countries, even though the low-income countries in many cases face a relatively higher burden of debt and debt service than the major debtors.

More serious still is the fact that the measures adopted for short-run adjustment in the debtor countries are undermining their prospects for coping with the debt problem in the longer run. Long-run adjustment calls for investment in the expansion and diversification of export capacity and import replacement, and it is precisely investment that has borne the brunt of the austerity programs. Per capita investment and consumption in the debtor countries will not, even on optimistic assumptions, regain their 1980 levels until 1990 or beyond. In many of the low-income countries recovery even to 1980 levels cannot be foreseen at the present time. Several leaders of debtor countries, in the course of their addresses to the 1985 UN General Assembly, emphasized their unwillingness to maintain heavy and prolonged transfers to foreign creditors at the cost of domestic deprivation. 3/ The Managing Director of the Institute for International Finance has stated that

> Even with reasonably strong export growth...the debt service burdens of some of (the non-oil developing countries) seem likely to return to excessive levels in 1985 and to crisis levels a few years later. 4/

There is a need for much greater efforts to develop the common interest of the international community as a whole in accelerating the recovery of the debtors. The creditor countries can only lose if the prostration of the debtors continues. The persistent decline in the flow of capital to the debtor countries needs to be reversed so as to relieve the foreign exchange constraints on growth and investment in these countries and thereby increase their capacity to meet their external commitments. The initiative of US Secretary Baker 5/ is directed to this end. Questions have been raised as to the adequacy of the resources envisaged under that initiative, the conditions proposed, and implications for the longer run. But the direction of the initiative in regard to additional flows of capital in support of adjustment with growth commands general acceptance.

An increased flow of capital to the debtor countries, including particularly the low-income countries, would fail in its purpose if it were not accompanied by appropriate macro-economic policies in creditor and debtor countries alike. Adjustment in the debtor countries clearly needs to continue, though its character needs to be substantially modified so as to minimize recourse to measures that depress the level of activity and maximize the restructuring of the economy with a view to improving its performance within a reasonable time frame.

But the creditor countries also have a part to play by achieving and maintaining a high level and rate of growth of business activity. The debt problem cannot be solved if commodity prices continue falling, and a recovery in such prices is not likely to be brought about at the levels of activity and rates of growth presently envisaged in the industrial countries for the immediate future. Nor can the debt problem be overcome at present levels of real interest rates. The situation calls for concerted policies on the part of the industrial countries to reduce interest rates to historical levels. A long-run solution to the debt problem requires macro-economic and open trade policies in the industrial countries that will promote a rate of growth of the value of imports from debtor countries that is substantially higher than the nominal rate of interest. The optimism generated by the export successes of certain debtor counties in 1984 was short-lived and in 1985 the exports of debtor countries as a whole appear to have levelled off or declined. A continuation of this trend would be disastrous. As the IMF <u>World Economic Outlook October 1985</u> has pointed out, a slowdown in economic activity in the industrial countries would have major adverse implications for developing countries, which "would severely strain the social consensus needed to maintain adjustment efforts in heavily indebted countries." <u>6</u>/

The development of an appropriate international response to the various issues outlined above calls for a dialogue between the governments of creditor and debtor countries involving also the international institutions and commercial banks. None of the existing fora is presently authorized to discuss these issues in depth, to review the general adequacy of present arrangements, including those for low-income countries, or to establish a framework and perspective for long-run solutions. Such a dialogue would not prejudice in any way the treatment of each case on its own particular merits. A major Committee of the UN General Assembly has adopted, by consensus, "Agreed Conclusions" containing the following passage:

> While countries recognize the unique circumstances of each case ... they will pursue, <u>inter</u> <u>alia</u>, a dialogue involving debtor and creditor countries, international private banks, as well as multilateral financial institutions exercising their responsibility in a spirit of mutual co-operation towards equitable, durable and mutually agreed approaches in support of positive adjustment and long-term growth. <u>7</u>/

The practical implementation of this consensus would be an important step forward.

The Situation at the End of 1985

The IMF staff has characterized the adjustment that has taken place in the balances of payments of capital-importing developing countries 8/ since 1982 as "dramatic" and has stated that its size and speed "caught most observers by surprise". 9/ The current account deficit of this group of countries was reduced from $104 billion in 1982 to $38 billion in 1984 and is expected to remain at the $42-44 billion level in 1985 and 1986.10/ IMF forecasters, who had projected a faster rate of reduction in current account deficits than most other analysts, found that even they had underestimated that rate by a considerable margin.

The rate of adjustment achieved was not the result of deliberate decisions as to the optimum pace of adjustment in each country. Still less did it reflect an agreed distribution of burdens between creditor and debtor countries. It was brought about quite simply by the availability of external finance which was itself severely constrained by the unwillingness of commercial banks to engage in new lending and of governments to add to the flow of official lending. IMF programs simply translated expectations of available funds into rates of adjustment according to certain well known formulae. The question of burden-sharing never arose for serious consideration in any forum whether within or outside the Fund.

The cost of adjustment was high, and was borne largely by the debtor countries. Many major borrowers as well as low-income countries suffered drastic declines in output, employment and standards of living, the poor being generally the hardest hit. In addition the economic outlook for the future was gravely affected by sharp declines in investment. This resulted not merely from the cutting back of output and growth prospects but also from the fact that much of the improvement in current account balances depended on reductions in imports, including imports of capital goods required for investment. The volume of imports of Latin American countries fell by about 36 per cent from 1981 to 1983 and of African countries by 17 per cent, followed by a recovery of no more than 2-3 per cent in both cases in 1984. Latin American imports appear to have changed little in 1985, but those of Africa may have dropped another 5-6 per cent.

It had been hoped that the sacrifices made by the debtor countries, albeit costly, would bring about a marked improvement in the world debt situation - that they would not merely prevent an international financial disaster, but would lead to a basic improvement in the position of the debtors, including their creditworthiness as seen by the commercial banks. Unfortunately these expectations have not been realized and concern regarding the vulnerability of debtor countries continues. Even countries whose performance has been applauded by the creditors in one year may find themselves in acute difficulties in the next year. Consequently, the hoped for resumption of voluntary lending by the commercial banks has receded further and further into the future, and fears of renewed crisis persist in the knowledge that a repetition of previous difficulties may find the debtors at the limit of their endurance. In the case of African countries, it is not foreseen, even on optimistic assumptions, that per capita incomes will rise very much from the low levels to which they had declined by 1984 unless donor countries make financial assistance available in much larger amounts than those presently contemplated, and unless the African countries themselves improve the utilization of their domestic and external resources.

Most economic forecasters assume that the bulk of the burden of adjustment will continue to be borne by the debtor countries. While some easing of the burden has been brought about by rescheduling principal, this does not involve real costs for the creditors since interest will continue to be paid on the amounts rescheduled. No agreed rescheduling of interest payments has occurred, (except to a limited extent under the auspices of the Paris Club) and while interest rates have declined somewhat, this has not brought corresponding relief to the debtors because of further declines in the prices of commodities that they export.

Expectations continue to be that the per capita incomes of many debtor countries will not regain pre-crisis levels until 1990 or later. As noted above, recovery of many of the low-income countries is not foreseeable at all at this time. Despite economic forecasts along these lines, there is a widespread tendency to assume that the world debt crisis has receded, and that the debt problem is now "manageable" and will remain so in the foreseeable future. The question, however, is whether the depression of the economies of the debtor countries below their potential represents a viable proposition over a period of years - viable not only economically but politically and socially as well. This remains to be seen.

Meanwhile economic conditions are becoming less favourable than those assumed earlier in 1985. Following a short-lived and partial recovery, the world economy has entered a new period of declining growth rates. The stimulus provided by the United States economy has weakened, and no other stimulus has emerged to take its place. Expectations reflected in the IMF World Economic Outlook, April 1985, were for a lower rate of growth in the industrial countries in 1985-1986 than in 1984 partially offset by higher growth rates in developing countries. The Outlook for October 1985 makes minor revisions in the 1985-1986 growth rates for industrial countries, but lowers the expected rates for developing countries by half a point for 1985 and four-tenths of a point for 1986 - both of them significant changes.11/

The slower momentum of the United States economy has been accompanied thus far by a welcome reduction in nominal interest rates and a moderate decline in the effective exchange rate of the dollar. A lowering of interest rates is of great importance for the countries that face debt-service problems. And for many countries a fall in the value of the dollar tends to reduce debt/export and debt service ratios, partly because a larger proportion of their debt than of their

exports is denominated in dollars, and partly because a decline in the
dollar may have a favourable effect on the dollar prices of the
commodities that they export. But of equal or greater importance is the
decline in import demand that is likely to result from lower growth
rates in the industrial countries. Moreover commodity markets and
prices had been weak even in 1984, and are therefore particularly
vulnerable to any further drop in demand. It is not difficult to
envisage situations in which the decline in interest payments owed by
debtor countries might be overshadowed by a fall in their export
earnings, and this did in fact occur in a number of countries in 1985.
If this tendency were to continue, the optimistic scenarios suggested
by forecasters in recent months would fall wide of the mark.

     The inability of countries, both industrial and developing, to
establish and maintain a trend of steady growth and rising living
standards is at odds with the worldwide spectacle of unemployed labor,
and surplus productive capacity. From the standpoint of their own
productive potential alone, there is no reason why living standards in
numerous developing countries should have to be held down to levels
considerably below those of the 1970s, or why they cannot expect to
regain those levels until 1990 or beyond. Labor and capital are
available in sufficient quantity in these countries to permit
substantially higher production and income levels than those now
prevailing provided that the international environment could be managed
in a more supportive manner that did not call for drastic reductions in
the level of business activity.

     Despite this, there has been a sharp and continuing deceleration
in commercial bank lending to developing countries. Morgan Guaranty
reports that following a 6 1/2 per cent increase in 1983, bank credit
to developing countries grew by only 2 per cent in 1984 and "is
unlikely to pick up for some time to come." 12/ US banks alone reduced
their exposure to developing countries by nearly 3 per cent. Net
voluntary lending to countries with debt problems has been curtailed,
new voluntary extensions of short-term trade credits having been more
than offset by net repayments of existing loans.

     The effect of bank efforts to limit concentrations of developing
country risk has been to lower exposure to developing countries
relative to bank capital by increasing their capital as well as by
constraining their lending. By the end of 1984 the ratio of outstanding
cross-border and foreign office non-local currency claims on developing
countries to the primary capital of US banks involved in international
lending had fallen to below the end-1977 level. The corresponding ratio
for the nine largest US money center banks was down to the end-1978
level. Since there is no sign of a resumption of voluntary lending or
of a significant easing of constraints on lending, the ratios are
expected to decline further during the years ahead. 13/

Historical Parallels

     In his book <u>International Trade</u> published in 1927, Taussig
described the pattern of international debt crises. Through recurrent

cycles of accelerating and decelerating lending by creditor countries, a point was generally reached at which "the debtor country has more to remit on interest account than to receive on principal account, and ... the remittance is effected by an excess of merchandise exports over imports". Taussig cited the history of the United States and of Argentina as illustrating, from the standpoint of the debtor countries, the successive waves of international borrowings followed by repeated crises.14/ It is noteworthy that during the period discussed by Taussig, debt service ratios reached levels comparable with those of today: the ratio of investment income payments to current receipts reached a level of 66 per cent in Argentina in 1889, forcing a renegotiation of debt in 1891. 15/

In a recent paper, Robert Solomon has pointed to strong similarities between the experience of the United States as a debtor in the nineteenth century and borrowing countries in recent times. The ability of US debtors, both sovereign and private, to pay interest on their debts was affected by economic conditions in the major industrial country - Great Britain. A recession in Britain lowered both the prices and the volume of exports of the United States. This in turn affected the tax revenues of the sovereign borrowers and the income of the railways and other private debtors. The result was often suspension of interest payments, often referred to as default.

Similar effects occurred when financial conditions became stringent in Britain and interest rates rose there. Capital flows to the United States fell off or ceased completely. And this, in turn, made it difficult or impossible for the American borrowers to continue interest payments.

This has a familiar ring. It is similar to the experiences of Brazil, Mexico, and other borrowers in recent times... 16/

During the 1920s the exports of debtor countries rose much more slowly than service payments so that the proportion of export earnings available to finance imports declined continuously. As a United Nations study of this period pointed out:

> The high return on the capital, however, was not an unmitigated advantage to the investors, since it contributed to undermining the balance of payments of the debtor countries and thus hastened and aggravated the collapse. The instability in the external transactions of debtor countries, only temporarily cloaked as long as foreign capital continued to enter, was all the more serious since a considerable part of that capital was lent on short or medium term. 17/

The subsequent collapse of the debtor countries under the impact of the decline in commodity prices during the Great Depression and the drying up of international capital flows is well known. In Chile debt service obligations in the depth of the Depression exceeded the total value of exports, whereas from 1926 to 1929 the debt service ratio had increased only from 5.5% to 9.2%. Similar orders of increase were experienced in other debtor countries.

As a result of the widespread defaults of the 1930s, most of the flow of capital to developing countries during the first two decades after World War II took the form of grants and loans from official bilateral and multilateral institutions, while private lending on market terms was relatively much less important. One of the principal considerations underlying the establishment of the World Bank in 1945 was that the channelling of private capital for reconstruction and development would be feasible only through an intermediary supported by the guarantee of the United States and other developed countries. Even under the relatively favorable conditions of this period, it did not take long for debt problems to build up. At the Annual Meetings of the IBRD and IMF in 1961, Eugene Black, President of the World Bank, felt it necessary to warn of the danger "that the machinery of economic development could be overloaded with foreign debt until it sputtered to a halt amid half-built projects and mountains of discarded plans".[18]/ In 1965 a study by the United States Agency for International Development (USAID) noted the large role of lending in development finance and concluded that softer terms constituted "the only practical solution for maintaining the net resource flow needed".[19]/

Despite the unique characteristics of each of the periods mentioned above, they have the following features in common with one another as well as with the debt problems of the 1970s and 1980s:

(a) the persistence of cycles in which the buildup of debt and debt service ratios was followed by crisis in one form or another and frequently by default.

(b) the acceleration of the onset of crises and their aggravation by efforts on the part of lenders - whether private or official - to maintain rates of return on capital at unduly high levels, and by excessive reliance on short and medium-term debt.

Mismanagement on the part of individual debtor and creditor countries or enterprises was also frequently in evidence. But the breadth and variety of the circumstances in which crises occurred make it clear that mismanagement could only have been an aggravating and not a fundamental factor. Taussig pointed out that the experience of the United States as a borrower in its early days of development was basically no different from that of Argentina or of scores of other countries. Comparing twentieth century Brazil with the United States of the previous century, Robert Solomon states that "In many respects, the United States was the Brazil of the nineteenth century".[20]/

The Origins of the Debt Crisis

The exceptional buildup of debt during the 1970s was initially the result of a deliberate decision by the governments of both lending and borrowing countries - a decision supported by the entire membership of the IMF. The rise in oil prices had resulted in the accumulation of large savings in the oil-exporting-countries well beyond their capacity to use productively within their own countries alone. On the other hand, the real incomes and savings of the oil-importing-countries were correspondingly reduced. Unless the surplus savings in the hands of the oil-exporting-countries could be channelled for investment or consumption elsewhere, there was a danger that the world economy as a whole would be thrown into a deflationary spiral to the detriment of oil exporters and oil importers alike.

In January 1974 the Managing Director of the IMF presented a note to the Committee of Twenty in which he indicated that oil-importing-countries would, in the short run, have to accept the deterioration of the current account of the balance of payments, since:

> Attempts to eliminate the additional current deficit caused by higher oil prices through deflationary demand policies, import restrictions, and general resort to exchange rate depreciation would serve only to shift the payments problem from one oil-importing country to another and to damage world trade and economic activity. 21/

Subsequently, in its communiqué of 13 June 1974, the Committee of Twenty noted:

> As a result of inflation, the energy situation, and other unsettled conditions, many countries are experiencing large current account deficits that need to be financed ... Sustained co-operation would be needed to ensure appropriate financing without endangering the smooth functioning of private financial markets and to avert the danger of adjustment action that merely shifts the problem to other countries (emphasis added).22/

These were the considerations underlying the decision to establish an oil facility to provide balance-of-payments support at low conditionality in 1974-1975. Any Fund member drawing on the oil facility was required 'to cooperate with the Fund in order to find appropriate solutions for its balance-of-payments problem'. This requirement of co-operation with the Fund was the same as that applicable to the Compensatory Financing Facility, but the character of the conditionality involved was somewhat different. Under the relevant decisions of the Executive Board on this matter 23/ member countries drawing on the oil facility were required to avoid 'competitive depreciation and the escalation of restrictions on trade and payments'; and to pursue 'policies that would sustain appropriate levels of economic activity and employment, while minimizing inflation.'

The financial resources available to the Fund for this purpose were, however, very small in relation to the scale of the problem created by the rise in oil prices.24/ Moreover certain influential Fund members had objections in principle to any assumption by the Fund of an intermediating or recycling role. Most of the requisite channelling of financial resources from surplus to deficit countries was therefore undertaken by the commercial banks, which thereby, in effect, took over the major part of IMF responsibilities for providing balance-of-payments support. They did so in the knowledge that the rate of return on foreign lending was substantially higher than on domestic lending, while the foreign loss ratio was relatively low. Some of the large US banks earned well over half of their total profits from foreign operations despite the fact that these accounted for a much smaller proportion of their total business.

It has been suggested that "the recycling of petrodollars explains only a fraction of the tremendous expansion in lending by international banks" and that there was substantial credit creation in the Eurocurrency markets. 25/ Efforts were made to bring these markets under control, but these were successfully resisted by the lending banks and by two of the central banks of the countries in which they were domiciled. 26/

In the first few years of recycling, the loans were made at relatively low nominal rates of interest, and real rates were often actually negative. Later, however, interest rates rose to unprecedented levels as a result of restrictive monetary policies adopted by the industrial countries to counter inflation. While the cost of servicing accumulated debts soared, the export earnings of the debtor countries dropped sharply as their export prices and volumes reacted to slackening business activity in the main industrial countries. This in turn led to a collapse of new lending by the commercial banks.

In its Annual Report 1983 the IMF explained the sharp setback in the current account balance of non-oil-developing countries from 1978 to 1981 as follows:

> The key consideration here is the generally unfavourable nature of the external economic and financial environment faced by these countries in recent years and the importance of certain major adverse influences almost wholly beyond their own control. The global recession, of course, has undermined the buoyancy of export markets in volume terms and has brought severe weakness in export prices for primary commodities. Meanwhile, continued increases in the import prices faced by non-oil developing countries had already contributed to the prolonged deterioration of their terms of trade (1982 having been the fifth consecutive year of such deterioration). Finally, the upsurge of interest rates that followed the general shift toward monetary restraint in the major industrial countries in 1979 imposed an unexpectedly heavy and lasting burden on

this group of countries, whose balance of payments structures already featured quite sizable debt service charges...

For the oil-importing developing countries, the entire deterioration of their combined current account balance from 1978 to 1981 can be ascribed to essentially the three adverse factors just enumerated. (emphasis added) 27/

Despite the obvious similarities between the situations that resulted from the deterioration in terms of trade of non-oil developing countries in 1978-81 and 1974-75 the Fund was not prepared to repeat the remedies that it had advocated and acted upon in the mid-1970s. While it had deliberately encouraged the financing of current account deficits in 1974, it now insisted on strong measures of adjustment to a set of circumstances very similar to those that had prevailed earlier. This was accompanied by a marked shift of position on conditionality. Previously Fund policies on conditionality had been evolving towards recognition of the importance of structural factors in balance of payments disequilibrium, and of the need for additional time and resources for structural adjustment by deficit countries. These trends were halted and reversed.

The reasons for this change of position are not altogether clear. 28/ At times it was suggested that the surpluses of oil-exporting countries were likely to be more persistent in the 1980s than in the 1970s and that adjustment to this state of affairs could no longer be postponed. Thus, in discussing issues of "global adjustment" in its World Economic Outlook for June 1981, the Fund staff stated that "the possibility of further increases in the real price of oil over the next few years cannot be discounted". 29/ Alternative scenarios through the mid-1980s explored in this study assumed that the real price of oil would either remain steady or continue to increase. Even the lower of these assumptions implied a current account surplus of oil-exporting countries of $50 billion in 1985, while on the higher assumption the surplus was likely to amount to $95 billion. 30/ These incorrect expectations probably had a profound influence on the policy stance of the Fund at that time.

A new source of difficulty was the exceptional upsurge in interest rates, particularly since debt levels were now much higher than they had been in the early 1970s. And high real interest rates have indeed continued much longer than had been generally expected. It could therefore be argued, at least with hindsight, that adjustment was needed if not to higher oil prices at least to higher levels of real interest rates, and this became still more apparent with the onset of the world debt crisis in the latter months of 1982.

This, however, meant that debtor countries were being required to adjust to interest rate levels that were the result of policies adopted by the industrial countries for domestic reasons, without adequate

consideration of their international repercussions. In their statement
on June 21, 1985 the Ministers and Governors of the Group of Ten (G-10)
took the view that "The international implications and interactions of
domestic economic policies should be given close attention in the
domestic policy-making process and in international consultations". 31/
And their Deputies acknowledged that there had, in certain instances,
been a "lack of mutual understanding of the impact of particular
policies and of an agreed analytical framework, which have sometimes
made international consensus on the appropriateness of policies more
difficult to achieve". 32/ Although the G-10 did not make any
commitment with respect to interest rates, there is a wide measure of
international agreement that real interest rates have been, and still
remain, too high. Even recent declines in nominal rates have been
partly or wholly offset, so far as developing countries are concerned,
by declines in the prices of primary commodities.

Thus a more balanced and symmetrical policy would not be limited
to insisting that debtor countries adjust to whatever levels of real
interest rates may emerge from the domestic policies of the industrial
countries. Interest rate levels should themselves be a subject for
surveillance and, if need be, adjustment. This reasoning lies at the
basis of proposals that appropriate Fund arrangements should be made to
do for increases in interest rates what the Compensatory Financing
Facility was intended to do for declines in commodity prices.

Factors in the Debt Crisis

World Development Report 1985 has suggested that "It is possible
... to exaggerate the role played by external disturbances in causing
debt difficulties. In most instances, countries that ran into trouble
had failed to adjust ..." 33/ According to the Report, the failure to
adjust was due to mistaken expectations in three important areas.
First, many oil importers assumed that the second oil shock could be
handled as easily as the first, and were therefore insufficiently
attentive to "policy reforms". Secondly, many countries borrowed
heavily in the expectation that the 1980-83 recession would be much
shorter than it turned out to be. And, thirdly, a number of countries
made plans for major investment programs on the basis of windfall gains
from commodity exports in the 1970s, and borrowed to complete these
programs assuming that subsequent price declines would be temporary.
34/ It would not be possible to examine all these points adequately
within the compass of the present paper and, indeed, the World
Development Report itself does not document the points in detail. Some
reflections may nevertheless be in order.

In the first place, the suggestion that it is possible to
"exaggerate" the role of external factors raises the question whether
the Fund was exaggerating when, in its Annual Report 1983, it stated,
as noted above, that the entire deterioration of the combined current
account balance of the non-oil-developing countries from 1978 to 1981
was due to three adverse factors "almost wholly beyond their own
control".

Secondly, the judgment that "in most instances" countries in difficulties "had failed to adjust" goes too far. Adjustment may well have been incomplete in many cases, especially where long-term structural adjustment was required. But, as pointed out by the Fund in its Annual Report 1983, the deterioration of the oil trade balance and of the non-oil terms of trade of oil-importing-developing countries, together with the increase in their net payments of interest abroad amounted to nearly $80 billion from 1978 to 1981, against a cumulative increase of only $53 billion in their total current account deficit. "The difference between these two figures", said the IMF Report, "reflecting changes in other elements of the group's current account, can be viewed as roughly indicative of the adjustments already made by 1981 to compensate in part for the adverse impact of the external factors identified here". 35/ (emphasis added)

Particularly impressive was the fact that the exports of these countries increased by over 60 per cent from 1978 to 1981 notwithstanding the world recession, with the result that in the aggregate these countries were close to balance on their non-oil trade accounts even in 1981. The Managing Director of the IMF drew attention to this "rather remarkable" achievement in the course of his address to the 1981 Annual Meetings of the Fund and Bank, and said that in many of these countries there had been "a rather clear tendency to adopt adjustment programs and abandon expansionary policies". 36/

As regards any mistaken expectations regarding the length of the recession, it is, of course, quite possible that this led to policy errors in some cases. But such mistakes are commonplace in all countries, and governments should be faulted only when the errors made are of major proportions and are in conflict with the best advice available to the authorities at the time the relevant decisions were made. For example, the expectation that the recession would not last as long as it did was shared, in the case of the United States, by the US Council of Economic Advisers, which stated in January 1980 that "The expected recession is likely to be mild and brief".37/ The US economy did rebound in 1981, and in January of that year the Council foresaw real growth of 3 1/2 per cent for 1982. In fact, however, following a rise of 2 1/2 per cent in 1981, there was a drop of 2.1 per cent in real GNP in 1982, resulting in a decline in GNP for industrial countries as a whole. Subsequently, in June 1981, the IMF World Economic Outlook detected "more weakness in real and nominal GNP growth than the forecast published by the Administration" 38/ but even so projected a rise in real GNP of the United States of 1 1/4 per cent from 1981 to 1982, and of 2 per cent in the course of 1982. As late as August 1981 the World Bank itself, referring to the decline in the growth rates of industrial countries in 1980, stated that "Their recession has probably now bottomed out, and recovery will begin in late 1981 or early 1982" - a forecast that was wide of the mark.39/

All in all, 1980-83 were highly confusing years for economic forecasters, and few reputations improved as a result of forecasts made during this period. But it does not seem to be the case that the expectations of most developing countries differed substantially from those communicated to them from responsible sources, including the international financial institutions. Perhaps it could be argued that developing countries should, in the light of experience, always expect the worst, and act accordingly. But developing countries already face sufficient constraints on growth without adding new ones. There is something to be said for the view that developing countries should push as hard as they can against the limits to growth without deliberately incurring serious dangers of inflation or external imbalance. Trend rates of growth might well prove to be higher under such an approach than they would be under more cautious policies, even if retrenchment became necessary from time to time.

More generally, World Development Report 1985 argues that "every major payments crisis in the 1970s and 1980s was preceded by large and growing budget deficits" and cites "a significant positive relationship between growing government deficits and the accumulation of foreign debt".40/ It would however, take much more than a simplistic correlation of this type to prove that fiscal imbalance was a major factor in the debt crisis of the 1980s. As Cline has argued:

> It is difficult to believe that more than thirty developing countries simultaneously went on a binge of fiscal irresponsibility. A far more reasonable hypothesis is that their similar and contemporaneous balance-of-payments problems were the result of a common external source, international economic disruption. Indeed, external shock eroded export earnings and tax revenues, thereby contributing to fiscal deficits. Moreover, the case of Chile illustrates that severe debt crises emerged even in countries with virtually no fiscal deficit. 41/

In addition to the factors referred to by William Cline, mention should be made of the sharp curtailment of imports in many debtor countries which had the effect of lowering tariff revenues, a principal source of government income in many cases. On the expenditure side, soaring interest rates increased payments on government debt, internal as well as external, while rising unemployment imposed additional burdens on governments. Thus the fiscal deficits constituted to a large extent a passive response of the government sector to the crisis rather than an active or originating source of internal disequilibrium. It should be borne in mind that a budget deficit is the residual of two much larger quantities and that a relatively small increase in expenditure and reduction in revenue can generate a proportionally much larger increase in the budget deficit.

On the other hand, the emphasis placed by the World Development Report on the importance of capital flight in certain cases is well taken. As the Report points out, capital flight was "massive" in Argentina, Mexico and Venezuela, and added to the difficulties experienced in Nigeria and the Philippines. "In such cases foreign borrowing was a recipe for disaster". 42/ As pointed out by Bacha, in

Venezuela a cumulative current account surplus recorded over the period 1979 to 1983 implies that the growth of indebtedness must have been due entirely to a net export of capital. In Argentina and Mexico net capital outflow accounted for about one half of the increase in foreign debt from 1979 to 1983. 43/

Even capital flight, however, has its external as well as internal causes. For one thing, capital flight often results in part from uncertainties in particular countries originating in instability or declines in external demand for their exports, or other external sources of pressure on the balance of payments such as from rising interest rates on the foreign debt. In some countries foreign banks have been encouraging the placing of deposits in industrial countries, a process facilitated in some cases by premature liberalization of exchange restrictions under the influence of the Fund and World Bank.

The World Development Report implicitly takes it for granted, moreover, that capital flight can always be prevented through the appropriate constellation of policies designed to support the operation of market forces, particularly avoidance of inflation, of overvalued exchange rates, of "repressive financial policies" that maintain real interest rates at negative levels during periods of rapid inflation, and high domestic protection which obstructs the servicing of foreign debt.

This is tantamount to saying that if a government can overcome all the political, social and economic tensions within the country through market-oriented policies, incentives to capital flight will cease to exist. This may or may not be true, but even if it were true, it does not follow that all governments can at all times meet the above conditions for avoiding capital flight. If a choice has to be made in cases where freedom of action is limited, many governments would prefer to regulate the flow of capital rather than abandon policy objectives that they consider fundamental. The Report does not discuss the cases of Brazil and the Republic of Korea, which appear to have been able to limit the amount of capital flight through exchange control.

An important question is how far the funds borrowed by developing countries during the 1970s were used productively. An IMF study of 20 middle-income and relatively high-income developing countries showed that the median ratio of savings to GNP rose from 18.0 per cent in 1968-72 to 21.7 per cent in 1978-81, while the median increase in the current account deficit amounted to only 1 per cent of GNP. All but 2 of the 20 countries surveyed had savings rates in 1978-81 that were equal to or higher than those of the 1968-72 period. The study concluded that "In general, it appears that increases in the indebtedness of the non-oil-developing countries have reflected primarily an exchange of debt instruments for additional physical capital". 44/ Experience in some of the low-income developing countries was less favorable, but this was often the result, at least in part, of adverse climatic conditions and, in some cases, military conflict.

The preceding discussion illustrates the inconsistency that has arisen between the diagnosis of the debt problem at the global level and at the level of individual debtor countries. At the global level it is generally acknowledged that the combination of recession and high interest rates in the industrial countries and the consequential deterioration in the balances of payments of developing countries were sufficient, or even more than sufficient, to account for the debt crisis that came to a head in 1982. On this reasoning, the problems that arose were due overwhelmingly to factors in the international environment beyond the control of the debtor countries. But at the level of individual countries the diagnosis is turned upside down and focuses on mismanagement of the economy. Since the crisis managers apparently have little or no expectation that there will be sufficient improvement in the international environment either as regards the level of real interest rates or as regards the rate of growth of demand for developing country exports, they are led to the conclusion that adjustment must take the form predominantly of severe compression of the growth and import demand of the debtor countries, accompanied by devaluation of exchange rates. The burden of adjustment is therefore borne mainly by the debtor countries, and this can be justified to the world at large only if it can be shown that the debtor countries were themselves predominantly responsible for their own undoing. The effort to document this proposition frequently requires a stretching of the facts of the case.

But the supreme irony is this. It turns out that the case by case diagnosis at the country level leads invariably to the same remedy regardless of the circumstances of each case - more or less drastic deflation and devaluation. Moreover this standardized formula is entirely unrelated to the factors which, according to the IMF, accounted fully for the debt emergency in the first place.

The Response to the Crisis

Great skill and resourcefulness were shown by the crisis managers of the IMF and governments and banks concerned in dealing with the onset of the debt crisis in 1982 and its immediate aftermath. The arrangements made were successful in preventing an international financial collapse. Programs for individual debtor countries provided for the rescheduling of amortization payments and a modest amount of "new money" 45/ to support the efforts of the countries to bring about a rapid reduction in their external deficits. As noted earlier, the speed of these reductions was quite remarkable, although achieved at heavy cost. In the space of only two years, from 1982 to 1984, the current account deficits of capital-importing developing countries were, according to the IMF, reduced from $104 billion to $38 billion. In 1983, the first year of this process, the reduction in the current deficit was achieved entirely by curbing imports, since exports of goods and services fell slightly. The further reduction in the deficit in 1984 resulted from an upturn in exports which made it possible for the value of imports to stage a limited recovery. Most of the 1984 rise in exports was, however, concentrated in the relatively more advanced countries, especially those with a capability for exporting manufactures. Many of the low-income countries experienced little change in the demand for their exports in 1984, and were therefore also unable to increase their imports. In 1985 the value of exports and imports of the capital-importing countries appear to have levelled off or declined.

According to the IMF, from January 1984 to April 1985 21 Fund members reached agreements with commercial banks restructuring amounts totalling $105 billion, equivalent to 20 per cent of their outstanding debts. The postponement of debt service on medium-term and long-term bank debt by developing countries was equivalent to 5 per cent of their exports of goods and services in 1983 and 4 per cent in 1984. 23 countries obtained 29 official debt reschedulings in 1983-84, all except two being conducted under the auspices of the Paris Club. 46/

The effect of rescheduling on debt service ratios is shown in Table I. Following some decline in the debt service ratios of market borrowers from 1982 to 1983, there was a slight increase in 1984, the effect of rescheduling being offset by the ending of grace periods. The further increase in 1985 was due to the weakness of export earnings.

In Sub-Saharan Africa the value of exports dropped from $24 billion in 1980 to $21 billion in 1981 and stagnated around the $20 billion level from 1982 to 1985, owing to the weakness of markets for primary commodities. On the other hand these countries were less affected by the curtailment of commercial bank lending, so that their indebtedness increased more rapidly after 1982 than that of the market borrowers. The result was a near-doubling of the debt service ratio of Sub-Saharan countries from 14.4% in 1980 to 28.2% in 1985, compared with a rise from 18.2% to 26.8% for market borrowers.

The cost of commercial bank rescheduling was extraordinarily high. The interest spreads charged on restructured loans ranged from 1 3/4 to 2 1/2 per cent over LIBOR in addition to which front-end negotiating fees of 1 per cent or more were levied. Moreover each rescheduling covered only amortization falling due over a 12 to 24 month period, and grace periods were limited to two or three years.

Mexico, Venezuela and a few other countries were able to negotiate better terms on reschedulings in 1984 covering amortization over much longer periods and involving lower spreads over LIBOR. Spreads were reduced to a range of seven-eighths to one and one quarter percentage points for these countries, and fees were reduced or eliminated. The Mexican agreement covered public sector maturities through 1990 and stretched payments out over fourteen years. Severe bunching of amortization is expected in 1987-90 and beyond, which may call for a stretching out of payments for periods as long as twenty years. Moreover the benefits of multi-year rescheduling need to be extended also to the smaller debtors, for whom the grace and repayment periods negotiated have been shorter and the interest spreads over LIBOR much larger.

Table I　Debt Position of Selected Groups of Countries, 1982-86[a]

(Billions of dollars; percentages)

	1982	1983	1984	1985	1986
External Debt, End of Year					
Capital-importing developing countries	749.1	796.9	829.5	865.1	895.7
Market borrowers	532.5	563.7	581.4	597.1	608.7
Small low-income countries	59.4	64.3	68.8	75.9	82.4
Sub-Saharan Africa[b]	51.1	53.7	57.1	62.1	66.5
Ratio of External Debt to Exports of Goods and Services					
Capital-importing developing countries	147.7	158.2	150.7	157.1	150.4
Market borrowers	147.0	156.4	146.9	150.5	141.8
Small low-income countries	317.0	335.9	345.2	388.5	387.8
Sub-Saharan Africa[b]	202.5	221.2	224.1	246.9	248.6
Ratio of Debt Service Payments to Exports of Goods and Services					
Capital-importing developing countries					
Debt service ratio	24.1	22.0	23.4	25.6	23.4
Interest payments ratio	13.9	13.3	13.6	13.8	12.2
Amortization ratio	10.2	8.8	9.8	11.7	11.2
Market borrowers					
Debt service ratio	26.7	23.7	24.9	26.8	24.0
Interest payments ratio	15.9	14.8	15.1	15.0	12.9
Amortization ratio	10.8	8.8	9.8	11.7	11.1

Table I (continued)

	1982	1983	1984	1985	1986
Small low-income countries					
Debt service ratio	19.2	20.7	23.8	28.7	28.8
Interest payments ratio	9.0	9.5	10.6	12.8	12.7
Amortization ratio	10.2	11.2	13.2	15.9	16.2
Sub-Saharan Africa					
Debt service ratio	19.4	21.6	23.3	28.2	28.4
Interest payments ratio	9.9	10.4	11.3	12.7	12.9
Amortization ratio	9.5	11.3	12.0	15.5	15.4

Source: IMF World Economic Outlook October 1985

Note: Capital-importing developing countries are defined by the IMF
as all developing countries except the eight Middle Eastern
oil exporters.
Market borrowers are defined as 34 countries that obtained at
least two-thirds of their external borrowings from 1978 to
1982 from commercial creditors.
Small low-income countries include 41 countries whose per
capita GDP did not exceed the equivalent of $410 in 1980, but
excluding China and India.
Sub-Saharan Africa comprises all African countries except
Egypt, Libyan Arab Jamahiriya, Algeria, Morocco, Nigeria,
South Africa and Tunisia.

a/   Data for 1985-86 are projections based on information
available on or before September 20, 1985.
b/   Excluding Nigeria and South Africa.

It has been stated that improved terms of rescheduling are a
reward for good performance - a somewhat paradoxical and self-defeating
policy since performance itself depends in part on the availability of
external resources and hence on advantageous terms of rescheduling.
The smaller countries can scarcely be blamed for believing that their
inability to secure better terms has more to do with the limited
leverage they have since in their cases much less is at stake for the
commercial banks because of their much smaller exposure to these
countries.

The External Environment for Adjustment

The undue emphasis of the short-term adjustment process on compression of imports by debtor countries was the result of two main factors - the inadequate recovery of real GNP and hence import demand in the European members of the OECD group, and the shortfall in net inflows of capital into the debtor countries. As shown in table II growth rates in the European countries have been below normal since 1980 and are expected to remain low through 1986. Growth rates in Canada, Japan and the United States surged temporarily in 1984 but are expected to decline in 1985-86.

Table II   Industrial Countries: changes in real GNP

(Percentage change from preceding year)

	1967-76	1980	1981	1982	1983	1984	1985	1986
Canada	4.8	1.1	3.3	-4.4	3.3	5.0	4.0	2.4
United States	2.8	-0.3	2.5	-2.1	3.7	6.8	2.6	3.3
Japan	7.4	4.8	4.0	3.3	3.4	5.8	4.4	4.0
European countries	3.8	1.5	-0.2	0.5	1.4	2.3	2.3	2.5
France[a]	4.7	1.1	0.4	1.8	0.7	1.3	1.0	1.7
Germany, Fed. Rep. of	3.5	1.9	-0.2	-1.0	1.3	2.6	2.1	3.1
Italy[a]	4.3	3.9	0.2	-0.5	-0.4	2.6	2.7	2.6
U.K.[b]	2.2	-2.5	-1.5	2.3	3.0	2.6	3.2	2.2
Total industrial countries	3.7	1.3	1.6	-0.2	2.6	4.9	2.8	3.1

Source: IMF, World Economic Outlook October 1985, table 2

a/   GDP at market prices.

b/   Average of expenditure income and output estimates of GDP at factor cost.

The weakness of the recovery in industrial countries, taken as a whole, was reflected in a marked difference between the recent behavior of commodity markets and the behavior characteristic of previous business upturns. UNCTAD has pointed out that although the volume of primary commodities exported by developing countries increased with the recovery in the industrial countries the gain in prices was weak and was limited to the early part of the upswing. The recovery in prices started towards the end of 1982 and reached a peak in the first quarter of 1984. The subsequent decline, which continued into 1985, took place despite rising business activity in industrial countries, and notwithstanding the fact that even the earlier gain in prices had failed to restore them to their previous peak - that of 1980. These price developments limited the export gains of countries dependent mainly on exports of primary commodities.47/

In addition to the incomplete recovery of the industrial countries, other factors tending to depress commodity prices in the face of inelastic demand were the pressures on commodity producers having external deficits to expand their production of primary commodities and to devalue their currencies or otherwise attempt to undercut the prices of their competitors. While measures of this kind would not necessarily have achieved the hoped-for objectives even if adopted by a relatively few countries, they were bound to be self-defeating in a situation in which a large majority of commodity-exporting countries were in balance of payments difficulties.

So far as the inflow of capital is concerned, Fund data show that most official borrowers - those countries that had derived two-thirds or more of their external capital in 1978-82 from official sources - experienced a decline in transfers and loans from these sources from 1981 to 1984; and that market borrowers - countries that had obtained at least two-thirds of their external borrowing from 1978 to 1982 from commercial creditors - had experienced a decline in such borrowing from $79.2 billion in 1981 to $9.0 billion in 1984. 48/

Increasing numbers of developing countries have been faced, for the first time since World War II, with a situation of negative net transfers - in which debt service payments exceed new external borrowing. For developing countries as a whole the negative net transfer has been estimated at $7 billion in 1984, but for Latin America alone such transfers amounted to $30 billion in 1983 and $27 billion in 1984. This made it necessary for the countries concerned to run trade surpluses if they were to avoid defaulting on their debt service obligations. The chairman of the US Federal Reserve Board, Mr. Paul Volcker, has noted that the exposure of US banks to developing countries has fallen by 25 per cent in relation to capital over the last three years and that "net new bank lending appears to have practically stopped this year (1985), adding to a sense of political and financial uncertainty and frustration among borrowers as they face the need to achieve sustained growth".49/

It should also be noted that commercial bank lending has been markedly pro-cyclical: the banks lend most readily when business is good. On the other hand, the availability of bank finance tends to contract with the onset of recession and in the event of deterioration of the cash flow of borrowers due to this or other influences. Thus the banks have themselves added to the liquidity squeeze and have tended to undermine the creditworthiness of their own clients.

The consequences of such a lending pattern, which are relevant for developed as well as for developing country borrowers, have been described by the Bank for International Settlements as follows:

> To put this view into perspective, it may be useful to imagine what would happen in a national context if during a recession banks were suddenly to cut off the flow of net credits to the corporate sector and to begin closing off existing short-term credit lines. The inevitable result would be a financial collapse which would threaten to engulf even soundly managed firms, including banks... Such a financial collapse ... would not permit any easy inference with respect to the quality of the pattern of bank lending and of corporate investment before the outbreak of the crisis, whereas the conclusion could safely be drawn that something had gone seriously wrong with the macro-economic management of the economy. 50/

Lending by multilateral financial institutions has been slowing down despite the severe foreign exchange constraints facing the debtor countries. IMF credit to capital-importing developing countries increased from $6.8 billion in 1982 to $10.6 billion in 1983, but it then dropped to $4.6 billion in 1984 and is expected by the Fund to decline further to $1.0 billion in 1985, following which net repayments to the Fund totalling $3.7 billion are expected in 1986. Similarly, at commitment levels projected prior to the Baker initiative net disbursements and net transfers by the World Bank showed a significant decline even in nominal terms. It was estimated that World Bank commitment levels would have to increase at an annual rate of at least 6.2 per cent in real terms over the levels reached in FY 1983 if net disbursements and net transfers were to remain relatively steady.

The adverse international environment manifested in weak commodity markets and the unaccustomed net transfer of resources by developing to industrial countries seriously aggravated the burdens borne by the debtor countries. They were forced into a degree of austerity that would not have been necessary if the international business climate had been more buoyant and if steps had been taken to maintain the flow of capital. The number of countries experiencing stagnation or declines in production increased steadily as the crisis deepened. The IMF Managing Director has stated that 58 countries that encountered major debt-servicing difficulties from 1981 to mid-1984 had to cut their imports by no less than 32 per cent from 1981 to 1983, while output actually fell over the same period. 51/

In some cases countries reduced their borrowing voluntarily, despite the adverse effects of the consequential curtailment of imports, because their own analyses of payments prospects led them to conclude that they could not afford additional debt, given prospective interest rates and export earnings.

Particularly ominous were the cutbacks in capital goods' imports by developing countries in 1982-84, reflecting the drop in domestic investment. However necessary the import decline may have been in correcting current account deficits the drop in capital goods' imports and investment was damaging from the standpoint of long-term adjustment. The crisis managers thereby took insufficient account of the fact that the measures introduced with strictly short-term goals in view were disrupting the prospects for more basic types of adjustment in the longer term.

As Professor Wallich, member of the Board of Governors of the U.S. Federal Reserve System, has pointed out:

> For many countries, bringing down debt/GDP and similar ratios and returning to voluntary financing implies changes more basic than the short term balance-of-payments adjustment sought by many of the Fund's arrangements with formal duration of one year or a little beyond... Structural changes may be needed enhancing the export base and substituting domestic production for imports.

Medium term adjustment designed to bring about such structural changes implies, as Professor Wallich indicates, greater resort to the Fund's extended facility programs and the World Bank's structural adjustment loans. 52/ Moreover the considerations referred to by Professor Wallich raise important questions as to the nature of the adjustment process.

The Nature of the Adjustment Process

In its World Economic Outlook April 1985 the IMF staff pointed to "the sheer magnitude of the adjustment that has occurred". 53/ On the other hand the 1985 report on Economic and Social Progress in Latin America published by the Inter-American Development Bank (IDB) reached the "fundamental conclusion" that "the adjustment process - in the sense of positive structural adaptation to a changed external situation - is barely beginning in most of the countries"54/, and the same statement is equally true of debtor countries outside Latin America.

A careful reading of the two statements indicates that there is no literal inconsistency between them. Both institutions would presumably agree that

(a) the rate of reduction of current account imbalances has been remarkable, but that

(b)   this does not imply that there has been
      much progress towards improved structural
      adaptation of the debtor countries to the
      external environment.

Nevertheless the use of the term "adjustment" to denote simply an
improvement in current account imbalance is confusing and is frequently
responsible for misleading the reader as to the nature and extent of
what has been accomplished.

If a country has an insufficient inflow of capital to allow it to
finance a current account deficit at existing levels, and if it cannot
draw upon reserves, it has no choice but to reduce its deficit by
whatever means may be available to it. The fact that a reduction in its
current account deficit is forced upon it by shortage of finance in no
way implies that its overall economic situation has improved in any
fundamental or significant sense. It may simply have reduced its level
of economic activity and import demand, and run down its inventories of
imported goods. Such enforced measures will not necessarily have
increased, even slightly, its capacity to maintain a normal level and
rate of growth of economic activity combined with external balance. As
pointed out by Professor Wallich in the statement cited earlier,
adjustment in this more fundamental sense is rarely attainable, at
least by developing countries, within the time horizon of one-year
stabilization programs.

What the IDB calls "positive structural adaptation" implies the
promotion of new or additional exports as well as substitution for
imports. Neither of these can be brought about quickly enough to affect
performance under a one-year program. Even where the problem is simply
one of shifting resources and incentives from non-traded to traded
goods, an exchange rate change will normally take much more than a year
to yield its results. More commonly, however, new investment will be
needed and the effects of such investment may lie even farther in the
future.

In view of this, most developing countries faced with stringent
short-term stabilization targets have found themselves compelled to
rely mainly on deflationary measures. And these deflationary measures
may well be an obstacle to the more fundamental structural changes
required for adjustment in the longer run. The obstacle may, indeed, be
double-edged - from both the supply and demand sides. Monetary and
fiscal contraction inevitably reduces the supply of savings whether
from private business profits or from personal incomes or, indeed, from
the public sector. At the same time the inducement to entrepreneurs to
invest may well be weakened since the prospects of additional markets
from import substitution or new external demand may be subject to all
kinds of uncertainties while the impact of reduced domestic demand is
immediate and unmistakable.

Thus the requirements of short-term stabilization programs may be completely at odds with longer-run structural change. To this extent attempts to "adjust" in too short a time-frame may seriously prejudice the more fundamental type of "adjustment" without which the underlying balance of payments problem cannot be said to have been solved at all .

It is true that Brazil, the Republic of Korea and some other countries demonstrated a remarkable resilience in taking advantage of the export opportunities offered by the United States market in 1984. These were, of course, countries that had developed a substantial capacity for the export of manufactures in preceding years so that the rise in United States import demand could be met by fuller utilization of the existing capacity to export in these countries. Even these countries will need, in the longer run, to undertake structural adaptation in the sense of enlarging, diversifying and, where necessary, modernizing their productive capacities. In the meantime the inducement to such structural adaptation has been weakened by the slowing down of economic growth in the industrial countries and by the growing uncertainties as to how far exporters can rely on being allowed even to maintain - let alone to extend - their existing footholds in industrial country markets.

Where the capacity to export manufactures is less well developed, or not developed at all, the responsiveness of the economy, whether to such short-term measures as devaluation or to longer-run efforts for structural change, is correspondingly weaker. That means that the achievement of short-term stabilization targets may have to depend even more on the cutting back of production and growth, so that the conflict between adjustment in the short-term and long-term senses is likely to be even more acute than in the countries with more developed industrial capabilities.

But austerity programs are not the only cause of reductions in investment in the debtor countries. An additional factor of great importance in many cases is the diversion of domestic savings to the payment of debt service. Up till the 1980s developing countries were in a position to make use of the net inflow of capital from abroad to add to the volume of domestic investment. That situation has been reversed, with the effects shown in Table III. As will be seen, in 1984 the proportion of domestic savings absorbed by net factor payments was extraordinarily high in a number of countries in all regions, the extreme case being Chile, where little more than a quarter of domestic savings was available for financing domestic investment, after taking account of net factor payments. Among other countries listed in the table the share of domestic savings allocated to net factor payments ranged from 12% in Colombia to 53% in Zambia.

The combined effect on investment of domestic recession and net factor payments abroad is shown in Table IV, which records marked declines from 1981 to 1984 in the proportion of domestic expenditure devoted to capital formation in various groups of developing countries. The experience of market borrowers and official borrowers

Table III   Selected Countries: Domestic Savings, Net Factor
Payments and National Savings, 1984

	Domestic Savings	Net Factor Payments	National Savings
Argentina	21.6	-8.8	12.8
Brazil	23.2	-5.4	17.8
Cameroon[a]	25.1	-5.3	19.7
Chile	14.2	-10.5	3.7
Colombia	18.5	-2.2	16.3
Ecuador	25.2	-8.0	17.1
Kenya	20.2	-2.7	17.5
Korea, Republic of	30.3	-3.5	26.8
Malaysia	33.8	-6.8	26.9
Mexico	30.9	-6.4	24.5
Peru	21.9	-6.9	15.0
Philippines	20.7	-3.7	17.1
Venezuela	30.9	-6.0	24.9
Zambia[a]	13.5	-7.2	6.2

Source: UN Department of International Economic and Social Affairs.

a/   Data are for 1983.

was similar in this respect. The proportional decline among market
borrowers was somewhat greater, but the level of investment ratios
among official borrowers was lower in 1984, as it had been in 1981.

The IDB study mentioned earlier found that in the case of the
Latin American countries the largest reductions in capital outlays had
taken place in industries producing for the domestic market, as
expected. But even in industries producing exportable goods favored by
strong real devaluation, investment in new productive capacity was,
according to the IDB study, "not significant," so that structural
adjustment was minimal. 55/ The same is likely to have been true of
most if not all of the African and some of the Asian countries.

Table IV Developing Countries: Gross Capital Formation,
1981 and 1984
(Percentages of GDP)

	1981	1984
Capital importing developing countries	26.5	22.0
Market borrowers[a]	26.8	20.7
Official borrowers[b]	20.5	17.4
Sub-Saharan Africa[c]	23.9	19.7

Source: IMF, World Economic Outlook October 1985, table 6.

a/ Countries that obtained at least two-thirds of their external borrowings from 1978 to 1982 from commercial creditors.
b/ Countries, except China and India, that obtained two-thirds or more of their external borrowings from 1978 to 1982 from official creditors.
c/ Excluding Nigeria and South Africa.

In Sub-Saharan Africa a particularly unfortunate combination of circumstances - partly, as the IMF points out, reflecting factors beyond the control of the countries concerned 56/ - added to the above-mentioned obstacles to the long-run adjustment process. The prolonged drought of recent years as well as military conflict in some areas have been an acute drain on limited foreign exchange and other resources as well as on the health and vitality of the working population. At the same time the weakness of industrial country demand for primary commodities had a depressing effect on exports from the region: as noted earlier, the value of exports from Sub-Saharan Africa dropped from $24 billion in 1980 to $21 billion in 1981 and stagnated around the $20 billion level from 1982 to 1985. Major exporters of manufactures, on the other hand, were able to increase the total value of their exports of all kinds by about one third from 1980 to 1985.57/ The pre-empting of foreign exchange resources by debt service as well as by imports of food in the African countries had a devastating effect on imports of investment goods and hence upon the investment required for strengthening the export and import substitution sectors, which in the case of Africa include the replacement of imported food supplies by domestic output.

Problems of the Official Borrowers 58/

Countries outside the group that borrowed heavily in private capital markets fall into two categories - those dependent mainly on official development assistance (ODA) and those relying to a major extent on official or officially-guaranteed export credits. Within the first of these categories, in only very few cases has there been any explicit recognition of the importance of increasing the debtor country's productive capacity through expanded investment. However, the fact that in a few cases an aid consortium or a consultative group did offer the financial support needed to enable the debtor countries concerned to undertake essential investment in addition to meeting debt service obligations indicates the lines along which better programs could be established for a much larger number of countries - including countries outside the ODA-dependent group. 59/

Countries belonging to the second group are among those whose debt problems have been considered in the Paris Club. Countries depending on export credits for a major part of their inflow of external resources have faced considerable difficulties resulting from restrictive policies applied by export credit agencies (ECAs) affecting the availability of insurance as well as its terms. Moreover the ECAs have often suspended insurance cover when negotiations on the rescheduling of a borrower's debts have opened, though short-term cover was frequently still available if short-term debt service obligations were met. Many ECAs found themselves in a situation where claims were running ahead of premiums and recoveries, and were thus compelled to impose the above-mentioned restrictions in order to comply with the requirement that they be self-supporting in the medium term. Cover has normally been restored on the completion of rescheduling, but in some cases suspension of cover has been known to last more than two years, and there have even been instances when cover has not been promptly restored even after bilateral agreements under Paris Club accords have been signed. 60/

The approach of the Paris Club to countries applying for the rescheduling of official debt has generally been to treat debt problems as if they were essentially balance of payments problems resulting from excess aggregate demand, with the solution therefore lying in demand restraint. As in most cases of commercial debt rescheduling, debtor countries have been required to reach a satisfactory agreement with the IMF. The rescheduling of debt, when granted, has been limited to consolidating periods of approximately the same length as a country's stand-by program with the Fund - often only one year. The concept of the debt problem as having a certain inherent dynamic over the long run, and of debt management as a problem of relating the evolution of debt and debt service obligations to the growth of productive capacity in the borrowing country has had little influence on the Paris Club proceedings, any more than on commercial bank rescheduling. In a few cases donor group meetings have been held in reasonably close proximity to debt rescheduling exercises, but debt was not a prominent item on the agenda, and the relationship between the approaches taken in the meetings was not always clear. 61/

This dichotomy between meetings on development aid and meetings on adjustment of the terms of public debt is a great weakness of present procedures. As a former chairman of the Paris Club has pointed out:

> The members (of the Paris Club) represent their governments as creditors, not as donors and governors of the IMF or the World Bank. Their responsibility is limited to adjusting the terms of the public debt...Governments grant concessionary assistance within the framework of other procedures. 62/

Failure to deal with the debt problem in the context of long-run development is not, of course, the result of faulty procedures alone, but such procedures certainly aggravate the problem.

Another serious shortcoming of Paris Club arrangements is the excessive time taken in carrying out the agreements reached. UNCTAD reports that the entire debt rescheduling process, from the moment the intent to reschedule is made known to the signing of the last bilateral agreement "may easily take from 12 to 18 months". In the case of successive debt reschedulings, the process may, in fact, be an uninterrupted one" - with the last stage of one rescheduling lasting until just before the Paris Club meeting convened to consider the next one". 63/

This brings us to a third set of difficulties associated with the Paris Club namely the recourse to repeated rescheduling that results inevitably from the shortness of the consolidation periods adopted. This imposes high costs on the debtor countries not only in terms of the expenditure of time by the senior officials involved, but also in terms of the repeated and cumulative damage to the creditworthiness of the countries concerned, and the complete disruption of any possibility of planning the course of the economy, including debt management, over a period of reasonable length ahead.

The World Bank reported in September 1984 that in the case of the Sudan, even if arrears then outstanding were consolidated and rescheduled on 1983 Paris Club terms with a 10 per cent interest rate, the Sudan would face debt service ratios averaging 80 to 90 per cent for the rest of the 1980s. 64/ Countries such as the Central African Republic, Madagascar, Somalia, and Zaire were facing similar difficulties. These impossible situations have arisen, according to the World Bank, because reschedulings in the last few years, mostly on conventional terms, gave short-term relief, but at the expense of increasing the debt service burden from 1984 onwards. The World Bank concluded that "unless corrective measures are taken, the external resource position of Sub-Saharan Africa is likely to become disastrous in the next few years." 65/ In other words, in the case of Sub-Saharan Africa, there is no sign that debt problems are in the process of being overcome.

Efforts to deal with debt difficulties in the low-income countries go back to the 1970s. In 1978 the UNCTAD Trade and Development Board adopted by consensus resolution 165(S-IX) providing for the retroactive easing of terms on official debt, including, in the case of the least developed countries, conversion of outstanding loans into grants. Thus far 17 creditor countries have reported measures favoring 58 individual developing countries and entities in amounts totalling $6.2 billion, of which $3.5 billion represents debt cancellation. Despite these steps, conditions have generally deteriorated in these countries. The international community has yet to take the measure of the African crisis. Thus far both official transfers and net long-term borrowing from official creditors other than the IMF show a downward trend. Repurchases and charges on loans from the IMF to Sub-Saharan countries will total $3.5 billion during 1985-7 and new aid from bilateral donors is already being used, at least in part, to repay the IMF. And prospects for commodity markets remain highly uncertain.

Prospects for the Debt Problem

There is, perhaps, no area of national or international economic policy-making in which scenario-building has been as influential as it has been in relation to the debt problem. The record, quite generally, of efforts to throw light on future economic trends even for such aggregates as gross domestic product and even for the major developed countries with massive statistical capabilities has been a dismal one, particularly in recent years of increased volatility and instability in the world economy. The very fact, noted earlier, that the major international institutions were unable to foresee the world debt crisis of the early 1980s in time to take action to prevent it should no doubt prompt a certain caution in appraising current views of prospects for the coming years.

From a very early stage of the crisis, the view prevailed that the situation was "manageable", that there were no generalized problems but only particular problems of individual countries, and that these problems would respond readily to treatment case by case through programs of adjustment under IMF supervision, supported by quite small amounts of new lending. No major efforts by creditor countries were envisaged, other than in the matter of bridging finance, and no new mechanism either within or outside existing institutions was considered necessary. Whether the scenarios that were developed by economists at the time provided any real basis for these views, or whether, on the contrary, these views themselves constituted the *a priori* assumptions on which the scenarios were based is debatable.

The idea that the present and prospective situation is manageable was based on a number of assumptions that included the following:

(a) that the OECD rate of growth will generally be
     maintained at 3 per cent and will in any case
     not fall very far below it; and that income

elasticities of demand for imports from developing countries will revert to the relatively favorable levels of the 1960s and 1970s instead of continuing the less favorable trends of the 1980s.

(b) that the slump in commodity markets will be reversed.

(c) that commercial bank exposure will rise by 6-7 per cent a year.

(d) that interest rates will fall somewhat further in both nominal and real terms.

(e) that the access of exports of debtor countries to the markets of creditor countries will be maintained.

(f) that debtor countries will continue to accept strong compression of consumption, investment and imports as well as the postponement of any significant recovery of living standards to the 1990s or even (in the case of African countries) beyond.

The weakest link in the chain is, of course, the last. It is impossible to foresee how long countries will be prepared to forego improvement in living standards.

But the other assumptions are also vulnerable, and it does not take much to cause serious difficulties for a significant group of countries, notably if the terms of trade continue to deteriorate for commodity producers or if interest rates tend to rise once more, or if a strong wave of protection sweeps over the industrial countries. As far as commercial bank lending is concerned, it is already clear that annual increases in exposure are much smaller than those previously stated to be the bare minimum, i.e. an average of 6-7 per cent a year.

One of the most influential private assessments of prospects was that of William R. Cline who has summarized his views as follows:

> Under central expectations for international economic variables (and politically acceptable growth rates in debtor countries), the projections showed that most major countries would show substantial improvement in balance of payments and relative debt burden, and that by the late 1980s, debt-export ratios would be back to levels previously associated with creditworthiness. A return to higher OECD growth would increase export volume and prices, an eventual easing of interest rates would moderate

interest payments, and a decline in the dollar
from its seriously overvalued level would raise
the dollar value of the export base. However,
the analysis also indicated that a critical
threshold of 2 1/2 to 3 per cent was required
for OECD growth to avoid stagnation or severe
deterioration   in   external   deficits   and
debt-export ratios for debtor countries.66/

     A series of scenarios prepared by the staff of the IMF and
World Bank from 1983 to 1985 were broadly supportive of the same point
of view, though with some differences on secondary aspects.   Two
particularly crucial assumptions were that the rate of increase of the
volume of exports of the debtor countries would be higher than real
interest rates on foreign debt and that total external private credit
to these countries would increase by more than 4 per cent a year.
There is no sign at all of the realization of the latter assumption,
and while export growth was substantial in 1984, it seems possible that
1984 was an exceptional year in that respect.

     It is implicit in the reasoning of the IMF and World Bank, as it
is explicit in that of William Cline, that the curtailment of growth
and living standards in debtor countries necessitated by their having
to bear virtually the entire burden of adjustment is "politically
acceptable". From the vantage point of 1985, it is possible to point to
the fact that the severe reductions in real incomes of many African and
Latin American countries in the immediately preceding years did not
lead to political upheaval, despite earlier fears in many quarters that
this would be the case.

     But the fact that the peoples of debtor countries have so far
tacitly accepted high unemployment and drastic losses of income does
not mean that they can be counted on to do so indefinitely. Still less
likely is it that they will tolerate indefinitely the deprivation and
undernourishment of children and other vulnerable groups entailed by
adjustment without growth, which has been documented by UNICEF. 67/.
The experiment of enforced and prolonged economic depression in the
Third World is a dangerous one that it would be imprudent to dismiss
with the facile characterization that it is "politically acceptable".
The fact that Brazil and Mexico, which had won universal acclaim for
their adjustment efforts in 1983-84, are now resisting the further
sacrifices that seem to be expected of them reflects the judgment of
their respective governments that indefinitely continued austerity is
not "politically acceptable" to their peoples. As Dr. Fritz Leutwiler,
former President of the Swiss National Bank and of the Bank for
International Settlements, put it:

          But quite a different bomb might explode,
     namely a political or social one. This will explode
     when these debtor developing countries have to
     conduct a policy of austerity over too long a
     period simply in order to service their debt. That
     is a bomb with a built-in time fuse.68/

The "Program for Sustained Growth" of the debtor countries put forward by US Treasury Secretary Baker at Seoul in October 1985 shows a clear recognition of the importance of making it possible for these countries to grow at rates that will be found "politically acceptable" by public opinion.

One of the key features of the scenarios is their high degree of sensitivity to relatively small changes in the assumptions made about certain basic economic parameters as well as about the macro-economic policies of both creditor and debtor countries. In setting out its own debt scenarios for 1985 to 1995 UNCTAD drew attention to "the rather substantial negative, collective impact of a set of slightly more pessimistic assumptions for a number of the key variables". 69/

In table V the IMF base line scenario set out in its World Economic Outlook October 1985 is compared with that given in the above-mentioned UNCTAD study. It will be seen that UNCTAD posits an OECD growth rate for 1985-90 that is only one-third of a percentage point less than that envisaged by the IMF. This, combined with a significantly lower estimate of the income elasticity of demand of OECD countries for imports from developing countries (1.5 as against the IMF's 1.9) and a higher nominal interest rate (11.0 as against the IMF's 8.7) is sufficient to cause a substantial reduction in the estimated growth rate of import volume of deficit developing countries and hence a one-third drop (from 4.8 per cent to 3.2 per cent) in the growth rate of real GDP in these countries.

There is a case, if only on precautionary grounds, for erring on the side of the less optimistic forecasts for the purposes of national and international policy-making. Such an approach seems particularly necessary in view of certain methodological limitations in the available scenarios.

Prospects for the debt problem are customarily analysed by relating the exports of debtor countries to the real exchange rates of these countries and the expected growth rates of the OECD countries. The proceeds of such exports together with any net inflow of capital will, after allowance for interest payments on foreign debt, determine the volume of imports and hence the rate of GDP growth that can be sustained by debtor countries.

This basic framework no doubt suffices for short-term analysis, but it leaves out of account the investment in new capacity that is needed for expanding and diversifying exports. As far as is known, there has been little or no research into the data that would be required for this purpose. 70/

What is clear, however, is that as the earlier citation from work by the IDB makes clear, in many debtor countries investment has fallen to the point at which the expansion and diversification of productive

Table V   Capital-Importing Developing Countries: a/
Base-line Scenarios of IMF and UNCTAD, 1985-90

	IMF	UNCTAD
Industrial Countries		
Growth rate of real GNP	3.1	2.8
Real LIBOR b/	8.7	11.0
U.S. GNP deflator	4.3	4.8
World Economy		
Change in world prices of manufactures in US dollars c/	6.8	7.4
Terms of trade between non-oil primary commodities and manufactures	0.2 d/	...
Capital-importing developing countries		
Growth rate of real GDP	4.8	3.4
Growth rate of total external private credit	4.7	6.0
Growth rate of import volume	6.7	5.2
Growth rate of export volume	5.8	4.3
OECD country income elasticity of demand for imports from deficit developing countries	1.9	1.5

Sources: IMF, World Economic Outlook April 1985, table III-1, World
Economic Outlook October 1985, table 50; UNCTAD, Trade and
Development Report 1985, pp. 137-140.

a/ There are substantial differences between the country coverage of
the two institutions. The main difference is that UNCTAD excludes
Southern Europe. For details see sources cited.

b/ London interbank offered rate on US dollar deposits. IMF:
three-month LIBOR; UNCTAD: one-year LIBOR.

c/ IMF assumes a 0.7 per cent fall in the real effective exchange
rate of the dollar in 1986 and a 4.1 per cent average annual
decline from 1987 to 1990. UNCTAD assumes a 3 per cent average
annual rate of decline of the dollar in terms of the SDR from 1985
to 1988, and no further change thereafter.

d/ Terms of trade projected as stable from 1986 to 1990.

capacity is minimal. In many of the low-income countries it is likely that the capital stock is being run down for lack of adequate maintenance and replacement.

Table VI sets out two scenarios for absorption, (i.e. domestic consumption and investment, public and private) in 1990, together with an estimate of actual absorption in 1985. Total and per capita figures are shown. The assumptions underlying each scenario are given in the "Memo items".

It emerges that in 1985 per capita absorption was 5 per cent lower than in 1980: since consumption fell less than investment, the average reduction in per capita investment must have been significantly greater than 5 per cent.

Even by 1990 per capita absorption would, on the optimistic assumptions of Scenario II , be no higher than in 1980 in the major developing country Eurocurrency borrowers, and would be slightly below the 1980 level in the least developed countries. In other deficit developing countries the situation would be appreciably better. On less optimistic assumptions per capita absorption levels in 1990, both in the Eurocurrency borrowers and in the least developed countries, would be 7 per cent below those of 1980.

In other words, during the years between 1985 and 1990 investment levels in many of the developing countries may well be insufficient to generate the export growth that is envisaged in all the various available scenarios - including those shown in table V. And this insufficiency is likely to continue into the 1990s unless OECD growth rates, interest rates and new capital flows to developing countries become more favourable. It should be noted that even the less optimistic assumptions in this context are not as unfavourable as the worst experience of the recent past.

Both the IMF and UNCTAD scenarios imply an unbroken period of economic expansion in industrial countries from 1983 to 1990 and beyond. The past record does not suggest that such a sustained expansion is at all likely. The profound implications of even a temporary slowdown in economic activity in the industrial countries have been clearly set out by the IMF staff. The staff acknowledges that a number of developments in 1985 had "served to underline the uncertainties in the staff's projections". 71/ For illustrative purposes the staff examined the consequences of a slowdown in the growth of industrial countries to 1 1/2 per cent in 1987 and 1988 followed by a weak recovery to 3 per cent growth in 1989-90, thereby reducing the average rate of growth expected for the period as a whole. This would have the effect of halving the projected growth of exports and hence of imports of developing countries, leading to a reduction in the annual rate of GDP growth from 4 3/4 per cent to a little over 3 1/2 per cent for 1987-88. Average per capita incomes would stagnate in such areas as the African and Latin American regions, and would be no

Table VI   Alternative Scenarios for Absorption
in Deficit Developing Countries

(Index numbers 1980=100)

	Absorption		
	1985	1990	
		Scenario I	Scenario II
Major developing country Eurocurrency borrowers	101	117	127
Least developed countries	109	124	130
Other deficit developing countries	120	138	143
Total	107	124	132
	Per capita Absorption		
Major developing country Eurocurrency borrowers	89	93	100
Least developed countries	95	93	99
Other deficit developing countries	107	111	115
Total	95	98	105
Memo items			
OECD growth rate, 1985–90		2.7	3.3
LIBOR, 1985–90 average		11.0	8.2
Manufactures price index 1985–90		7.4	9.6
Private debt: rate of increase 1986–90		5.0	6.0
$/SDR index (1980=100)	77	84	92

Source: UNCTAD.

higher in 1988 than a decade earlier. According to the Fund staff "Such a trend would severely strain the social consensus needed to maintain adjustment efforts in heavily indebted countries". 72/

It should be noted that, as the Fund staff points out, this illustrative exercise does not allow for any possible effects of a slowdown in industrial country growth in intensifying protectionist pressures and in reducing concessional and non-concessional capital flows. In other words, it is quite likely that the impact on developing countries of such a slowdown in industrial countries is understated. The understatement would be even greater, of course, if the slowdown were of more than two years' duration.

Prudence requires that contingency plans be made for such an eventuality. The knife-edge character and precariousness of the outlook for the debt problem raise the gravest doubts about the validity of the idea that the debt problem is "manageable". They also pose questions about any strategy for dealing with the debt problem that implies that present methods of improvisation on a case by case basis will prove to be adequate to cope with all and any difficulties, and ups and downs, that may arise. The ad hoc methods for crisis management characteristic of 1982-83 have not been tested under conditions in which a number of the biggest debtors get into difficulties simultaneously - this could well be a characteristic of the next major crisis.

The Common Interest in Co-operative Solutions

The main criticism that has to be made of the international response to the debt crisis is not that that response was initially designed with only the short run in view: given the pressures of the moment, short-term rescue operations were inevitable. The real problem is that once the immediate threat to international stability had been contained, nothing was done to plan ahead for the longer run, taking advantage of the fact that the debtors and creditors have fundamental interests in common.73/ Indeed the latter concept of convergence of interests never emerged clearly as a basis for a long-run international debt strategy.

The creditor countries have nothing to gain from prostration of the debtors. On the contrary, the greater the disruption of debtor country economies brought about by programs of austerity, and the more acute the inner tensions resulting from efforts of various social groups in debtor countries to escape the effects of the austerity programs, the less likely is it that debt service obligations will be fulfilled on a steady, reliable and continuing basis, and the more probable is it that political instability or upheaval followed by repudiation will be the ultimate outcome.

But the creditor countries have an even more direct and immediate interest in the economic recovery of the debtors. The pre-empting of an

unusually large proportion of the export earnings of developing
countries by debt service requirements has reacted sharply upon
production and employment in the manufacturing sectors of the
industrial countries. UNCTAD has shown that in the third quarter of
1984 total OECD exports to developing countries were running at an
annual rate some $46 billion lower than the 1980-81 average,
three-quarters of the reduction occurring in OECD Europe. Making use of
trade-employment coefficients published by the ILO, UNCTAD estimates
that the above contraction of exports corresponds to a cumulative loss
of close to 7 million man-years of employment in Europe and close to
one million man-years in the United States and Canada over the
three-year period 1982 through 1984. These totals understate the
overall impact on employment levels to the extent that the trade
balance adjustment has taken the form of export expansion to developed
countries not matched by an expansion of imports from them.74/ On the
other hand it may to some extent overstate the impact by not allowing
for the employment effects of interest receipts by industrial countries
from developing countries. Even so, employment considerations underline
the common interest of creditor and debtor countries in easing the
impact of debt service obligations on the import capacity of debtor
countries.

We shall return to the question of articulating the common
interest of creditors and debtors in the concluding section of this
paper.

Conditions for Solving the Debt Problem

Proposals for debt reform are the subject of a separate report to
the Group of Twenty-four by Professor Paul Krugman (UNCTAD/MFD/TA/34).
Conclusions may, however, be drawn from the analysis contained in the
present paper regarding the conditions that would have to be satisfied
if there is to be reasonable assurance of solving the debt problems in
a manner satisfactory to all concerned.

Those conditions relate to the international environment within
which debtor and creditor countries must reach a mutual accommodation.
Such accommodation would be greatly facilitated if it took place in a
context of worldwide economic expansion. There is no escaping the need
for adjustment by both debtors and creditors, but such adjustment can
be made most readily, and with the least danger of social tension or
conflict, if the general trend of all economies is upward, and if
domestic consumption and investment are meeting at least the minimum
social and economic needs of all countries.

As shown above, there are substantial differences of opinion among
those who have analyzed the outlook for the debt problem, which are
reflected in divergent policy conclusions. But there are several
fundamental points on which they are all agreed and which constitute
certain of the major assumptions on which their projections depend, as

set out at the beginning of the section on Prospects for the Debt Problem. These points may be restated as follows:

(a)   The OECD countries must achieve and maintain an adequate rate of growth of their economies;

(b)   interest rates must be significantly reduced;

(c)   there must be a sustained recovery in the volume and prices of primary commodity exports;

(d)   the access of debtor countries to the markets of creditor countries must be maintained or improved;

(e)   new lending by official institutions and commercial banks should be sufficient to sustain a net transfer of resources to the debtor countries, particularly the low-income countries.

The above points have been set out in qualitative terms and it would be much more difficult to get agreement on quantifying them. In particular, as noted above, some analysts continue to believe that severe compression of demand in the debtor countries is a viable policy for these countries for several years to come, and this colors their evaluation of the minimum conditions for success under points (a) to (e) above. Obviously the need for higher rates of OECD growth, or declines in interest rates, or recovery in commodity markets, or improved market access, or increased borrowing is pro tanto less, the greater is the willingness of debtor countries to absorb the consequences in the form of lower living standards.

But the tradeoff between creditor and debtor country obligations is, as we have seen, not as straightforward as implied above. This is because of the fact that persistent economic depression in the debtor countries would prevent them from investing in the structural changes needed to enable them to grow out of the debt problem. It is therefore the contention of the present paper that current international policies do not constitute a viable option for solution of the debt problem even if the debtor countries were prepared to continue their austerity programmes for an indefinite period ahead.

The need for adjustment to take place in a context of growth has already gained a large measure of international acceptance, as evidenced in the Baker initiative. 75/ What is not yet fully agreed is the full measure of change in international policies that adoption of the principle of adjustment with growth implies. So far the shift is seen merely in terms of modest increases in resource flows into the debtor countries together with greater involvement of the World Bank so as to introduce a longer term development dimension into the adjustment process.

These changes fall far short of what would be required to solve the debt problem. In the first place, OECD growth rates of the magnitude currently projected are unlikely to provide the necessary impetus to the exports of the debtor countries because they will not suffice to restore the strength of the markets for primary commodities. The lesson of 1985 is that an average OECD growth rate of 2.8 per cent was not sufficient to prevent the prices of primary commodities from declining by over 10 per cent. No solution to the debt problem is possible unless commodity prices recover on a sustained basis.

The concern about inflation that inspired macroeconomic policy in the 1970s and the first half of the 1980s cannot be set aside completely, but for the time being at least its weight in policy-making could be considerably reduced without significant risk. Under present conditions, OECD growth rates could and probably should be stepped up towards the limits dictated by the available supplies of primary commodities - namely foodstuffs and raw materials.

Some increase in the prices of final goods is likely if primary commodity markets recover. But this does not mean that a cumulative process of inflation is inevitable. Macroeconomic policy should henceforth be directed towards obtaining the social consensus on income distribution that is required to permit a recovery in commodity markets without thereby inducing a resumption of wage-price spirals. This is admittedly an ambitious goal, but by no means an unattainable one.

Interest rates are still much too high, especially in real terms. They are too high not only in relation to the debt problem but also from the standpoint of raising the level of investment and growth in the industrial countries themselves. So long as the authorities in the latter countries take the steps needed for achieving higher domestic employment while holding aggregate expenditure to levels consistent with available labor and capacity, there is no reason why monetary policy should not be relaxed to the extent required to return interest rates to their historical real levels. Next to worldwide economic expansion, a major reduction in nominal and real interest rates is the most important contribution that could be made to the solution of the debt problem.

There is no need to dwell on the need for resisting and rolling back protectionism in the industrial countries. Apart from the strong case that can be made in this regard in terms of the dynamics of world growth and trade to the advantage of all countries, it is simply not possible for the debtor countries to meet their debt service obligations if their efforts to earn the foreign exchange required for this purpose are frustrated by trade restrictions in the industrial countries.

A reversal of the present net transfer of resources from the debtor countries would speed up their recovery by increasing their capacity for investing in structural adjustment at home. The one danger here is that if the interest rates charged on the new inflows of capital are too high the immediate relief may be purchased at the cost of greater difficulties later on. This reinforces the case for lower interest rates discussed above, and also suggests an additional argument for much greater involvement of the World Bank as a low-cost channel for re-lending funds raised in private capital markets.

The Case for an Intergovernmental Dialogue

A number of ideas have been advanced in several quarters in recent months that reflect the search of the international community for new directions in dealing with the debt problem. Particularly noteworthy in this regard was the statement made at the Annual Meetings of the Bretton Woods institutions in Seoul in October 1985 by Secretary of the US Treasury James Baker.

It is recognized that in the first stage following the crisis of 1982 it was necessary to take certain emergency measures to protect the international financial and monetary system by assisting the countries that had encountered debt-servicing difficulties to meet their obligations. The initial objectives were, on the whole, achieved, but at a painfully high cost to the debtor countries. These countries were required, under the system of crisis management adopted, to shoulder most of the burden. The austerity programs characteristic of this first period involved not only severe reductions in living standards, even in countries, and in social groups within countries, at the lower end of the income scale, but also an even sharper cutting back of the investment outlays on which long-run development and structural change depended.

There are still those who believe that the situation remains "manageable" as it is, and that all that is needed is the fortitude to persevere along the lines already established since 1982. Increasingly, however, it has come to be understood that the present strategy has been taken as far as it will go, and that more of the same could undermine the economic and political stability of the debtor countries.

The financial packages put together by the IMF in conjunction with certain creditor governments and the commercial banks were of a strictly short-term nature, consisting essentially of a rescheduling of amortization falling due and a small amount of new money. They were not intended to set forth medium or long-range programs for restoring an adequate rate of growth and investment, nor even of restoring a degree of creditworthiness of the debtors that would lead to a resumption of voluntary lending by the commercial banks.

At the Seoul meeting, US Treasury Secretary Baker proposed a "Program for Sustained Growth" of the debtor countries incorporating three elements:

First and foremost, the adoption by principal debtor
countries of comprehensive macro-economic and structural
policies, supported by the international financial
institutions, to promote growth and balance of payments
adjustment, and to reduce inflation.

Second, a continued central role for the IMF, in
conjunction with increased and more effective structural
adjustment lending by the multilateral development banks
(MDBs), both in support of the adoption by principal
debtors of market-oriented policies for growth.

Third, increased lending by the private banks in
support of comprehensive economic adjustment programs.76/

The Secretary said further that adequate financing could be made
available through a combination of private creditors and multilateral
institutions working cooperatively, but only where there were
reasonable prospects that growth would occur: the latter would depend
upon the adoption of "proper economic policies" by the developing
countries. Such policies should include increased reliance on the
private sector; the mobilization of domestic savings and facilitating
efficient investment, both domestic and foreign, through appropriate
reforms; and "market-opening measures" and trade liberalization. 77/

Secretary Baker envisaged that disbursements by the World Bank
and the Inter-American Development Bank to "principal debtors" might be
increased by roughly 50 per cent from their current annual level of
nearly $6 billion. Net new lending by private banks to "heavily
indebted, middle-income developing countries" would need to be in the
range of $20 billion for the next three years. As far as low-income
debtors were concerned $2.7 billion of IMF Trust Fund resources might
be used, possibly supplemented by other funds, in support of
comprehensive economic programs. In addition, consideration should be
given to "a bolder approach, involving more intensive IMF and World
Bank collaboration" in support of such programs.

Secretary Baker's statement was welcomed in Seoul as pointing to
new directions for the international community as well as for the
debtor countries themselves in dealing with the debt problem. At the
same time it was universally understood that much would depend on how
the program would be worked out in concrete terms. In particular, the
means would have to be sufficient to achieve the ends, and this would
require substantially larger capital flows than those indicated,
especially after taking into account the needs of countries outside the
group of "principal debtors." The venture was to be a cooperative one,
calling for commitments by commercial banks and international financial
institutions as well as by debtor and creditor countries.As the
chairman of the US Federal Reserve Board, Mr. Paul Volcker, pointed
out, Secretary Baker's program "implies a very large cooperative

effort". It was, he said "a tall order" but there had fortunately been a lot of experience in this field, and some "concrete successes". 78/ Clearly a program on such a scale, and involving so many countries, institutions and individuals, would need to be negotiated under auspices having the mandate and range of responsibility for dealing effectively with such matters.

A number of debtor countries have proposed a "political dialogue" on the debt problem. The use of this phrase has raised questions in the minds of creditors, who are concerned about the content and consequences of such a dialogue. Would it simply mean the creation of the long-feared debtors' cartel designed to bring political pressure to bear upon creditors to agree to concessions that might be costly for the banks or the taxpayers of the creditor countries, or perhaps even for both?

In fact, however, an analysis of the events of 1982-85 would show that the debtors have behaved with considerable caution and prudence in the face of extraordinary domestic difficulties and tensions caused by drastic declines in real income within periods as short as two or three years.

It would seem rather that the term "political dialogue" may be understood as a multilateral dialogue among governments as opposed to the kind of dialogue that takes place between creditor banks and various state or private entities of individual debtor countries, or even between debtor countries and official creditors.

The point has been made that since the existing machinery has been able to handle the problems arising up till now, what reason can there be for complicating matters by setting up new machinery?

A possible reply is that there are certain issues of importance to both debtors and creditors that cannot be discussed adequately in existing multilateral forums. Indeed if there were any existing multilateral forum that could be given the requisite competence to act on all the matters arising between the parties, the debtors would no doubt regard such a move as responsive to their request for a political dialogue. What is important is to bring together, in a single negotiation and decision-making process, the multiplicity of interdependent factors (including trade, as well as money and finance) many of which are the sole responsibility of governments and can only be settled in a comprehensive forum having the right to tackle an agenda as broad as the scope of the problem itself.

Such a forum could take up precisely those aspects of Secretary Baker's Program that call for further study and elaboration. It could do so in a manner designed to emphasize the important interests and objectives that creditors and debtors have in common with one another.

A co-operative effort could be made to develop a strategy for accelerating the recovery of the debtor countries and preventing damage to their economies through the diversion of an excessive proportion of current income to the payment of debt service. Such an approach makes sense not only in terms of the debt problem per se but also in terms of minimizing the adverse effects on employment in the creditor countries resulting from unduly severe reductions in the import capacities of the debtors.

If such an approach is rational, and in the common interests of all parties, why has it not been adopted hitherto? One possible reason is that the process of multi-year rescheduling has been mistaken for a long-run strategy. As a prominent United States banking official has pointed out, it is an illusion to suppose that multi-year rescheduling represents a long-term solution to the debt crisis:

> In summary, multi-year rescheduling, as currently formulated, does not address the key development issues embedded in the current crisis. It does not bring together the relevant participants - the banks, the multilateral development institutions, the IMF and the creditor and debtor governments - to begin working out desirable and feasible adjustment programmes over the medium term. For this reason, multi-year rescheduling cannot be seen as a prelude to the resumption of voluntary lending by the banks. 79/

A more basic reason for the failure to develop the common interests of debtors and creditors may be that a strategy of the type envisaged would involve a more balanced sharing of the costs of adjustment, and that there is no way of guaranteeing an adequate rate of return on the additional costs that would be incurred by creditors. Consequently all rescue operations have been designed to transfer the maximum share of costs to the debtors short of provoking default. This solution is, however, sub-optimal in the sense that under conditions in which the debtor economies are constrained, as they are now, by shortages of foreign exchange, additional investments by the creditors would actually enhance the probability of realizing the expected rate of return on existing debt in good time.

Solutions much closer to optimality are often achieved in debt problems that arise within the limits of a single country. Thus cases of bankruptcy within an industrial country are usually subject to legislation providing for substantial protection for debtors against creditors, which may involve major relief from contractual obligations of the debtors in the interests of promoting their recovery. But the fact that both debtors and creditors operate within a single legal framework in such cases and that there is a judicial authority capable of enforcing its decisions provides certain assurances to the creditors that are not available to them with as much certainty in cases involving sovereign immunity of the borrowers.

It has nevertheless been suggested by another distinguished banking official that

> What is needed is some international variation on the Chapter 11 approach to workouts under the United States Federal Bankruptcy Law. We need to have the ability to help countries in difficulty, due to events outside their control, to reorganize their external indebtedness on the basis (i) of an impartial assessment of their prospects for earning foreign exchange on a fair trading basis, (ii) of their need and access to new money for sound development and restructuring requirements and (iii) of their demonstrated commitment to necessary structural adjustments and reasonable austerity measures. As in all cases of <u>force majeure</u> or "unforeseen circumstances," the settlement procedure in such cases should be designed to spread the burden of adjustment and loss of profit or delays in repayment on an equitable basis between the various actors in the drama, creditors, borrowers and the taxpayers of both the capital exporting and importing countries. 80/

What would be the work program or agenda of the kind of forum that could tackle the issues set out above? Obviously it would be for the forum itself to decide, but one could imagine some or all of the following matters coming up for discussion:-

1. The creation of an international environment conducive to the solution of the debt problem.

2. The conditions for adjustment with growth, including structural change in the debtor countries.

3. Measures for the long-term restructuring of debt and elimination of bunching of maturities.

4. Adjusting debt service to the capabilities of the debtors, including the establishment of appropriate interest rate levels.

5. The transfer of resources.

6. Special problems of low-income countries: improving the performance of the Paris Club.

7. The impact of banking regulations on treatment of the debt problem.

8. Steps to be taken in the event of changes in circumstances beyond the control of those affected.

Intergovernmental discussion of such matters, whether in an existing forum or in a new one, would not be designed to supersede the responsibilities of existing institutions. It would seek rather to consider those aspects of the debt problem that existing institutions have not tackled, for whatever reason, and how those aspects might best be handled in the future within the present institutional framework.

One source of opposition to the convening of a dialogue on such matters as those set out above is the idea that such generalized discussion of the debt problem would undermine the case-by-case approach, an approach that Secretary Baker strongly supported in his statement at Seoul.

There is, however, no necessary contradiction between the examination of general issues in an intergovernmental forum and the continuation of the case-by-case approach in dealing with specific problems of particular debtors. There is, in fact, no dispute that each case of debt crisis has its own special characteristics that need to be taken into account in devising adjustment programs. But that does not mean that it is impossible or improper to define certain generally accepted principles governing such programs. In the absence of such general principles, the case-by-case approach means that the terms and conditions of each rescheduling operation are set by a lengthy bargaining process and hence ultimately by the leverage that each party to the process is able to mobilize in its own favor. Since the leverage of small countries is quite limited the lack of guidelines has resulted in their being generally unable to achieve improvements in terms corresponding to those accorded to some of the larger debtors.

At the conclusion of a review of the world economic outlook carried out by the UN Economic and Social Council in July 1985, the President of the Council, Ambassador Tomohiko Kobayashi of Japan, delivered a summing up of the discussion that received the general support of all groups of countries. The Council later decided to transmit the President's statement to the General Assembly for further consideration. In the course of his summing up, the President, addressing himself to the debt problem, made the following observation:

> A difference of opinion seems to exist between those who argue for the current case-by-case approach and those who plead for a more general and intergovernmental dialogue between creditors and debtors. However, I think that this conflict is more apparent than real, and that close consideration will show that these approaches are not incompatible and that there is ground to expect greater convergence when the matter has been more fully explored.81/

Subsequently, the Committee on the Review and Appraisal of the Implementation of the International Development Strategy for the Third United Nations Development Decade adopted by consensus "Agreed conclusions" that included the following passage:

> While countries recognize the unique circumstances of each case, they also agree that, since adjustment cannot be divorced from the external environment in which it must take place, there are other elements, identifiable in many cases, which need to be accounted for. They also agree that there are shared responsibilities in respect of which debtor and creditor countries, as well as multilateral financial institutions have an essential role to play. In the broader context of these considerations, countries will intensify their efforts towards solving the debt problems of the developing countries. They will pursue, inter alia, a dialogue involving debtor and creditor countries, international private banks, as well as multilateral financial institutions exercising their responsibility in a spirit of mutual co-operation towards equitable, durable and mutually agreed approaches in support of positive adjustment and long-term growth. 82/

These ideas provide a useful basis on which to establish a more adequate framework for achieving international cooperation on the debt problem than exists at the present time.

FOOTNOTES

1. IBRD-IMF, Summary Proceedings, Annual Meetings of the Boards of Governors, 1961 (Washington, D.C. 1961) p. 12.

2. UNCTAD document TD/99 paragraph 78.

3. For example, Mr. Jose Sarney, President of Brazil stated on 23 September 1985 that "Brazil will not pay its foreign debt with recession, nor with unemployment, nor with hunger." (United Nations document A/40/PV.4, page 22.)

4. André de Lattre, Restoring Bank Lending: Policies for Interdependence, in Adjustment with Growth, edited by Khadija Haq and Carlos Massad, North South Roundtable, Islamabad, 1984, p.32.

5. The content of the Baker initiative is set out in the last section of this paper.

6. Op. cit. p. 22.

7. United Nations document A/40/48, page 8.

8. That is, all developing countries except the eight Middle Eastern oil exporters.

9. International Monetary Fund, World Economic Outlook April 1985, Washington, D.C., 1985, page 51.

10. International Monetary Fund, World Economic Outlook October 1985, Washington, D.C., 1985, table 32.

11. The 1985 growth rate for developing countries was reduced from 4.0 in the April Outlook to 3.5 in the October Outlook, and the 1986 growth rate from 4.5 to 4.1.

12. Morgan Guaranty Trust Company of New York, World Financial Markets, July 1985, p.1.

13. Ibid.

14. F.W. Taussig, International Trade, New York, 1927.

15. Raymond F. Mikesell, The Capacity to Service Foreign Investment, in U.S. Private and Government Investment Abroad, University of Oregon, 1962, pp. 382-383.

16. Robert Solomon, The United States as a Debtor in the 19th Century, Brookings Discussion Papers in International Economics, The Brookings Institution, May 1985, p. 19.

17. International Capital Movements during the Inter-War Period, United Nations publication, Sales No.: 1949, II.D.2, p. 66.

18. IBRD-IMF, Summary Proceedings, Annual Meetings of the Boards of Governors, 1961 (Washington, D.C. 1961) p. 12.

19. USAID, A Study on Loan Terms, Debt Burden and Development (Washington, D.C. 1965) p. 38.

20. Op. cit. p. 21.

21. International Monetary Fund, Annual Report 1974, p. 26.

22. International Monetary Fund, International Monetary Reform: Documents of the Committee of Twenty, Washington, D.C., 1974, p. 221.

23. Executive Board decisions 4134-(74/4) of 23 January 1974 and 4241-(74/67) of 13 June 1974 as recorded in International Monetary Fund, Annual Report 1974, pp. 108 and 122-123.

24. In addition, increases in regular Fund charges from mid-1974 as well as the market-related charges established on the oil facility caused problems for the low-income countries. This led to the creation of an interest subsidy account for the benefit of over 60 low-income countries making drawings on the second oil facility.

25. See Otmar Emminger, The International Debt Crisis and the Banks, Intereconomics, May-June 1985, p. 109.

26. Ibid.

27. IMF, Annual Report 1983, p. 34.

28. For a short time after the oil price increases of 1979 and 1980 some consideration was given in the Fund "to means that it might use to facilitate the movement of funds to countries that may not have sufficient access to funds from private sources. Many countries may require considerable time to carry out necessary structural adjustments, and may need both financial assistance from the Fund and the Fund's help in devising realistic programs of structural adjustment". (Annual Report 1980, p. 3). This kind of approach, with its emphasis on structural adjustment and facilitating "the movement of funds" was soon discarded in favor of more conventional programs oriented towards short-term adjustment and relying heavily on deflation.

29. IMF, World Economic Outlook, June 1981, Washington, D.C., 1981, p. 10.

30. Ibid, pp. 14-15.

31. Statement by the Ministers and Governors of the Group of Ten agreed at their meeting in Tokyo on June 21, 1985 paragraph 4 (iii).

32. Group of Ten, The Functioning of the International Monetary System, June 1985, paragraph 37.

33. World Bank, World Development Report 1985, p. 55.

34. Ibid, pp. 55-56.

35. Op. cit. p. 34.

36. IMF Survey, 12 October 1981, p. 313.

37. Economic Report of the President, Washington, D.C., January 1980, p. 67.

38. Op. cit. p. 67.

39. World Bank, World Development Report 1981, Washington D.C., August 1981 p. 10.

40. Op. cit. pp. 60-63. As an example of excessive public sector investment inefficiently carried out, the World Bank (op. cit. p. 40) cited the case of Peru, where, it was stated, an oil pipeline was constructed "that was bigger than the capacity of Peru's oil fields". But this pipeline construction was presumably based on the same information that had led the World Bank in 1979 to classify Peru with Ecuador and Venezuela as having "large deposits of heavy oils" (World Development Report 1979 p. 40). As far as the efficiency of Peruvian public enterprise in the oil industry is concerned, the World Bank had this to say in 1983: "Where national oil companies are sufficiently technically competent and financially independent to undertake complex capital-intensive exploration programs (as they are, for example, in Argentina, Brazil, India, Peru and Yugoslavia) the Bank will consider supporting their efforts." See World Bank, The Energy Transition in Developing Countries, Washington, D.C. 1983, p. 34.

41. Journal of Development Planning No. 16, United Nations, New York, 1985, pp. 26-27.

42. Op. cit. pp. 63-64.

43. Edmar Bacha, Questions and Answers on the Latin American Debt, June 1984 (mimeo).

44. IMF World Economic Outlook 1983, Washington D.C. 1983, pp. 140-144.

45. The money was "new" only in the sense that total exposure of the lending banks increased. It did not mean that the creditors lent more than they received. What they did was to relend part only of the interest that was being paid to them on past loans.

46. IMF, Annual Report 1985 p.82.

47. UNCTAD Trade and Development Report 1985, pp 23-25

48. IMF, World Economic Outlook October 1985, table 38

49. Financial Times, August 22, 1985, p.1.

50. <u>Fifty-third Annual Report</u>, 1 April 1982 - 31 March 1983. (Basle 1983), p. 130.

51. J. de Larosière, Address to the Institute of International Finance, May 10, 1985. IMF Survey, May 27, 1985.

52. Henry C. Wallich, The International Debt Situation in an American View, Remarks to the Verein fuer Socialpolitik, Frankfurt, February 8, 1985, p. 10.

53. <u>Op. cit.</u> p. 51.

54. <u>Op. cit.</u> p. 3.

55. <u>Op. cit.</u> p. 37.

56. IMF, <u>Annual Report 1985</u> p.14.

57. This statement, like the rest of the paragraph is based on the IMF <u>World Economic Outlook October 1985</u>, which includes the following countries in the group of "major exporters of manufactures": Argentina, Brazil, Greece, Hong Kong, Israel, Republic of Korea, Portugal, Singapore, South Africa and Yugoslavia.

58. As noted in footnote <u>b/</u> to Table IV the term "official borrowers" is used by the IMF to denote those countries, except China and India, that obtained two thirds or more of their external borrowings from 1978 to 1982 from official creditors.

59. For further details see UNCTAD Document TD/B/980, paragraphs 29 and 33-4.

60. For additional detail see UNCTAD, <u>Trade and Development Report 1985,</u> paragraphs 278 to 294.

61. UNCTAD Document TD/B/980 paragraphs 35-6.

62. Michel Camdessus, Governmental Creditors and the Role of the Paris Club, in <u>Default and Rescheduling</u> edited by David Suratgar, Euromoney Publications Limited, 1984 p. 128.

63. UNCTAD, Document TD/B/980, paragraph 65.

64. <u>Toward Sustained Development of Sub-Saharan Africa</u> (Washington, D.C.: World Bank, 1984), p.13. The debt service ratios reflect interest and principal owed but not necessarily paid.

65. <u>Ibid</u>, P.13.

66. William R. Cline, International Debt: From Crisis to Recovery? American Economic Review, May 1985, p.186.

67. See <u>The Impact of the World Recession on Children</u>: edited by Richard Jolly and G. A. Cornia, Pergamon Press 1984; and <u>Within Human Reach: A Future for Africa's Children</u>, UNICEF, 1985.

68. Bank for International Settlements Press Review, 12 October 1984.

69. UNCTAD, Trade and Development Report 1985, United Nations Sales No. E. 85. II. D.16 .p.141.

70. In Trade and Development Report 1985 paragraphs 233-249 UNCTAD analyzes the dynamics of debt, investment and exports.

71. World Economic Outlook October 1985, Washington, D.C,1985. p. 27.

72. Ibid, p. 22

73. For further discussion of this aspect, see Sidney Dell, Crisis Management and the International Debt Problem, International Journal XL Autumn 1985, Toronto, Canada .

74. UNCTAD, Trade and Development Report, 1985, p. 119.

75. The content of the Baker initiative is set out in the last section of this paper.

76. Boards of Governors, 1985 Annual Meetings, Seoul, Republic of Korea, Press Release No. 13. October 8, 1985, p.3.

77. Ibid, p.5.

78. Address in Toronto, Canada, 28 October 1985.

79. Lawrence J. Brainard, Current Illusions about the International Debt Crisis, World Economy, March 1985, pp. 4-5. Lawrence J. Brainard is a Senior Vice President and Head of International Economic and Political Analysis at the Bankers Trust Company in New York.

80. David Suratgar, The International Financial System and the Management of the International Debt Crisis in Default and Rescheduling, ed. David Suratgar, Euromoney Publications, 1984, p. 159. David Suratgar is a Director of Morgan Grenfell and Co. Ltd.

81. United Nations document A/40/525, p.6.

82. United Nations document A/40/48, page 8.

PROSPECTS FOR INTERNATIONAL DEBT REFORM

Paul Krugman*

The purpose of this paper is to provide a guide to thinking about proposals for international debt reform. The paper is in five parts. The first part reviews briefly the background to the current situation. The second part establishes a conceptual framework for thinking about the objectives of debt reform schemes. The third part provides an analytical summary of some of the better-known proposals for debt reform. The fourth part then evaluates the main elements in these reform proposals in terms of the criteria advanced in the second part. Finally, the last part reviews the discussion and suggests some conclusions.

I. BACKGROUND TO THE PROBLEM

The two debt crises

For the most part the international debt problem is a problem of two regions, the middle-income borrowers of Latin America and the poor nations of Sub-Saharan Africa. Table 1 provides some comparisons of the debt situation of these two groups of countries. The important point to stress is that, apart from the fact that both have high levels of debt, the two groups look very different. The Latin American nations have borrowed primarily from private bankers. By contrast, the poor African nations have relied on public lending, both from governments and from multinational agencies such as the World Bank, for most of their borrowing. Because the bulk of African borrowing was on concessional terms, the average interest rate paid on African debt is much less than that on Latin American debt, a gap which increased with the sharp rise in market interest rates after 1980. Finally, we should note that, although low-income Africa is comparable in population to high-debt Latin America and has levels of debt (although not of interest payments) relative to GNP and exports that are even higher than those of the Latin American debtors, the total value of African debt is far less. This of course reflects the poverty of the continent. It means that when we turn to the arguments for debt reform, Africa will weigh heavily in political and humanitarian terms but is not a major factor in the stability of the financial system.

*The author is Professor of Economics, Massachusetts Institute of Technology, Cambridge, U.S.A. January 1986.

The Latin American debt crisis

The facts of the Latin American crisis are too familiar to need restatement. The special feature of the Latin American crisis is of course that the reliance on bank lending has made it in the first instance a banking problem. We do not know whether Latin America actually has too much debt in the light of its future economic prospects, and at times the question seems almost irrelevant. At least proximately, the Latin American crisis is one of confidence, related in only a loose way to economic fundamentals. Given Latin America's predominant reliance on relatively short-term private capital, bankers' worries translate almost immediately into balance-of-payments crises. This has led to a preoccupation with the problem of getting the banks to maintain and increase their exposure, with both policymakers and analysts sometimes failing to ask where the process is leading.

The concentration of claims on Latin America in the hands of commercial banks, and the resultant concern over the stability of the financial system, can also lead us to lose sight of the fact that Latin American debt is not all that large relative to the world economy. For the sake of comparison, we can calculate that a complete write-off of all United States claims on Latin America would represent a once-and-for-all cost to the United States roughly equal to that of one extra percentage point of unemployment for one year; this is also roughly comparable to the terms of trade loss the United States suffered annually as a result of the first oil shock. The point is that the OECD countries are certainly able to afford substantial write-downs on their claims on Latin America, if that becomes necessary. (This is a fortiori true of Africa, whose debts are an order of magnitude smaller.)

The African debt crisis

The debt crisis in Latin America has attracted much more attention than financial problems in Africa, for understandable reasons. The sums of money involved are much smaller in Africa, and the prevalence of official claims in the debt of low-income countries means that the difficulties of Africa do not much affect the solvency of commercial banks. Furthermore, African financial problems have developed in a less dramatic way than those of the Latin American countries. Nonetheless, low-income Africa is in debt difficulties serious enough to warrant designation as a crisis.

The financial squeeze on low-income Africa has developed in a more muted way than that on Latin America, because of the role of official lending, but has the same basic elements. Interest rates on African debt lagged much further behind market rates than Latin America's, but they did rise, increasing the interest burden. More important, net capital inflows declined. In 1980 low-income Africa received net private capital inflows of almost a billion dollars, financing about 17 percent of the current account deficit. By 1984 these flows had turned somewhat negative. Official flows not only failed to make up this shortfall, they actually declined slightly in nominal terms. Thus low-income Africa was forced to reduce its trade deficit by more than one and a half billion dollars.

What made this especially difficult was that Africa was at the same time experiencing a sharp terms-of-trade deterioration. The continued weakness of commodity prices despite OECD recovery from the 1980-82 slump has hit sub-Saharan Africa particularly hard. The need to reduce trade deficits in an unfavourable environment, while by no means the only source of Africa's difficulties, has certainly contributed to a decline in living standards that has been quite literally disastrous.

Coping with the debt problem

The Latin American strategy

The essential idea underlying the ad hoc debt strategy adopted toward Latin America in 1982-3 was that the region's debt problem was one of liquidity rather than solvency. The official view at least was that, given time, the debtor countries would be able to recover the confidence of financial markets, both because of their own efforts and because the world economic picture would improve. On the other hand, the balance-of-payments crises created by the cut-off of bank lending could force countries into a moratorium on payments and even repudiation of debt before the situation would have time to right itself. What was needed, then, was to find a way to avert default, through temporary ad hoc measures, until the storm had passed.

We will discuss the theoretical rationale for official involvement in this process in the next section. For now, let us simply note the main elements of the strategy as it emerged in 1983. These were: debt rescheduling; "involuntary" new lending by commercial banks; austerity on the part of debtor countries; and a central role as mediator and supplemental lender by the IMF.

The African strategy

If the debt strategy adopted toward Latin America may be described as ad hoc, that adopted toward Africa may hardly be described as a new strategy at all. The slower motion deterioration in Africa's financial position, and the secondary role of private credit, meant that the innovations required to deal with the crisis of market borrowers could be at least temporarily avoided. African debt problems have continued to be handled within traditional channels: rescheduling via the Paris Club mechanism, tied to IMF conditionality.

The results of ad hoc strategies

The debt strategy adopted toward Latin America in 1982-3 was essentially designed to buy time. Clearly it succeeded in that aim. A major financial crisis was averted, and at the end of 1985 had still not arrived. What we need to know first is how costly this strategy has been, and second whether it is a strategy that will continue to work.

The first point to note is that the financial stabilization in Latin America since 1983 has been achieved by a different mix of financing and adjustment than the original strategy envisioned. The plan had been that while countries would reduce their current account deficits, banks would continue to provide new lending that would finance at least some of the interest payments. What happened was that on one side the debtor countries moved into trade surplus much more sharply than had been anticipated, while on the other hand banks failed to deliver the expected increase in their exposure. In 1984 the exposure of banks to Latin America actually fell slightly, a process which seems to have accelerated in 1985. The counterparts to this failure of private lending to live up to expectations were, first, a much more drastic adjustment of trade balances than anyone either predicted or found desirable, and second, a dominant role of official sources rather than private creditors in providing whatever new money did become available.

The second point is that the adjustment has placed an extreme burden on high-debt nations. The major Latin American debtors have suffered a 15-20 per cent reduction in the resources available for domestic use per capita, which was reflected in a decline both in living standards and in real capital formation. The chief causes of this decline were the need to run huge trade surpluses, and the recessions that were generated in large part to help the countries achieve these surpluses.

The African experience was quite different. Although private capital inflows vanished, official lending continued. Between new official lending and the "financing" provided by rescheduling and growing arrears, low-income Africa has been able to continue to run sizable, though reduced, non-interest current deficits. The problem is that the growth of debt has not been controlled: indeed, since both rescheduling and capitalization of arrears in effect create new debt at increased interest rates, the growth of African debt is beginning to look explosive.

What we can see, then, is that the post-1982 debt strategy has been very costly: a huge adjustment burden has been placed on market borrowers, while official borrowers have continued to get more deeply indebted. The next question is whether, despite these costs, the strategy is working.

Prospects for the ad hoc debt strategy

The financial outlook for market borrowers

The intention of the Latin American debt strategy as originally formulated was to buy time until adjustment in the debtors and, even more important, recovery in the world economy restored creditor confidence. At that point the countries would regain normal access to the capital market and both "involuntary" lending and the imposition of conditionality on the countries could come to an end.

What is immediately clear is that the restoration of normal capital market access is as far away as ever. Press reports as of November 1985 indicate that secondary sales of developing country debt place a substantial discount on that debt: Brazil's debt changes hands at 75-83% of face value, Mexico's at 78-82%, Peru's at 32-36% (Economist, Nov.22).

This raises the question of whether it will be possible to get banks to accept further increases in exposure. If they were unwilling to do this in 1984 and 1985, what will make them willing in 1986 and 1987? If it is possible at all, it will require new incentives. The Baker Plan, which we will discuss below, is an effort to provide both an explicit carrot and an implicit stick to get banks lending again.

The more basic question, however, is whether a resumption of the original strategy makes sense. There are reasonable grounds for questioning this, even if one believes that the debt strategy as of 1983 was in fact reasonable at the time.

1986 vs. 1983

In many ways the middle-income countries with private debt will enter 1986 in a substantially better situation than the one in which they entered 1983. The recovery in the United States has at least stabilized their export prices, and contributed to a considerable rise in export volume. Nominal interest rates have fallen, even if real rates remain high by previous standards. Most important, the countries have demonstrated an ability to adjust, and even to resume limited economic growth, that is greater than many observers expected to see.

The improvement in the current situation, however, may be more than offset by the lack of any comparable prospects. In early 1983 it was reasonable to presume that the external environment of developing country debtors would improve sharply as industrial countries recovered and real interest rates fell to more normal levels. As it turned out, outside North America the recovery has failed to develop much strength, and real interest rates have remained high. Growth in the United States has slowed now that much of the slack has been taken up, and OECD growth has slowed with it. In contrast to 1983, early 1986 will not offer the likely prospect of a dramatic improvement in the world economy over the next few years.

This means that much of the rationale for the debt strategy adopted in 1982-3 seems less applicable now. The point of that strategy was to play for time, waiting in particular for the effects of recovery in the OECD. Now that the period of rapid recovery, such as it was, seems to have run its course, a strategy of postponement makes much less sense. We will formalize that insight below, when we show that the case for "defensive" lending rests not on a belief that such lending leads with certainty to full repayment, but rather on a belief that playing for time is productive, raising the probability of repayment. In 1983 the subjective discount placed by bankers on their developing-country claims may well have been larger than it is today, but there was a stronger case for believing that delay would reduce that discount.

Nonetheless, the United States has proposed a plan for international debt that, at least at first glance, seems to be a revival of the 1982-3 approach. The plan proposed by Treasury Secretary Baker at Seoul has as its publicized centrepiece the provision of a fund of new money by commercial banks over the next three years. The provision of financing would be contingent for each country on appropriate adjustment policies. Thus, as usually described, the Baker plan has the same outline as the post-1982 strategy: involuntary lending coupled with conditionality. It is unclear who would enforce the conditionality, but on reflection the creditor country governments might well decide to put it in the hands of the IMF.

Given the doubts we have raised, this may seem like an unlikely plan to get very far. However, on closer observation it becomes clear that the Baker Plan strays further from the post-82 strategy than it at first appears to. The reason is that the plan actually calls for the new money from the banks to be matched by comparable sums of official money, chiefly from the World Bank and the Inter-American Development Bank. To put this in perspective, the lending by commercial banks under the Seoul proposal would increase their exposure at an annual rate of only 2.5 per cent. Judging from past experience, the actual growth in exposure will be much less than this because of the "leakages" we described above. (From end-1982 to first quarter 1985, 24 billion dollars of new money from banks translated into only a 10 billion dollar increase in exposure.)

The result is that in practice the Baker Plan would be likely to turn into a situation where new lending comes predominantly from official sources, and in which the new lending is in any case of very modest size. In quantitative terms the financial picture for Latin merica under a successful Baker Plan might look very much like 1984: continued large debtor trade surpluses, with small current deficits financed for the most part by official rather than private capital.

Africa's prospects

The African question is not so much one of mobilizing funds as of achieving adjustment. Nonetheless, the same contrast between 1983 and 1986 is present. A few years ago there seemed at least a reasonable chance that a sustained OECD recovery would restore real commodity prices to historical levels, making trade balance adjustment for the nations of Africa feasible without extreme domestic cost. If low-income Africa's terms of trade had improved sharply, the traditional mechanism of rescheduling could arguably have worked. At this point, however, while a recovery of real commodity prices is a possibility -- since we do not really know why they have been so weak -- there is no longer a strong presumption that the near term will in fact see a more favourable external environment.

II. A CONCEPTUAL FRAMEWORK FOR DEBT REFORM

The debate over international debt reform should be viewed as part of a broader debate over the appropriate degree of involvement of creditor country governments and international agencies in the debt problem. Clearly this debate is primarily about intervention in the debt problems of market borrowers, and does not apply directly to the problems of official borrowers in Africa, where governments and agencies are themselves the creditors and cannot help but be involved. Thus, our discussion of the conceptual framework for debt reform must take as its starting point the case of countries that have primarily borrowed from private sources. Nonetheless, the discussion is not without relevance to the problems of official borrowers as well. We will indicate as we go along how arguments over appropriate intervention in private debt carry lessons for appropriate management of official claims.

Let us begin, however, by focussing on the problem of market borrowers. The Latin American situation is that levels of foreign debt that seemed reasonable and justified during the 1970s have come to be regarded by private creditors as excessive, and are no longer willingly held. In this situation a continuation of business as usual is impossible: rescheduling of debt-service obligations is inevitable, and, as we have suggested, creditors do not appear to expect to receive full payment even in the long run. Why, however, should this situation require a role for creditor country governments and international agencies? In previous episodes of international debt difficulties, such as the 1930s, the problem of debt was largely left up to the debtors and private creditors. By contrast, even the ad hoc strategy adopted by creditor country governments and the IMF during 1982-5 presumed that international bank debt was a matter of official concern and worth at least some commitment of official funds. Proposals for a more comprehensive strategy, which typically envision a larger role for governments and multilateral agencies, presume an even stronger justification for intervention. Before we turn to a description of specific proposals, it is important to consider the conceptual justification for the role of creditor country governments and international agencies in the debt situation. At the same time, we also need to examine the choices facing debtor country governments; these governments of course have no choice about involvement, but their incentives need to be clarified.

We begin by adopting a narrow view, one that both focusses exclusively on the interests of creditor country governments and identifies that interest as solely one of attempting to preserve the value of banks' claims on developing countries. This view is helpful in allowing us to see clearly the purely financial justifications for an official role. It is also helpful in that it defines a minimal justification for rescheduling and new lending by official creditors. In fact, however, the interests of governments and multinational agencies go beyond this purely financial issue, and arguably should go well beyond it. Thus, we also need to discuss the broader justifications for an official role to stabilize the world economic and political situation, and also to serve humanitarian objectives. Finally, we need to consider the problem from the point of view of the debtor countries.

Once we have described the justifications for intervention, we can turn to the options. This means first discussing the possible dimensions of reform in terms of restructuring and perhaps reducing the debt, as well as changing the way adjustment is managed. Once we have laid out the possible dimensions of reform, we can take a preliminary overview of options for reform.

The narrow financial argument for an official role

Even if multinational organizations were simply the agents of the creditor countries, and even if the creditor countries were interested only in recovering as much as possible of the money lent to developing countries, there would be a strong case for official involvement in the working out of the debt problem. This case rests on two points. The first is that, while it is in the collective interest of creditors to maintain and even increase their exposure to problem debtors rather than provoke a mutually harmful default, individual creditors have an incentive to pull out; this "free rider" problem will be difficult to resolve without an official role. (The experience of the last year suggests that it may be hard to resolve even with an official role.)

The second point is that creditors and debtors are locked in a bargaining game in which each party has an incentive to try to commit itself to a tough position, yet in which both parties will lose if mutually inconsistent commitments prevent agreement. Official bodies, most notably the IMF, can help here by serving a mediating role, establishing focal points for agreement that might otherwise not be achieved.

The case for defensive lending

The starting point for our analysis must be an understanding of the crucial point that it is often in the interest of creditors to reschedule debt obligations and even to lend more to problem debtors rather than demand payment, when the effect of such a demand will be to increase the probability of default. That is, it is in the interest of creditors to engage in "defensive lending" to protect the value of their existing claims on a country.

The structure of the debt of market borrowers in 1982 was based on the assumption of continued access to world capital markets, so that principal and at least part of interest could be met out of new borrowing. When this access was cut off, a demand on the part of their creditors for full payment of their obligations could not have been met. If creditors were to try to collect, the countries would be forced to declare a moratorium on payments at best, a repudiation of debt at worst. While a complete repudiation was and remains unlikely, clearly creditors who forced a country into default could not expect to receive full payment on their claims.

On the other hand, if the creditors allowed the countries to delay payment by rescheduling principal and offering new loans to cover part of the interest due, there was in 1982 a reasonable prospect that in time normal access to capital markets would be restored, and that the existing creditors would then be able to reclaim the full value of their claims. This was not a certainty; it has been recognized all along that the improvement in the world economic environment and successful policy adjustment of the debtors required for a return to free borrowing was by no means guaranteed. However, the expected value of existing claims on debtor nations, given a programme of rescheduling and new loans, was clearly higher than it would have been in the absence of such a programme.

Against the improvement in the value of existing claims on developing countries resulting from new lending creditors must set the costs of the increase in their exposure. By definition a problem debtor is a country which may not fully pay its debts, and any new loan runs the risk of non-payment. From the point of view of the creditors, then, the case for defensive lending involves a tradeoff between the increase in the value of existing claims and the risk of losses on the new lending.

The important point is that even if the risk of non-payment on new loans is substantial, and even if the improvement in the probability of payment on existing debt that can result from additional lending is modest, it is still in the interests of creditors to engage in a good deal of defensive lending.

To see this, it is helpful to consider a simple algebraic model of defensive lending. (The analysis is closely related to that of Cline (1984), but corrects what appears to be a confusion over the treatment of multi-year programmes of defensive lending.) Let us suppose that a problem debtor's debt is valued by creditors at a discount from its face value equal to the fraction d. That is, the creditors expect to receive only a fraction 1-d of the payments due to them. Let us also suppose that by lending the country more money, and thus increasing their exposure, the creditors believe that they can raise the expected fraction of debt repaid to 1-d* ; i.e., the discount from face value can be reduced to d* < d. Also, let e be the value of the new lending as a fraction of the existing debt.

The benefit to the creditors from their defensive lending is the reduction in their expected losses on existing debt: d-d* times the value of that debt. The cost of the defensive lending is the risk of losing the new loans: d* times the value of the new lending, or d*e times the value of existing debt.

Clearly a programme of defensive lending is worth doing as long as the benefits exceed the costs, that is, as long as

$$e < (d-d*)/d*$$

Now we can actually get a direct estimate of d* by looking at the discount at which banks sell claims on developing countries to one another. We noted above that claims on debtor nations sell at values ranging from 32-36 per cent of par for Peru to 75-83 per cent for Brazil and Mexico. For the biggest debtors a conservative estimate might be that, given a programme of defensive lending, creditors expect to receive 75 cents on the dollar of their debt. To ask how much defensive lending this justifies, we need to know how much less the debt would be worth in the absence of new lending. Suppose, for example, that without new lending banks could expect to receive only 50 cents on the dollar. Then defensive lending would be worth doing as long as e < (.5 - .25)/(.25) = 1.0 -- that is, banks should be willing to double their exposure in order to protect their original investment.

It is common to think of defensive lending in terms of the annual rate of growth of banks' exposure rather than in terms of the total increase over the course of the programme. The maximum justifiable rate of growth depends, of course, on the number of years the lending is expected to continue. Table 2 takes as given that a programme of defensive lending will reduce the discount on existing debt to 25 percent, and shows how the maximum justifiable rate of growth of exposure depends on the discount without such a programme and on the length of time that the programme is expected to continue. The conclusion that is apparent from the table is that plausible numbers can justify a quite rapid growth in banks' exposure. For example, if one thinks that defensive lending will reduce the discount from 50 to 25 per cent, banks should be willing to increase their exposure at 14 per cent a year for five years.

Calculations of this sort, implicit or explicit, suggested in 1982-3 that it was definitely worthwhile for banks to avert default by continuing lending to problem debtors. (Whether it is still worthwhile is a question to which we will return.) The problem, however, is that what we have shown is that such lending is in the creditors' collective interest rather than their individual interest. The first hurdle that any debt strategy must cross is to get creditors to act in their own interest.

The free rider problem

Our brief analysis of defensive lending compared the costs of new lending with the benefits to the creditors as a whole. The immediate problem faced by creditors is that there may not be anyone prepared to serve this group interest.

Certainly no bank or other potential lender who is not already owed money by a problem debtor will be prepared to lend in the situation we have described. Taken in isolation, a new loan is simply unprofitable: if we ignore the defensive value of new lending, a dollar lent to a problem debtor immediately becomes worth only 75 cents. (This need not be strictly true if the loan pays a higher-than-market interest rate. However, given the size of the discount, the premium on the rate needed to attract new lenders would be so high as itself to provide an incentive for default.)

New lending must, then, come from the existing group of creditors. Even these creditors, however, may not have the individual incentive to lend. Each creditor will of course be better off if other creditors do the defensive lending while its exposure remains constant or even falls. And if everyone tries to "free ride" in this way, there may not be any single creditor with a large enough stake to be willing to take on the burden of defensive lending for the group of creditors as a whole.

One of the recurrent concerns of those watching the debt crisis has been the following scenario: the burden of defensive lending is borne only by a core group of large banks that are able to act in a cooperative manner. Although these banks expand their exposure at a rapid pace, smaller banks do not go along and indeed reduce their exposure. The result is that, even with the core banks lending the maximum that they can justify on defensive grounds, the net capital flow to debtor nations is small and perhaps even negative, so that the countries are given little incentive to continue to play the game. This scenario seems to have largely come to pass in the last year.

The importance of the free rider problem for the issue of debt reform is that it provides an immediate justification for official involvement in the situation to insure a continuing flow of lending.

That is, it gives a clear-cut reason why the IMF and other official bodies should seek to coerce the banks into lending in their own interest. It may also provide a justification for official lending, but let us set aside this aspect until we have considered a second justification for official involvement.

Bargaining and mediation

Suppose that creditors can in some way overcome the free rider problem and agree to maintain and to some extent increase their collective claims on a problem debtor. The next problem is one of reaching an agreement with the debtor. Both the creditors and the debtor are better off with an agreement than with a rupture of relations; if that happens, the creditors will not receive payment and the country will be subject to retaliation. There is, however, a range of possible agreements, some more favourable to the debtor, others more favourable to the creditors. The debtor will of course want generous lending and some concession on interest rates; the creditors will want to minimize the rate of growth of their exposure and will want to be compensated for their risk by receiving a premium over market interest rates.

The problem raised by this conflict of interests is that it might lead to a failure to reach any agreement at all. Each party will want to tilt the outcome to its advantage, and will therefore try to commit itself to accept only solutions that are sufficiently in its favour. Thus political leaders in debtor countries may attempt to make some minimum terms a domestic political necessity, while lead banks assert that the smaller banks will not go along with concessional interest rates or substantial new lending. If both sides are successful in making commitments, they may unfortunately find that they have eliminated any possible ground for agreement. Thus the problem is that the incentive to bargain hard may lead to a failure to reach any bargain.

The potential role for official bodies in this case is that of mediator. A third party -- in practice the IMF -- can simultaneously dictate the adjustment policies of the debtor nation and the volume of new finance that the banks must provide. Each party may complain about the terms of the solution, but if the IMF has sufficient credibility, each party will also realize that failure to go along will sharply reduce the chances of reaching agreement, which is to everyone's disadvantage. Thus if all goes well the IMF can create a "focal point" for agreement between creditors and debtors.

Obviously this role depends on the IMF having sufficient credibility. Where does this credibility come from? In part it may come from the willingness of creditor country governments to back up the IMF with pressures on banks to go along, and sanctions against countries that fail to cooperate; in part from the fact that the IMF is better able than the banks to dictate and monitor the policies of debtor countries; in part from the usefulness of IMF conditionality as an excuse for painful policies that countries would have undertaken in any case. A final source of the IMF's ability to play a role, however, is the fact that it is itself an important source of funds. This brings us to the most controversial part of this issue: the case for official lending as a part of debt strategies.

The case for official lending

The narrow financial argument for official involvement in international debt issues is, as we have seen, essentially that creditors need to be coerced into engaging in the defensive lending that is in their own interests. This seems to suggest that the funds for defensive lending should come from the creditors themselves. How, then, can we justify the fact that some of the lending to problem debtors is in fact provided by official sources such as the IMF, the World Bank, and industrial country governments?

For countries that have largely borrowed from official sources, the answer is of course that these sources are themselves the major creditors. That is, even if those agencies and governments that have lent to low-income Africa in the past were now to take a purely financial view of their interests, it would make sense for them to continue lending to protect their investment. The controversial question, however, is whether official lending should play an increased role for countries that have borrowed primarily from private sources.

One answer is to point to justifications for official involvement that go beyond the narrow financial issue of maximizing the value of claims on the debtor nations. We consider these justifications below. Even with this narrow objective, however, it is possible to offer two justifications for at least some official lending.

The first justification is that efforts to overcome the free rider problem are imperfect in their effect, so that in practice only part of the creditors provide all of the defensive lending. There is then a danger that the rate of growth of exposure of these creditors required to provide an adequate flow of capital may be more than they are willing to offer, even though the level of defensive lending is still appropriate for the creditors as a whole. In this situation official finance can take some of the burden off these core creditors, making the debt strategy feasible when this would not otherwise be the case.

The other justification is that official lending enhances the ability of the IMF and other official bodies to play the mediating role described above. That is, the credibility of an IMF-proposed solution will be substantially enhanced if the other parties know that agreement will bring several billion dollars of IMF and other official funds with it.

One question that is often raised is whether official lending to problem debtors constitutes some form of "bail-out" for the creditors. The usual answer is that it does not, because the IMF receives market interest on its lending, and because the creditors are simultaneously increasing rather than reducing their exposure. As it is sometimes put, it is a "bail-in" rather than a bail-out. In fact, however, official lending is costly, because it, like private loans, carries a risk of non-payment that is by definition substantial for a problem debtor. And official lending takes the place of defensive lending that banks would have found it in their interest to undertake in any case (though they might not have been able to act in their own interest). So the answer is that official lending does constitute a bail-out -- which is not to say that it is necessarily undesirable.

Broader arguments for intervention

So far we have focussed on the narrowly financial case for government intervention, by which we mean justifications for intervention designed purely to minimize the loss in value of creditor country claims on problem debtors. Such a narrow focus is useful as a way of isolating some key arguments. Clearly, however, this is not the whole of either the actual or the appropriate reason for official concern and intervention. This is especially true because multilateral agencies, while powerfully influenced by creditor-country concerns, are not simply these countries' agents. Thus, we turn next to some broader arguments for an official role.

Safeguarding the financial system

One important argument for official concern about the debt problem is that losses by banks can have larger consequences than if the losses were simply to occur to individual bondholders. The reason is the role of banks as financial intermediaries. This role means both that banks are highly leveraged, with their net worth much less than their assets, and that insolvency by major banks could disrupt the workings of the financial system.

The key point is that although bank claims on problem debtors are only a small fraction of the wealth of the industrial countries, in aggregate they considerably exceed the net worth of the banks. Some illustrative figures are provided in table 3. These figures show that if the problem debtors were to repudiate all or most of their debt, the effect could be to put many of the major United States banks out of business. This in turn could disrupt the normal functioning of financial markets. If the monetary authorities of the United States and other industrial countries were to remain passive in the face of these disruptions, the result could be a severe monetary contraction reminiscent of the early 1930s.

Now in fact even in the worst case this will not happen. The Federal Reserve and other monetary authorities have sufficient instruments available to keep the banking system operating, and are both able and willing to supply enough liquidity to prevent a debt repudiation from leading to a depression. The problem is instead that the rescue operation that the Federal Reserve is certainly capable of mounting would lead to a de facto nationalization of the major United States banks. This would be administratively, politically, and ideologically awkward. The United States Government and the governments of other industrial countries would certainly prefer to avoid this happening, even at the cost of a mixture of coercion and bail-out of the banks.

Trade-finance linkages

The consequences of debt problems for the industrial countries of course go beyond the banking system. The rapid shift of debtor nations into trade surplus from 1981 to 1984 had as its counterpart a sharp fall in industrial country exports to these countries, and to a lesser extent a rise in debtor exports to the OECD. This trade finance linkage is often cited as a reason for official concern with the debt problem.

This issue is often stated as a simple one of employment: lost exports to developing countries cost jobs in the United States and other industrial nations. To put the issue this way is, however, to oversimplify. The overall level of employment in industrial countries is not really constrained by an inability to generate demand. Rather, the problem is that the governments of these countries are unwilling to allow demand to grow because of concerns about inflation. Let us suppose that Latin American demand for United States exports had not fallen so much from 1981 to 1983; then the Federal Reserve, which is clearly attempting to restrain growth so as to avoid reigniting inflation, would have found itself obliged to be more restrictive in its monetary policy. To a first approximation, one may reasonably assert that the debt crisis has had no effect on aggregate employment in the industrial world.

The real trade-finance issue is less simple. It concerns the effects of the debt crisis on the composition of employment in the industrial countries, and through this on the sustainability of the world trading system. Although the employment effects of import cuts and export promotion by debtors can be offset by employment creation elsewhere, for the individuals and firms affected the loss is nonetheless real. The political consequences are serious, particularly in the United States. With export demand from developing countries sharply reduced, United States firms that have relied on these exports no longer see the maintenance of a relatively open world trading system as an important objective, removing one of the main supports of a liberal trade policy. At the same time, as debtor countries attempt to increase their exports they stir up protectionist responses. These combined effects increase the strain on a world trading system that is already in serious difficulty because of the over-valued dollar and persistent high unemployment in Europe.

What is particularly worrisome about the trade-finance linkage is that it has the potential of feeding on itself. If the industrial countries respond to the attempts of debtor nations to run trade surpluses with protectionist measures, this will deepen the financial problems of these nations, forcing them into more urgent efforts to promote exports and restrain imports. This may seem to be an unrealistically self-defeating loop for the industrial countries to get into, but an examination of the level of much public discussion is not encouraging. The recent proposals for a retaliatory tariff against Brazil on the grounds that it runs an excessive trade surplus suggest that many influential policy makers either do not understand or choose not to understand the trade-finance linkage.

Political and security consequences

An obvious and important reason for official involvement in the debt problem is the concern that debt problems could lead to political instability. The different actors in the debt situation have widely varying political views and objectives, but one need not accept the foreign policy goals of any particular group to be worried about the political consequences of the severe austerity we have documented above.

The fact is that so far the political consequences of the debt crisis have been remarkably subdued. In Latin America the drift since 1982 has if anything been toward increased democracy and civilian rule. Africa presents a less favourable picture. On the whole, however, the political instability that one might well have expected from the sharp deterioration of living standards and the rise in unemployment has not materialized.

This is of course no guarantee that the political consequences will remain mild. Concern about the eventual consequences of "debtor fatigue" -- especially if, as we have suggested, creditors are increasingly seen as not living up to their side of the bargain -- is or should still be a major justification for official involvement.

Social and humanitarian concerns

The social and humanitarian issue as a reason for official involvement in the debt crisis is listed last here, not because it ought to be last in importance, but because realistically it carries much less policy weight than the other concerns. Nevertheless, there is a degree of altruistic interest in the welfare of others in the economically advanced nations.

Where social and humanitarian concerns could play a significant role in creditor-country policy is in Africa. As we have noted, African debt is small in absolute terms, constituting less than 10 percent of developing country debt and less than 5 percent of the private bank claims on developing countries. Yet the debt is a severe burden because of the poverty of the African economies. Indeed, for large numbers of Africans the ability of their governments to cope with debt problems may literally be a life and death issue. What this means is that debt relief that is substantial from the point of view of the people of Africa might not loom large to the creditor nations.

The interests of the debtor countries

So far we have examined the incentives for intervention by creditor-country governments and international agencies that presumably reflect a somewhat broader set of interests. The third set of players is the debtor country governments. How do they fit in?

The incentive for a debtor not to pay is obvious. The question for debtors is therefore what are the incentives to accept the burden of debt service rather than declaring a moratorium or otherwise failing to honour the terms of the original loans. These incentives may be grouped under four headings: maintenance of current capital flows, maintenance of the option of future access to the international capital market, maintenance of trading relationships, and a set of broader concerns.

The first incentive is unambiguous: if a country is receiving current capital inflows that exceed debt service, and a failure to maintain full debt service would cut off these funds, then a debt moratorium would actually worsen the country's cash flow. Equally, a country has nothing to gain from unilateral action on debt if it is running a non-interest current-account deficit. Here there is a sharp contrast between Africa and Latin America. The low-income African countries as a group, despite the fall-off in capital inflows described above, continue to receive net inflows that substantially exceed their interest payments. By contrast, the Latin American debtors have, since the onset of the debt crisis, been running large non-interest surpluses, and in some cases even overall surpluses on current account.

The second incentive is a real concern but much more difficult to quantify. A country may choose to service its debt, even though this worsens its current cash flow, in order to retain the flexibility of future access to world capital markets. There are at least two levels of uncertainty about this incentive. The first is the question of how costly a loss of future ability to borrow would be; there is a theoretical economic literature on this issue, but that literature is notably lacking in operational content. Furthermore, there is a good deal of dispute about the link between payment of debt and future ability to borrow. How long would a country that unilaterally wrote down its debt have to wait before it was once again able to raise money on international markets? For that matter, how long will it be before countries that do <u>not</u> take such action are again able to borrow? The truth is that we have very little idea.

Concern over trade access is a major reason why debtors have been willing to adjust as much as they have. Under some scenarios, a debt moratorium or repudiation could set in motion a cascading series of legal actions that would strangle the country's normal channels of international trade. Whether this would happen in fact -- indeed, whether creditor country governments would allow it to happen -- is more doubtful, but the risk that it might happen is not something we can dismiss completely.

Finally, debtor countries, like creditors, have interests that go beyond narrow financial ones. International debt is part of a much broader network of economic and other linkages. Some of these linkages are quite direct: if Mexico or Brazil were to take a hard line on debt, they might find the United States even less forthcoming on issues of protectionism and immigration than it has been. Others are fuzzier: there is surely at least some linkage between a government's ability to appear credible in its domestic policies and its demonstrated willingness to honour international commitments.

The noteworthy point is that three of the four incentives for debtor countries to maintain debt service are of highly uncertain magnitude, and that the certain incentive applies only to the low-income official borrowers. What this means is that while African debt reform must wait on the creditors, there is always the possibility that Latin American debt "reform" will take the form of refusal by the debtors themselves to pay in full. Such an action by debtors would clearly run more risks than a debt reform agreed to by all parties. It remains, however, a fairly likely outcome.

Possible dimensions of debt reform

We have now described a number of arguments for the involvement of international organizations and creditor country governments in the developing country debt problem. As we have seen, from 1982 to 1985 this involvement took the form of a series of *ad hoc* interventions rather than a concerted plan of international debt reform. Discussion of international debt reform is once again in the air. Before we can discuss actual proposals for reform, however, we need to understand what debt reform would mean.

The answer is of course that a debt reform plan could have several possible dimensions. To introduce some order into our discussion, it will be useful to review these possible dimensions of debt reform.

The essential point may be briefly stated. In the absence of debt reform, debtor countries would be forced either to run large trade surpluses to service their debt, or to declare unilateral moratoria on debt service and risk the consequences. If one proposes a reform scheme, one must make two crucial choices. The first is that of procedural reform vs. reduced adjustment burden. That is, will the debt reform simply try to improve the way in which the current level of financing is provided, or will it attempt to reduce the level of trade surplus that the debtor countries are obliged to run? To the extent that a debt reform does allow countries to run smaller trade surpluses, the issue then becomes one of stretch-out vs. write-down. That is, is the reduced burden on the country a temporary relief that must be compensated for by increased payments in the future, or is it provided by reducing the present value of the country's obligations? Obviously a debt reform scheme can combine all of these features, but it is useful to begin by thinking of them separately.

Procedural reform vs. reduced adjustment burden

Many proposals for international debt reform call for a revision of procedures that will not affect the required trade performance of debtors -- except to the extent that the new procedures work, and the old do not. A good example is a switch from year-by-year rescheduling to multi-year rescheduling agreements. This does not change the expected payments of the debtors: nobody expects that on net the problem debtors will repay principal on their medium and long-term debt over the next few years. What it does do is reduce the number of recheduling negotiations that must take place, and -- it is to be hoped -- minimize the risk that such negotiations could break down.

Procedural reforms may be valuable, and in fact there has been some move to adopt such proposed procedural reforms as multi-year rescheduling, longer maturities on new loans, creation of secondary markets, and so on. What procedural reforms do not do is reduce the burden of adjustment on the debtor countries. If Brazil's principal is rescheduled for the next four years instead of being rescheduled in four separate negotiations, this does not change the fact that Brazil is required to run a trade surplus large enough to pay interest on its debt less any net new lending. That is, procedural reforms can deal only with technical financial issues, not with the fundamental economic problem of servicing the debt. It is of course possible that an otherwise sound debt strategy will fail because of technical issues, so that procedural reforms are not to be neglected. But if "debtor fatigue" will undermine a debt strategy that is working perfectly at a technical level, then it is necessary to go beyond procedural reform to reduce the adjustment burden.

Stretch-out vs. write-down

To reduce the current adjustment burden on a debtor country -- that is, to reduce the size of the trade surplus that a country is required to run -- the country must of course be allowed on net to pay less to its creditors currently. The issue of stretch-out vs. write-down is whether the creditors as a group are fully compensated for this reduced current receipt. In a strech-out plan, the reduction of current debt service is in effect relent to the country at market interest, so that the increased claims on the country's future earnings fully offset the reduced current payments. The <u>ad hoc</u> debt strategy since 1982 has of course been one of stretch-out in this sense. Some debt reform schemes that would radically change the nature of the debt, such as the Bailey plan described below, may also be regarded as strech-out rather than write-down schemes because the new financial instruments they introduce are expected to be seen by creditors as equal in value to the conventional loans they replace.

Suppose, however, that one concludes that debtor nations either cannot, even in the long run, pay the present value of their current debt or should not be obliged to do so. Then stretch-out is not enough, and must be supplemented with write-downs that reduce the present value of the debt. The best-known example of a write-down proposal is of course the Rohatyn plan that calls for a conversion of developing country debt to long-term debt at a reduced interest rate. Although the face value of this debt might be unchanged from the original debt, its market value would of course be less; thus in effect a write-down would have taken place.

Reforming conditionality

We have emphasized the effect of debt reform on the size of the trade balance adjustment that countries are obliged to make. In fact, however, the debt burden has not been solely defined by the trade balance adjustment. As part of the "conditionality" that the IMF imposes as a condition for lending, nations must agree to changes in specific domestic policies as well. These domestic policy changes typically include budget restriction and credit constraints as well as measures targeted at the trade balance specifically.

The important point is that the policies demanded under IMF conditionality place a high weight on fiscal discipline and control of inflation through demand restriction. As a result, they may have imposed more severe recessions and greater shortfalls in economic growth than were necessary to acheive the actual improvements in trade balances. Although most debt reform schemes do not address this issue, many observers -- including, apparently, some United States government officials -- believe that countries should be allowed to achieve their trade surpluses with more "expenditure-switching" and less "expenditure-reducing" policies, thus reducing the domestic sacrifice needed.

The experience of Brazil during 1985 lends some credence to this view. Brazil essentially defied domestic conditionality, failing to reduce its budget deficit or reduce an inflation rate in excess of 200 per cent. Nonetheless, Brazil continued to run a very large trade surplus, and at the same time experienced a notable revival of economic growth to more than 6 percent.

The issue of reforming conditionality is an extremely important one. To address it adequately, however, would require a careful discussion of the macro-economics of high-debt developing countries, something that is beyond the scope of this paper. Thus our discussion of debt reform focusses on the financial aspects of reform, even though the method of adjustment may be equally important.

Who pays for reform?

Not all reform carries a price tag. Procedural reform, if well conceived, should make all parties better off. If promises of future payments are credible, a stretch-out does not reduce the value of creditors' claims. But a write-down, or a stretch-out that lacks credibility and is perceived as a write-down, involves a cost that someone must bear.

The key point here is that the structure of the debt means that private creditors can be made to bear only limited costs of reform. Private claims on developing countries are primarily loans from banks whose capital is small relative to their assets; their deposits are to a large extent explicitly insured and to an even greater extent implicity insured by the desire of creditor country governments to protect their financial systems. In other words, only the stockholders can be made to swallow losses, and the bank stockholders are not a large enough group to finance any very generous debt reform. As can be seen in table 3, any large write-down would threaten the solvency of the largest banks.

The clear implication is that a debt reform that does involve a large element of write-down would have to be officially financed. This is true even for those countries that have borrowed primarily from private lenders, and is <u>a fortiori</u> true of countries, especially in Africa, that have borrowed from official sources. Thus to the question of who pays for debt reform, the answer must be that if the price is large the bill falls on taxpayers in the creditor countries.

A preliminary view of reform options

In Section III we examine explicitly the most influential reform proposals that have been offered. It is, however, useful to begin with a preliminary overview of the elements that appear in many of these proposals. Aside from fairly minor procedural changes, there seem to be three main ideas for debt reform. The first is to change the <u>nature</u> of the claims that banks have on developing countries, either by handling the process of financing in ways contrary to normal banking practice or

by converting bank loans into some other kind of asset. The second is
to change the ownership of the claims by consolidating the debt of
developing countries in the hands of a new intermediary, with existing
creditors now having claims on that intermediary. Finally, the third
idea is to change the value of the claims by reducing interest rates or
otherwise providing debt forgiveness.

Changing the nature of the claims

The argument for a change in the nature of the claims on problem
debtors may be considered as analogous to the argument, common in
business, that the term of lending for a project should be matched to
the likely returns from that project. If an investment is expected to
yield returns only gradually over a twenty-year period, financing that
investment with three-year loans is setting oneself up for financial
trouble.

The analogy with countries is as follows: the expected net
payments to creditors of high-debt developing countries are not at all
well matched with their legal debt-service obligations. Since debtor
countries are expected to run current account deficits for the
foreseeable future, their nominal indebtedness will grow over time.
This is in fact what everyone expects, and is generally regarded as
sustainable as long as GNP and exports grow faster. But servicing the
loans will require that existing debt be retired, and even if all
principal is rescheduled will not allow that debt to grow. The result
will be a perennial need for new financing, and thus (perhaps) a
continual risk of crisis.

What many reformers have proposed is that the de facto expectation
that debt will grow, not shrink, be reflected in the nature of
creditors' claims. Two ideas in particular have emerged. The first is
that interest as well as principal be included in rescheduling
agreements, so that the exposure of existing creditors grows
automatically. The point is that the current debt strategy calls for
new lending by the existing creditors, and this lending is to all
intents and purposes forced rather than voluntary. In the view of its
advocates, rescheduling interest would simply make this process
explicit, and perhaps more effective.

The other principal idea is that conventional debt be converted
into equity-like claims on a country's foreign exchange earning
capacity. Assuming that this capacity grows, the payments on these
claims would then automatically grow over time.

Changing the ownership of claims

Many debt reform proposals envisage elimination of the direct
claims of private creditors on developing countries. Instead, these

claims would be assumed by an official agency of some kind -- prominent candidates are either a new agency or a new arm of the World Bank. The private creditors would in turn acquire claims on the new agency. Some proposals add that these claims would be insured by creditor country governments.

Creation of a new official intermediary to hold developing country debt is appealing for four main reasons. First, by insulating the banks from the direct consequences of any national failure to pay such an intermediary would in effect safeguard the financial system. Second, once debt is consolidated in a single agency's hands the free rider problem discussed at length above will no longer obtain. Third, creation of an intermediary has technical advantages as a way of bypassing certain accounting and regulatory obstacles to debt reform. Finally, the process of transfer of claims to such a new intermediary is in some schemes also the vehicle for an official buyout of debt.

Changing the value of claims

Some debt reform proposals call for strictly limited reductions in bank claims on developing countries, such as reductions in spreads above LIBOR and reduction of fees. These proposals could be financed by the banks themselves, which is to say by their stockholders. Realistically, bank stockholders do not themselves value claims on debtor nations at par. Reductions in spreads and fees might well raise the expected value of claims on debtors even though it lowers the legal obligation, and thus may not impose any costs at all.

A write-down of debt large enough to make a major difference in national obligations, on the other hand, would threaten the solvency of major banks. Thus official funds would have to be injected. This could be accomplished, for example, by creating a new official intermediary that buys up bank claims at a moderate discount and then restructures its claims on debtors at strongly concessional rates; the difference between the payments received by this intermediary and its obligations to the banks would then be met by creditor country governments.

III. A SURVEY OF MAJOR REFORM PROPOSALS

The purpose of this section is to review some of the proposals for debt reform that have received the most attention. This is not intended as a comprehensive review of all proposals, which would involve considering at least three dozen proposals, many of them similar to one another, many of them clearly misconceived. In any case a number of surveys of this kind already exist. Instead the intention here is to discuss proposals that are both representative and at least potentially sensible.

Following our earlier discussion, the proposals will be grouped under four headings. First are proposals for procedural reform that are not intended to change the burden on the debtor nations themselves. Next are proposals to change the nature of the claims on developing countries in such a way as to reduce their current debt service without reducing the value of these claims to creditors. Third are proposals to consolidate claims in the hands of a new financial institution of some kind that becomes an intermediary between the banks and the debtor nations. Finally are proposals to write down the debt, perhaps sufficiently so as to require injection of official money.

Procedural reforms

Multi-year rescheduling

Continued rescheduling of debt for at least the next several years is taken for granted even by those most optimistic about the debt situation. Since the rescheduling must happen, there is a strong case to be made for doing it now rather than in repeated negotiations. The counter-argument is that creditors want to keep debtors on a "short leash" so as to be able to enforce sufficiently stringent adjustment policies. Increasingly, however, the control gained by this short leash has come to seem illusory. Thus, multi-year rescheduling has come to seem mutually advantageous to both sides.

Multi-year rescheduling and the next proposal, lengthening of maturities, are unique among the proposals we will consider here in that they have already been put into practice in a major way. In September 1984 Mexico negotiated a rescheduling that covered principal due over the period 1985-1990. This negotiation also involved a conversion of some debt into longer maturities. As a partial compensation for the loss of their "short leash", banks were given a mechanism for calling off the rescheduling if they are dissatisfied with Mexican policy (this process is tied to the IMF's Article IV consultations with the Mexican Government).

The shift to multi-year rescheduling is, as we have noted already, a good example of a purely technical change. It does not change the cash flow position of the debtors, since there was no question that debt would be rescheduled in any case. The gain is instead one of increased certainty and reduced risk that technical factors will give rise to a crisis.

Longer maturities

A conversion of debt to longer maturities is to some extent a substitute for rescheduling. Again, some conversion of this kind was a part of the September 1984 Mexican package.

More extensive conversion to longer maturities is a feature of a number of debt proposals. The well-known Rohatyn proposal, which we will discuss below, includes a restructuring of debt into 15-30 year bonds as one of its elements; similar lengthening of maturity characterizes related proposals by Kenen and others.

Some proposals have gone even further. In particular, Gutentag and Herring (1985) have proposed elimination of principal repayment altogether, by issuance of consols to replace existing debt.

Insurance and secondary markets

The two proposals considered above are aimed at smoothing out the relations between banks and creditors. A different kind of technical proposal is essentially interbank in its orientation. These are schemes to help banks spread the risks of their claims on developing-country debtors, either by insuring the risks or by selling some of their claims on a secondary market.

One might ask why these schemes require official help; why don't the banks themselves create these markets? In fact some secondary sales do take place -- the prices on those sales are important clues to the expectations of the banks. Attempts have also been made to develop private insurance arrangements, although apparently without success. The argument of proponents of a deliberate policy of encouraging risk-spreading is that the markets are too thin, and that it is desirable to have either governments or official agencies serve as market-makers. (An alternative hypothesis is that moral hazard problems are inhibiting the development of these markets. We will return to this possibility in Section IV of the paper.)

Insurance and secondary markets would be essentially the same in their implications for both banks and the financial system as a whole. In each case the risk of default by a particular developing country would be spread more widely, presumably both improving the position of a bank itself and also reducing the threat that such defaults could leave banks that participated heavily in North-South lending insolvent. Nonetheless, policy proposals for the two cases are quite different.

Proposals for official encouragement of insurance, advanced by among others Witteveen (1983), Lever (1983), and Zombanakis (1983), envisage the creation of an official insurance institution. This institution, in addition to charging a fee, would restrict its operation to particular classes of loans, say those associated with high-conditionality IMF programmes. The important point, however, would be that, in the event of a failure to pay, the losses would have to be absorbed by the institution and thus indirectly by creditor-country governments.

By contrast, proposals for encouragement of a secondary market, of which Gutentag and Herring (1985) is the best known, cast official institutions in the role of market-makers rather than risk-bearers. In the Gutentag-Herring proposal the IMF purchases some loans and "packages" them for resale, thereby creating a secondary market without itself taking a permanent stake in that market.

Changing the nature of claims

The purpose of changing the nature of claims on debtor nations is to bring the time profile of their debt service obligations into line with a plausible path of repayment, and thus to limit or eliminate the need for the countries to raise further new money. Proponents of these schemes usually believe that the new instruments they create will ease the problems of the debtors without reducing the value of the claims to creditors.

In a logical sense we might think of proposals for new instruments as being simply an extension of the idea of converting debt to longer maturities. However, the three proposals we will consider -- interest capitalization, indexed loans, and exchange participation notes -- all involve creation of securities that are in effect of longer maturity than consols. That is, they would create a situation in which the nominal value of a claim on a debtor grows rather than shrinks over time. This is sufficiently unconventional to warrant discussion under a separate heading.

Interest capitalization

The debt strategy developed in 1982-3 relied on new lending by existing creditors as an essential ingredient. That is, in effect the strategy called on banks to convert part of their interest receipts into increased claims rather than actually collect them. At the same time, we know that such relending of interest depends on collective action by creditors that is difficult to enforce, and in fact the growth of bank exposure in high-debt developing countries has ceased. This leads to the natural suggestion that the process of capitalization of interest receipts be made explicit. Interest capitalization has been widely discussed among bankers and government officials, but has found its way into few published debt reform proposals. Three exceptions are Dornbusch and Fischer (1984), who eventually opt for a limited write-down instead, Krugman (1985), where the idea is treated favourably but no specific proposal is offered, and most recently an explicit proposal by Robichek (1985).

The advantages sought by advocates of interest capitalization are in part similar to those sought by advocates of multi-year rescheduling. An agreement to capitalize interest over a period of several years would reduce the need for repeated negotiations over additional finance. More important, however, is the hope that an explicit process of interest capitalization would do better at coping with the free rider problem than the informal pressures that are supposed to lead creditors to relend interest under the current strategy.

Opposition to interest capitalization seems to stem from two sources. First, some banks are concerned that if the process of relending interest is made automatic the incentives for countries to pursue effective adjustment will be reduced. This is of course the "short leash" idea revisited. Second, capitalization of interest would raise difficult problems of accounting and bank regulation, since it would go against what is normally regarded as sound practice to count loans whose interest is automatically relent as performing loans.

Indexed loans

One reason why the ability of countries to repay debt can be expected to grow over time is inflation, which, other things being equal, reduces the real burden of debt service. Several proposals for debt reform suggest that the time profile of debt service can be brought more into line with likely repayment paths by converting debt into loans whose principal is indexed to some measure of inflation, such as United States wholesale prices or world export prices. Such debt would bear a correspondingly lower rate of interest, so that initially debt-service payments would be reduced. Eventually the indexation of the principal would mean larger debt service than otherwise, but this would come at a time when inflation had made such payments easier.

Indexed loans have been proposed as part or all of a debt strategy by a number of authors. Exactly why they have not been taken more seriously is somewhat puzzling -- part of the larger puzzle of why indexed financial instruments are so rare in general except under extreme inflation. In any case, we may note that the sharp disinflation in the industrial countries makes the importance of indexation less than it would have been a few years ago.

Exchange Participation Notes

One of the more intriguing suggestions for a change in the nature of claims on developing-country debtors has been the proposal of Bailey (1983) that fixed-interest claims be replaced with shares in a country's exports, which he calls Exchange Participation Notes. Related proposals have suggested alternatively that debt service be limited to a fixed share of export earnings and that any difference between these payments and normal debt-service obligations simply be capitalized at the loan interest rate.

The idea of Exchange Participation Notes takes the logic of matching obligations to likely net payments one step beyond indexation. It does so by taking into account not only growth in ability to pay due to inflation but also growth in real export capacity (presumably related to economic growth in general).

If there were no uncertainty, Exchange Participation Notes would amount simply to another way of achieving the same goals as interest capitalization. Since in fact the growth of exports is uncertain, however, EPNs would distribute risk differently. On one side, countries would find their risk reduced, because their obligations would vary with their actual earnings. On the other side, banks would find themselves exposed in a direct way to country export uncertainty. (It is of course arguable that, given the possibility of default, banks are de facto exposed to this risk in any case.)

Changing the ownership of claims

Many debt reform proposals have as their centerpiece the transfer of claims on high-debt developing countries from private creditors to an official institution. Such proposals may be divided into two groups. First are proposals that call for official takeover only of the incremental role of commercial banks, i.e., that call for an official institution to provide new lending to debtor nations. Second are proposals that call for an overall takeover of debt, with banks receiving claims on the new institution in exchange.

Official incremental lending

Two proposals for official incremental lending have received substantial attention. One is the plan proposed by Soros (1984), who proposes that a new International Lending Agency take over the role of private bank involuntary lending. The ILA would borrow its funds on the private market, enabled to do so by guarantees provided by industrial-country governments. Charges on both creditors and debtors would be used to build up a capital base which would, if all went well, eventually allow the government guarantee to be withdrawn.

Mahbub ul Haq (1984) has proposed that the IMF consolidate new lending packages under a Debt Refinancing Subsidiary, which would in effect act as an intermediary between lenders and the debtor nations.

Official takeover of debt

Finally we come to the most famous of debt reform proposals, the Kenen (1983) and Rohatyn (1983) plans.

Kenen's plan is the milder of the two. He calls for the creation of a new entity, the International Debt Discount Corporation, which would offer to buy up loans to a specified list of countries at a modest discount from face value (10 percent in the original proposal). The discount would allow the IDDC to offer some interest forgiveness to the countries; the IDDC would also extend the maturity of debt.

Rohatyn's plan similarly calls for a buy-out of debt by an official agency -- he suggested the IMF, the World Bank, or a new agency created for the purpose. In contrast to the Kenen plan, however, this agency would buy debt with its own, low-interest bonds, presumably implying that banks would take a substantial capital loss (although this loss might be minimized for accounting purposes). The agency would then offer debtor countries both a stretch-out of debt and a reduction in interest rates, with the intention of reducing debt service to no more than 25 to 30 percent of exports.

As we will see in our quantitative discussion of debt relief below, to reduce debt service to the levels suggested by Rohatyn would require that either the discount at which debt is acquired would have to be large enough to place the solvency of major banks in question, or there would have to be a substantial injection of official funds in some form. While no formula is proposed, Rohatyn has made it clear that he would envisage that some of the losses would be absorbed by industrial country governments rather than by the private creditors.

Changing the value of claims

The final category of possible debt reform is that of debt relief pure and simple: writing down the claims on developing countries (typically interest rather than face value) so as to provide a reduction in their debt-service obligations at creditors' expense.

Few debt reform proposals allow explicitly for any write-down. The reason is obvious. On one hand, the size of developing-country debt relative to bank capital and earnings implies that any very large debt forgiveness cannot come entirely at the expense of bank stockholders without threatening the stability of the international financial system. On the other hand, the political climate is very unfavourable for any official injection of funds that can be seen as a bail-out for countries or banks. Thus, most debt reform proposals seek a "technical fix" that avoids the necessity for a large reduction in the present value of debt.

Nonetheless, the possibility of a substantial write-down is clearly apparent to many observers, and a few write-down schemes have been proposed.

A mild interest write-down proposal is offered by Dornbusch and Fischer (1984), who propose that interest rates on developing-country debt be reduced moderately for only the next few years. The intent is to provide some immediate debt-service relief but to limit the impact on the value of loans sufficiently so that the solvency of banks is not put at risk.

Congressman Schumer (1983) proposed a comprehensive interest rate reduction for troubled debtors, sufficient to ensure that, together with a strech-out of maturities, the burden of debt service would be reduced to levels comparable to those in Rohatyn's plan. The problem of bank solvency was not treated in his proposal, though the magnitude of the debt relief would surely make this an issue.

Finally, we have already noted that the Rohatyn plan contains a major element of debt relief.

IV. EVALUATING REFORM PROPOSALS

We have now described some of the major proposals for international debt reform. Our next task is to ask how these proposals stand up in the light of the conceptual framework developed in the previous section and the facts of the situation as described earlier.

The purpose of this discussion is, as we emphasized at the beginning of the paper, to provide an analytical basis rather than to make a final pronouncement.

Procedural reforms

Our discussion of procedural reforms mentioned multi-year rescheduling, extension of maturities, and the closely related issues of secondary markets and insurance. The first two seem clearly sensible and, as we noted, have already to some extent been put into effect. Insurance and secondary markets are, on the other hand, of much more questionable desirability.

Multi-year rescheduling and extension of maturities

The argument for multi-year scheduling and for lengthening of maturities is the straightforward one that problem debtor countries will not repay principal on net in the medium term whatever the banks do. Since this is the reality, one might as well recognize it explicitly and avoid unnecessary negotiation -- saving political and managerial resources for issues where the outcome is in fact negotiable.

The only argument against this is the alleged need to keep countries on a short leash. The point is of course that the banks do not have any ability to pull on that leash, because no creditor can in fact withdraw except at the expense of some other creditor. If the banks should at some point find that it is in their collective interest to call a country in default and invoke sanctions against it, they will surely not need the excuse of repeated rescheduling negotiations to do this.

Secondary markets and insurance

Several proposals urge that creditor governments and/or multilateral lending agencies encourage spreading of risk, either by acting as market-makers for secondary markets in developing-country loans or by providing new insurance facilities. It is not at all clear that this is a good idea. In fact, our conceptual framework, if anything suggests that it would be counterproductive.

There are two cases for encouraging a secondary market or insurance scheme. The first is the belief of some analysts that, by allowing a wider sharing of risk, it would encourage increased new lending to problem debtors. The second is the belief that risk-spreading would lessen the vulnerability of the financial system to a debt-created crisis.

The first of these arguments is definitely wrong. Under normal circumstances an increased ability to diversify risk may encourage new lending. For lending to problem debtors, however, the obstacle to voluntary lending is not the uncertainty but the expected return: claims on high-debt countries are not regarded as worth their par value, and no potential lender will voluntarily choose to convert a dollar into 80 cents, even if the 80 cents are risk-free. This also means that an insurance scheme, unless it is intended to serve as a disguised subsidy, will have to involve very high premiums -- high enough so that the cost of insuring a dollar's worth of claims is enough to reduce the value to something like 80 cents. Clearly, availability of such costly insurance will not bring new lenders into the market.

The second argument may have some validity. As we have seen, the risks to the financial system posed by developing-country debt stem not so much from the sheer size of that debt as from the way its ownership is concentrated in the hands of a few highly leveraged banks. It is possible that, with well-developed secondary markets and/or insurance markets, these vulnerable banks would choose to accept some losses or pay some insurance premiums in order to reduce their exposure, and that this would have the systemic benefit of reducing the risks of insolvency among major banks.

The major problem is, however, that the concentration of debt in the hands of a relatively small group, while it increases systemic vulnerability, is also a key to the maintenance of involuntary lending, which is essential to the current debt strategy. As we have seen, there is a conflict between the collective interest of creditors, which may call for defensive lending, and the individual interest of particular banks. To overcome this conflict we require collusive action on the part of the banks. If the ownership of claims on debtors becomes more widely diffused, the "free rider" problem becomes more severe -- and we have seen that it is already so severe that involuntary lending has ground to a halt.

In fact, we might argue that secondary markets or insurance would pose a moral hazard problem. Existing creditors who sold off some of their claims or took out insurance would then have a reduced incentive to participate in reschedulings and new loans. This would in turn reduce the value of the loans sold through the secondary market and reduce the expected return of the insurers.

It is worth recalling that the trend under the post-1982 debt strategy has been increasingly to rely on a core group of banks to provide new money. A larger secondary market/insurance market would erode the incentives of these banks to participate. Taken by themselves, then, these particular technical reforms would probably make the situation worse rather than better.

Changing the nature of claims

We have discussed three types of changed claim -- capitalization of interest, indexed loans, and exchange participation notes. Since indexing has lost some of its interest with lower inflation, however, let us focus on the other two.

Interest capitalization

The case for interest capitalization, like the case for multi-year rescheduling, is that it simply makes explicit something that must happen in any case. In the absence of interest forgiveness the nominal debt of developing countries with debt problems must be allowed to grow over time, and thus some relending of interest is essential. Why not, then, make the process explicit? There are two advantages to doing this. The first is the usual one of avoiding repeated renegotiations that take valuable managerial resources and also run the risk of a rupture. The second is that an explicit process of interest capitalization might help to "lock in" the banks that would otherwise be acting as free riders and failing to participate in the provision of new money.

One argument against interest capitalization rests on technical accounting grounds. The <u>de facto</u> interest capitalization under the post-1982 debt strategy, in which "new money" provided by existing creditors was used to pay interest, allowed banks to continue to report all of their interest receipts as income. Under current regulations explicitly capitalized interest could not be counted in this way, so that banks' reported income would drop. Since banks are in fact uncertain about the extent to which their claims will in the end be honoured, the current practice certainly overstates bank earnings; but counting none of the interest that is capitalized would go to the other extreme and would understate the earnings.

The other argument against interest capitalization is once again a version of the "short leash" argument: if the provision of new money is made institutionally too easy, debtor countries will not make sufficient adjustment efforts.

The problem is that the system of relending to cover part of interest, which was designed among other things to avoid the accounting problems associated with involuntary growth in exposure, has not been working. Banks have not been expanding their exposure, and countries, far from doing too little adjustment, have moved further into trade surplus than either was intended or is desirable. Thus, the time may have come to search for ways to accommodate interest capitalization within the accounting and regulatory framework.

Exchange participation

The appeal of exchange participation notes or some other system that allows debt service to grow with export earnings may be most strongly conveyed by numerical example. Suppose that a country is paying an interest rate of 10 per cent on its debt, and that this debt is three-and-one-half times the value of exports. Even with complete rescheduling of principal, the country would then have to make interest payments of 35 per cent of exports. Suppose, however, that the country's dollar exports can be expected to grow at 6 per cent a year: 3 per cent real, 3 per cent inflation. Then interest payments would shrink to 17.5 per cent of exports within 12 years, and 9 per cent in 24 years. The country might well prefer a more level debt burden.

Suppose now that all of the debt were converted to Bailey-style Exchange Participation Notes, entitling its owners to a fixed share of export revenues. If exports are definitely expected to grow at 6 percent, so will earnings on the notes. A straighforward calculation shows that the owners of the notes should consider a 14 percent share of exports as valuable as the original debt. Since 14 percent is a fairly modest number, the debt problem would thus seem to be solved.

This is not merely an accounting trick. In fact, the reasons why the case for Exchange Participation Notes looks so favourable are

precisely the reasons for which calculations such as those of Cohen
(1985) suggest that developing-country debtors ought to be solvent: the
ultimate burden of servicing debt is greatly reduced by growth and
inflation.

Despite the apparent favourable aspects of an exchange
participation scheme, Bailey's proposal and other related ones have met
with a generally negative response. There are three main complaints
about this kind of scheme, all of which seem on reflection to be fairly
weak.

The first criticism is that the novelty of proportional claims on
national export earnings would disturb financial markets, leading to an
excessive depression in the value of bank stocks. This may be true; but
it would seem then to be an argument against ever introducing any new
financial instrument.

The second criticism is that proportional claims on a country's
exports would not be credible; if exports were to grow rapidly,
countries would then be unwilling to honour their commitments. This is
true. However, conventional loans also have this problem, in reverse,
in that countries become unwilling to honour them if exports are low.
One might suppose that the incentive to meet foreign obligations and
thus retain normal access to world markets would be stronger for
countries doing well on those markets than for countries doing poorly,
and that the exchange participation might therefore be, if anything,
less subject to sovereign risk than are fixed-interest loans.

Finally, an objection to any shift to a new form of asset is that
it would force an accounting change. As long as the claims of banks on
developing countries are not transformed, and as long as the secondary
markets remain marginal, the banks can carry the loans on their books
at face value. With a change in their nature the loans would probably
have to be "marked to market", revealing a significant capital loss. If
other objections to exchange participation are surmounted, however,
this loss need be no larger than the losses that are already built into
bank stock prices. While there is a good case for avoiding
under-reporting of banks' true earnings that would result from interest
capitalization, it is not clear what purpose is served by seeking to
avoid reporting a loss which is genuine (in an expected sense at least)
and is probably already discounted by the market.

As in the case of interest capitalization, the point is that the
post-1982 strategy of reducing current debt service by relending
interest seems to have broken down. If that strategy were working
smoothly, it could reproduce the pattern of payments that are envisaged
under exchange participation without posing the awkward problems of
creating a new instrument, making it credible, and devising appropriate
accounting and regulatory treatment. Unfortunately, that is not the way
things are, so that more unconventional strategies now begin to make
more sense.

New institutions

Both the Kenen and Rohatyn plans for debt reform stress the creation of new institutions in whose hands debt would be consolidated. Despite the wide attention given to these plans, however, the advantages and disadvantages of a new official intermediary have not been as clearly discussed as they should be. We will discuss these advantages and disadvantages in general, then turn briefly to the content of these actual proposals.

Advantages of a new intermediary

Why is there any advantage in converting the direct claims of banks on countries into claims on an intermediary which in turn becomes the new creditor? Most proposals for such an intermediary are not too clear on this, but we can in fact identify at least four advantages (which must of course be set against disadvantages).

The first advantage is that once debt is concentrated in an intermediary's hands, the free rider problem will of course cease to be an issue. This advantage depends, however, on getting the potential free riders to be part of the consolidation, which may not be easy. Precisely those banks that are most likely to be able to free ride in the absence of an intermediary will also have the least incentive to transfer their claims to that intermediary. Thus this advantage may not be as easy to grasp as one might imagine.

The second advantage is that to the extent that a debt reform does involve an element of officially financed debt relief, an intermediary provides an easy channel for this relief. For example, in Rohatyn's plan the new institution buys out bank claims with bonds that offer less than market interest rates, and in turn reduces the interest rates on developing-country debt. An official contribution to debt relief would then naturally take the form of a subsidy that allows the instiution's lending rate to be below its borrowing rate.

The third advantage is in fact closely related: an official intermediary would offer a more attractive channel than other options for insulating the financial system from the effects of a major repudiation or write-down of developing country debt. Since the losses would now occur in the first instance to the intermediary rather than to the banks that have become its creditors, industrial country governments would be able to insure their solvency by aiding the intermediary, rather than having to undertake the de facto nationalization of the banking system that we described above.

The final advantage is a technical one, but possibly quite important. Creation of an intermediary might serve as a way to cut through the accounting and regulatory objections to unconventional

schemes such as interest capitalization and exchange participation.
Since this may not be obvious, it deserves a little more discussion.

Consider the example of interest capitalization. As we saw, this
could have a devastating impact on the reported earnings of banks,
because none of the capitalized interest could be counted as income.
Suppose, however, that banks exchange their claims for claims on an
official intermediary. There is then nothing to prevent the
intermediary from allowing debtor nations to capitalize some of their
interest. To do this would require that the intermediary initially be
able to borrow so as to pay interest to the banks; if claims on the
intermediary are guaranteed by a consortium of governments, as they
would have to be in any case, this should not be a problem.

Disadvantages of an intermediary

The most obvious disadvantages of an intermediary are that its
creation might turn into a bail-out either for the banks or for the
countries. In addition there is the problem, stressed by Cline (1984),
that consolidation of bank claims would take banks "off the hook",
eliminating the possibility of new involuntary lending.

The concern about a bail-out for banks is certainly justified.
Developing-country creditors do not expect with certainty that they
will be repaid; as we have seen, secondary market evidence suggests
that much of the debt is subjectively discounted by 20 percent or more.
A buy-out by a new intermediary at anything close to par would thus
indeed constitute a bail-out. Thus, in order to avoid a bail-out it
would be necessary that an intermediary make an effort to buy debt at a
discount comparable to what it would have been worth otherwise. Many
observers are sceptical about whether this is actually the way it would
turn out. We may note, however, that we have a reasonable idea about
what value banks place on their developing-country claims, and a
buy-out at much more than this would be conspicuous and would not go
unremarked in the United States Congress.

The concern about a bail-out for countries is equally realistic,
and perhaps not as easy to assuage. Basically the worry is that an
official creditor would not be as tough as private claimants. Without
the incentive of profit or the risk of bankruptcy, and with foreign
policy concerns tending to impinge on financial ones, an official
intermediary might tend to let debt restructuring slip into debt
forgiveness on a scale unintended by its founders. Against this, all
one can suggest is that the example of the IMF shows that it is not
impossible to create multilateral agencies that are fairly
tough-minded. In particular, any new organization would be under the
baleful eye of a populist United States Congress, so that with
appropriate institutional design one might not have to worry about
excessive willingness to give money away.

Beyond these concerns is the point emphasized by Cline, that debt consolidation will give creditors a chance to wash their hands of the debt problem and thus to cease involuntary lending. This point needs to be understood clearly. It has two aspects: the known need for an expansion of exposure, and the need for flexibility.

The first point is the familiar one that without a large write-off of debt we must expect the nominal indebtedness of problem debtors to grow rather than shrink over the near future. Under the post-1982 strategy this was supposed to be dealt with by new involuntary lending by existing creditors. Once these existing creditors have exchanged claims on the countries for claims on an official body they have no further stake in the countries and thus no incentive to continue lending.

This means that any new lending after a debt consolidation must come from official sources. The most plausible source is the new intermediary itself, which now has the same stake in defensive lending that the original creditors had. The problem is that in order to make this new lending the intermediary must itself borrow new money. It is not clear why this should be regarded as an insuperable problem. Admittedly the new lending will take place at an expected return below market rates, because of the continued risk of non-payment; but if the intermediary has been brought into existence properly it will have been compensated for this in advance by the discount at which it acquired bank claims.

A stronger argument is the loss of flexibility. If unanticipated developments required more lending than initially anticipated, the original creditors would no longer be on call to provide more involuntary loans. Again, however, what this requires is that the intermediary itself be able to borrow; if this can be arranged, there is no reason why the intermediary cannot then capitalize interest or make new loans. When it does this, of course, it will take losses in an expected sense. On the other hand, favourable developments will constitute gains for the intermediary. Ideally the discount at which the debt was acquired will offset the expected losses, though actual losses may be either more or less.

It is clear that many things could go wrong in the establishment and operation of a new intermediary. It would be misleading to assume that everything could be made to work out perfectly. On the other hand, a realistically sceptical view about such an intermediary should not be contrasted with an idealized view of the ad hoc debt strategy, which has also not worked out as it ideally might.

Debt relief

As we have noted, few proposals for debt reform make explicit allowance for debt relief, because the cost of such relief is seen as too large to be borne by banks, while a government assumption of the losses is politically unacceptable. The major exception is the Rohatyn plan, which calls for a combination of debt relief and stretch-out to lower debt service to permanently tolerable levels. Nonetheless, debt relief of some kind is clearly at least implicitly on the agenda, and the prospects need to be discussed.

Quantitative tradeoffs

As crucial background to the discussion of debt relief we need some idea of the tradeoff between reducing debt service and the capital losses to creditors. The original Kenen and, to some extent, Rohatyn proposals seem to have been marked by a failure to appreciate the size of capital losses that would occur if debt were written down sufficiently to make current debt service payable out of current export earnings. On the other hand, critics of these plans may not have noticed that the decline in interest rates during 1985 has made the size of these capital losses a good deal smaller. In other words, a Rohatyn-type plan, though it still implies large capital losses, looks substantially better now than it did when he first proposed it.

Consider the following example, intended to be representative of the situation of middle-income problem debtors. Suppose that a country has a debt-to-export ratio of 350 per cent, with this debt paying market interest plus a risk premium, and that it is proposed to convert this debt into long-term loans at a reduced interest rate, so as to reduce current debt service to a manageable level. How much will the present value of the claims be reduced?

The answer depends on three things. First is the initial interest rate. We will consider two cases: a "1984" case in which that rate is 14 per cent, and a "1986" case in which that rate is only 10 per cent. Second is the maturity of the new loans; we consider 15 and 30 years. Finally is the level of acceptable debt service; we consider 30, 25, and 20 per cent of exports.

Table 4 shows the value of the new claims as a percentage of the face value of the old claims under these different assumptions. The first part of the table conveys the point that has been made by critics of the Rohatyn plan, that debt relief large enough to produce an acceptable level of debt service would produce extremely damaging losses for the banks. For example, to reduce debt service to 30 per cent of exports -- still a heavy burden -- at 1984 interest rates would have required that banks take a 39.7 per cent capital loss on their debt.

Now it should be pointed out that claims on problem debtors are already implicitly discounted to some extent. If written-down debt carries a smaller discount than before, the net loss to the banks will be reduced. However, the numbers in the first part of table 4 are so large that the net loss would still be crippling, certainly putting the solvency of some major banks at risk.

The second part of table 4 shows that the decline in the interest rate makes this tradeoff a little less stark. Indeed, in one case -- 30 percent debt service and 30 year loans -- the reduction in value is no more than the current market discount on Brazilian and Mexican debt. This may seem to suggest that by writing down the debt in this way banks could actually offer debt relief without reducing the true value of their assets. It is unlikely, however, that the new loans would be valued by the market at par. Thirty percent debt service remains a heavy burden (though Brazil and Mexico paid more than this in 1984), which would still pose some risk of eventual failure to pay. Thus it is not true, or at any rate not yet true, that a once-and-for-all write-down of debt is in the banks' own interest. And an attempt to reduce the debt service to a level where the incentives for non-payment were much less would impose unacceptable losses on the banks, requiring some kind of official contribution to protect the financial system.

We should note, however, that this discussion of tradeoffs applies only to the Latin American case of large bank debt. Since the sums of money are much smaller and are primarily officially held, debt forgiveness for low-income Africa would carry neither the price tag nor the risks of relief for middle-income market borrowers. While this is not a likely outcome, all the debt of Africa's poorest countries could be written off with only slight budgetary impact on OECD countries and a minor impact on bank net worth.

Critique of debt relief plans

We have now seen that a debt relief plan sufficient to make the debt- service burden tolerable without new money would induce capital losses such that an official bail-out would probably be necessary. The basic criticism of such plans is the argument that this capital loss is unnecessary, because of the prospects for growth in countries' ability to service their debt. Converting the debt into long-term loans without ensuring a supply of new money requires that the country run a constant nominal trade surplus despite the fact that its exports can be expected to increase in volume and price. By allowing debt to expand, we can keep the initial debt-service burden manageable without such a large reduction in present value. This thinking underlies both the post-1982 debt strategy, with its reliance on involuntary lending, and such unconventional proposals as interest capitalization and exchange participation.

In the discussion of exchange participation above we saw that, given the same assumptions about initial debt and interest rates as are made in table 4, together with growth in exports of 6 per cent a year, a permanent devotion of 14 per cent of export revenues to debt payments would be sufficient to maintain the present value of the debt. By contrast, to reduce initial year payments to 20 per cent of exports using only the conventional instrument of long-term loans would reduce the value of the debt by 46 per cent.

Thus the basic criticism of debt relief schemes along the lines of the Rohatyn plan is that they are unnecessarily expensive because of their failure to take account of inflation and growth.

How might such debt relief schemes be defended? The answer is presumably to argue that while a debt strategy that allows for rising debt may look good on paper, it is not in fact feasible. The process of involuntary lending has indeed apparently run aground, unless the Baker plan can get it restarted. The remaining argument must be that such proposals as interest capitalization and exchange participation raise too many difficulties to be workable.

We have already noted that the arguments against debt relief lose much of their force in the African case. Nonetheless, even if debt relief is to be provided to Africa, it will arguably do more good for any given degree of relief if it is also combined with measures to ensure a continuing inflow of capital. Thus, for both market and official borrowers debt relief designed to solve the problem once and for all without allowing debt service to rise with growth and inflation is a bad bargain. However, there is no necessary reason why a debt relief scheme cannot also include a provision for such growth.

Combining debt relief with new money

The critique of debt relief just presented was a critique of the particular form in which the most popular plans are presented, namely, a reduction of the cash flow burden on countries achieved purely through debt relief without new money. However, there is no reason in principle why some debt relief could not be combined with a flow of new money. This might allow a smaller debt write-down, hopefully sufficiently smaller to make official bank bail-out unnecessary.

The problem of course is that countries that have in effect repudiated part of their debt are not likely to have access to new borrowing thereafter. However, one can conceive of two ways in which this problem might be circumvented.

The first is to arrange for the write-down to be, at least in a legal sense, a voluntary choice by the banks rather than an action of the debtor governments. This would require the establishment of a financial intermediary, which would buy up the debt from banks at less than par, but not at less than the current secondary market rate. The intermediary could then pass on the saving in the form of debt relief to the countries. Since the countries had not actually defaulted on their debt, there would be no legal obstacle to resumption of lending. At the same time, if the reduction in the debt burden were sufficient to restore confidence, new lenders might once again be willing to come forth. Of course, relying on this would be taking a serious risk.

The alternative would be to rely on official lending to reduce the cash flow burden after a moderate debt relief. This lending could take the form of conventional new loans. Alternatively, if the debt were assumed by a new intermediary, the intermediary could engage in interest capitalization or even exchange participation.

The advantage of such schemes would be that they could not only limit the amount of debt relief to a level that would not endanger the financial system, they might even limit the loss to the discount already placed on bank claims, and thus leave the banks no worse off. As always, the disadvantage is that they could be mishandled and end up as bail-out schemes.

V. CONCLUSIONS

This paper has touched on many issues. It does not attempt to make any particular recommendation for international debt reform in this section, but aims rather to review the key points of the preceding discussion.

The current state of international debt

The starting point for any discussion of the prospects for international debt reform must be an acknowledgement that the strategy adopted in 1982-3 for dealing with the debt crisis has not worked out as intended, and appears to have run aground. That strategy was based on the presumption that policy reforms in the debtor countries plus economic recovery in the industrial countries could restore normal conditions within a few years. The plan for market borrowers was that banks would continue to lend to problem debtors as an interim measure; the plan for official borrowers was that time would be provided through conventional rescheduling. At the same time, countries would pursue plans of manageable austerity. Normality would be restored when banks recovered confidence in market borrowers, and official borrowers were able to resume normal debt service.

As it turned out, the lending by banks did not materialize on anything like the scale envisaged. Correspondingly, Latin American debtor countries adjusted their trade balances more than anyone expected. These trade balance improvements were, however, achieved through austerity programmes of great severity, producing extraordinarily sharp falls in living standards. Meanwhile, the growing debt of low-income Africa still seems out of control.

At the end of 1985 the prospects for a return to normal capital markets seem if anything more remote than in 1983. The world economic recovery that was supposed to end the debt crisis has now run its course, leaving no strong reason to expect a major improvement in the

external environment of debtors over the next few years. Yet banks
continue to be unwilling to lend, and appear to value
developing-country debt at well below par.

Hopes for a revival of the 1982-5 debt strategy now rest on the
Baker plan for a new round of defensive lending by private banks,
matched by an equal commitment of funds from multilateral agencies.
Even if the Baker plan is accepted by the banks, however, past
experience suggests that it will at best only restore a situation
something like that of 1984, in which debtors ran huge trade surpluses,
and modest capital inflows were supplied predominantly by official
lenders.

The disappointing results of the post-1982 debt strategy provide
the impetus for a reconsideration of the case for debt reform.

Procedural reform

Many proposals about international debt are essentially procedural
reforms, in the sense that they change the mechanics of debt finance
without changing the cash flow of debtors. Of these, some seem clearly
sensible -- notably proposals to lengthen maturities and carry out
multi-year rescheduling.

Other proposals, to encourage the development of insurance
arrangements and secondary markets, are not as well thought out. They
will not produce new capital inflows to problem debtors. Indeed, by
diluting the incentives of creditors to engage in collective action
they might well reduce the ability of creditors as a group to engage in
new lending to defend the value of existing claims. That is, such
proposals might exacerbate the already serious problem of failure of
banks to expand their exposure.

In general procedural reforms have only limited usefulness. They
can help to prevent a debt strategy from foundering unnecessarily on
technical problems, but they cannot get that strategy afloat if it has
run aground on more fundamental issues.

Changing the nature of claims

Some important proposals call for changing the nature of the
claims that banks hold on developing countries. The general idea is to
replace the dependence of the current strategy on "involuntary" lending
by some mechanism whereby banks' exposure grows automatically. The most
influential of these ideas are interest capitalization and exchange
participation.

These proposals have problems. Changing the nature of claims would pose difficult accounting and regulatory issues, and there is concern that uncertainty about the meaning and reliability of the new techniques of financing would be disruptive. On the other hand, these proposals only seek to make explicit the reliance of debt service on new lending that was implicit in the strategy of 1982-5. It was easy to criticize such proposals when it was believed that involuntary lending would provide a way to accomplish the same ends; allowing new money to be formally separated from debt service is a good way to keep the accountants and regulators away. Since the process of involuntary lending has in fact ground to a halt, however, these proposals deserve a second look.

A new intermediary

The well-known Kenen and Rohatyn plans had as their centerpieces the creation of new intermediaries to take over claims on developing countries. At the time this idea was quickly rejected, because the creation of such a middleman would remove the incentive for new lending by the banks. Now that this new lending has been shown to be less forthcoming than expected, however, the idea of an intermediary is worth re-examining.

A re-examination shows that assumption of claims by a new institution could have some important benefits. It might provide an answer to the problems of collective action that have plagued the debt strategy. It would insulate the world financial system from the risk of disruption by sovereign debtors. It would provide a channel for official contributions toward debt relief, if these should be deemed desirable. And it would be useful as a way to get around some regulatory and accounting problems with such schemes as interest capitalization.

On the other hand, there are still serious problems with such an intermediary. The main objection in the end is probably that, unless handled with great skill, creation of such an institution could degenerate into a bail-out of banks and countries to an unintended degree.

Debt relief

Proposals such as Rohatyn's that call for a once-and-for-all write-down of debt sufficient to leave debt service manageable are extremely costly. This is true even though the fall in interest rates during the past year has made such schemes less costly than before. To bring debt service to 20-30 per cent of the *current* exports of high-debt nations simply through stretch-out plus reduced interest rates would impose losses that would threaten the solvency of major banks.

The point is that such extreme measures seem unnecessary. By allowing debt to grow at a modest rate, well below the likely rate of export growth, the same levels of debt service could be achieved with much smaller write-downs. The problem, of course, is getting the debt to grow; under the 1982-5 strategy this was supposed to be accomplished by involuntary bank lending. If this cannot be arranged, there is still a strong incentive to try a more innovative approach rather than accept the necessity of massive write-downs.

Some debt relief could, however, be granted without threatening the solvency of banks. It is conceivable that a debt reform that combined some debt relief at banks' expense with a change in the nature of claims could reduce the discount on developing-country debt so much that it actually leaves banks better off.

Debt relief to low-income official borrowers would be much less costly. Like relief to market borrowers, however, it would make most sense if combined with a mechanism that allows for continuing capital inflow.

Prospects for debt reform

It should be clear from the discussion in this paper that there is no simple panacea for the international debt problem. While some debt reform schemes look as though they should allow a smooth resolution of the issue, in practice they would pose tricky problems of implementation. No one proposal stands out as a clear answer.

The point is, however, that something must be done. It is possible that an updated version of the 1982-5 strategy, built around some version of the Baker plan, will be enough to buy time until things finally improve enough to restore voluntary lending and normal debt service. At this point, however, the odds on this look substantially less good than they did in early 1983. So we should be willing at least to consider a more comprehensive reform.

Table I: Debt Indicators, 1984

	Low-income Africa	Western Hemisphere
Debt/GNP 54.5	46.0	
Debt/Exports	278.1	280.0
Interest/GNP	2.1	4.6
Private debt as % of total	18.4	84.0
Total debt ($ billion)	27	351

Source: World Bank, World Development Report, 1985 and IMF, World Economic Outlook, 1985.

Table 2: Justifiable rates of exposure growth under defensive lending */

	Number of years lending is expected to last		
	3	5	10
Discount in absence of new lending			
.25	0.0	0.0	0.0
.35	11.2	6.7	3.4
.50	23.1	13.9	6.9
.75	36.6	22.0	11.0

*Assuming discount on claims given defensive lending of 0.25. For explanation of calculation, see text.

Table 3: Share of claims on developing countries
in bank capital, March 1984

	9 largest United States Banks	All United States Banks
7 problem debtors *	142.5	92.8
All developing countries	262.6	163.7

Source: UNCTAD, Trade and Development Report, 1985.

* Argentina, Brazil, Chile, Colombia, Mexico, Peru, Philippines.

Table 4: Value of loans as percent of par under
debt relief schemes *

A. Initial interest rate = .14		
	Maturity of loans	
	15	30
Debt service as % of exports		
30	53.7	60.3
25	44.8	50.3
20	36.8	40.2
B. Initial interest rate = .10		
	Maturity of loans	
	15	30
Debt service as % of exports		
30	66.6	81.4
25	55.5	67.9
20	44.4	54.3

*Assuming initial debt/export ratio of 3.5.

REFERENCES

Bailey, N.(1983): "A safety net for foreign lending", Business Week, January 10.

Bergsten, F.,Cline, W.R. and Williamson, J.(1985): Bank lending to developing countries: the policy alternatives, Institute for International Economics, Washington.

Cline, W.(1984): International debt: systemic risk and policy response, Institute for International Economics, Washington

Cohen, D.(1985): "How to assess the solvency of an indebted nation", Economic Policy (November).

Guttentag, J. and Herring, R.(1985): The current crisis in international banking, Washington: Brookings Institution.

ul Haq, M.(1984): "Proposal for an IMF debt refinancing facility", address to UNESCO, July 6.

Kenen, P.(1983): "Third world debt: sharing the burden, a bailout plan for the banks", New York Times, March 6.

Krugman, P.(1985): "International debt strategies in an uncertain world" in Cuddington and Smith, eds. The international debt problem. World Bank.

Kyle, S.C. and Sachs, J.(1984): "Developing country debt and the market value of large commercial banks", NBER Working Paper no. 1470.

Lessard, D.and Williamson, J.(1985): Financial intermediation beyond the debt crisis, Institute for International Economics, Washington.

Lever, H.(1983): "The international debt threat", The Economist, July 9.

Robichek, W.(1985): "External debt relief", Journal of Development Planning, no.16.

Rohatyn, F.(1983): "A plan for stretching out global debt", Business Week, February 28.

Soros, G.(1984): "The international debt problem: a prescription", New York: Morgan Stanley investment research memorandum.

Witteveen, J.H.(1983): "Developing a new international monetary system: a long term view", Per Jacobsson lecture (Sept.)

Zombanakis, M.(1983): "A way to avoid a crash", The Economist, April 30.